SENSATIONALIZING THE JEWISH QUESTION

STUDIES IN CENTRAL EUROPEAN HISTORIES

EDITED BY

THOMAS A. BRADY

AND

ROGER CHICKERING

VOLUME XXXIX

BARNET HARTSTON

SENSATIONALIZING THE JEWISH QUESTION

SENSATIONALIZING THE JEWISH QUESTION

Anti-Semitic Trials and the Press in the Early German Empire

BY

BARNET HARTSTON

BRILL
LEIDEN · BOSTON
2005

This book is printed on acid-free paper.

Library of Congress Cataloging-in-Publication Data

A C.I.P. record for this book is available from the Library of Congress.

ISSN 1547-1217
ISBN 90 04 14654 7

PRINTED IN THE NETHERLANDS

For Gloria Leifer-Hartston

CONTENTS

LIST OF ILLUSTRATIONS

ACKNOWLEDGMENTS

As often happens for historians, the idea for this book first occurred to me as I was researching in a different direction. Laboring alone in the vast reading room of the Federal Archive in Koblenz, I sat for hours on end with a frustratingly disorganized carton of newspaper clippings from the collection of the Bavarian aristocrat Friedrich Karl Reichsfreiherr von Fechenbach zu Laudenbach. The collector, an eclectic man who had bounced back and forth during the last decades of the Nineteenth Century between support for Conservatives, anti-Semites, and the Catholic Center Party, amassed thousands of clippings from newspapers across Germany on various topics of political interest. As I flipped through loose articles in cartons labeled "Anti-Semitic", however, I began to notice something intriguing. Carton after carton of articles included references to court cases involving discussions of the "Jewish Question". These cases included several ritual murder allegations, numerous criminal trials involving Jewish defendants, and innumerable libel trials involving both anti-Semitic agitators and those that opposed them. Even more surprising than the number of these trials was the breadth of press coverage that often accompanied them. Fascinated by these trial stories, I gradually abandoned my earlier work and began instead to investigate the role of the press and the courtroom in the development of anti-Semitism during the *Kaiserreich.*

Of course, my freedom to pursue this new course would never have been possible without the generous financial assistance from the Deutscher Akademischer Austauschdienst (DAAD), the Center for German and European Studies at the University of California, Berkeley, the Department of History at the University of California, San Diego, and the administration of Eckerd College. I am also grateful to the archivists at the Bundesarchiv Koblenz, Bundesarchiv Berlin-Lichterfelde, Brandenburgisches Landeshauptarchiv Potsdam, Geheimes Staatsarchiv Preussischer Kulturbesitz, and the Staatsarchiv der Freien und Hansestadt Hamburg. It is impossible for me to name here all the individuals who assisted me during my repeated visits to these archives, but I am thankful for their helpfulness and professionalism.

My thanks to Roger Chickering and Thomas Brady for allowing me to be a part of their wonderful series, and to Julian Deahl, Hendrik van Leusen, and Boris van Gool at Brill for all of their assistance. Diethelm Prowe has also kindly given me permission to use material that originally appeared as part of my article "Reluctant Justice: Government Legal Intervention on behalf of Jews in Imperial Germany" *German Studies Review* Vol. 27 Nr. 1 (February 2004): 83–102.

I am also indebted to a number of colleagues and friends at the University of California, San Diego for their guidance in the early stages of my research, including Allan Mitchell, Cynthia Truant, Cynthia Walk, and John Marino. I would like to express my special gratitude to David Luft, a valued mentor and friend, who helped to shape me both as a researcher and a teacher, and who has had a profound influence on this project. Thanks also to my many colleagues at Eckerd College for their encouragement and advice, especially Mary Abdoney, who was diligent in finding me even the most obscure of sources.

This work also would never have been possible without the help of many additional friends and colleagues both in San Diego, St. Petersburg, and in Germany. Special thanks go to Theresa Smith and Phoebe Kropp for helping me to remain focused, and to my dear friends John Lee, Kelline Rodems, John Ferrari, and Henry Sanabria both for their moral support and for providing much needed distractions. I also owe a debt of gratitude to my friends who made me feel at home in a foreign land, especially Tim and Sabine Cox, and Joachim, Molly, Stephen, and Manu Klein.

Finally, I would like to thank the members of my family. My sisters Heidi and Eve, and my brothers Amos, David, and Paul have all been sources of strength, even from thousands of miles away. My mother Gloria has had as profound an influence on my work as she has had on my life. Her compassion and energy, as well as the example she sets as a successful scholar and teacher gives me daily inspiration. Last, but certainly not least, I should mention that I am eternally grateful to have Helene Gold in my life. Her unconditional love, her generous spirit, and her limitless patience with my academic obsessions have not only made this book possible, but have made every day with her a true blessing.

ABBREVIATIONS

AZdJ	Allgemeine Zeitung des Judenthums
BABL	Bundesarchiv Abteilung Berlin-Lichterfelde
BAK	Bundesarchiv Koblenz
BLHA	Brandenburgisches Landeshauptarchiv Potsdam
GStA PK	Geheimes Staatsarchiv Preußischer Kulturbesitz
LAB	Landesarchiv Berlin
NAZ	Norddeutsche Allgemeine Zeitung
StH	Staatsarchiv der Freien und Hansestadt Hamburg
StPK	Staatsbibliothek Preußischer Kulturbesitz

INTRODUCTION

The founding of the German Empire in 1871 was an event that seemed to hold great promise for the Jews of Central Europe. The Prussian Law of Emancipation, which had been passed in 1869, now became valid for the entire German Reich—thus abolishing any remaining restrictions on Jewish civil rights and assuring equality before the law.[1] The relaxation of these social restrictions allowed Jews to move into occupations that had previously been excluded to them. Prominent Jews quickly assumed important positions in the political life of the new state, including Eduard Lasker and Ludwig Bamberger as leading figures in the National Liberal Party and Gerson von Bleichröder as a powerful banker and associate of Otto von Bismarck. German Jews also shared the general optimism of their countrymen, whose high hopes in the early 1870s were buoyed by their new status as a world power and by the promise of a seemingly limitless economic boom. But all was not well for long. In the mid-1870s, Germany would suffer both a serious economic downturn and a political shift away from liberalism; these changes would also be accompanied by a dramatic backlash against Jewish emancipation.

In early 1873, the German stock exchange, bloated by irrational exuberance and undermined by rampant corruption, collapsed in a fury of selling. Although the economic stagnation that followed over the next two decades would have considerable social and political repercussions, these would pale in comparison to the psychological impact of the initial collapse.[2] The German Reich, which had waited so long for glory, unity, and prosperity, now seemed to be brought to its knees by mysterious financial manipulations. Someone had to be responsible. For ordinary Germans, many of whom lost their savings in the crash, the responsible parties seemed to be those who

[1] Amos Elon, *The Pity of It All: A History of the Jews in Germany 1743–1933* (New York: Metropolitan Books, 2002), 205.

[2] Jacob Katz, *From Prejudice to Destruction: Anti-Semitism, 1700–1933* (Cambridge: Harvard, 1980), 247. See also the classic work by Hans Rosenberg, *Grosse Depression und Bismarckzeit* (Frankfurt: Ullstein, 1976).

had energetically advocated the "Manchesterite" ideas of cutthroat capitalism—the leaders of the National Liberal Party.[3] Because this party had prominent Jewish leaders, because several Jewish businessmen were implicated in financial scandals, and especially because of traditional stereotypes about Jews and capitalism, public anger was often expressed in rhetoric that attacked the influence of German Jews. Opponents of Bismarck and his National Liberal allies in the Reichstag were quick to take advantage of this public discontent by printing a series of anti-Semitic attacks in leading political newspapers.

The first significant salvo in the German press was fired by a journalist named Otto Glagau in the *Gartenlaube*, a popular middle-class journal which by the mid-1870s sold between 380,000 and 460,000 copies and claimed an estimated two million readers.[4] Glagau, who was rumored to have lost his own money in the stock market crash, tried to bring his middle-class readers closer to conservative politics by outlining a common enemy, the Liberal-Jewish-"Manchesterites". Although the anti-Semitic content of his first articles was relatively modest, growing criticism from liberal and Jewish leaders encouraged Glagau to make even more strident attacks.[5] Eventually, Glagau's articles described indolence and dishonesty as inherent Jewish characteristics and demanded the exclusion of Jews from prominent positions in German society. His most infamous claim, however, was that 90% of all promoters (*Gründer*) and stock exchange speculators were Jews.[6]

Perhaps even more influential than the actual content of Glagau's allegations was the exaggerated and almost paranoid tone of his

[3] This despite the fact that the Jewish National Liberal leader Eduard Lasker first denounced the rampant corruption of many publicly-traded companies before the crash in a Reichstag speech in February 1873. Lasker's public revelations were later explained by anti-Semites as a pre-emptive strike to lead public opinion away from Jewish responsibility for the imminent crash. See Otto Glagau, *Der Börsen- und Gründungsschwindel in Berlin* (Leipzig, 1876), x.

[4] The two different estimates come from Fritz Stern, *Gold and Iron: Bismarck, Bleichröder, and the Building of the German Empire* (New York, 1977), 501, and Hermann Zang, *Die "Gartenlaube" als politisches Organ* (Würzburg, 1935), 14. Either estimate indicates an impressively large readership.

[5] So Glagau claimed when he later published his collected articles in a two-volume book. See Glagau, xxiv–xx. For more on Glagau's articles, see Katz, *From Prejudice to Destruction*, 249–252.

[6] Peter Pulzer, *The Rise of Political Anti-Semitism in Germany and Austria* (New York: Wiley, 1964), 89.

rhetoric. He suggested that this was not just a matter of a few unscrupulous Jewish financiers, but part of a vast conspiracy to establish Jewish dominance in all Christian lands. As he put it: "The Jews always push us Christians to the side, press up against the wall, and rob us of the very air to breathe. They have actually established their dominance over us . . . From baptized government ministers to Polish beggars, they form a single chain which united together makes common cause against Christians at every opportunity."[7]

Glagau's articles quickly inspired two new serialized "exposés" in leading political newspapers that had also been critical of Bismarck and the National Liberals. In June of 1875, as Glagau's articles were continuing their run in the *Gartenlaube*, a self-proclaimed financial expert named Franz Perrot penned a series of articles in the *Kreuzzeitung* called "The Era of Bleichröder-Delbrück-Camphausen and the New German Economic Politics". These articles restated many of Glagau's charges against Jews and National Liberals and presented these attacks in a similar conspiratorial tone. But Perrot placed a special emphasis on the ties between Otto von Bismarck and the Jewish banker Gerson von Bleichröder; he even alleged that Bleichröder was the real leader of the Empire: "[Bleichröder] is the great financial and economic *spiritus familiaris* of the new Reich . . . the intellectual author of our entire economic policy."[8]

Perrot's articles were a particular affront to Bismarck, not only because of the nature of his charges, but also because of the origins of the *Kreuzzeitung* as a newspaper. Formally named the *Neue Preußische Zeitung*, the *Kreuzzeitung* (so nicknamed for the cross on its masthead) had been founded in 1848 as an attempt by leading Junkers to create a newspaper that represented their own interests. Its founders had included several wealthy aristocrats, including Otto von Bismarck himself.[9] The *Kreuzzeitung* had originally aligned itself closely with Bismarck upon his assumption of power in the 1860s. This loyalty had disappeared quickly, however, as many Conservatives in the

[7] Otto Glagau, *Der Börsen- und Gründungsschwindel in Berlin* (Leipzig, 1876), xxx as quoted in Massimo Ferrari Zumbini, *Die Wurzeln des Bösen: Gründerjahre des Antisemitismus von der Bismarckzeit zu Hitler* (Frankfurt: Vittorio Klostermann, 2003), 141.

[8] Quoted in Stern, *Gold and Iron*, 187.

[9] Meinolf Rohleder and Burkhard Treude, "Neue Preussische (Kreuz-)Zeitung," in *Deutsche Zeitungen des 17. bis 20. Jahrhunderts*, ed. Hans-Dietrich Fischer (Pullach bei München: Verlag Dokumentation, 1972), 209–210.

early 1870s came to believe that Bismarck had abandoned their party for an alliance with the National Liberals. As Perrot's articles demonstrated, by the mid 1870s, the *Kreuzzeitung* had come to view Bismarck as an opponent, and even a bitter enemy.

The attacks of Glagau and Perrot were quickly adopted by another newspaper hostile to Bismarck, the radical Catholic daily *Germania*. At the time of Glagau and Perrot's articles, Bismarck was in the midst of launching the *Kulturkampf*, a campaign of intimidation against the newly founded Catholic Center Party and against papal influence in Germany. The *Germania*, therefore, eagerly adopted Glagau and Perrot's allegations of a Jewish-liberal conspiracy behind Bismarck and began to print "exposés" of its own. The *Germania* articles added a new twist: the Jews and liberals had initiated the *Kulturkampf* in order to hide their own illicit financial activities.[10]

Collectively, then, the articles in the *Gartenlaube*, the *Kreuzzeitung*, and the *Germania* used anti-Semitic rhetoric to attack Bismarck and his liberal allies in the Reichstag. This does not necessarily mean that the authors of these articles or editors of these newspapers did not truly harbor anti-Jewish sentiments. In fact, Glagau, Perrot, and many of the *Germania* editors would continue to use anti-Semitic rhetoric throughout their careers. These articles, however, helped to set a new precedent for using anti-Semitic attacks as a political weapon.

The publication of Wilhelm Marr's *The Victory of Jewry over Germandom* helped to reinvigorate the debate over the so-called "Jewish Question" in 1879. Marr's book is an unrelentingly pessimistic account of how the Jewish race had finally emerged victorious during the 1870s in its 1800 year long battle with the German race. Marr suggested that Jewish dominance was a forgone conclusion not only in Germany, but in the rest of Europe as well.[11] This paranoid racial argument seemed to strike a chord in a German society still reeling from economic stagnation, where both liberalism and tolerance seemed to be on the wane. But the overall importance of Marr's treatise was accentuated by two other factors. First, despite the overall pessimism of his book, Marr concluded with a call to action: he founded the first explicitly anti-Jewish political organization in Germany, which would

[10] Paul Massing, *Rehearsal for Destruction* (New York: Harper & Bros., 1949), 14–15.
[11] Pulzer, *The Rise of Political Anti-Semitism*, 50–51.

eventually become known as the *Antisemitenliga*.[12] Marr was also the first to coin the expression "anti-Semitism" (*Antisemitismus*)—a term that would quickly take on an obvious symbolic importance both to Jews and to those across the globe who sought to attack them.[13]

Although Marr and his *Antisemitenliga* never became a force in German politics, his call to action inspired a number of other politicians, journalists, and agitators to launch their own anti-Semitic organizations.[14] By the mid-1880s, a multiplicity of anti-Semitic clubs and political parties had emerged across Germany, and with them a variety of anti-Semitic newspapers were founded to carry on the attacks first started by Glagau, Perrot, and Marr. In addition, men such as Max Lieberman von Sonnenberg, Ernst Henrici, and Bernhard Förster all began to use public speeches and the power of the press to spread their anti-Semitic worldview and make a name for themselves as political leaders. Although these men and their organizations never challenged the established political parties for power, they did have a public voice and image that was often disproportionate to their actual numbers.

The rise of these political anti-Semites coincided with the rise of Adolf Stöcker as a political leader and a source of anti-Semitic rhetoric. Stöcker, who possessed a degree of credibility and visibility because of his position as court chaplain to the Kaiser, first founded a Christian Social Workers' Party in 1878. At first, Stöcker's political party was not designed with anti-Semitism as a major component. Stöcker's main goal was to win Berlin workers away from Marxist socialism and convert them to a more reliable Christian socialism that would be loyal to religious values and monarchical authority.[15] After a catastrophic showing in the elections of 1878, however, Stöcker searched for other methods of winning a public following in Berlin. Then, in September of 1879, undoubtedly inspired

---

[12] Ibid.

[13] Katz, *From Prejudice to Destruction*, 261. See Ferrari Zumbini, 168–174 for a discussion of the controversial origins of this term.

[14] The number of members in the *Antisemitenliga* never seems to have exceeded 40, and by 1881 it was struggling to attract more than a handful of activists. By the mid 1880s, many former *Antisemitenliga* members had become involved in the larger *Deutsche Antisemitenbund*. See LAB A Pr. Br. Rep. 030, Polizeipräsidium Berlin, Nr. 14942 and 14961.

[15] Pulzer, *The Rise of Political Anti-Semitism*, 90–91.

by the success of Wilhelm Marr's anti-Semitic pamphlet which had appeared the previous February, Stöcker gave his first public speech on the "Jewish Question". This speech marked a significant change in course for Stöcker and his party, who would henceforth become known primarily for their anti-Semitic worldview.[16]

Although the activities of all of these various political anti-Semites were never tightly coordinated, they had a significant overall impact. Several of these activists, led by Bernhard Förster, joined together to sponsor an Anti-Semitic Petition that demanded among other things a new Jewish census, the exclusion of Jews from positions of authority, and limits to Jews in certain professions. Förster and his colleagues managed to gain over 250,000 signatures for the petition by 1882, and although the petition was ignored by Bismarck, it nonetheless demonstrated the potential attractiveness of anti-Jewish rhetoric for mobilizing a mass audience.[17]

The depth and breadth of this new anti-Semitism in Germany, however, cannot be measured merely by the rather modest successes of independent anti-Semitic parties and organizations. A true appraisal must also include the fact that after 1879, anti-Semitic rhetoric once again became a consistent part of the debate between leading political parties and their representative newspapers. Whenever liberal and Jewish newspapers in Berlin attacked the machinations of Stöcker, Förster, or Henrici, opposition newspapers such as the *Kreuzzeitung* and the *Germania* jumped in quickly to respond. They did so not necessarily out of any love for the individual agitators themselves (although the *Kreuzzeitung* editors did ally strongly with Stöcker), but because they realized that anti-Semitism provided a powerful weapon to use against liberal political opponents. Although the intensity of these press debates over the "Jewish Question" would ebb and flow over the next several decades, they were an almost constant presence in German political life.

Before 1880, debates over the "Jewish Question" in the German press tended to revolve around the same social and economic rhetoric as the 1875 articles of Glagau and Perrot. But in the years thereafter, press debates were increasingly peppered with references to

[16] Katz, *From Prejudice to Destruction*, 260; Pulzer, *The Rise of Political Anti-Semitism*, 93–94.

[17] Katz, *From Prejudice to Destruction*, 272. Tellingly, the petition was rejected on purely formal grounds and Bismarck made no public comment on its content.

sensational court cases both within and outside Germany. These *causes célèbres* included a variety of libel trials between Jews and anti-Semitic agitators, a number of criminal trials involving Jewish defendants, and several sensational ritual murder cases.

Highly publicized trials involving anti-Semitism were not unique to the German Empire; this was, after all, the era of the Panama Scandal and the Dreyfus Affair. The Dreyfus case was a seminal event in French history, which deepened existing political rifts and left the country divided for almost a decade. The spectacle of a Jewish officer standing trial for high treason also captivated international attention and caused a rethinking of the "Jewish Question" throughout Europe. Historians, however, have often treated the Dreyfus Affair as an aberration, an extreme episode that was unique to France. In Germany, which had its own record of significant anti-Jewish agitation, there does not seem to have been any single anti-Semitic event in this era that left such a distinct impression in German culture or politics. As one German historian put it simply: "It should be noted that a political scandal of great significance, such as developed after 1894 in France with the Dreyfus Affair, did not occur under the banner of modern anti-Semitism in the German *Kaiserreich*."[18]

While it may be true that no single anti-Semitic scandal in Imperial Germany reached the severity and intensity of the Dreyfus Affair, it would be a mistake to assume that Germany was without similar episodes. In reality, the German political scene of the 1880s and early 1890s was dominated by public discussions of the Jewish Question—debates that were often sparked by press coverage of specific trials and scandals with anti-Semitic overtones. Many of these cases involved similar social and political issues as the Dreyfus Affair, provided the same sensational atmosphere, and had lasting effects on German society. Perhaps most importantly, the continuous drumbeat of these cases helped to keep the "Jewish Question" almost constantly in the public eye. The main purpose of this book, then, will be to examine the general nature of these anti-Semitic affairs, assess their role in German politics, and evaluate their overall effect on the development of German anti-Semitism.

---

[18] See Gerald Kolditz, "Zur Enwicklung des Anti-Semitismus in Dresden während des Kaiserreichs," in *Zwischen Integration und Vernichtung: Jüdisches Leben in Dresden im 19. und 20. Jahrhundert.* Dresdner Hefte, vol. 45 (Dresden: Dresdner Geschichtsverein, 1996), p. 45 n. 8.

CHAPTER ONE

AN EMPIRE TRANSFORMED: POLITICS, ANTI-SEMITISM, AND THE LAW IN THE TIME OF BISMARCK

The rise of political anti-Semitism in late nineteenth-century Germany was accompanied by a number of legal cases that provoked public debates about the rights of Jews and the nature of Judaism. The growth of anti-Jewish sentiment or the fervent activity of anti-Semitic agitators, however, cannot alone account for the appearance of such anti-Semitic *causes célèbres*. This chapter will single out four additional social and political trends that combined to increase the effectiveness of the courtroom as a public forum for discussing the "Jewish Question":

- A previous history of sensational political trials
- The explosive growth of the political press
- Significant reforms in the legal system
- New forms of electioneering

Political Trials in the Early Empire

Sensational public trials and scandals were a relatively common fixture of political life in the early German Empire. Throughout his tenure as Chancellor, Otto von Bismarck tried to use government prosecutors and the legal system as weapons in the struggle against his many adversaries. The frequent arrest and prosecution of those who criticized the government was designed to silence or intimidate political opposition. But the legal prosecution of these "enemies of the Reich", or *Reichsfeinde*, often had just the opposite effect. Through sensational trials, opposition politicians and journalists could use the courtroom as a forum for attracting public attention to their cause and furthering their own political agenda.

As Bismarck's primary *Reichsfeinde*, the socialists and their leaders, August Bebel and Wilhelm Liebknecht, were the most prominent targets of government prosecution. Bismarck viewed these two men as serious threats to German social and political stability. In reality, however, their power seemed to be in decline in the early 1870s as Prussian military victories and the unification of Germany caused a wave of nationalism that drowned out socialist calls for international brotherhood.[1] Because of their previous abstention in a Reichstag vote for war credits, Bebel and Liebknecht had a difficult time defending themselves from Bismarck's charges that they were traitors to their country. In fact, because of their public statements of opposition to the Franco-Prussian war, Bebel, Liebknecht and their colleague Adolf Hepner were arrested in December of 1870 and charged with conspiring to overthrow the German state. The trial against these three men opened in Dresden in March of 1872; however, contrary to the hopes of Bismarck, the case proved to be a significant political victory for the socialist parties.

Wilhelm Liebknecht was determined to use this public trial to rehabilitate his socialist party and socialist ideology in general. Thus, from the first day onward, Liebknecht tried to use the trial as a public forum to proclaim his innocence and spread Marxist propaganda. As a biographer of Liebknecht wrote: "With such bold affirmation of his ideals, Liebknecht turned the trial into a seminar on his beliefs . . . For fourteen days, Liebknecht lectured the courtroom—and through the journalists, the nation—on the principles of social democracy."[2] Although Liebknecht and Bebel were convicted and sentenced to two years in prison, their trial was a propaganda success. Among those persuaded by the trial to join the movement were the former liberal Johann Jacoby and the future leader of the Bavarian socialists, Georg von Vollmar.[3] In addition, in the year after the trial, party membership increased by fifty percent. Two decades later, books re-telling this trial story were still being printed by the socialist Vorwärts publishing house.[4]

---

[1] Because of the relative weakness of Social Democracy in the early 1870s, a more concentrated government persecution did not begin until after 1878. But even in the early days of the new Reich, Bebel and Liebknecht were treated as dangerous political figures.

[2] Raymond Dominick, *Wilhelm Liebknecht and the Founding of the German Social Democratic Party* (Chapel Hill: Univ. of North Carolina, 1982), 212.

[3] Ibid., 215. The third defendant in the trial, Hepner, was acquitted.

[4] For instance: *Der Hochverraths-prozess wider Liebknecht, Bebel, Hepner vor dem Schwurgericht zu Leipzig vom 11. bis 26. März 1872* (Berlin: Vorwärts, 1894). Trials remained an important political forum for the socialists through the "heroic period" of 1878–1890 and after. See Alex Hall, *Scandal, Sensation and Social Democracy: The SPD Press and Wilhelmine Germany 1890–1914* (Cambridge: Cambridge Univ. Press, 1977).

The socialists, however, were not the only *Reichsfeinde* to face prosecution. As part of his long battle to weaken the power of the Catholic Church within Germany, Bismarck brought a series of prosecutions against editors of various Catholic newspapers. The height of this *Kulturkampf* came in 1874, after a journeyman attempted to assassinate Bismarck in the small town of Kissingen. Bismarck was not seriously hurt, but the fact that the suspect admitted having been motivated by the anti-Bismarck editorials of various Catholic newspapers moved the Chancellor to action. Bismarck ordered prosecutors across Germany to confiscate any example of potentially dangerous newspaper articles, from the large Catholic papers down to the smallest church newsletters.[5] The Chancellor himself kept a close eye on this campaign against the Catholic press and repeatedly put pressure on the Justice Minister and State Prosecutors to step up their legal campaign against Catholic journalists.[6]

This wave of persecution and prosecution climaxed with the arrest of Paul Majunke, editor of the leading Catholic daily, the *Germania*.[7] Majunke, who was also a prominent Centrist Reichstag delegate, had already been tried and sentenced to one year in prison for slandering the Kaiser, the Chancellor, and other government ministers. However, because he had parliamentary immunity once the next Reichstag session started, Majunke decided to leave the country temporarily and return later to take his seat in parliament. When Majunke returned on December 11, 1874, he was quickly arrested and brought to the Plötzensee prison despite his parliamentary immunity. This arrest caused a heated debate in the Reichstag, and even many deputies who were loyal to Bismarck saw this as an abuse of power by the Chancellor and a challenge to the legal standing of parliament.

---

[5] See GStA PK, I. HA Rep. 90 Staatsministerium, Nr. 2411 pp. 198–9; GStA PK, I. HA Rep. 77 Ministerium des Innern, Abt. II Sec. 8 Tit. 380 Nr. 33 Band 1, p. 2.

[6] For example, see the letter from the Justice Minister to the office of the *Oberstaatsanwalt* on February 1, 1875. GStA PK, I. HA Rep. 84a Justizministerium, Nr. 43758, p. 2.

[7] The *Germania* was frequently forced to change its chief editor because of impending trials and prison sentences for libel. The editor Paul Kosciolek, for example, worked for the *Germania* for less than two years, but was prosecuted seven times and sentenced to almost 3 ½ years in prison. Kosciolek eventually fled the country for England, but other editors were arrested to prevent them from escaping similar prosecutions. See Letter from the Polizei-Präsident von Madai to the Minister of the Interior von Puttkamer in GStA PK, I. HA Rep. 77 Ministerium des Innern, Abt. I, Sec. 8, Tit. 54a, Nr. 45, pp. 53–55.

A majority of the Reichstag passed a resolution of protest, which labeled the arrest of Majunke an attack on the Reichstag as a whole.[8]

Soon after the protest resolution, however, rumors spread that Bismarck was threatening to resign over the matter and dissolve the Reichstag. This threat was directed primarily toward the liberals, who knew that a new election might threaten their power base and disrupt their tenuous alliance with the Chancellor. Faced with this possibility, most liberal deputies backed down from their earlier position. A few days later, when the Center party opposed the Chancellor on another matter in the Reichstag, the liberal deputies took the opportunity to attack the Center party and proclaim their support for Bismarck.[9] The Chancellor had called the Reichstag's bluff, and Majunke was forced to serve out his prison sentence.

Although legal campaigns against men like Bebel, Liebknecht, and Majunke brought national attention to the German legal system, these cases paled in comparison to the Arnim trial of 1874, which involved a power struggle between Bismarck and the ambassador to Paris, Harry Graf von Arnim.[10] The antagonism between Bismarck and Arnim was based partially on their contrasting personalities, but it was also caused by strong ideological differences. While Bismarck wanted France to remain an isolated and weak democratic state, Arnim believed that France would be much more stable and less threatening if it were again governed by a monarchy. In Arnim's opinion, and in the opinion of many other *Junker* aristocrats, a republican France might threaten to disintegrate into anarchy or spread political radicalism over the borders into Germany. Beyond these differences with Bismarck over diplomatic strategy, Arnim also had an ulterior motive for starting intrigues against the Chancellor. Arnim aspired to replace Bismarck, and, in hopes of eventually forcing his rival out of office, Arnim cultivated his personal ties to the Kaiser, as well as relations with other prominent *Junkers* who were hostile to Bismarck's pro-liberal policies.[11]

---

[8] Otto Pflanze, *Bismarck and the Development of Germany*, vol. 2 (Princeton: Princeton Univ. Press, 1990), 236–237.

[9] Ibid.

[10] The best source on the Arnim trial is still George Kent, *Arnim and Bismarck* (Oxford: Oxford Univ. Press, 1968).

[11] According to Kent, the Emperor sympathized with Arnim's view of the French situation, and the Chancellor waged a difficult battle to maintain his own authority in determining foreign policy. Kent suggests that because of his own political

The struggle between the two men continued behind the scenes for many years. But when Arnim attempted to use his connections to international newspapers to print editorials and secret diplomatic documents that would be embarrassing to Bismarck, the Chancellor's tactics became more aggressive.[12] Arnim was quickly dismissed from diplomatic service and charges were filed against him for stealing secret documents. A dramatic trial in November and December of 1874 brought national and international attention to this personal battle. Trial transcripts were printed in many national newspapers, and supporters of both sides waged a battle in the press and in the parliament. Eventually, Arnim was convicted of abusing his position as ambassador and was sentenced to three months in prison. Rather than go to prison, however, Arnim exiled himself from Germany.[13] After his conviction, Arnim continued to appeal to the Emperor for rehabilitation. But the anonymous publication of *Pro Nihilo*, a scathing review of the case thought to have been written by Arnim himself, hindered any chance for clemency. Two years later, Arnim was tried in absentia for treason and *lèse-majesté* and was sentenced to five years in prison. He died a few years later in exile.[14]

While Harry von Arnim was crushed in his attempt to unseat Bismarck as Chancellor, the scandal caused by his arrest and subsequent trial turned this incident into a national political issue. Because the Arnim case provided those who were unhappy with the *Kulturkampf* or with Bismarck's liberal policies an opportunity to vent their anger at the Chancellor's leadership, discussion of the trial became a

uncertainty, Bismarck was reluctant to move against Arnim despite the obvious risk of keeping him in the position of ambassador. See Ibid., 106.

[12] There were several incidents of embarrassing revelations being printed in foreign papers, but the most serious example happened in April 1874, when *Die Presse*, from Vienna, published documents that seemed to suggest that the *Kulturkampf* could have been avoided if Bismarck had only followed Arnim's advice. These "revelations" were followed by a political debate in which Catholic and ultra-Conservative newspapers attacked Bismarck, and more moderate newspapers like the *Norddeutsche Allgemeine Zeitung* did their best to defend the Chancellor and attack Arnim. Ibid., 129–143.

[13] This mild sentence is a sign of the independence of the Berlin City Court (*Stadtgericht*) in the face of immense political pressure from Bismarck. The prosecutor had asked for thirty months in prison, but received only a fraction of that sentence. This verdict was thus viewed by many of Bismarck's enemies as a considerable victory. After a prosecutorial appeal, however, Arnim's sentence was lengthened to one year. Pflanze, *Bismarck and the Development of Germany*, 232.

[14] Kent, *Arnim and Bismarck*, 176–183.

central part of the existing political debate. For instance, while ultra-Conservative and Catholic newspapers often cited the Arnim case as an example of the Chancellor's cruelty and ruthlessness in dealing with his political opponents, liberal newspapers like the *Berliner Tageblatt* would make the counter-charge that Arnim had been part of an international ultramontane conspiracy to weaken Bismarck and thus hurt the National Liberals.[15]

In the wake of the financial and economic crisis of 1873, public discontent continued to rise, and many of Bismarck's enemies became even more strident in their opposition. After Eduard Lasker of the National Liberal Party rose in the Reichstag in February of 1873 to attack government officials and wealthy conservatives for corruption, an intense public debate broke out over responsibility for the economic crisis. Many of Bismarck's opponents held him personally responsible. This was especially true of most ultra-Conservatives, who, already angered by Bismarck's abandonment of them in favor of the National Liberals, now became some of his bitterest opponents.

In addition to the anti-Semitic articles and books mentioned earlier, some of the most vicious attacks came from a small newspaper called the *Deutsche Eisenbahnzeitung*, which later changed its name to the *Deutsche Reichsglocke*. This newspaper, founded in 1874, featured almost constant personal criticism of Bismarck by some of his most vocal adversaries: Joachim Gehlsen, the founder and editor of the newspaper; Otto von Löe, a writer and publisher; and Dr. Rudolf Meyer, a prominent economist. These attacks eventually resulted in multiple charges of libel against all three, which in turn led to a series of sensational trials in 1876 and 1877.

The trials against Meyer, Gehlsen, and von Löe proved to be politically embarrassing both for Bismarck and for his Jewish banker Gerson von Bleichröder. Bismarck's refusal to testify in the trials was used by these defendants to show his lack of concern for the due process of law. It also allowed them to claim that the trials were part of a pattern of abuse of the legal system by Bismarck that extended from the Arnim trial onwards.[16] Although Bismarck's oppo-

---

[15] Ibid., 161–162.

[16] Among von Löe's offending articles was one that criticized Bismarck for unfairly influencing the German justice system in the Arnim case. Löe's response to the libel charges was printed as a 120 page pamphlet, *Appellations-Rechtfertigungsschrift in der Untersuchungsache von Löe.* This pamphlet was almost entirely a defense of Arnim

nents were never successful in forcing the Chancellor to testify, they did force many other prominent men such as Gerson von Bleichröder and Wilhelm von Kardorff to take the witness stand. None of the defendants ever provided proof that their allegations against Bismarck were true, but through insinuation and innuendo they were able to put both Bismarck and Bleichröder on the defensive. Unfortunately for Gehlsen and his associates, these propaganda successes did not translate into legal victories. After repeatedly being jailed for his articles, Gehlsen finally fled the country for Switzerland.[17] Soon after, Meyer was convicted and sentenced to 14 months in prison. Instead of imprisonment, Meyer also chose voluntary exile.[18] Despite these defeats (or perhaps because of them) men like Gehlsen and Meyer became martyrs for those committed to the struggle against "*Das System Bismarck.*"

Another prominent critic of Bismarck, Otto von Diest-Daber, also found himself in legal trouble because of his criticism of the Chancellor.[19] Diest, who had previously counted himself as an ally of the Chancellor, gradually became angry at Bismarck for abandoning his *Standesgenossen* for the liberal parties. Like Gehlsen and Meyer, Diest-Daber felt that Bismarck was partly responsible for the wave of speculation and corruption that led to the financial crisis of 1873. After several letters that pleaded with the Chancellor to change his policies were returned unopened, Diest-Daber finally gave up and followed another tack. In 1874, he published *Geldmacht und Sozialismus* (Financial Power and Socialism), a book which alleged that Bismarck

---

and an attack on Bismarck for abusing the legal system. Otto von Diest-Daber, a witness for Meyer, would later include a small chapter on Bismarck's treatment of Arnim in his pamphlet *Bismarck und Bleichröder. Deutsches Rechtsbewußtsein und die Gleichheit vor dem Gesetze. Lebenserfahrungen aus Akten, Tagebüchern, Briefen, u.a. Ein ernster Mahnruf an jeden wahrhaften und festen Patrioten* (München: Th. Wenng, 1899).

[17] Pflanze, *Bismarck and the Development of Germany*, 318.

[18] Meyer moved to London, then became a farmer in Canada, and finally ended up in Vienna. Throughout his exile, Meyer continued to attack "Das System Bismarck" with vigor and bitterness. Fritz Stern, *Gold and Iron: Bismarck, Bleichröder, and the Building of the German Empire* (New York: Knopf, 1977), 508.

[19] Diest was a Conservative Junker who had once served as a *Landrat* in the Rhineland. As the son of a Prussian general, he eagerly volunteered for service in the Franco-Prussian war at age 50. Diest later became enraged when he was not granted the Iron Cross despite assurances that he would receive it. This disappointment apparently contributed to an already active streak of paranoia and anti-Jewish sentiment. See Ibid., 503.

had been less than truthful about his management of the *Welfenfonds*.[20] Diest-Daber soon followed with *Das sittliche Boden im Staatsleben* (The Moral Foundation of Civic Life), which made further charges against the Chancellor. He also served as a primary defense witness at the libel trial of Rudolph Meyer, and he alleged that the banker Gerson von Bleichröder had committed perjury in that case in order to protect the Chancellor. As a result of his efforts, Diest-Daber was placed under police surveillance, and he was eventually prosecuted himself for libeling Bismarck.[21]

In his first trial at the Royal City Court of Berlin in November 1877, Diest-Daber was found guilty of having spread accusations that were either false or unprovable. He was sentenced to three months in prison.[22] Diest claimed, however, that he had not put forward a strong defense in this case because he wanted to avoid a public confrontation with Bismarck. In his appeal, Diest decided to make a stand. He demanded that Bismarck be brought in to testify under oath and that the records of Bleichröder's *Diskontobank* be entered into evidence. When the appeals court denied these requests, Diest was left with little more than his own testimony to support his case. He spoke for nearly four hours in his own defense, arguing that he had never intended to libel anyone and claiming that "he had only acted in the interests of the Fatherland." His defense attorney, the same attorney who had defended Harry von Arnim, also argued that the evidence did not support a charge of libel. But both Diest and his attorney argued in vain; the original verdict was upheld.[23]

This, however, was far from the end of Diest-Daber's crusade. He even authored two more short anti-Bismarck pamphlets while awaiting

[20] The confiscated exchequer of Hanover, which Bismarck allegedly used to "reward" his political supporters.

[21] See surveillance file in BABL R 43 #1455, Alte Reichskanzlei (Stammakten).

[22] Otto von Diest-Daber, *Lebensbild eines muthigen Patrioten, zu seinem achtzigen Geburtstag. dargestellt von einem Deutschen* (Berlin: Hermann Walther Verlagsbuchhandlung, 1901), 58.

[23] Ibid., 58–66. His defense attorney was August Munckel, a leading criminal lawyer from Berlin. Munckel may have been assigned to this case against his will since his own politics were quite different from those of Diest-Daber. Munckel served as an outspoken liberal Reichstag deputy, a member of the Prussian House of Representatives, and a member of the Charlottenburg city council. He went on to participate in many other sensational trials, including as an attorney for Joachim Gelsen in his trial for libeling Bismarck, for Edmund Kantorowicz in the "Kantorowicz Affair", for Heinrich Bäcker in the Stöcker-Bäcker trial, and for Isidor Löwe in the "Judenflinten Affair" (all discussed later in this book). See Benjamin Carter Hett, *Death in the Tiergarten* (Cambridge Mass.: Harvard Press, 2004), 124.

his prison sentence.[24] In the second, he explicitly charged Bleichröder with six instances of perjury. Diest assumed that this would cause Bleichröder to file libel charges against him, and he hoped that a new trial would give him another opportunity to prove his innocence in a court of law. When Bleichröder refused to prosecute, Diest decided to file his own libel charges against Bismarck. But these charges were first ignored and later dismissed by the legal authorities. Although all of Diest-Daber's legal efforts amounted to sharp personal defeats, these proceedings were still an embarrassment to the Chancellor and a source of propaganda for other anti-Bismarck agitators. Although no charges of wrongdoing were ever proven in court, as in the Meyer and Gehlsen proceedings, the disclosure of the intimate relations between Bismarck and his Jewish banker, Gerson von Bleichröder, was the source of new rounds of insinuations and allegations in the anti-Bismarck press.[25]

The series of trials involving Gehlsen, Meyer, and Diest-Daber thus provided a forum for the expression of political opposition to Bismarck and his policies. However, these trials also provided a public forum for anti-Semitism. Many of the allegations against Bismarck were linked to his relationship with Gerson von Bleichröder. For many of Bismarck's opponents, this relationship was no coincidence, but proof that Bismarck stood under the control of a vast Jewish conspiracy. While the spread of anti-Semitism may not have been a major goal of those who first publicized these trials, it was certainly not an undesired side effect. Years later, anti-Semitic agitators such as Hermann Ahlwardt would refer back to the trials of Gehlsen and Diest-Daber in order to fuel their own campaigns against the

[24] As a result of the conviction, Diest-Daber was also dismissed from the army. Because of this, Diest became obsessed with reclaiming his lost honor and become almost paranoid about those who he claimed were conspiring against him. In his next two pamphlets *Zur Klarstellung des anonymen Schriftstückes* and *Drei Monaten Gefängnis*, he charged that the government and leading newspapers had suppressed any mention of his defense, and alleged that several illegal court decisions had been made in order to make sure he was convicted.

[25] Over the next twenty-five years, Diest waged a constant propaganda campaign against his arch-rival Bismarck. Diest's campaign to regain his honor included further lawsuits, speeches by friends in the Reichstag, and several pamphlets. The last of these, *Berichtigung von Unwahrheiten in den Erinnerungen des Fürsten Bismarck und Deutsches Rechtsbewusstsein* (Zurich: C. Schmidt, 1899), was published more than a year after Bismarck's death. It showed that even twenty years later none of the bitterness had disappeared.

Jewish "domination" of the German government. Few defendants of these early trials became intimately involved with the anti-Semitic political parties formed after 1879, but the public debates caused by their printed propaganda and by their actions in the courtroom set an important example for later anti-Semitic agitators.[26]

It is not at all surprising, therefore, that when political anti-Semitism increased in the 1880s, anti-Semitic agitators should have chosen (or been forced) to use the courtroom as a forum for making their case to the German public. After all, while German government officials and bureaucrats often expressed anti-Jewish attitudes, radical political anti-Semitism was still, at its core, an ideology of opposition. Professional agitators of the next few decades, such as Otto Glagau, Otto Böckel, and Hermann Ahlwardt, were all steadfast in their patriotism and loyalty to the Kaiser, but they did not always show the same enthusiasm for the Chancellor and his policies. Thus, in the late nineteenth century, radical political anti-Semites often formed a super-patriotic opposition to more liberal or moderate German government coalitions—they always did battle with what they considered the predominance of Jewish influence in German society. Because these men often failed to win Reichstag mandates, and because their newspapers were often too small or poorly run to attract a mass readership, sensational trials often became the most effective way to broadcast their message to a wider audience.

The Role of Newspapers in Imperial Germany

Another reason why public scandals and trials became so common in the first few decades of the *Kaiserreich* was the increased role of

[26] Some anti-Semitic newspapers in the early 1880s rejected Gehlsen as a traitor and a servant of the Jews. See Gehlsen's obituary in *Berliner Ostend-Zeitung* 23 December 1880 #150. Other anti-Bismarck agitators of the 1870s, including Otto von Diest-Daber, Otto Glagau and Franz Perrot, developed indirect links to the anti-Semitic parties. Glagau refused to join a specific faction, but he served as president of the Second International Anti-Jewish Congress at Chemnitz in 1883 and published an influential anti-Semitic journal called *Der Kulturkämpfer*. Franz Perrot later became a supporter of Freiherr von Fechenbach zu Laudenbach, who actively funded anti-Semitic journalists and politicians. And although Diest-Daber never joined any of the anti-Semitic parties, he doubtless was glad to see his allegations of perjury against Bleichröder revived several times in the next 20 years as anti-Semitic propaganda.

the political press in German society. Political newspapers had existed previously in Germany, but they had reached a relatively limited audience and were often strictly controlled by official censors. After 1848 and especially after 1870, the Prussian and German governments granted the press more freedom of expression. Thereafter, newspapers quickly assumed a highly significant role in German political and cultural life.

During Bismarck's tenure as German Chancellor, the number of newspapers increased dramatically, as did the number of subscribers. Although many prominent non-political journals and newspapers were created during this time, the most rapid development came in the political press.[27] The new role of the Reichstag in Germany encouraged political leaders to use the press to rally public support for their own agendas. As Kurt Koszyk has noted: "Never before were journalists so eager to be politically active . . . and never before were political groups so interested in using a media that could allow them to quickly spread their ideas and thus gain new political converts. . . ."[28] The press was an essential instrument since it was the only medium that could bring political debates to a large number of people on a daily basis. Thus, while parliamentary speeches and public rallies were important political tools, the political press could describe these events to a regional and even national audience.[29]

It has ordinarily been argued that the emergence of the German political press occurred in four fairly distinct stages: the Conservative press arose primarily during the 1850s, the liberal press during the 1860s, an independent political Catholic press in response to the *Kulturkampf* in the 1870s, and a powerful socialist press in the period thereafter.[30] While this model does reflect the eras in which different

[27] It should be noted that even newspapers and journals that claimed to be non-political or *überparteilich* often carried articles with a political subtext or even explicit political content. The popular family journal *Gartenlaube*, for example, attracted a broad reading audience but had clear National Liberal tendencies. This "unpolitical" magazine was an unexpected source of controversy after it printed Otto Glagau's 1874 articles, which viciously attacked Bismarck and denounced the role of German Jews in the financial collapse of 1873. Walther Oschilewski, *Zeitungen in Berlin: Im Spiegel der Jahrhunderte* (Berlin: Haude & Spenersche Verlagsbuchhandlung, 1975), 86. See also Hermann Zang, *Die "Gartenlaube" als politisches Organ* (Würzburg: 1935).

[28] Kurt Koszyk, *Deutsche Presse im 19. Jahrhundert* (Berlin: Colloquium Verlag, 1966), 127.

[29] Ibid., 127.

[30] Ibid., 130.

branches of the political press began to flourish, it is a simplification of a much more complex pattern of development. Catholic newspapers such as the *Kölnische Volkszeitung* and the *Deutsche Volksblatt* (Stuttgart), for example, existed as early as the 1860s, while many prominent Conservative newspapers like the *Reichsbote* were not founded until the 1870s. Although most historians agree that the basic political constellation in Germany was complete by 1870, the political press was still in its formative years at the time of unification. The period between 1870 and 1895, therefore, was a time of journalistic growth and maturation for newspapers across the political spectrum.

The newspaper was a particularly important instrument for the parliamentary opposition in the German Empire. Although the Reichstag was not without influence as a political body, it provided little opportunity for opposition politicians to make their presence felt. Representatives from opposition parties often had little practical hope of reversing government policies, and many thus relied on the political press to take their case to the German people. During the decade of the *Kulturkampf*, the number of Catholic newspapers increased from approximately 100 to 221, and the number of subscribers to Catholic newspapers doubled to over 626,000.[31] In addition, new liberal, ultra-Conservative, and anti-Semitic newspapers were founded in the 1880s to voice the opposition of these groups to Bismarck's policies. Of course, in the years after the lapse of the Anti-Socialist Laws in 1890, the number of socialist newspapers increased dramatically as well. Indeed, during the last decades of the Nineteenth Century all political factions, and even many individual political leaders, sought to control their own newspapers in order to carry their message directly to ordinary voters. By 1895 there were more than 36 different political dailies in Berlin alone.[32]

During the time of Bismarck, there were several large publishing houses that printed non-political specialty journals and pamphlets along with their political newspapers. The *Germania-Verlag*, for instance, was responsible for printing the Catholic newspaper *Germania*. However, it also produced thousands of political and religious pamphlets, along with several local and regional newspapers such as the *Deutsches Volksfreund, Nordische Volkszeitung, Sächsische Tageblatt*, as well as the pop-

[31] Ibid., 179.
[32] Ibid., 160.

ular weekly *Das Schwarze Blatt.*[33] The publishing house of Rudolph Mosse, which owned the liberal *Berliner Tageblatt*, also printed specialty journals such as the *Zeitschrift für Dampfkessel und Machinenbetrieb* and the *Bäder-Almanach* for farmers and gardeners. In addition to an increase in the overall number of newspapers during this period, individual newspapers were also growing in size and sophistication. The *Vossische Zeitung*, for example, had four editors during the 1850s. By the end of the century, the same newspaper had an editorial staff of over 500.[34] This staff was responsible for a range of new features, including sections on foreign events, culture, business, and advertisements. Over the last decades of the century, the *Berliner Tageblatt* also added a large staff to work on free supplements such as the satirical *Ulk, Deutsche Lesehalle, Technische Rundschau, Haus Hof Garten, Handels-Zeitung*, and the illustrated *Weltspiegel.*[35]

Despite this kind of impressive growth, the press was still a long way from becoming a modern mass medium. Although the government kept subscription statistics for most newspapers, the exact number of readers for each newspaper is still difficult to estimate. By the mid-1870s, the *Berliner Tageblatt, Volks-Zeitung* and *Vossische Zeitung* each had close to 30,000 postal subscriptions or *Abonnements.*[36] However, the number of people who actually read these newspapers was probably much higher since these papers were also sold on the street and were usually available at inns, restaurants, and taverns. For smaller newspapers, this indirect form of distribution was far more important than subscriptions. The Dresden newspaper *Deutsche Reform*, for example, claimed that it was one of the most widely read anti-Semitic newspapers in Germany due to the fact that it was available in thousands of inns and restaurants. Although this is probably a gross exaggeration, it is also proof that such newspapers relied on "indirect" circulation to reach their audiences.[37] Using colportage

[33] Ibid., 177.
[34] Ibid., 160.
[35] Ibid., 282.
[36] Ibid., 281.
[37] A critic of the *Deutsche Reform* claimed that it was available in 20 restaurants at most. He also accused the editor, Alexander Pinkert-Waldegg, of inflating the number of subscriptions to 3500, when it really had only 1600 subscribers. See C.H. Rittner, *Zur Abwehr! Herr Alexander Pinkert (genannt Egon Waldegg) als Chef-Redakteur der Deutschen Reform und Vorsitzender des Deutschen Reform-Vereins zu Dresden und meine Thätigkeit als verantwortlicher Redakteur der Deutschen Reform und Schriftführer des Deutschen Reform Vereins* (Dresden: Selbstverlag, 1882). Because the number of subscribers was

and distribution in political rallies, even the smallest of newspapers could attract significant public attention. It is also worth noting that the political effectiveness of a newspaper was not always proportional to the size of its readership. Since the German political press formed a kind of community in and of itself, polemical attacks by one newspaper often provoked responses from other rival newspapers. Thus, even the smallest newspaper could sometimes affect the course of national political debate.

In the race to attract a broader reading public, German newspapers commonly relied on polemical articles, exposés of political or personal scandals, and coverage of sensational trials. For the anti-Semitic press, these kinds of stories were particularly important. Anti-Semitic newspapers often struggled to maintain a minimal circulation, and the fact that they were usually filled with the same redundant anti-Jewish rhetoric did not make them attractive for most readers. In fact, the anti-Semitic publisher Theodor Fritsch repeatedly lamented the inability of anti-Semitic newspapers to do more than repeat old stereotypes and preach to a small group of already dedicated followers.[38] For these papers, sensational scandals and trials involving Jews or anti-Semitic agitators provided a welcome source of new material to demonstrate the importance of the anti-Semitic movement and the gravity of the struggle against Judaism. Throughout the *Kaiserreich*, then, the political press and especially the anti-Semitic press became adept at both generating and exploiting public scandals and trials.

---

often seen as an indirect sign of popular support for a certain political faction, newspapers commonly accused each other of falsifying and inflating subscription statistics. These charges were especially common against the larger liberal newspapers in Berlin.

[38] *Antisemitische Correspondenz* July 1886 #6 in BAK *ZSg. 113* Sammlung Fechenbach #23. Theodor Fritsch was one of the most influential anti-Semitic leaders in Imperial Germany, but worked primarily behind the scenes as an organizer and publisher. Fritsch's Hammer Verlag published the infamous *Handbuch der Judenfrage*, which was reprinted numerous times and allegedly influenced a young Adolf Hitler. Fritsch is fascinating for a number of other reasons. According to Massimo Ferrari Zumbini, Fritsch published a plan to build Aryan "garden cities" more than two years before the famous book by Ebenezer Howard, and his mix of environmental reform and racism undoubtedly inspired the later *Blut und Boden* ideology of Heinrich Himmler and Walther Darré. Fritsch's long life-span (1852–1933), and his eventual membership in the Nazi party also means that he is frequently cited as a link between the anti-Semitism of the Second Reich and that of the Third. Massimo Ferrari Zumbini, *Die Wurzeln des Bösen: Gründerjahre des Antisemitismus von der Bismarckzeit zu Hitler* (Frankfurt: Vittorio Klostermann, 2003), 321–324, 422.

The Courtroom in Imperial Germany

While the growth of the German press often served to encourage scandals to satisfy an eager audience, changes in the German legal system also helped to make the German courtroom an ideal forum for political theater. This trend was not unique to Germany. In fact, the important role of trials as an extension of political debate had been a common theme throughout both early-modern and modern Europe—especially in France. In her 1993 book *Private Lives and Public Affairs: The Causes Célèbres of Prerevolutionary France*, Sarah Maza discussed how scandalous trials in eighteenth-century France, publicized in popular legal briefs, or *mémoires judiciaires*, helped to transform French political culture and open a new alternative public sphere for political debate. Several other important books have examined the political role of the courtroom in nineteenth-century France, including Eduard Berenson's recent book *The Trial of Madame Caillaux* and various works on the Panama Scandal. Of course, a multitude of works have been written on the Dreyfus Affair, which is perhaps the most significant political trial of the Nineteenth Century. Taken together, these books show how the courtroom played an important role in French culture as both popular entertainment and as a platform for the public discussion of national issues. These trials were never merely about the guilt or innocence of individual defendants; they were political as well as ideological battlegrounds.

While much of the historical literature on nineteenth-century political trials has focused on the French example, public fascination with *causes célèbres* was typical across Europe during this period. As Hannah Arendt wrote in reference to the Dreyfus Affair:

> It is characteristic of the period that a miscarriage of justice could arouse such political passions and inspire such an endless succession of trials and retrials, not to speak of duels and fisticuffs. The doctrine of equality before the law was still so firmly implanted in the conscience of the civilized world that a single miscarriage of justice could provoke public indignation from Moscow to New York.[39]

That equality before the law should have been a concern in places such as Paris, London, or New York is perhaps expected, but the

[39] Hannah Arendt, *The Origins of Totalitarianism*, vol. 1, *Anti-Semitism* (New York: Harcourt, Brace & World, 1968), 91.

fact that it was of equal concern in Imperial Germany may seem a bit surprising. Many legal historians agree, however, that the period after 1870 saw the final victory of legal positivism in Germany over other approaches to the legal system. This legal positivism was characterized by the radical separation of public and private law, by the insistence on treating the law in isolation from political, social, and ethical questions, and by the conviction that the legal order could be construed by value-free deduction. But most importantly, in this legal framework, all citizens were judged to be formally equal before the law.[40]

After 1870, the courtroom in Germany gradually became a buffer between the bureaucratic establishment and public opinion. Judges were no longer viewed as mere officials of the state, but as arbiters between the official establishment and society at large.[41] The court system, therefore, became an independent forum in which rival public figures, often representing rival ideologies, could do battle on a public stage. To put it in the language of Habermas, the development of legal positivism in effect created a new independent public sphere for the discussion of political issues. Alongside the Reichstag, the newspaper, and the political club, the courtroom became a crucial platform for spreading political propaganda and resisting governmental authority. Of course, it would be simplistic to argue that this new political sphere did not exist in Germany before 1871 since there were examples of sensational German trials long before the Franco-Prussian War. But the liberalization of the judicial system, the development of modern mass politics and a mass media, and the extremely volatile political atmosphere after 1870 gave added importance to alternative political forums such as the courtroom.

The triumph of legal positivism was accompanied by practical reforms in the German legal system. In 1878 the *Reichsrechtsanwaltsordnung* (Imperial Lawyer's Code) finally opened admission to the bar and established a free legal practice. While there were still some restrictions on the behavior of lawyers, such as localization and fixed fee schedules, the new system allowed an attorney "to champion any-

---

[40] Michael John, "Constitution, Administration and the Law," in *Imperial Germany*, ed. Roger Chickering (Westport CT: Greenwood Press, 1996), 201.

[41] Otto Kirchheimer, *Political Justice* (Westport, CT: Greenwood Press, 1961), 14–15.

thing and anyone, regardless of reason of state, as long as he does not show himself unworthy of the respect and trust which his profession demands."[42]

These legal reforms also enhanced the role of German courts as a forum for political opposition. Because an open bar meant that attorneys would no longer be strongly linked to the government or restricted along narrow class lines, opposition parties could now seek legal advice and representation from lawyers who were more supportive of their cause. These legal reforms allowed for a great increase in the number of lawyers available to the public, and thus allowed members of the lower classes, whose cases had formerly been rejected by the closed bar, to hire their own lawyers.[43] In addition, the fact that the German courts were now designed to be entities independent of governmental or partisan influence meant that, at least in theory, the court of law could serve as an effective arbiter of truth in public debates. Journalists or politicians accused of some wrongdoing, for example, might initiate a lawsuit (or provoke one) in order to have the chance to present their case before a jury. Often, the victorious party in such a suit would make speeches or write articles claiming to have been vindicated through an impartial legal process, while the defeated party would inevitably claim that the justice system had worked imperfectly or had been corrupted by some outside force.[44] Thus, after the 1870s, legal procedures often took on a special cultural and political significance, and *causes célèbres* (or attempts at producing them) became a more frequent fixture of German society.

Although these legal reforms were successful in creating the impression of an impartial German *Rechtsstaat*, in reality the German judicial system still operated under the strong influence of governmental

[42] Ernst Fuchs as quoted in Konrad Jarausch, *The Unfree Professions: German Lawyers, Teachers, and Engineers 1900–1950* (New York: Oxford Univ. Press, 1990), 9.

[43] Previously, poorer citizens had been forced to depend on lay practitioners. In the year after the *Reichsrechtsanwaltsordnung* took effect (1879), the number of lawyers in Berlin increased from 98 to 250. By 1886 there were 362 lawyers in Berlin. See Kenneth Ledford, *From General Estate to Special Interest: German Lawyers 1878–1933* (New York: Cambridge Univ. Press, 1996), 249–250.

[44] Anti-Semites who lost their legal proceedings would often claim that the impartial German legal system had been corrupted by an outside force, namely the presence of Jewish judges and lawyers, the influence of the "*Judenpresse*", and the power of Jewish lobbying groups.

authority. First, it was very difficult for a law student to advance through the judicial system without having the proper ideological pedigree. Candidates for judicial positions were required first to serve terms as *Referendare* (judicial apprentices) and then as *Gerichtsassessoren* (assistant judges). Only the presiding judge of the *Oberlandesgericht* (High Superior Court) could decide the acceptance of a candidate to these positions, and his decisions could not be appealed. Under these conditions, many judicial candidates with ties to socialism found it difficult to achieve judicial appointments.[45] Even after reaching the position of *Referendar*, candidates were often evaluated for further promotion according to their ideological reliability. Controversial or "disloyal" *Referendare* could be dismissed from their posts at any time. In addition, candidates with private incomes enjoyed distinct advantages over others because of the long period of training before an assignment to a permanent post. Finally, senior judicial appointments were reserved almost exclusively for those who had served as government prosecutors and thus demonstrated their loyalty to the German state.[46] These factors assured a judiciary that would be politically uniform and loyal to the government.

Although legal reforms opened the justice system to lawyers of various political orientations, there was still little chance for a defendant of modest means or radical political opinions to be judged by a jury of his peers. The court system was now set in a strict hierarchy. The *Reichsgericht* in Leipzig served as the highest court of appeal; under it were 13 *Oberlandesgerichte* (High Superior Courts), 94 *Landgerichte* (Superior Courts), and thousands of *Amtsgerichte* (District Courts). At the higher levels, a panel of judges presided over legal cases. Although many cases at the Superior Court or District Court levels were heard either before lay-judges or before juries, this did not necessarily mean that ordinary citizens played a significant part in the administration of justice. The *Schöffengerichte* (Courts of Lay Assessors) were comprised of one tenured judge and two lay-judges chosen from the public, while the *Schwurgerichte* (Jury Courts) were comprised of a panel of jurors. However, the selection procedure for both lay-judges and jurors was complex and decisions were often made on an extremely narrow social and political basis which mil-

[45] Hall, *Scandal, Sensation and Social Democracy*, 48.
[46] Ibid., 48–49.

itated against any genuine popular representation.[47] Thus, it was extremely rare for members of the lower classes or those with radical political affiliations to be selected as lay-judges or jurors.

Finally, the reforms of the 1870s did not weaken the power of the government prosecutor (*Staatsanwalt*) in the legal process. Prosecutors had complete control of the preliminary investigation of a case, and were usually the sole arbiters to decide when criminal charges should be filed. A prosecutor could take a defendant into "investigative custody" (*Untersuchungshaft*) without filing official charges and could keep him there if there was any suggestion of a flight risk or a danger to the state. The prosecutors were also given direct instructions from the Chancellor and other high government officials on what action to take against perceived "enemies of the Reich." Since the prosecutor was the direct representative of government authority in the courtroom, he could sometimes put enormous pressure on judges and jurors to deliver a conviction and an appropriate sentence. As the *Preußische Jahrbücher* suggested in 1895: "In Prussia the administration of justice is in the hands of the state prosecutor, mitigated only by the right of veto of the courts in cases of extravagant demands by the former."[48]

Despite these significant limitations, however, the public image of the court system was changing dramatically. Because it was no longer seen as a government instrument, but an arbiter of truth, the German courtroom proved attractive for politicians and public figures who were desperate to find a kind of official validation for their beliefs and actions. Because of the increased press coverage of public trials, a court proceeding could also serve as an opportunity to make a case to those beyond the walls of the court itself in the "court of public opinion".

---

[47] Ibid., 46–47. According to Hall, commissions to select lay-judges in Prussia consisted of nine people: the chairman of a local District Court, an appointed government official, and seven men appointed by the local district councils—who owed their positions to the Prussian three-class voting system. Selections for jurors in the *Schwurgerichte* were also made by these commissions and were submitted to a panel of judges who could accept or reject their recommendations.

[48] *Preußische Jahrbücher* as quoted in Hall, *Scandal, Sensation and Social Democracy*, 216 n. 41.

Politics in a New Key: Anti-Semitism and Electioneering

The particular effectiveness of political trials and scandals as propaganda was also directly tied to a transformation in German politics in the last decades of the Nineteenth Century. Traditionally, German political life had been centered on committees of local notables that included prominent businessmen, judges, lawyers, and landowners. These informal groups were usually independent of any regional or national political organization, and they could even vary internally in their political affiliation. In the early years of the German Empire it was these elitist organizations, not modern mass campaigning, which determined electoral success. From the very beginning of the new Reich, however, a new kind of popular politics began to challenge this traditional *Honoratiorenpolitik* or "politics of notables". Local election committees began to lose significance in the political process as the lower classes became more politically involved. No longer could a candidate rely on his political connections and social status to maintain his parliamentary seat. In the early *Kaiserreich*, therefore, candidates found it increasingly necessary to actively campaign in their home districts to mobilize popular support.[49]

Most historians point to the 1890s as the crucial decade in the transformation from the old politics of notables to a more modern popular political system. However, the seeds of this transformation were sown decades earlier. The introduction of universal manhood suffrage at the beginning of the Reich inevitably led to a greater degree of communication and activism at the local level. Thus, elitist committees were quickly faced with what one historian has called "politics in a new key."[50]

This increased political mobilization and activism was especially apparent among German Catholics during the *Kulturkampf*. Bismarck's anti-Catholic measures forged a broad range of disparate social groups into a unified Catholic Center Party. During the first six years of the *Kaiserreich*, voter participation in national elections increased from 51 to 61 per cent—a trend that was fed primarily by the mobiliza-

[49] James Retallack, *Notables of the Right: The Conservative Party and Political Mobilization in Germany, 1876–1918* (Boston: George Allen and Unwin, 1988), 3.

[50] Ibid., 2. Retallack takes the phrase from Carl Schorske's article "Politics in a New Key: An Austrian Triptych," *Journal of Modern History* 39 (1967): 343–386.

tion of new Catholic voters. Studies have shown that between 1874 and 1881, 97 to 99 percent of all voting Catholics supported Center Party candidates.[51]

The Center Party was not the only party to appeal directly to the masses instead of committees of notables. Although still small and relatively disorganized in the early years of the Empire, the socialists worked hard to mobilize the urban masses. Eventually, the growing fear of a mass socialist party provoked the Anti-Socialist Laws of 1878, but it also encouraged other political parties to abandon their traditional political methods for a more modern approach.

The German Conservative Party was faced with an especially critical problem: how to maintain their traditional *Junker* elitism while also gaining access to a broader electorate. For many Conservatives who hoped to turn their party into a true conservative *Volkspartei*, the adoption of anti-Semitic rhetoric seemed to be a perfect solution. Especially in 1880, after Marr's successful pamphlet, the start of Stöcker's agitation, and Förster's Petition, anti-Semitism seemed to be on the rise—especially among the lower-middle class in Berlin. Many Conservatives thus strongly supported the work of Adolf Stöcker and published their own anti-Semitic attacks in newspapers such as the *Kreuzzeitung*. Conservatives also decided to enter into a loose alliance with Berlin anti-Semitic agitators in the hope of drumming up popular support among the lower classes in Berlin. After the Conservatives failed to make substantial gains in the 1881 elections, however, many moderate Conservatives began to question whether political anti-Semitism carried more risks than potential advantages. Not only had the expected electoral windfall failed to appear, but more radical anti-Semitic agitators such as Ernst Henrici were seen by many Conservatives as unreliable and a potential threat to public order. Moderate Conservatives, therefore, quickly became wary of associating the party with these potentially socialistic or anarchistic rabble-rousers or "*Radauantisemiten*".[52]

After 1880, therefore, two wings of the Conservative Party developed. On the one hand, moderates such as Otto von Helldorf-Bedra

---

[51] Brett Fairbairn, "Political Mobilization" in *Imperial Germany*, ed. Roger Chickering (Westport, Conn.: Greenwood Press, 1996), 312.

[52] Richard Levy, *The Downfall of the Anti-Semitic Political Parties in Imperial Germany* (New Haven: Yale Univ. Press, 1975), 25–28.

sought to bring the Conservatives back into power through cooperation with Bismarck and with a moderate alliance with the Free Conservatives and National Liberals. On the other hand, there were the ultra-Conservatives—especially the editor of the *Kreuzzeitung*, Wilhelm von Hammerstein—who despised these liberal alliances and desired an independent course for the party. Hammerstein forged a close relationship with Adolf Stöcker, and he continued to use anti-Semitic rhetoric in the hope of driving a wedge between his moderate Conservative rivals and the National Liberals.

By the late 1880s, this split between moderate and ultra-Conservatives widened to the point that the two wings of the party publicly attacked one another on the issue of anti-Semitism. The power struggle between these two factions eventually led to a heated battle at the Conservative Party conference in December of 1892. During this conference, a sensational anti-Semitic trial—the "Judenflinten Affair"—played an influential role in pushing the Conservative Party, at least temporarily, to officially adopt anti-Semitism as a part of its party platform.

The Conservatives were not the only political party to have internal dissention about the use of anti-Semitic rhetoric. Traditionally, historians have asserted that Catholic leaders in late nineteenth-century Germany seemed to be relatively immune to the temptation of anti-Semitism.[53] Although the leading Catholic newspaper in Berlin, the *Germania*, did frequently produce anti-Semitic articles, many historians have suggested that these articles should be seen as an "unfortunate episode in an otherwise harmonious relationship" between Catholics and Jews.[54] Peter Pulzer and Richard Levy, for example, have argued that on the few occasions when Catholic politicians and editors engaged in attacks on Judaism, moderate Catholic leaders such as Ludwig Windthorst and Ernst Lieber used their powerful influence to silence these attacks.[55] Thus, any public expression of anti-Semitism by Catholic politicians and journalists was the exception, not the norm. As Peter Pulzer stated: "From the 1880s onward,

[53] See Kurt Wawrzinek, *Die Entstehung der deutsche Antisemitenparteien*, Historische Studien (Berlin, 1927).

[54] Paul Massing, *Rehearsal for Destruction: A Study of Political Anti-Semitism in Imperial Germany* (New York: Harper & Bros., 1949), 216–217 n. 38. This quote does not represent Massing's interpretation.

[55] Peter Pulzer, *The Rise of Political Anti-Semitism in Germany and Austria* (New York: John Wiley & Sons, 1964), 276; Levy, *The Downfall of the Anti-Semitic Political Parties*, 14.

the Centre [Party] not only refused to embrace anti-Semitism, but also went out of its way to denounce it."[56]

In addition to the influence of Windthorst and Lieber, Peter Pulzer also cites several other reasons for this Catholic "immunity" to anti-Semitism. He contends that the infamous *Germania* articles had been caused by anger at Jewish politicians who had supported the *Kulturkampf* in the mid-1870s. Once anti-Catholic legislation began to wane, however, the impetus for Catholic anti-Semitism largely disappeared. Pulzer also suggests that because of their own suffering during the *Kulturkampf*, Catholics were reluctant to persecute other minority groups or endorse a program of religious hatred.[57] Thus, both Pulzer and Levy argue that Catholic regions provided relatively infertile ground for candidates from anti-Semitic political parties, and they insist that this resistance was a crucial contributing factor to the failure of political anti-Semitism.[58]

The theory of Catholic "immunity" to anti-Semitism, however, has met with significant criticism. As early as 1949, Paul Massing suggested that Catholic hostility to "Jewish Liberalism" remained strong long after the end of the *Kulturkampf*. According to Massing, "Catholic decisions to use or abstain from political anti-Semitism were as little governed by Christian principles as were those of the Protestant Conservatives. Political, not ethical or religious considerations were the primary determinants of Catholic Jewish relations."[59] Recently, Olaf Blaschke has leveled an even more serious blow to the notion of Catholic "immunity" to anti-Semitism. By examining newspapers and pamphlets along with the literature and culture of regional Catholic associations, Blaschke has demonstrated that anti-Semitic stereotypes and the use of anti-Jewish rhetoric were pervasive in Catholic culture during the *Kaiserreich*. While many Catholic politicians and journalists openly rejected the anti-Semitic parties, they usually did so not out of any desire to defend the rights of German Jews, but instead out of a desire to avoid the most radical extremes of the Berlin Movement. Catholic leaders tended to reject the racial or "unchristian" rhetoric of anti-Semitic agitators, while

[56] Pulzer, *The Rise of Political Anti-Semitism*, 274.
[57] Ibid., 274.
[58] Ibid., 276–277; Levy, *The Downfall of the Anti-Semitic Political Parties*, 4–5.
[59] Massing, *Rehearsal for Destruction*, 216–217 n. 38.

at the same time acknowledging that there was a true "Jewish Question" which required action. Thus, as Blaschke put it:

> Despite what they felt were 'justified complaints' about Jews, [Center Party leaders] kept their distance from the 'rowdy anti-Semites.'[60] ... The methods of the anti-Semitic parties were seen as inappropriate, while the Center Party, on the other hand, felt it had better ideas that it knew how to put into practice. Criticism was leveled at anti-Semitic parties far more for accusations of ineffectiveness than for their anti-Semitism as such ...[61]

For Blaschke then, the Catholic reticence to work with anti-Semitic agitators did not represent a reluctance to engage in criticism of Jews or Judaism. Thus, despite the occasional speeches of Windthorst and Lieber which condemned the excesses of the Berlin Movement, there is no reason to speak of Catholicism acting as a bulwark against anti-Semitism in the *Kaiserreich*.[62]

The (at best) rather mixed record of the Center Party and the Catholic press in regard to anti-Semitism is not necessarily surprising considering that the party was itself a patchwork of different social constituencies. Forged by the pressures of the *Kulturkampf*, the Center Party contained Catholic groups that had relatively little in common except for their religion. The party leader during the 1880s, Ludwig Windthorst, was a Hanoverian politician who fostered strong ties to liberal leaders. His main rival, Burghard von Schorlemer-Alst, was a Westphalian landowner who had ties to ultra-Conservative Junkers like Wilhelm von Hammerstein. During the 1870s, Windthorst and Schorlemer-Alst fought together against the *Kulturkampf* laws. Once the restrictions of the *Kulturkampf* began to ease, however, these two men (and their respective factions) frequently battled over control of the party. While the moderate Windthorst retained his leadership of the parliamentary *fraktion*, agrarian-conservatives like Schorlemer-Alst quickly built a power base in peasant organizations in Westphalia, Silesia, and Bavaria. Under the leadership of Schorlemer-Alst, Freiherr von Hoiningen, and Freiherr von Thüngen-Roßbach,

---

[60] Olaf Blaschke, *Katholizismus und Antisemitismus im Deutschen Kaiserreich* (Göttingen: Vandenhoeck und Ruprecht, 1997), 127.

[61] Ibid., 122–123.

[62] Ibid., 87. Blaschke suggests that Anti-Semitism fulfilled five functions for German Catholics: it focused anti-modern sentiment, provided a simplified worldview, maximized unity, compensated for a sense of vulnerability, and helped Catholics to cope with political and ideological competition. See Ibid., 131–143.

Catholic peasant organizations embraced anti-Semitism as part of their Catholic social-reformist platform.[63] Their use of anti-Semitic rhetoric was in part a product of genuine anti-Jewish sentiment among the peasant population. However, anti-Jewish speeches and articles were also an extension of the internal party battle to prevent any political alliances by moderates with the "Jewish" National Liberals.

Although Schorlemer-Alst and his agrarian allies never succeeded in wresting control of the party away from Windthorst, their efforts were certainly influential in forging Catholic reaction to the Jewish Question. Some Catholic newspapers, such as the *Germania*, joined Schorlemer-Alst in making frequent use of anti-Jewish rhetoric in attacks on liberal politicians. Liberal Catholics like Ludwig Windthorst, on the other hand, occasionally used the rival *Kölnische Volkszeitung* to pointedly denounce the excesses of anti-Semitism.[64]

While Catholic politicians usually vigorously differentiated themselves from the most radical of anti-Semitic agitators, they were generally not afraid to use anti-Semitic rhetoric to attack their political rivals—especially in times of intense political conflict. During the 1870s, "Jewish-liberal" served as a common epithet in Catholic newspapers, and Catholic leaders of this period, like their Conservative counterparts, frequently tried to "beat Bismarckian Liberalism with the anti-Semitic stick."[65] Although Bismarck eventually broke with the liberals, many Catholic politicians continued to see the liberals as their primary enemies. Thus, even long after the *Kulturkampf* had faded, Catholic newspapers continued to revive anti-Jewish rhetoric as a political weapon.[66]

The inconsistent record of the Catholic press on anti-Semitism created frustration and disappointment among both anti-Semites and

---

[63] *Der Kulturkämpfer* Heft 56 (15 April 1882): 35–7. Schorlemer-Alst, founder of the *Westfälischen Bauern-Verein*, consistently objected to the methods of anti-Semitic parties and dismissed their radical platform; however, he also claimed to have "fought energetically his entire life against the many outrages perpetrated by the Jews in commerce and trade". Speech quoted in *Pfälzer Zeitung* (Speyer) 24 April 1893 #111 in BAK *ZSg. 113* Sammlung Fechenbach #14.

[64] Margaret Lavinia Anderson, *Windthorst: A Political Biography* (New York: Oxford Press, 1981), 259.

[65] Pulzer, *The Rise of Political Anti-Semitism*, 273.

[66] In contrast to the conclusions of Pulzer and Levy, Uriel Tal concludes that anti-Jewish sentiment was common in Catholic circles not only during the height of the *Kulturkampf*, but also throughout the 1880s, particularly in the Rhineland, Westphalia, and Bavaria. Uriel Tal, *Christians and Jews in Germany: Religion, Politics, and Ideology in the Second Reich, 1870–1914* (Ithaca: Cornell Univ. Press, 1975), 90–91.

liberals. Anti-Semitic agitators such as Max Liebermann von Sonnenberg and Otto Glagau, for example, consistently praised the activities of Schorlemer-Alst and the Catholic peasant organizations. Occasionally, they even considered the *Germania* a sympathetic ally to their own cause. However, anti-Semitic leaders also expressed their distaste for Ludwig Windthorst and their disappointment that he and his liberal allies had prevented the Center Party from taking a forceful stand on the Jewish Question. As Liebermann von Sonnenberg's anti-Semitic *Deutsch-Soziale Correspondenz* (formerly *Deutsch-Soziale Blätter*) wrote in frustration in 1894: "What does it matter if the Center press occasionally prints articles tinged with anti-Semitism? That will not bother the Jews as long as these articles remain the exception and protection of the Jews remains the rule . . ."[67]

The reaction of German liberals to the Center Party's position on anti-Semitism was equally mixed. While liberal newspapers were not always fond of Windthorst himself, they often praised him for resisting the more conservative and more anti-Semitic elements of his own party. These same newspapers, however, were quick to condemn even the slightest sign of anti-Jewish rhetoric in the Catholic press. Liberal journalists frequently attacked the *Germania* for its use of anti-Jewish rhetoric and openly worried that the Center Party as a whole might begin to follow the *Germania*'s example.[68]

Given the important role of anti-Jewish rhetoric in the contentious political debates of early Imperial Germany, it is easy to see why anti-Semitic scandals and trials became a frequent battleground both for rival political parties and for individual factions within those parties. Libel trials, criminal trials, and ritual murder allegations provided an excellent propaganda opportunity for ultra-Conservatives and radical Catholics to use against their liberal opponents and against any in their own parties that might seek to ally with them.

[67] *Deutsch-Soziale Blätter*, 30 July 1894 #86, quoted in Uwe Mazura, *Zentrumspartei und Judenfrage (1870/71–1933): Verfassungsstaat und Minderheitenschutz* (Mainz: Mathias Grünewald Verlag, 1994), 171–172.

[68] While liberal and Jewish newspapers commonly attacked the *Germania* for its anti-Semitic rhetoric, not all German Jews remained hostile to the Center Party. Throughout the *Kaiserreich*, the Center party gradually attracted voters among orthodox and conservative-agrarian Jews in Bavaria and Silesia. In fact, the number of Jews who supported Center Party candidates increased from 1–2% between 1867 and 1878, to 2–4% between 1879 and 1892, and finally to 5–6% between 1893 to 1902. Many liberal and reform oriented Jews, however, continued to view the party with suspicion. See Tal, *Christians and Jews in Germany*, 189.

CHAPTER TWO

FIGHTING WORDS: LIBEL TRIALS, JEWS, AND THE CULT OF HONOR

During the last decades of the Nineteenth Century, demonstrations of personal honor became an obsession both among Junkers and members of the German middle class. The depth of this fascination with honor is demonstrated by the dramatic increase in the number of duels fought in the 1870s and 1880s.[1] The causes of this revival of dueling culture are complex and controversial; however, they certainly include the already highly stratified and militarized nature of Imperial German culture, the gradual weakening of old aristocratic privileges, and the seemingly ominous growth of socialism and working-class power. In a sense, the resurgence of dueling in fin-de-siècle Germany can be seen as a reaction against modernity—an attempt to reinforce traditional values against the perceived social and moral degeneration of the modern world.

Although dueling was still considered a criminal act in Imperial Germany, it was usually punished with a slap on the wrist or a small jail sentence. A refusal to duel, on the other hand, could have much more serious consequences—including public humiliation and even dismissal from the military. The hypocritical attitude of German authorities toward the duel is especially evident in the practices of the German Honor Courts (*Ehrengerichte*). These courts had originally been designed to forestall duels by providing judgments in matters

[1] Kevin McAleer, *Dueling: The Cult of Honor in Fin-de-Siècle Germany* (Princeton: Princeton Univ. Press, 1994), 23. This book differs from two previous works on the subject of dueling: V.G. Kiernan's *The Duel in European History: Honor and the Reign of the Aristocracy* (Oxford: Oxford Univ. Press, 1988), and Ute Frevert's *Ehrenmänner: Das Duell in der bürgerlichen Gesellschaft* (München: Beck, 1991). While Kiernan argued that the duel was the last bastion of aristocratic honor in modern society, Frevert claimed that the duel was a bourgeois institution thoroughly integrated into middle-class culture. McAleer, on the other hand, finds a theoretical middle ground. While he insists that middle-class interest rejuvenated the duel in fin-de-siécle Germany, McAleer also claims that the duel maintained a thoroughly aristocratic character and, through the standard of "*Satisfaktionsfähigkeit*" (capability of giving satisfaction), remained a matter of *Standesehre* (class honor).

of military honor. By the 1880s, however, these courts seemed to be having the opposite effect. Although officials of the Honor Courts discouraged dueling, they also now offered to attend the duels to make sure they were properly carried out.[2]

Despite a considerable number of challenges, however, the number of actual duels involving Jews and anti-Semitic agitators during the time of Bismarck was negligible. One reason these challenges rarely led to violence is that the acceptance of a challenge would have meant acknowledging that an opponent was "*satisfactionsfähig*" (capable of giving satisfaction). Acceptance was thus an indirect recognition of an opponent's honorable status, and it granted a legitimate claim to a certain amount of esteem.[3] For anti-Semitic agitators confronted by a Jewish opponent (and vice versa), this was not a desirable outcome—even if the duel was resolved successfully. Thus, instead of resorting to pistols or swords, anti-Semites and their Jewish and liberal opponents often turned to a less dangerous public forum to defend their honor—the German courtroom.[4]

Although most German officers eschewed legal proceedings as an unacceptable substitute for the duel, many politicians and journalists found that libel trials offered many of the same benefits as a duel, without the danger of bloodshed. The victor in a libel trial could publicly proclaim his virtue and courage, while the defeated party might still portray himself as an innocent martyr. A libel trial also had the extra benefit of allowing political agitators to do what they did best—play to the "court of popular opinion." Libel trials were often effective in building (or destroying) the reputations of participants, especially when one party could rely on the trial coverage and commentary of a friendly political newspaper. Of course, for those participants in libel trials who owned newspapers, sensational coverage of their own trials could both enhance their public reputation and boost sales and subscriptions.

Although anti-Semitic agitators preferred the courtroom to the duel, many found that battles in the German courtroom could be almost as hazardous as the tip of a blade or an exchange of gunfire.

---

[2] McAleer, *Dueling: The Cult of Honor*, 89.

[3] Ibid., 155.

[4] Duels in France between Jews and anti-Semites seem to have been more common. See, for instance, Robert Nye, *Masculinity and Male Codes of Honor in Modern France* (New York: Oxford Univ. Press, 1993), 205–210.

Cross-examination by attorneys, criticism by judges, and significant fines or jail sentences were serious risks that awaited any defendant. Even when anti-Semitic agitators were plaintiffs instead of defendants, they still ran the risk of having their personal character and political record impugned by hostile attorneys. Thus, each political skirmish inside the courtroom had the potential to turn into a battle for political survival.

This chapter examines a series of anti-Semitic libel trials that served as an extension of contemporary political debates, as a platform for discussion of the Jewish Question, and also as a forum for the defense of personal honor. While these trials are only a small sample of those that occurred during the 1880s and 1890s, they clearly demonstrate the way that the battle over the "Jewish Question" was fought in the courtroom (and the press) as much as in the Reichstag or on the streets.

The Kantorowicz Affair

After Adolf Stöcker's first anti-Jewish speeches in late 1879, the anti-Semitic movement steadily gained strength in Berlin. Stöcker's speeches, Heinrich von Treitschke's articles in the *Preußische Jahrbücher*, and the founding of several local anti-Semitic newspapers all fanned the flames of religious (or racial) intolerance. But the single most dramatic event in this so-called *Berliner Antisemitismusstreit* did not involve either Stöcker or Treitschke.[5] The Kantorowicz Affair, as it soon became known, centered on a simple slap delivered by a Jewish businessman on a Berlin tram. This rather trivial altercation quickly developed into a *cause célèbre*. What began as a simple feud over personal honor eventually sparked an intense debate on the "Jewish Question" in the Berlin press and led to a significant intensification of anti-Jewish sentiment in Berlin and across Germany.

---

[5] The book *Berliner Antisemitismusstreit* (The Berlin Anti-Semitic Conflict), edited by Walther Boehlich, focuses specifically on the series of pamphlets and articles surrounding the Treitschke-Mommsen debates on the "Jewish Question." These "scholarly" debates did have an effect on public perceptions of the Jewish Question, but they were only one contributing factor to the rising anti-Jewish agitation in 1880. I have here used the term *Antisemitismusstreit* to refer more broadly to the intense public debate over the "Jewish Question" between 1879 and 1881.

On November 8, 1880, two men boarded a horse-drawn tram in the center of Berlin. They were the 30 year-old Dr. Bernhard Förster and his colleague, 29 year-old Dr. Carl Jungfer. Both men were teachers at the *Friedrichs-Gymnasium*, and both were also active supporters of the Anti-Semitic Petition that had recently started to circulate through Berlin.[6] As they sat in the tram, the two men engaged in a loud and very public discussion of Stöcker and the "Jewish Question." In particular, Förster and Jungfer condemned Jewish influence in Germany and expressed their gratitude that Stöcker's growing popularity had already led to the defeat of a "Jewish" city councilman named Wolfgang Strassmann.[7] These loud comments were clearly meant to rouse the ire of Jewish passengers, and in this they succeeded. Edmund Kantorowicz, a 35 year-old Jewish salesman from Posen, rose to exchange insults with Jungfer and Förster. At the next stop, all three men got out of the tram, and the argument became even more heated. When Jungfer tried to dismiss Kantorowicz with the comment "Oh, you're only a Jew!", Kantorowicz responded by slapping him on the back of the neck. Förster immediately called for a policeman, and the parties were separated without further incident. This seemingly insignificant confrontation, however, was not quickly forgotten.

The day after the incident, Kantorowicz wrote a letter to the director of the *Friedrichs-Gymnasium* and to the liberal *Berliner Börsen-Courier*. The letter described the confrontation in detail and added that, although Jungfer had agreed to a duel with Kantorowicz after the incident, a note had later arrived declaring Kantorowicz "*unsatisfactionsfähig*" (incapable of providing satisfaction) and refusing to fight. Kantorowicz's letter did not demand any action against the teachers by school authorities, but simply defended his own reputation and proclaimed: "Naturally, these men no longer exist as far as I

---

[6] According to Richard Levy, Bernhard Förster had the idea to start the Anti-Semitic Petition while attending a Wagner festival in Bayreuth during the summer of 1880. But contrary to Levy's implication, the Kantorowicz Affair was not a cause, but a result of Förster's already growing involvement with anti-Semitism. Förster was also Friedrich Nietzsche's "much despised" brother-in-law. His wife, Elizabeth Förster-Nietzsche, edited Nietzsche's work after his death to give it a more nationalistic and anti-Semitic interpretation. See Richard Levy, *The Downfall of the Anti-Semitic Political Parties in Imperial Germany* (New Haven: Yale Univ. Press, 1975), 21; Fritz Stern, *The Politics of Cultural Despair: A Study in the Rise of the Germanic Ideology* (Berkeley: Univ. of California Press, 1961), 283–284.

[7] Strassmann had converted to Christianity years before.

am concerned."[8] Soon after his letter to the *Friedrichs-Gymnasium*, Kantorowicz decided to write to the district militia office (*Landwehr-Bezirkskommando*) to suggest that an Honor Court (*Ehrengericht*) investigate Förster's behavior in the tram and his refusal to duel.[9] In these letters, however, Kantorowicz confused Jungfer with Förster, and asserted that it was Förster who had received the slap. This was probably an honest mistake by Kantorowicz, but it would later come back to haunt him.

In response to these public letters, both Förster and Jungfer sent statements to a prominent newspaper, the *National Zeitung* that corrected Kantorowicz's misidentification and portrayed the entire incident in a much different light.[10] While Förster and Jungfer boasted of their own honor (and Förster's military record), both men also repeated their claim that Kantorowicz was "*unsatisfactionsfähig*" because of his conduct and his reputation. Jungfer, therefore, claimed that his only viable alternative was to file a civil suit instead.

Long before the two parties could present their case in civil court, however, local (and national) newspapers took sides in the case and began to use the incident to argue their own views on the Jewish Question. The *Berliner Börsen-Courier*, for example, a liberal newspaper owned by George Davidsohn, became the champion of Kantorowicz's cause.[11] In a lead story, the *Börsen-Courier* responded to the argument that Kantorowicz was "*unsatisfactionsfähig*" by showing that he had served faithfully in the Prussian army and had earned the Military Service Cross and the Campaign Medal (*Feldzugsmedaille*). "As the Fatherland called on its sons to do battle," the article continued, "Kantorowicz served as a fully qualified and obligated citizen."[12] In fact, the *Börsen-Courier* compared the Kantorowicz

[8] Simplicius Simplicissimus, "Der Fall Kantorowicz als Symptom unsere Zustände," reprinted in *Beiträge zur Geschichte der antisemitischen Bewegung vom Jahre 1880–1885*, ed. Max Liebermann von Sonnenberg (Berlin: Selbstverlag des Herausgebers, 1885), 8. See also an artcle from the *Allgemeine Zeitung des Judenthums* in Karsten Krieger, ed., *Der "Berliner Antisemitismusstreit," 1879–1881*, Teil 2 (München: K.G. Saur, 2004), 633–642.

[9] For more on Honor Courts and their powers, see McAleer, *Dueling: The Cult of Honor*.

[10] The editors of the *National Zeitung* were not at all sympathetic to Jungfer and Förster, but perhaps felt obliged to print the statements in order to avoid a lawsuit over the matter of mistaken identity.

[11] As a liberal paper under Jewish ownership, the *Börsen-Courier* had always been a favorite target for anti-Semitic attacks.

[12] Quoted in Simplicissimus, "Der Fall Kantorowicz," 15.

incident to another recent confrontation in Hanau, where a Jewish man had killed an anti-Semitic officer in a duel. Both incidents, the paper suggested, were cases of honorable and justified self-defense.[13] Finally, the *Börsen-Courier* also used the Kantorowicz incident to condemn Adolf Stöcker and the anti-Semitic movement, and it demanded that school teachers who were active in preaching hatred be removed from the classroom.

In the following days a full-fledged press war occurred over the honor of Kantorowicz and his two opponents. The *Berliner Börsen-Courier* boasted that Kantorowicz had received hundreds of telegrams congratulating him for his actions, including many from non-Jewish admirers. The *Volkszeitung*, the *Berliner Tageblatt*, and several other liberal newspapers also joined the *Börsen-Courier* in condemning this incident as the "newest fruit of [Adolf] Stöcker's disseminations."[14]

Because of their own anti-liberal inclinations, the Catholic and ultra-Conservative press could not resist attacking the liberal press for their support of Kantorowicz. For example, although the Catholic *Germania* explained that it did not condone the behavior of Jungfer and Förster, it printed a long exposé that accused Kantorowicz (who was a maker and seller of liqueurs) of fraudulent business practices. The *Germania* reported that in 1873 the firm Hartwig-Kantorowicz had been convicted of using false labels to suggest that their product was authentic Benedictine liqueur. According to the *Germania*, the judge in that case ruled that the firm had behaved in a manner that was "dishonest, disloyal, and unworthy of an upstanding businessman."[15]

---

[13] *Berliner Börsen-Courier* 11 November 1880, quoted in Simplicissimus, "Der Fall Kantorowicz," 9–10. In the Hanau incident, Lieutenant von Kapphengst allegedly slandered the *Referendar* Goldschmidt by calling him a "Jew-boy." Goldschmidt responded with a challenge. Although challenges between anti-Semites and prominent Jews and liberals were common, the Hanau case is one of the few to have been followed to a fatal conclusion. A little more than a decade after the Hanau duel, a similar conflict in France provoked a sharp debate on the Jewish question. In that case, an anti-Semite named Marquis des Morés fought a duel and killed a Jewish officer in the French army. Although Morés was eventually acquitted of criminal charges, the French Minister of War, Freycinet, made a point of attending the Jewish officer's funeral. See *Berliner Volksblatt Vorwärts* 28 June 1892 #148 in StH Polizeibehörde, Abteilung IV, Politische Polizei (Bestandnummer 331–3): S 576 Teil I.

[14] *Berliner Tageblatt* as quoted in Simplicissimus, "Der Fall Kantorowicz," 19.

[15] *Germania* as quoted in Simplicissimus, "Der Fall Kantorowicz," 24. In the weeks after the Kantorowicz incident, the *Germania* and the ultra-Conservative *Kreuzzeitung*

Kantorowicz responded to these accusations with a letter published in the *Börsen-Courier*, which explained that the earlier case had been a routine dispute over trademarks. He argued that his firm had previously used that trademark for over a decade and added that previous court rulings had allowed him to continue this practice. Despite Kantorowicz's protests of innocence, however, the anti-Semitic press did not hesitate to use this story to attack his reputation. Anti-Semitic newspapers now gleefully referred to Kantorowicz as the "Schnapps-Jew" or the "well-known trademark forger."[16]

Anti-Semitic agitators soon published a pair of anonymous pamphlets that vilified Kantorowicz and even challenged his military credentials. One of these pamphlets, "The Kantorowicz Case as a Symptom of our Situation," written under the pseudonym Simplicius Simplicissimus, recounted both the original confrontation on the tram and the press debates that had followed. For the anti-Semitic author, it was Kantorowicz who had provoked the confrontation by interfering in a private discussion. The actions of Förster and Jungfer, on the other hand, were very much akin to the actions of a brave soldier fighting against Germany's enemies:

> At this moment, shouldn't these two men have been overcome by the feeling that breaking off their conversation [in the face of Kantorowicz's objections] would be a sign of cowardice? Wouldn't this be the same as a commander of a brigade of storm troopers yelling 'Drop your weapons!' at the moment he should be yelling 'Forward! Hurrah!'? Anyone who can still feel German will understand what we mean.[17]

---

printed daily reports and commentaries under headlines such as "On the Jewish Question." These articles would often comment on the progress of the Kantorowicz case, criticize the "*Judenpresse*," or report on "typical Jewish behavior" in other German cities. *Germania* was not the only Catholic newspaper to criticize Kantorowicz and the "*Judenpresse*." In fact, even the *Kölnische Volkszeitung*, a major Catholic daily which later developed a reputation for tolerance and moderation, printed vicious attacks against the Berlin "*Judenpresse*." The hostility of these articles reflected both current political (and journalistic) rivalries as well as lingering hatred over the *Kulturkampf*. Catholic attacks on Kantorowicz were often mixed with condemnations of liberal hypocrisy. As the *Kölnische Volkszeitung* wrote: "The same newspapers that now lament the Jew-baiting, and who set heaven and earth in motion against anti-Semitic endeavors were once the most avid supporters of the persecution of Jesuits and ordinary Catholics." *Kölnische Volkszeitung* 14 November 1880 #314 Erstes Blatt.

[16] Simplicissimus, "Der Fall Kantorowicz," 24–27.

[17] Quoted in Ibid., 9. Of course, in this version of the Kantorowicz confrontation, Jungfer had been surrounded by a crowd of Jews (9 to 1!) and was already weakened and slowed by a chronic foot injury. This explains how a Jew could have had the "courage" to assault an honorable German man. Other anti-Semitic newspapers and pamphlets claimed that Kantorowicz had attacked Jungfer from behind.

The anonymous pamphlet also claimed that the Kantorowicz incident had now become far more than a personal feud. It had become a symptom of "the grave sickness of our Jewish-infected state-body (*Staatskörper*)." Thus, the slap delivered by Kantorowicz was not merely directed against Dr. Jungfer; it was "a slap in the face of the German people!"[18]

The polemics in the German press soon brought public comment by the Berlin city council. A few weeks earlier, several anti-liberal and anti-Semitic newspapers had printed editorials accusing the liberal Councilman Strassmann of stealing cement from city building projects. Using these kinds of allegations, a loose coalition of anti-Semites, Conservatives, and radical-Catholics succeeded in defeating Strassmann in the November 1880 elections. Strassmann, however, was elected in a second district and then re-appointed as chairman of the city council. Since the Kantorowicz Affair occurred just a few days after the election, it provided an easy opportunity for Strassmann and the rest of the city council to strike back at their anti-Semitic opponents.

On November 11, only three days after the Kantorowicz incident, the liberal politicians Otto Hermes and Paul Langerhans demanded in a city council meeting that that the Municipal Executive Council (*Magistrat*) take action against Jungfer and Förster. Hermes made a long speech attacking both Stöcker and the Anti-Semitic Petition, and he argued that anyone engaging in such hateful agitation was not qualified to serve as an educator. Councilman Hermes also attacked Jungfer and Förster personally, suggesting that their teaching abilities did not rise above the standard of mediocrity. Although a school official named Cauer responded that the Municipal Council had little power in such cases, he did express sympathy for the comments of the liberal city councilmen, and he assured the council that the behavior of the two teachers would be investigated by the provincial school board.[19] The next day, the anti-Semitic press, along with Conservative and radical-Catholic newspapers, blasted Cauer and the

[18] Ibid., 41–42.

[19] *Kreuzzeitung* 12 November 1880 #266A. A few days later the *Magistrat* advised that the school board should open a disciplinary hearing against the two teachers, and suggested that they be relieved of their duties while the hearings were underway. *Kreuzzeitung* 13 November 1880 #267A.

city council for taking a position on the incident before the investigation had been completed.

In the meantime, the discussion of the Kantorowicz Affair in the national press had turned the incident from a local into a national issue. On November 14, many prominent Berlin intellectuals and politicians released a statement to the Berlin press that was designed as a response to the infamous Anti-Semitic Petition started by Bernard Förster. Several prominent non-Jews, including Theodor Mommsen, Rudolph Virchow, and Heinrich Rickert signed this counter-petition, which was nicknamed the "Statement of the Berlin Notables." Although this statement did not mention Kantorowicz by name, and although the signers claimed it had been conceived before the Kantorowicz incident, many in the anti-Semitic press argued that the uproar over the Kantorowicz Affair had been the crucial factor in motivating its dissemination.

A few days later, Albert Hänel, a liberal politician from Kiel, made an interpellation in the Reichstag to demand a government response to the growing furor in the public and the press. This triggered the infamous *Judendebatte* of 1880, which consisted of two full days of polemics on the Jewish Question by delegates from across the political spectrum. On the first day, the debate centered on the general issue of the government's attitude toward Förster's Anti-Semitic Petition. No explicit mention of the Kantorowicz case was made, although city councilmen like Hermes and Strassmann came under direct attack for their domination of Berlin city affairs. On the second day of the Reichstag debate, however, several speakers turned their attention directly to the Kantorowicz Affair. A deputy named Strosser began his speech by complaining that the debate had so far been too general in focus. Strosser claimed to want to "illuminate the genesis of this interpellation a bit more closely."[20] For Strosser, the source of this controversy was the fact that a Jewish businessman, well known for his fraudulent practices, had slandered and assaulted honorable German men and then dared to use his political connections in an attempt to ruin them. Strosser also singled out the city council, and especially Hermes and Langerhans, for having criticized Förster and Jungfer before any official investigation had taken place. After all the recent "financial revelations"

[20] Simplicissimus, "Der Fall Kantorowicz," 156–157.

about Kantorowicz, Strosser claimed, the liberals and Jews were surely sorry that they had selected this man as their champion.

This attack on Kantorowicz brought a response from one of the most prominent liberal deputies and one of the most respected scientists in Germany, Rudolf Virchow. Although he admitted having no personal knowledge of the case, Virchow proceeded to defend Kantorowicz's reputation from the Reichstag floor. He argued that the previous conviction of Kantorowicz's company was not in a criminal court but in a civil court. Thus, according to Virchow, any suggestion that Kantorowicz had been convicted of criminal fraud was ludicrous. Virchow also claimed that several other firms had been prosecuted for similar reasons, and that this was a simple disagreement over trademark rights and in no way a criminal matter. Virchow also defended the comments of several city councilmen and the disciplinary proceedings against the two teachers. Apparently, school officials had previously warned Förster about making offensive remarks in front of Jewish students. Thus, Virchow claimed, this incident was not an isolated case, but part of a pattern of anti-Jewish harassment. Finally, Virchow used the Kantorowicz incident to attack the "real" source of the anti-Jewish furor, Adolf Stöcker. Virchow claimed that Stöcker's latest speeches had gone so far, "that one might believe he would end by demanding the extermination of all Jews."[21]

The vitriol displayed in the Reichstag only served to arouse public passion over the Jewish Question even more. In the weeks ahead, agitators like Adolf Stöcker and Ernst Henrici held dozens of rallies that were attended by thousands of people. In response, Jewish and liberal leaders initiated several public meetings of their own in the hopes of finding a strategy for fighting the spread of anti-Jewish sentiment. Anti-Semitism seemed to be raging out of control throughout Germany, and people across the political spectrum pointed to the Kantorowicz incident as the spark that had ignited the blaze.

Meanwhile, as all of Berlin argued over the "Jewish Question," the disciplinary proceedings against Jungfer and Förster continued. Despite a petition in support of the two teachers from some of their students and teaching colleagues, the disciplinary court of the provincial school board censured both teachers for their behavior and fined

[21] Ibid., 181.

Förster 90 Marks.[22] Eventually, both men were dismissed from their teaching positions. But this was not all. Because of his involvement in the Kantorowicz Affair, Förster, the "brave anti-Semitic soldier," was also dismissed from his position as a Prussian officer.[23]

Jungfer and Förster responded to these setbacks by launching a new legal campaign. In addition to pressing charges against Kantorowicz, they lobbied the Public Prosecutor's Office (*Staatsanwalt*) and the Senior Public Prosecutor (*Oberstaatsanwalt*) to charge Otto Hermes and Paul Langerhans with slander for their critical comments in the city council meeting. When their repeated pleas were rejected, Förster and Jungfer instead filed a private suit against the men. Unfortunately for the two teachers, these charges were also dismissed on the grounds that the councilmen were only making fair comments on matters of public interest. To add to this frustration, Förster and Jungfer were forced to pay the court costs for each failed attempt to charge these men with slander. After nearly a year of disappointment, the two teachers were finally given another legal forum for regaining their honor: after a brief investigation, the Berlin public prosecutor decided to charge Edmund Kantorowicz with both slander and assault for the incident in the tram.

While the participants waited for the case against Kantorowicz to come to trial, public attention shifted to other anti-Jewish incidents, such as the anti-Jewish violence in Pomerania. But Bernhard Förster was never completely out of the public spotlight. In the intervening months, Förster gave many speeches that attacked Kantorowicz, his supporters in the "*Judenpresse*," and individual members of the Berlin city council. Unfortunately for Förster, however, he would again achieve notoriety in March 1881 for another physical altercation.

In the months after the Kantorowicz incident, two students who had been active in the anti-Semitic movement developed a rivalry with Förster over personal and philosophical differences. After several heated public exchanges, these students, Schramm and Roland, challenged Förster to a duel. After Förster refused to acknowledge this challenge, however, Schramm and Roland decided to take matters

---

[22] The liberal *Volks-Zeitung* reported that 159 of the 400 Gymnasium teachers in Berlin signed the petition supporting Förster and Jungfer. *Volks-Zeitung* #298 Erstes Blatt.

[23] As Kantorowicz's lawyer, August Munckel, recounted. *Berliner Tageblatt* 5 January 1882 #7 Erstes Beiblatt.

into their own hands. After telling Förster's housekeeper that they wanted to offer him surprise birthday congratulations, the two students confronted Förster in his own study. A brief struggle ensued in which Förster was punched and beaten with a cane. Eventually, Förster reported the incident to police, who then filed charges against both Schramm and Roland.

For the anti-Semitic press, the "brave soldier" of the Kantorowicz case had now become a martyr to his cause. The small *Berliner Ostend-Zeitung* and the *Hallesches Thorbote*, for instance, both put out extra-editions dealing with the affair. As the *Hallesches Thorbote* wrote: "This morning at 7 AM, the esteemed defender of our holy national movement, Dr. Förster, was attacked in his apartment by two men armed with clubs. Despite a heavy resistance, Dr. Förster was unable to stop his attackers. Unfortunately, he must now spend his own birthday severely injured and bedridden in his room."[24] The liberal press, however, was far less sympathetic to Förster's plight. Many newspapers implied that Förster was as disreputable as those who had attacked him, and they concluded that this incident was just a case of one anti-Semitic rabble-rouser attacking another. Needless to say, Förster demanded a stiff sentence for his attackers, who had robbed him of his honor and dignity. This case, therefore, joined the Kantorowicz Affair as part of Förster's campaign to regain his personal honor and defeat his enemies in the Berlin "*Judenpresse*."

Förster and Jungfer's day in court in the Kantorowicz matter finally arrived on August 30, 1881. The small Court of Lay Assessors was filled with spectators, and several reporters covered the trial for leading Berlin newspapers. Kantorowicz was charged with three crimes: slandering Jungfer, slapping Jungfer, and then libeling Förster through a purposeful misidentification in a letter to the *Berliner Börsen-Courier*. The defendant, Kantorowicz, was the first to testify. He assured the court that Jungfer and Förster had purposely provoked the incident, and he stated that as the two were taken to the local police station, they were already using the public attention they had garnered to advertise a meeting of Adolf Stöcker's Christian-Social Party. After Kantorowicz finished his testimony, Jungfer gave his own fairly straightforward account of the original incident. He claimed

---

[24] Quoted in *Berliner Börsen-Courier* 1 April 1881 #166, in LAB A Pr. Br. Rep. 030, Polizeipräsidium Berlin, Nr. 15220, p. 22.

that he had not meant the conversation to be overheard, and had harbored no desire to provoke Kantorowicz or anyone else on the tram. Förster, on the other hand, admitted that he had noticed several Jews on the tram, but claimed to have decided to proceed with his anti-Jewish remarks anyway.

After Förster's testimony, and after several witnesses confirmed that Kantorowicz had slapped Jungfer, the prosecutor claimed to have proven his *prima facie* case. Although he admitted that Kantorowicz had been provoked, he argued that the defendant had no right to publicly slander two educated public officials with epithets such as "insolent fool." The prosecutor added that the use of violence against Jungfer, and the subsequent libel (by misidentification) of Förster in the press were in no way justified, and must be punished. The prosecutor, therefore, asked the judges to sentence Kantorowicz to a 30 Mark fine for the libel of Jungfer, a 60 Mark fine for the libel of Förster, and one week in jail for the slap.

Kantorowicz's attorney, the renowned August Munckel, responded by claiming that Kantorowicz's actions had not only been justified, but had been honorable. Munckel claimed that any slanders on the tram canceled each other out, and that any libel resulting from the case of mistaken identity was unintentional and should be forgiven. Munckel ended his speech by again claiming that Jungfer and Förster had provoked the incident and had received exactly what they deserved.

The three judges in the Court of Lay Assessors retired only a short time before returning with a verdict. They agreed with Munckel that the slanders on the tram canceled each other out. However, they agreed with the prosecutor that a slap was unjustified, and therefore must be punished. In addition, the judges believed that the misidentification of Förster was not an accident, but part of a campaign to destroy his reputation. Kantorowicz thus received a total sentence of one month in jail for both libel and assault. A subsequent appeal by Kantorowicz was heard by the Berlin Superior Court I in January of 1882. This hearing reduced the total sentence to a 100 Mark fine, but the conviction of Kantorowicz was upheld.[25]

[25] *Berliner Tageblatt* 5 January 1882 #7 Erstes Beiblatt. The arguments in the second trial were much the same as the first. This time, the prosecutor also expressed his distaste for the actions of all parties involved, including those of Förster and Jungfer. However, he still maintained that the slap was an unjustified response. The

On the day after Kantorowicz's conviction, Förster appeared in another Berlin court for the trial against Schramm and Roland. The two students were charged with both assault and unlawful entry. Schramm tried to defend his actions by claiming that a previous failure to respond to a slander had resulted in an investigation by an Honor Court and his dismissal as an officer. Therefore, he argued that a less than vigorous response to Förster's insults may have hurt his own chances of regaining his rank. Schramm claimed to have tried repeatedly to challenge Förster to a duel, but in each case he failed to elicit a response. As Schramm testified: "Because I didn't receive any answer for several days, there was no other way to prove that there was no cowardice on my part except to go to Förster's apartment."[26] Schramm admitted that he did strike Förster on the head with his staff, but claimed that the blow was a "symbolic one" and had not been delivered at full force. As for the subsequent struggle, this was simply a matter of self-defense, since he had simply repelled Förster's attempts to attack him. Förster responded that the blows he had received from the two students had not been "symbolic," and he claimed to have needed three weeks in bed to recover fully. After a summary of the evidence, the prosecutor asked that Schramm be sentenced to two months in prison and that Roland be sentenced to 20 days. The judges deliberated for thirty minutes before finding both students guilty of illegal entry and assault. The judges, however, viewed both the injuries to Förster and the damage done by the illegal entry as minimal, and so they sentenced each defendant to a very lenient penalty: a small fine and eight days in jail.[27]

The sentence in this case was quickly appealed by the prosecutor, and a new hearing was ordered less than a week later. In this new trial, Förster made a point of claiming that as soon as he had been struck on the head by Schramm, he had immediately grabbed for his sword to return the attack. Förster also claimed to have pursued the two students down the stairs and given one a scar on the head before being wrestled to the ground by his assailants. This time,

---

judge reversed the verdict on the "unintentional" libel of Dr. Förster, but upheld the conviction for assault.

[26] Quoted in *Kreuzzeitung* 1 September 1881 #204B.

[27] *Kreuzzeitung* 1 September 1881 #204B.

however, Förster's public proclamation of his own bravery backfired. In ruling on this appeal, the lead judge commented that since Förster had taken his sword with the aim of attacking rather than defending himself, his own actions had been unjustified. Although the judge upheld the original verdict against the students, he reduced the already minimal sentence even further.[28]

On the surface, then, these trials were victories for both Förster and for German anti-Semitism. As one might expect, the verdict against Kantorowicz was seen in the anti-Semitic press as a public defeat for both Jews and liberals. Anti-Semitic newspapers took special enjoyment in ridiculing George Davidsohn and the *Berliner Börsen-Courier*, who had so emphatically supported Kantorowicz. The anti-Semitic *Berliner Ostend-Zeitung*, for example, ran a page-long article that mocked Davidsohn and sarcastically described the "hero" Kantorowicz leading a Jewish military parade.[29]

A victory for anti-Semitism, however, did not necessarily mean a victory for Förster and Jungfer. After all, the punishments given to Kantorowicz and Schramm were relatively slight, while Förster had been stripped of both his teaching position and his military rank. Thus, despite the "favorable" verdicts, Förster was still unsatisfied by his courtroom experiences. In the months after these verdicts, Förster made several more attempts to regain his lost honor, both inside and outside the courtroom. Days after the Kantorowicz verdict, Förster challenged Kantorowicz's defense attorney, August Munckel, to a duel because of disparaging remarks he had made in his closing arguments. The *Berliner Figaro* reported that Munckel refused the duel because it violated his professional duties as a lawyer.[30] And Munckel was not the only participant in the Kantorowicz affair to be challenged. Otto Hermes, the city councilman, also rejected Förster's offer of a duel.

---

[28] *Berliner Tageblatt* 8 December 1881 #575 Beiblatt.

[29] *Berliner Ostend-Zeitung* 4 September 1881 #204 Beilage. This issue also included the story of a "second Kantorowicz" named Marcuse. After he was asked to give up his seat for the wife of a man named Müller, Marcuse not only refused, but also threatened to slap Mr. Müller. The newspaper sarcastically reported that "the Oriental prudently failed to carry out his threat after noticing the strong handworker fists of Mr. Müller." Rather than instigating a brawl, Müller instead called for a policeman. The *Ostend-Zeitung* promised its readers that legal action would follow.

[30] *Berliner Figaro* September 1881 #227 in LAB A Pr. Br. Rep. 030, Polizeipräsidium Berlin, Nr. 15220, p. 140.

Thus, frustrated by the outcome of his legal campaign (and disappointed by Bismarck's failure to react to his Anti-Semitic Petition), Förster declared his intention to leave Germany in order to found a utopian colony in South America. This colony, called "*Neu Germania*," would allow a new start for Förster and his followers, free from corruption and Jewish influence. In his farewell speech to a meeting of Berlin anti-Semites, Förster made it clear that a primary source of his decision to flee was the infiltration of Jews into the legal system. As he put it:

> As far as law is concerned, such a thing no longer exists. Judges can no longer grasp and understand the legal paragraphs that lie before them—a miseducation of judges has now begun. One could just as well replace legal verdicts with a game of dice since the former is a matter of pure chance.[31]

Förster reserved special contempt for Kantorowicz's defense attorney, August Munckel, who apparently represented all that was wrong with the reformed German legal system. Finally, Förster ended his speech by expressing his own exasperation:

> Gentlemen, if I still wanted to remain here, then I must have one thing above all—and that is my right (*Recht*)! Since this has so often been denied to me, and since I now realize I will never receive justice if I continue to be so persecuted and slandered, I believe that staying would eventually force me to become—yes gentlemen, I must say it—a *revolutionary*! And therefore I would rather leave![32]

For those anti-Semites who stayed behind, however, the Kantorowicz Affair—and the conflict with the Berlin city council—remained a vital part of their propaganda. For several months afterward, the *Magistrat*, the school board, and the city council all found themselves embroiled in a series of libel suits against anti-Semitic agitators. Although several of these trials resulted in libel convictions and fines for anti-Semites, each one also re-ignited public passions over the

---

[31] Police surveillance report in LAB A Pr. Br. Rep. 030, Polizeipräsidium Berlin, Nr. 15221, pp. 33–37. Other anti-Semites expressed similar sentiments.

[32] Quoted in *Neue Deutsche Volkszeitung* 26 January 1883 #21; see LAB A Pr. Br. Rep. 030, Polizeipräsidium Berlin, Nr. 15221, p. 38 (Italics mine). Bernhard Förster's efforts in South America were just as fraught with controversy as his activities in Berlin. After a few years, financial difficulties and internal dissension caused Förster's Paraguayan colony to disintegrate. In 1889, frustrated by his failures, Förster committed suicide.

Kantorowicz Affair and the "Jewish Question."[33] Even years later, Kantorowicz's slap was still being used for public propaganda. When the Reichstag discussed responsibility for the March 1884 anti-Jewish violence in the Pomeranian town of Neustettin, Adolf Stöcker addressed his liberal opponents in the Reichstag with these words:

> The Minister's statements lead to the conclusion that the first provocation in the Neustettin riots came from the Jews. That doesn't surprise me; The Jews have always provoked first. In Berlin it was a Jew who struck the first blow. (Call from the Left: 'Henrici!') Henrici never hit anyone, it was Kantorowicz![34]

Otto Glagau, Karl Hapke, and the Fight Against "Jewish Justice"

Bernhard Förster's concerns about a Jewish domination of the German justice system were shared by many other anti-Semites, as well as by some Conservatives and Catholics. In the late 1870s and early 1880s, many Germans came to believe that Jews were disproportionately represented among lawyers and judges, and this perception led to occasional public debates over the role of Jews in the German justice system. Not surprisingly, in rare cases when anti-Semitic agitators found themselves in court facing a Jewish judge, the combination could be explosive. There were several such confrontations in the 1880s and 1890s, but the most sensational cases included a well-known anti-Semitic journalist named Otto Glagau and an obscure pastor named Karl Hapke.

To understand the atmosphere surrounding the Glagau and Hapke cases, it is first necessary to understand the nature and degree of resistance to the growing numbers of Jews in the German justice system. Although Jews had been allowed to study law in many German states before 1870, they were prevented from becoming judges or high justice officials throughout the North German

[33] A partial list of cases: Magistrat and Horowitz vs. Limprecht and Ruppel, Liebermann vs. Hermes, Liebermann vs. School Board, Madai vs. Liebermann, Basedow vs. Liebermann.

[34] Quoted in *Reichsbote* 16 March 1884 #65 from BAK ZSg. 113 Sammlung Fechenbach Nr. 19. Ernst Henrici gave a speech in Neustettin that was blamed for several months of anti-Jewish unrest. See Chapter 3 for more on Henrici and Neustettin.

Federation. In Prussia, the Law on Jewish Relations of 1847 did grant more opportunities for Prussian Jews, but it only permitted Jews to take over state and community offices as long as they did not involve "judicial, police, or executive power."[35] The public justification for restrictions on Jews in the justice system was that Jewish judges could not administer a religiously based oath to Christian citizens. Thus, even when the Prussian government allowed Jews to become judicial apprentices (*Referendare*) and assistant judges (*Gerichtsassessoren*) in the 1850s, it still prevented them from achieving the highest positions in the German justice system.[36]

The emancipation laws of July 1869 removed these restrictions, however, and after some initial hesitation the German government announced its intention to allow Jewish *Gerichtsassessoren* to become judges. In the next few years, the number of Jewish judges increased dramatically. By 1881, there were 123 Jewish judges in Prussia in both District Courts (*Amtsgerichte*) and Superior Courts (*Landgerichte*).[37] The German government also announced its intention to appoint Jewish prosecutors; however, not a single one was appointed in Prussia throughout the *Kaiserreich*. One explanation for this is that a prosecutor was often considered a more prestigious position than a judge since he was a direct representative of state power in the court.[38] Judgeships, on the other hand, were considered more appropriate

[35] Barbara Strenge, *Juden im preußischen Justizdienst 1812–1918: Der Zugang zu den juristischen Berufen als Indikator der gesellschaftlichen Emanzipation* (Munich: K.G. Saur, 1996), 68. Before 1848, only Baden, Württemberg and Hesse regularly appointed Jews as attorneys. Konrad Jarausch, "Jewish Lawyers in Germany, 1848–1938: The Disintegration of a Profession," *Leo Baeck Institute Year Book* 36 (1991): 173.

[36] These were usually stages in the preparation of a law student for higher judicial office, but they could also lead to other careers in the legal field. After a four-year clerkship, *Referendare* could take the Assessor's exam. After passing this exam, the *Gerichtsassessoren* closely aided judges in their legal duties. See Strenge, *Juden im preußischen Justizdienst*, 102. Baptized Jews had significantly more chance of serving in higher administrative and legal posts than those who maintained their Jewish confession. Karl Friedenthal, for example, served as the Prussian Agricultural Minister (1874–1879), Martin Simson became the president of the Imperial Court (*Reichsgericht*) in 1879, and Heinrich Friedberg served as Prussian Justice Minister (1879–1889). All three had been baptized as children. Tillmann Krach, *Jüdische Rechtsanwälte in Preussen* (Munich: C.H. Beck'sche Verlagsbuchhandlung, 1991), 16.

[37] Strenge, *Juden im preußischen Justizdienst*, 162.

[38] Ibid., 158–9. There were a few Jewish prosecutors in the rest of Germany. The first was Eduard Silbermann, who took office in 1879 in Bavaria. See Monika Richarz, ed., *Jüdisches Leben in Deutschland*, vol. 1 (Bloomington: Indiana Univ. Press, 1991), 160.

for members of the middle-class, and most judges tended to be from the *Bildungsbürgertum* instead of the landowning classes. Therefore, at least initially, there seemed to have been less opposition among political and social elites to allowing Jews to become judges.[39]

As the number of Jewish judges multiplied in the early Reich, so did the number of Jewish private lawyers. The biggest increase came after the Imperial Lawyer's Code (*Reichsrechtsanwaltsordnung*) of June 1878, which opened the German bar to all qualified applicants and established a legal practice relatively free of state interference. From this point onward, private practice offered Jews the possibility of both a stable income and significant social prestige.

By the early 1880s, Jewish law students also began to opt for private law since it seemed that the doors to the elite law positions such as judges and prosecutors were once again being shut. As Barbara Strenge argues in her book on Jews in the Prussian justice system, the brief period of legal liberalization and tolerance that began in 1869 had come to an abrupt end by the late 1870s. Strenge asserts that the number of Jewish judges did increase after 1880, but at a much slower rate than in the years after unification. Thus, the return of intolerance and the rise of political anti-Semitism pushed Jewish students away from being judges and prosecutors, and into the field of private law.[40] The disproportionate number of Jewish lawyers was already noticeable in December of 1880, when 53 of the 261 private attorneys in Berlin were Jewish (20%).[41]

As one might imagine, there was considerable opposition to the liberal legal reforms of the 1870s among Conservatives and anti-Semites. Most Conservatives were outspoken in their demands for a limitation on the number of private attorneys, and some even demanded repeal of the open bar. They worried that the competition between lawyers would lead to a loss in professional integrity,

---

[39] Strenge, *Juden im preußischen Justizdienst*, 154. This applies primarily to judges of the District Court or Superior Court levels. Higher courts were more prestigious and were usually closed to practicing Jews. For more detailed statistics on Jews in the justice system, see Krach, *Jüdische Rechtsanwälte in Preussen.*

[40] Strenge, *Juden im preußischen Justizdienst*, 164–165.

[41] Ibid., 170. In 1893, 25% of all Prussian lawyers were Jews, although Jews comprised only 3% of the population. The statistics for Berlin and Prussia were not always representative of Germany as a whole, but the conspicuous presence of so many Jewish lawyers in Berlin seemed to magnify their importance. Helmut Heinrichs et al., *Deutsche Juristen jüdischer Herkunft* (Munich: C.H. Beck'sche Verlagsbuchhandlung, 1993), 136.

and they feared that a growing class of leftist-liberal middle-class lawyers might eventually create a "legal proletariat" that would challenge the power of governing elites.[42] These Conservatives, however, also associated liberalization in the legal profession with so-called "Manchesterite competition" and Jewish influence. Thus, calls for a special restriction of Jewish judges and Jewish attorneys usually accompanied their calls for general limitations on lawyers.

As early as the mid-1870s, articles began to appear in many Catholic and Conservative newspapers that complained about the growing "infiltration" of Jews into the German legal system.[43] In July 1878, an especially polemical article called "The Jewish *Referendarius*" appeared in the Catholic-conservative *Schlesische Volkszeitung*. The article not only suggested that all Jews be removed from the legal system, but also demanded that the emancipation laws of 1869 be reversed. Soon after this article was published, the Jewish law clerks (*Referendare*) of the Breslau Appellate Court (*Appelationsgericht*) filed a libel suit against the newspaper. The lead editor of the *Schlesische Volkszeitung* was eventually convicted and fined, but the trial received widespread public attention and brought the journalist a significant amount of public sympathy.[44]

Public attacks on the "Jewification" of the justice system continued over the next several years, spearheaded by men like Adolf Stöcker. In his political rallies and his various newspapers, Stöcker suggested that Jewish judges and attorneys could never represent the interests of the German people. In one newspaper article, he even warned that Germans were in danger of allowing their entire judicial system to fall under Jewish control.[45] However, while these kinds of polemical articles and speeches did arouse some popular interest in the issue, they did not inspire any explicit legislation against Jewish participation in the legal system.

---

[42] Strenge, *Juden im preußischen Justizdienst*, 166.

[43] Ibid., 195. See also Peter Pulzer, "Religion and Judicial Appointments in Germany 1869–1918," *Leo Baeck Institute Year Book* 28 (1983): 185–204. Pulzer writes mostly about official discrimination after the turn of the century, but his inclusion of the Catholic perspective in debates over judicial appointments is an important addition. His article shows that polemical attacks on Jewish judges and lawyers were common occurrences, even in times when the number of Jews in judicial positions was stagnant or in decline.

[44] Strenge, *Juden im preußischen Justizdienst*, 195–196.

[45] Ibid., 202.

The rising number of libel suits against anti-Semitic agitators and the increasing number of Jewish judges were two trends that would almost inevitably produce a public conflict. It is likely that there were many objections to Jewish judges raised in the decade before 1880, but neither the political interest nor the organized anti-Semitic parties existed to turn such incidents into anti-Jewish propaganda. After Stöcker's appearance, and especially after the furor caused by the Kantorowicz Affair and the *Judendebatte* of 1880, public conflicts between Jewish judges and anti-Semites received far more public attention.

In mid-December 1880, the ultra-conservative *Kreuzzeitung* reported on a trial in Wittenberge where a local minister, Pastor Boit, was summoned to testify as a witness. Boit knew beforehand that the lead judge in the case was of Jewish ancestry, so he sent a letter to the court asking to be sworn in by a Christian judge. In this letter, Boit claimed that if his request was refused, he would add the words "through Jesus Christ to everlasting salvation" to the ordinary secular oath, which normally only included the words "so help me God." On the day of the trial, the Jewish judge insisted on swearing in Boit, and the pastor responded by repeating the oath with his own phrase added on the end. According to the *Kreuzzeitung*, the judge rejected this oath as invalid and ordered Boit to recite the official oath or face punishment. When Boit refused, the court fined him 30 Marks and ordered him to pay all court costs.[46]

The *Kreuzzeitung* criticized this verdict as an assault by a Jewish public official on the Christian religion. The newspaper claimed that by law an oath was only invalidated if a significant phrase was left out or if an added phrase explicitly weakened or contradicted the official oath. Obviously, the *Kreuzzeitung* wrote, the invocation of Jesus could not be interpreted as weakening or contradicting the oath in any way.[47] Apparently, the appeals court agreed. When Boit's appeal reached the Superior Court in Neuruppin a few days later, the judges overturned the fine, and claimed that the added phrase did not alter the validity of the oath.[48]

The *Kreuzzeitung* interpreted this verdict as a victory for the right of ordinary Germans to be free of Jewish influence. After a liberal

---

[46] *Kreuzzeitung* 22 December 1880 #300.
[47] Ibid.
[48] *Kreuzzeitung* 24 December 1880 #302.

newspaper criticized a Berlin priest for a similar act of defiance a few weeks later, the *Kreuzzeitung* wrote an angry article condemning Jews for once again attempting to destroy Christianity.[49] Adolf Stöcker also made use of the Wittenberge case in a speech to his Christian-Social Party. Stöcker claimed the case would have far-reaching implications, and he joked that by starting such a controversy, the Jewish judge in Wittenberge had proven that not all Jews were clever.[50]

However, Stöcker's prophecy that the Wittenberge case would have a long-lasting impact proved false. The case disappeared from the headlines and was soon replaced by other scandals, including the anti-Jewish violence in Pomerania (see Chapter 3). But this episode was merely a prelude to the more dramatic cases that were to come a few months later. The next conflicts involving Jewish judges took place in local Berlin courts, in a series of episodes surrounding a little-known Jewish judge named *Amtsgerichtsrath* Lion and a baptized judge named *Landgerichtsrath* Friedberg.[51] The controversy surrounding these men received widespread publicity and helped to bring the issue of Jews in the German justice system into the national headlines.

Glagau and the Jewish Judges

Otto Glagau was best known as the founder and editor of the anti-Semitic journal *Der Kulturkämpfer*.[52] Although not affiliated with any particular party or anti-Semitic faction, Glagau was often viewed—and undoubtedly viewed himself—as one of the most prominent anti-Semites in Germany. Glagau was neither a quiet nor a modest man. He frequently claimed to have single-handedly weakened the National Liberal Party in late 1870s, and he often complained that leading Conservative and anti-Semitic politicians used his articles and speeches

[49] *Kreuzzeitung* 16 January 1881 #13.

[50] Ibid.

[51] *Amtsgerichtsrath* and *Landgerichtsrath* were honorary titles given to tenured judges at the District Court and the Superior Court respectively. Otto Glagau claimed that the lead judges of two of three Courts of Lay Assessors (*Schöffengerichte*) in Berlin's District I (where many libel cases were heard) were Jewish. *Der Kulturkämpfer* Heft 57 (1 May 1882): 36–37.

[52] The title of the journal refers not to the anti-Catholic measures, but to Glagau's 1880 book *Des Reiches Noth und der neue Culturkampf* (Osnabruck: B. Wehberg, 1880). Glagau was not Catholic, although he later claimed to be one of the leading opponents of the liberal-Jewish inspired anti-Catholic campaigns.

in their election campaigns without giving him any credit.[53] Glagau's arrogance and his strident anti-liberal and anti-Jewish rhetoric also made him a frequent target for libel charges throughout the late 1870s and early 1880s. For Glagau, these trials were a thing of pride and honor. As *Der Kulturkämpfer* boasted after a court hearing on libel charges filed by a Jewish journalist:

> His many opponents have been utterly unsuccessful in proving any untruths on his part, and this particular case is only designed to discredit him in public opinion . . .[54]
>
> What satisfaction, what jubilation for the plaintiffs and their *Volk*, if they could only discredit [him] in public and expose [him] as a 'slanderer'![55]

Glagau's arrogance, however, quickly turned to anger and frustration when a series of libel charges in the early 1880s repeatedly brought him in front of judicial panels that included both practicing and baptized Jews. The confrontations that followed would threaten to ruin Glagau's reputation and honor, and would eventually convince him that the justice system in Imperial Germany was thoroughly corrupted by Jewish influence.

In late 1880, Glagau's *Der Kulturkämpfer* printed an article that claimed J.F.H. Dannenberg, the editor of a small newspaper called *Die Börsenhalle*, had been involved in several shady investments. Dannenberg demanded a retraction, and after Glagau's refusal, he sued for libel. The case was sent to the Berlin District Court I in June of 1881. Of the three judges set to preside over the case, two were Jewish, including the lead judge, *Amtsgerichtsrath* Lion. However, after one of the Jewish judges asked to be removed from the case, the trial was postponed.[56] When the case was rescheduled several weeks later, it came before three Christian judges, and Glagau won a quick acquittal.

---

[53] *Der Kulturkämpfer* Heft 42 (15 September 1881): 36–38.

[54] *Der Kulturkämpfer* Heft 26 (15 January 1881): 38–40.

[55] *Der Kulturkämpfer* Heft 34 (15 Mai 1881): 33–8. Glagau devoted a significant amount of this journal to his own courtroom exploits or setbacks—in part because he felt that his heroic struggle was not being covered adequately by the mainstream Berlin press. In this same article, Glagau claims that he could have raised legal objections that would have caused this suit (Hesdörffer vs. Glagau) to be dismissed. But he decided to let the trial go forward in order to publicly prove his innocence (and to give himself another opportunity to publicly attack his liberal and Jewish opponents).

[56] Cases in the District Court were heard by one lead judge and two *Schöffen*, or

In October of the same year, Dannenberg appealed the case to the Berlin Superior Court I. The lead judge for this appeal was *Landgerichtsrath* Gartz, and another member of the three-judge panel was *Landgerichtsrath* Friedberg, who was reported to be a nephew of the baptized Prussian Justice Minister, Heinrich von Friedberg.[57] This appeal did not go as Glagau had anticipated. As he later recounted in an angry article in *Der Kulturkämpfer*, any attempts he made to question Dannenberg's evidence or argue on his own behalf were rudely interrupted by Gartz. According to Glagau, the judges never allowed him to present a full defense, and instead quickly adjourned to consider a verdict. The appeals court found that Glagau had acted with "uncommon carelessness" in claiming Dannenberg was involved in shady investments without checking to see if this was actually the case. Because of Glagau's previous involvement in libel trials, the judges sentenced him to a hefty 500 Mark fine.[58]

Glagau responded with a very long article in *Der Kulturkämpfer* that angrily denounced the corruption of the German court system that had been caused by Jewish-liberal influence. Glagau attacked the appeal judges, who he claimed had lost all sight of justice and impartiality in their rulings. As he wrote: "Which verdict is now the correct one, that of the Court of Lay Assessors (*Schöffengericht*), where two men from the people sat next to a judge, or that of the criminal court (*Strafkammer*), where three judges presided?"[59] Glagau's open contempt for the judges was also targeted toward court reporters,

---

lay-judges from the public. Thus, these District Courts (*Amtsgerichte*) were often called Courts of Lay Assessors (*Schöffengerichte*). In the first hearing of the Glagau-Dannenberg case, it was a Jewish lay-judge who asked to be replaced.

[57] Dr. Heinrich von Friedberg was born into a Jewish family in 1813 and baptized at the age of sixteen. He was a student of Friedrich Karl von Savigny and eventually became a leading jurist. Friedberg was later one of the leading contributors to the Imperial Penal Code (*Reichsstrafgesetzbuch*), and he served as a major figure in the justice reforms of the 1870s. He held the position of Secretary of the Imperial Justice Office (*Staatssekretär des Reichsjustizamtes*) from 1876–1879 and then served as Prussian Justice Minister from 1879 to 1889. He was eventually granted nobility in 1888. For a more detailed biographical sketch see Robert Kuhn, *Deutsche Justizminister 1877–1977* (Köln: Bundesanzeiger Verlagsges., 1977).

[58] *Der Kulturkämpfer* Heft 45 (1 November 1881): 25–34. Glagau admitted that the names on the various lists of investors did not necessarily match (Donnenburg, H. Dannenberg, etc.), but he insisted that his report was made in good faith. He even volunteered to print a retraction—although he suggested that any retraction would be framed with his own commentary on Dannenberg's true character.

[59] *Der Kulturkämpfer* Heft 45 (1 November 1881): 25–34.

who Glagau claimed were in on a conspiracy against him. According to Glagau, when any reporters sent word to leading newspapers that he was doing well in court, these newspapers (dominated by Jews, of course) would refuse to print reports of the trial. In order to earn a living, therefore, these court reporters would either distort the true picture of the proceedings or only report when Glagau met with difficulties. Thus, he claimed, the "*Judenpresse*" was making sure that the German public never got the true story.[60]

Not surprisingly, Glagau was determined to appeal the case again and reclaim his lost honor. This appeal was made to the Berlin Supreme Court (*Kammergericht*) in January of 1882. The Supreme Court claimed to have no right to overturn the second verdict or to question the sentence. But the Supreme Court did decide that the Superior Court had erred in two relatively minor matters: the punishment for non-payment of the fine was too high and an entire page of the offending article was censored instead of just the offending sentences. However, these two errors were serious enough for the Supreme Court to order the case back to the Superior Court for a further hearing.[61]

When the case resumed in the Superior Court, it came before the same three-judge panel that had previously treated Glagau rudely and found him guilty. This time Glagau tried a new approach. He asked that one of the judges, *Landgerichtsrath* Friedberg, be removed from the panel because, even if he was not currently a practicing Jew, he was biased because of his Jewish ancestry. Glagau claimed in a new *Kulturkämpfer* article that this tactic was not unheard of, and that other anti-Semites had repeatedly asked Jewish judges to remove themselves from cases where there might be an appearance of bias. In fact, Glagau claimed that one Jewish editor even took his revenge

[60] Glagau listed many prominent newspapers and criticized almost all of them for buying the same "Jewish-influenced" report of the trial proceedings. Even ultra-conservative and some anti-Semitic newspapers came under fire for printing this unflattering version. *Der Kulturkämpfer* Heft 45 (1 November 1881): 25–34.

[61] Glagau again devoted several pages of his journal to this hearing under the title of "*fiat justicia, pereat mundus*". Once again venting his anger at the court system, Glagau complained that although the case was sent back to a lower court because of judicial errors, he was still being held responsible for a majority of the court costs. (This is because his own grounds for reversal were overruled.) Glagau claimed that these court costs were now climbing into the hundreds of Marks, and could easily bankrupt him even if the criminal fine were eventually reduced. *Der Kulturkämpfer* Heft 53 (1 March 1882): 37–39.

by demanding that a Christian judge remove himself from a court case.[62] Nevertheless, Glagau's objection to Friedberg was overruled after a short delay, and the case continued.[63] The Superior Court made short work of the case—adjusting the problematic parts of its first ruling and upholding the original sentence.

But Glagau was not yet ready to rest. He appealed a second time to the Supreme Court, using another technicality as his main grounds for appeal. This time, Glagau made a long speech to the court about the corruption of Jewish judges and denounced Judge Friedberg in particular for being biased due to his Jewish ancestry. After one of the Supreme Court judges interrupted Glagau to ask him how he could call Friedberg a Jew when he had been raised as a Christian, Glagau responded with a monologue on his views of race. He argued that Orthodox Jews were preferable to Reform Jews, who were themselves preferable to baptized Jews and their direct descendants. Glagau declared that no baptized Jews should be allowed to serve in the German justice system until the fifth generation, and that Jews should never be allowed to lead any major court. The Supreme Court judges listened patiently, but then rejected his attempt to have Friedberg removed. The fine of 500 Marks remained, and Glagau was now forced to pay several hundred additional Marks for the court costs of all his appeals.[64]

Although the Dannenberg case was finally over after two years, five different appeals, and dozens of hearings, Glagau's struggles with Jewish judges were far from over. While the Dannenberg case was still winding its way through appeals, another of Glagau's enemies sued him for libel. A man named Ferdinand Biermann claimed that a *Kulturkämpfer* article falsely suggested that he had cheated German officers out of their money. This second case came to the Berlin District Court I in May of 1882. The presiding judge was *Amtsgerichtsrath* Lion, a Jew.[65]

---

[62] During the Kantorowicz Affair of 1880, a Dr. Bram wrote to the *Vossische Zeitung* to pose this (rhetorical) question: "Isn't a Jew allowed to reject *Amtsgerichtsrath* Wilmanns as a judge because he has no trust in Wilmanns' ability to be unbiased?" Wilmanns, the author of the 1876 book *Die goldene Internationale und die Nothwendigkeit einer Sozialen Reformpartei*, was a judge in a Berlin Commercial Court (*Handelsgericht*). I have uncovered no evidence that Wilmanns' position was ever directly challenged because of his views on the Jewish Question.

[63] *Der Kulturkämpfer* Heft 57 (1 May 1882): 36–37.

[64] *Der Kulturkämpfer* Heft 69 (1 November 1882): 38–40.

[65] This was not the first confrontation between Lion and an anti-Semitic agitator. In March 1882, Julius Ruppel, the editor of the notorious *Berliner Ostend-Zeitung*,

Glagau's conflict with Lion started almost immediately. When Glagau demanded that the charges be dropped because the plaintiff had not presented the proper forms, Lion refused and merely ordered the forms to be added later. Glagau called this an act of improper judicial interference, but Judge Lion overruled all of his objections. Then, as expected, Glagau objected to Lion as a judge because of his bias in matters relating to anti-Semitism. As a legal precedent, Glagau referred to the first hearing of the Dannenberg case, where a Jewish lay-judge had recused himself. Glagau also claimed that Judge Lion had previously recused himself from another case for similar reasons. Although Lion claimed that he had never removed himself from a case for reasons of bias, he did grant a postponement to consider the motion.[66] Glagau's motion was eventually denied, and when the case resumed he was found guilty of libel and sentenced to a 100 Mark fine.

Glagau immediately decided to appeal the Biermann case. However, unfortunately for him, the appeals court was once again the Superior Court I, with Gartz and Friedberg at its head. Glagau immediately made several motions—to remove Gartz for his behavior in the Dannenberg case, to remove Friedberg due to his Jewish ancestry, and to remove all three because of their previous judicial errors. The court took two weeks to consider these motions, but in the end denied all three. Then, once the case resumed, Glagau delivered a long speech attacking Lion's many judicial mistakes and his obvious bias. But Judge Gartz rejected all these complaints and once again treated Glagau in the same rude manner as he had in the Dannenberg case. As Glagau admitted later in *Der Kulturkämpfer*, he was sure that the original guilty verdict would be upheld.

But then something unexpected happened. After reviewing the article in question, the three judges decided that there was no evidence

had been charged with libeling a Jewish banker named Schüler. Ruppel objected that as a Jew, Lion could not be an impartial judge in this case. The issue was sent to the Superior Court for review, and Ruppel's objection was eventually overruled. Ruppel tried to use §24–27 of the legal code to argue that Lion was biased in this matter and should be recused. *Die Post* 18 March 1882 #76 and 7 April 1882 #95 in LAB A Pr. Br. Rep. 030, Polizeipräsidium Berlin, Nr. 15220, p. 338.

[66] *Der Kulturkämpfer* Heft 58 (15 May 1882): 34–7. In an earlier libel case against Glagau (Hesdörffer vs. Glagau), Judge Lion had removed himself from the case for unspecified reasons. Lion, however, claimed that this had nothing to do with Glagau's identity, but was "*zufällig*."

of libel in this case—they overturned the previous verdict and erased the 100 Mark fine. Glagau was stunned and elated. He reported in *Der Kulturkämpfer* that the majority of the audience in the courtroom had been Jewish, and that after his acquittal, they each looked like they had been convicted themselves. But Glagau's acquittal in front of a "Jewish judge" did not lead him to the conclusion that the legal system had worked or that Jewish judges could be impartial. Instead, Glagau claimed that it had been proven that the new legal system was almost like a lottery, and that justice was left up to chance. In the end, Glagau took little solace in his victory in the Biermann case. He was still faced with a large fine from the Dannenberg case, and, worse yet, he still felt that other Berlin newspapers were printing distorted reports on the two trials. All in all, Glagau left these cases with a sense of disillusionment about the state of the justice system and skepticism about the possibility of getting a fair hearing in a legal system "dominated" by Jews.

The Hapke Incident

While Glagau's campaign against Jewish judges met with little success, public discussion of his cases did reach a significant audience and inspired others to follow his example. In January 1883, only a few weeks after the end of the Glagau vs. Biermann case, the issue of Jewish judges and their impartiality returned to the national political stage as the result of the so-called "Hapke Incident." This incident took place rather unexpectedly during a libel trial involving another prominent anti-Semite, Max Liebermann von Sonnenberg.

Liebermann von Sonnenberg was a major figure in the swarm of libel suits and counter-suits during the early 1880s. In addition to being the co-founder of the first *Deutscher Volksverein*, Liebermann was also editor of the anti-Semitic *Hallesches Thorbote* and later the *Neue Deutsche Volkszeitung*. In 1881 and 1882, Liebermann fought an almost constant polemical battle with editors of various Berlin liberal newspapers, and these debates often degenerated into personal attacks. For instance, Liebermann was repeatedly forced to defend himself against charges of financial improprieties and suggestions that his last name implied he might have Jewish ancestors.[67] As a result of these

[67] See *Berliner Tageblatt* 22 October 1881 #495. This newspaper argued that the

kinds of exchanges, Liebermann became involved in a large number of libel trials. In fact, at one time he even had hearings for three separate cases on a single day. In early 1883, one of these cases unexpectedly became a national scandal. After five different liberal newspapers alleged that he was in default on several unpaid debts, Liebermann decided to file libel charges against all of the editors. This particular libel case came to trial at the Berlin District Court I. The presiding judge on the three judge panel was once again *Amtsgerichtsrath* Lion, a Jew.[68]

Unlike Glagau, however, Liebermann seemed to have no intention of attacking Lion's competence in this trial. He was determined to use the trial to clear himself once and for all of charges that he had failed to pay off several promissory notes (*Ehrenscheine*) in a timely manner. But early in this trial something happened that turned the spotlight away from the main issues of the case and, at the same time, turned the trial into a *cause célèbre.* One of the first witnesses, Pastor Karl Hapke, refused to testify unless he could be assured that the judge administering the oath was a Christian.[69] Lion advised Hapke that he had no right to make such demands, and warned him that a refusal to testify might bring severe penalties. When Hapke again refused to take the oath, Lion sentenced him to a 300 Mark fine—giving him the maximum possible fine because of the "demonstrative character of the refusal."[70] The judge also assigned all court costs to Hapke, and postponed the trial indefinitely.

This incident turned Hapke into an instant celebrity. Many Conservative and anti-Semitic newspapers praised him as a martyr who would rather face prison than allow his religious beliefs to be

name Liebermann was traditionally Jewish, while Liebermann himself claimed it had been adopted by Jews from old Christian nobility.

[68] The charges of unpaid debts first originated in the 1881 election campaign in which Liebermann was a candidate. The *Vossische Zeitung* first printed the accusations on December 10, 1881. In addition to the editor of the *Vossische Zeitung* (Stephany), the other defendants were from the *Berliner Börsen-Courier* (Klaußner), *Berliner Presse* (Bäcker), *Volks-Zeitung* (Berghausen), and *Kleinen Journal* (Zeblicke). Several well-known attorneys defended these editors, including Erich Sello and August Munckel.

[69] Hapke, the pastor of the Bethlehem-Kirche in Berlin, already had a long association with anti-Semitism—he was one of the early signers of the Anti-Semitic Petition to Bismarck. However, it appears that he was still relatively unknown outside anti-Semitic circles. See Strenge, *Juden im preußischen Justizdienst*, 203.

[70] *Staatsbürger Zeitung* 9 January 1883 #6.

violated.[71] The anti-Semitic *Staatsbürgerzeitung*, for example, portrayed Hapke as a strongly religious man who was being persecuted for standing firm on a matter of principle:

> It can hardly be contested that it is a kind of religious persecution (*Gewissenszwang*) to force a Christian clergyman to take an oath, one that still has a religious character due to the invocation of God, in front of a Jew who denies Christ as both Savior and Redeemer. It is impossible for us to believe that the laws of a Christian state would want a devout Christian to be brought under this kind of compulsion.[72]

The ultra-conservative and Stöckerite press also treated the Hapke incident as a matter of religious freedom—that is, a matter of Christians having the freedom to follow their own conscience in a Christian country. While Stöcker's *Reichsbote* complained about the current "oath crisis" (*Eidesnoth*), the ultra-Conservative *Kreuzzeitung* claimed that this issue had "only progressed into its first stage, and would sooner or later become a burning controversy."[73]

Hapke also did his best to rally public support for his actions by printing a statement in the anti-Semitic *Deutsches Tageblatt.* This statement read, in part: "It remains . . . a public calamity and a deep humiliation for every Christian German to have to take an oath before such non-Christians, who hate and despise the savior of our souls and nourish themselves from Talmudic wisdom."[74] In this same statement, Hapke also proclaimed that he would never back down, and he encouraged other patriotic Germans to support his efforts with public protests and petitions. Hapke's friends quickly started a petition to the Reichstag, but Conservative politicians did not wait for the petition to arrive.[75] On January 22, 1883, just a few days after Hapke refused the oath, the Conservative deputy Maltzahn-Gültz proposed legislation that would make sure Christians would

---

[71] Strenge, *Juden im preußischen Justizdienst*, 204.

[72] *Staatsbürger Zeitung* 9 January 1883 #6.

[73] *Berliner Tageblatt* 10 January 1883 #15 Morgen; *Kreuzzeitung* 10 January 1883 #7. It should be noted that Stöcker's opinion was not necessarily shared by other Protestant groups. The editors of the *Evangelische Kirchliche Anzeiger*, for example, encouraged their brethren to stay out of the Hapke controversy. They offered this comment: "It is self-evident that the obligations of a Christian oath cannot be influenced if a non-Christian administers it in the name of the king." As reported in *Berliner Tageblatt* 13 January 1883 #21.

[74] As reported in *Jüdische Presse* 8 March 1883 #10.

[75] LAB A Pr. Br. Rep. 030, Polizeipräsidium Berlin, Nr. 15221, p. 90.

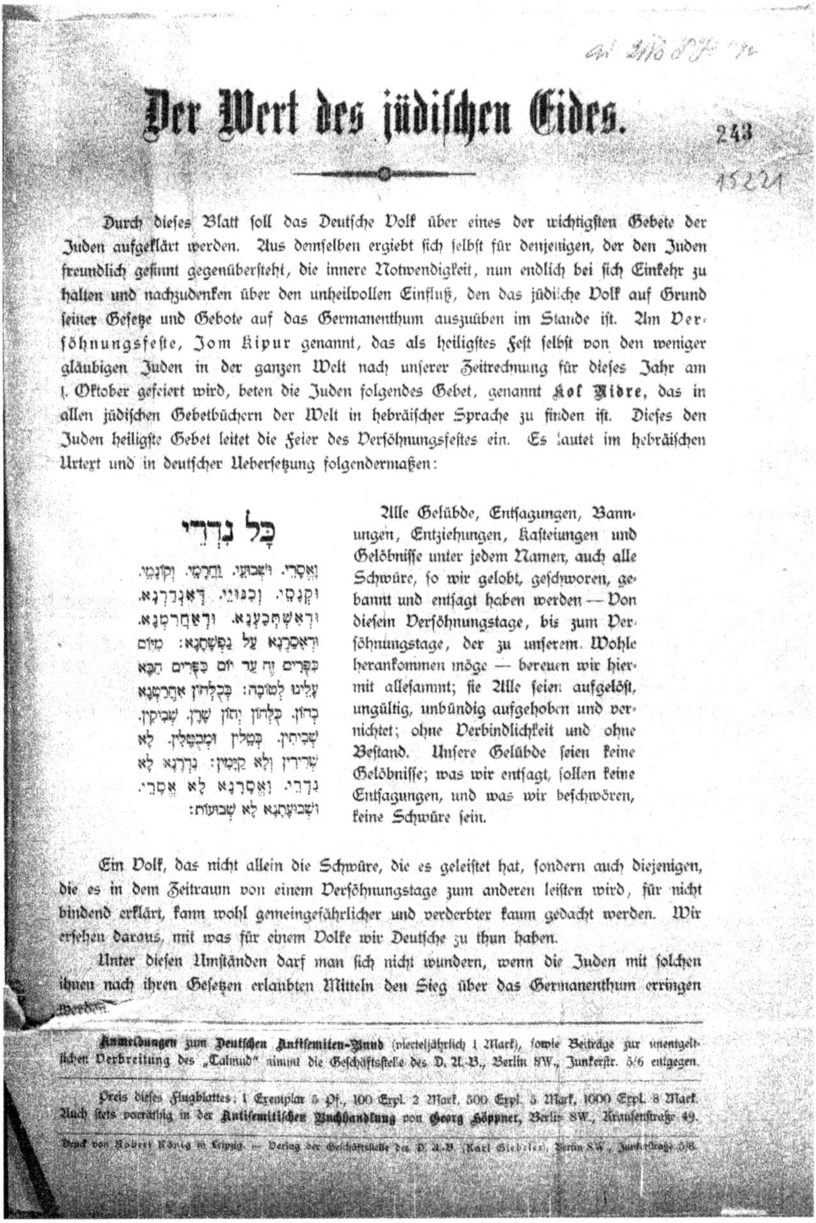

Der Wert des jüdischen Eides.

Durch dieses Blatt soll das Deutsche Volk über eines der wichtigsten Gebete der Juden aufgeklärt werden. Aus demselben ergiebt sich selbst für denjenigen, der den Juden freundlich gesinnt gegenübersteht, die innere Notwendigkeit, nun endlich bei sich Einkehr zu halten und nachzudenken über den unheilvollen Einfluß, den das jüdische Volk auf Grund seiner Gesetze und Gebote auf das Germanenthum auszuüben im Stande ist. Am **Versöhnungsfeste, Jom Kipur** genannt, das als heiligstes Fest selbst von den weniger gläubigen Juden in der ganzen Welt nach unserer Zeitrechnung für dieses Jahr am 1. Oktober gefeiert wird, beten die Juden folgendes Gebet, genannt **Kol Nidre**, das in allen jüdischen Gebetbüchern der Welt in hebräischer Sprache zu finden ist. Dieses den Juden heiligste Gebet leitet die Feier des Versöhnungsfestes ein. Es lautet im hebräischen Urtext und in deutscher Uebersetzung folgendermaßen:

כל נדרי

ואסרי. ושבועי. וחרמי. וקונמי.
וקנסי. וכנויי. דאנדרנא.
ודאשתבענא. ודאחרמנא.
ודאסרנא על נפשתנא: מיום
כפרים זה עד יום כפרים הבא
עלינו לטובה: בכלהון אחרטנא
בהון. כלהון יהון שרן. שביקין.
שביתין. בטלין ומבטלין. לא
שרירין ולא קימין: נדרנא לא
נדרי. ואסרנא לא אסרי.
ושבועתנא לא שבועות:

Alle Gelübde, Entsagungen, Bannungen, Entziehungen, Kasteiungen und Gelöbnisse unter jedem Namen, auch alle Schwüre, so wir gelobt, geschworen, gebannt und entsagt haben werden — Von diesem Versöhnungstage, bis zum Versöhnungstage, der zu unserem Wohle herankommen möge — bereuen wir hiermit allesammt; sie Alle seien aufgelöst, ungültig, unbündig aufgehoben und vernichtet; ohne Verbindlichkeit und ohne Bestand. Unsere Gelübde seien keine Gelöbnisse; was wir entsagt, sollen keine Entsagungen, und was wir beschwören, keine Schwüre sein.

Ein Volk, das nicht allein die Schwüre, die es geleistet hat, sondern auch diejenigen, die es in dem Zeitraum von einem Versöhnungstage zum anderen leisten wird, für nicht bindend erklärt, kann wohl gemeingefährlicher und verderbter kaum gedacht werden. Wir ersehen daraus, mit was für einem Volke wir Deutsche zu thun haben.

Unter diesen Umständen darf man sich nicht wundern, wenn die Juden mit solchen ihnen nach ihren Gesetzen erlaubten Mitteln den Sieg über das Germanenthum erringen werden.

Anmeldungen zum Deutschen Antisemiten-Bund (vierteljährlich 1 Mark), sowie Beiträge zur unentgeltlichen **Verbreitung** des „Talmud" nimmt die Geschäftsstelle des D. A.-B., Berlin SW., Junkerstr. 5/6 entgegen.

Preis dieses Flugblattes: 1 Exemplar 5 Pf., 100 Expl. 2 Mark, 500 Expl. 5 Mark, 1000 Expl. 8 Mark. Auch stets vorräthig in der **Antisemitischen Buchhandlung** von **Georg Höppner**, Berlin SW., Krausenstraße 49.

Druck von Robert König in Leipzig. — Verlag der Geschäftsstelle des D. A.-B. (Karl Giebeler), Berlin SW., Junkerstraße 5/6.

Fig. 1. "The Value of a Jewish Oath"—A pamphlet on the Kol Nidre and Jewish oaths distributed by the Deutsche Antisemitenbund in September of 1892. Prosecutors pursued, but then quickly dropped, charges against those responsible for the pamphlet. Courtesy of the Landesarchiv Berlin.

swear their oaths before judges of the same religion. This legislation would have effectively removed most Jewish judges from serving in their positions. The proposal, however, received only minimal support in the full Reichstag and was quickly voted down.[76]

While anti-Semites and Conservatives did their best to turn Hapke into a heroic martyr for religious freedom, liberal newspapers wasted no time in cutting his image back down to size. Several newspapers argued that this incident was not the spontaneous reaction of a religious man, but a well-planned publicity stunt designed to bring public attention to anti-Semitism.[77] The *Berliner Tageblatt* went even further. It not only questioned Hapke's motives in this case, but also attacked his personal character. On January 19, 1883, the *Tageblatt* printed a story that accused Hapke of marrying a 21 year-old girl only two months after her older (and quite wealthy) husband had died of an illness. Although the *Tageblatt* was careful with its language, the clear implication was that Hapke had less than honorable motives for befriending the couple in the first place, and was far from the man of conscience that the Conservative and anti-Semitic press had championed.[78]

Despite his newfound celebrity, Hapke still faced a possible jail sentence if he refused to take the oath once the Liebermann trial resumed. To avoid this possibility, Hapke tried to appeal Judge Lion's ruling to a higher court. Although his fine for refusing the oath was cut in half, the appeals court upheld the ruling and ordered him to testify or face further punishment. Hapke then petitioned the Kaiser to overturn the fine and change the law to prevent such circumstances from reoccurring. When this effort also proved fruitless, Hapke did his best to postpone the resumption of the trial by using a variety of excuses.[79] For Liebermann, who may have otherwise admired

---

[76] Strenge, *Juden im preußischen Justizdienst*, 205.

[77] Ibid., 204.

[78] *Berliner Tageblatt* 19 January 1883 #31 Morgen Erstes Beiblatt.

[79] According to the *Neue Deutsche Volkszeitung*, Hapke claimed that a June trial date was inconvenient since he intended to visit Bad Ems for health reasons. The *Berliner Tageblatt* added that Hapke hoped to postpone the trial until Judge Lion was on vacation since he would probably be replaced by a Christian judge. In this way, Hapke could testify and avoid further punishment, while still claiming to have maintained his defiant stand. Unfortunately for him, additional delays pushed the trial back to November, long after Lion had returned from his vacation. See *Neue Deutsche Volkszeitung* 7 June 1883 #129 and *Berliner Tageblatt* 16 August 1883 #379.

Hapke's actions, these delays were agonizing. Liebermann had already waited 18 months to rehabilitate his reputation, and, as one newspaper reported, he was very angry with Hapke for delaying the case with a self-aggrandizing stunt.[80]

The Liebermann trial finally resumed on November 19, 1883. Hapke again was called as a witness and ordered to take the oath. He refused once again, but this time he tried to present several mitigating factors. He claimed, for instance, that his memory of the facts of the case was no longer clear, and he feared that he might contradict his own previous statements. Judge Lion assured Hapke that he only had to swear to recount the events as accurately as he could, but Hapke offered several other excuses as to why he could not testify. As it became clear that Judge Lion was losing patience, Hapke finally agreed to take the oath if he could read it himself. Lion commented that this was usually reserved for the hard of hearing, but he agreed to allow this measure to avoid further controversy.[81] With this compromise, the Hapke incident reached an anticlimactic end. Hapke's actual testimony was brief and almost completely irrelevant to the Liebermann case.[82]

Although Hapke and his allies tried to claim that he had not compromised his principles in reading the oath himself, many liberal newspapers suggested that Hapke never had the courage of his convictions and backed down when faced with serious consequences. Most liberal papers viewed the outcome of the affair as a complete humiliation for Hapke and an important victory over intolerance. As the *Berliner Tageblatt* stated: "... the law has triumphed, and another of those worshippers of intolerance will not attempt to follow in Hapke's footsteps anytime soon."[83]

The outcome was also an unsatisfactory one for Liebermann. Despite Hapke's interference, Liebermann actually won his case

[80] *Neue Deutsche Volkszeitung* 7 June 1883 #129.

[81] This request also had a precedent. In a separate trial involving Liebermann a month earlier (Gerhardt vs. Liebermann), the anti-Semitic politician Wilhelm Pickenbach was called as a witness. He asked the presiding judge, again Judge Lion, to allow him to read the oath himself. After Lion told him that he had no right to ask for this special treatment, Pickenbach took the oath without further complaint. *Hallesches Thorbote*, 4 September 1883 #131 in LAB A Pr. Br. Rep. 030, Polizeipräsidium Berlin, Nr. 11453, p. 98.

[82] *Freie Zeitung* 20 November 1883 #222.

[83] *Berliner Tageblatt* 20 November 1883 #544 Abend.

against the five editors. This victory, however, proved to be a hollow one. In issuing their decision, the judges claimed that many of the financial allegations against Liebermann had proven to be true, and they suggested that his failure to pay debts would probably result in an investigation by an Honor Court (*Ehrengericht*). These conclusions hardly served to rehabilitate Liebermann's reputation. In addition, Liebermann's appeal for punitive damages was rejected, and in a related suit, Liebermann himself was convicted of libel and fined 150 Marks.[84] Despite his best efforts, the charges of financial improprieties dogged Liebermann for the rest of his political career.

The efforts of Glagau and Hapke to remove Jewish judges from their positions were thus a complete failure. But before writing these incidents off as a colossal defeat for German anti-Semitism in general, it is important to gauge their effects on the press and the public. While these incidents may have had little effect on the justice system, they did provoke sharp political debate and provide a new rallying point for anti-Semitic agitators. Moreover, it is important to remember that the number of Jewish judges was, in fact, restricted in the 1880s, even if this trend had little to do with these particular incidents. Finally, these cases should not be viewed alone, but as part of a broader public debate on the moral fitness of Jews and their ability to assimilate into German society. In the next decade, additional controversies would arise over the baptized Justice Minister Friedberg and over Jewish attitudes toward legal oaths. Thus, the cases involving Glagau and Hapke were only the first skirmishes in a long and brutal war.[85]

---

[84] *Neueste Nachrichten* 8 December 1883 #334. This suit (Polakowsky vs. Liebermann) was filed against Liebermann by the *Vossische Zeitung*'s informant for its anti-Liebermann story, a former Christian-Social named Polakowsky. In trying to defend his own honor against the charges of financial improprieties, Liebermann had viciously attacked Polakowski for his public betrayal. This trial was also judged by Lion—this time without major incident. However, the conviction of Liebermann in the Gerhardt vs. Liebermann case was followed by strong criticism of Judge Lion in the anti-Semitic *Deutsches Tageblatt*. Lion responded by filing (and winning) a libel suit against the editor. As reported in *Berliner Tageblatt* 1 March 1884 #103 Morgen Erstes Beiblatt.

[85] The issue of religious oaths periodically reappeared in anti-Semitic propaganda. Ironically, in 1897, Liebermann von Sonnenberg sponsored a successful Reichstag bill to reintroduce denominational oaths in court proceedings. It was the only successful legislation ever sponsored by an anti-Semitic delegate. Levy, *The Downfall of the Anti-Semitic Political Parties*, 168.

The Stöcker Trials: Politics and the Perjured Pastor

Although he was undoubtedly the most renowned anti-Semitic politician in Germany, and although he constantly attacked liberal and Jewish leaders in his speeches and articles, Adolf Stöcker managed to avoid the kind of libel trials that were so typical of other anti-Semitic leaders. Stöcker's speeches in the Reichstag were protected by parliamentary immunity, and his influence on several newspapers such as the *Reichsbote*, the *Christlich-Soziales Correspondenzblatt*, and *Das Volk* was exerted only indirectly. Thus, various chief editors would usually serve as the target for law suits instead of Stöcker himself. Because of his strong anti-Semitic rhetoric and his prominent position as *Hofprediger* (Court Chaplain), it was inevitable that Stöcker would be the target of political attacks. However, unlike many other anti-Semitic politicians, Stöcker preferred to answer these attacks in the press and in the Reichstag rather than inside the courtroom.

Stöcker became more sensitive to public criticism as his relations with the Conservative Party became more tenuous. In the early 1880s, most Conservatives had viewed Stöcker's Christian-Social Party as a promising ally that might attract radical workers away from socialism and toward conservative politics. In addition, Stöcker's fiery speeches and anti-Semitic rhetoric seemed to contain the kind of demagogical populism that many hoped would finally turn the Conservative Party from a party of elites into a party of the masses.[86] However, after the agitation of the early 1880s failed to produce substantial Conservative electoral gains or to reduce the power of German socialism, Stöcker's relationship to the Conservative Party gradually became more controversial. Many moderate Conservatives, like the party leader Otto von Helldorf-Bedra, began to regard Stöcker and his anti-Semitic rhetoric as an obstacle to a pro-Bismarck coalition with the Free Conservatives and National Liberals. Right-wing Conservatives like Baron Wilhelm von Hammerstein, on the other hand, fiercely defended Stöcker and strongly opposed Conservative participation in a centrist Bismarckian *Kartell.* This internal party

---

[86] See James Retallack, *Notables of the Right: The Conservative Party and Political Mobilization in Germany 1876–1918* (Boston: Unwin Hyman, 1988) for a more thorough discussion of the attempt to turn the Conservative Party into a more "demagogical" organization. See also my Chapter 6 on the attention to "demagogy" in the Tivoli Program of 1892.

battle and the controversy surrounding Adolf Stöcker continued to grow throughout the 1880s.

In part because of the growing concern with Stöcker within the Conservative Party, liberal attacks on Stöcker's integrity reached a crescendo in the Reichstag election campaign of 1884. Many liberals apparently hoped that these attacks would either drive a wedge through the Conservative Party or at least weaken the party's radical right wing. In the midst of the election campaign, the liberal *Berliner Volkszeitung* and *Vossische Zeitung* both published sharp attacks on Stöcker's honesty and integrity. Rather than defend himself in court, Stöcker once again responded indirectly through attacks by the Stöckerite *Christlich-Soziales Correspondenzblatt* and *Reichsbote.* But when a small liberal newspaper called the *Freie Zeitung* labeled him a liar and an embezzler, and dared him to sue in court, Stöcker decided to change his strategy. This time, he decided to haul his attackers into court; it was a decision he would regret for the rest of his political life.

The *Freie Zeitung* was a small Berlin newspaper associated with Eugen Richter's liberal *Freisinnige* Party. In October of 1884, the editor, a Jewish journalist named Heinrich Bäcker, published an extra-edition under the title "On the Characteristics of Court Chaplain Stöcker." This article was essentially an election flyer that was designed to damage Stöcker's image and thus help his *Freisinnige* opponent, Rudolph Virchow. The primary argument of this article was that, despite repeated charges of untruthfulness and corruption, Stöcker had never dared to defend his reputation by taking his opponents to court. The *Freie Zeitung* complained that even after a former Stöcker aide named Emil Grüneberg had leveled extremely serious charges against him, Stöcker still declined to sue for libel.[87] As the article continued: "Although Grüneberg publicly voiced the gravest of accusations, Stöcker still did not dare to bring his former friend into court. Any honorable man in public life would have done this. That Stöcker fails to call on a judge to act against Grüneberg gives the

[87] Grüneberg had worked with Stöcker in the late 1870s and even served as a Christian-Social Reichstag candidate in 1878. Soon after, however, Grüneberg developed a bitter rivalry with Stöcker and left the party. He took his revenge a few years later by selling his own diary and private recollections of Stöcker to the liberal *Volkszeitung.* Soon after, Stöcker and Grüneberg reconciled their differences—but the damage had already been done.

clear impression that Grüneberg's charges are true."[88] The *Freie Zeitung* then went on to repeat many of Grüneberg's charges: that Stöcker employed convicts in his party organization, that he plotted to undermine the reputation of rival ministers, and that he used church funds to finance his political campaigns. The *Freie Zeitung* also linked Stöcker to the two 1878 assassination attempts on the Kaiser, since the two assassins, Nobiling and Hödel, were alleged members of the Christian-Social Party. The article concluded by asking readers: "Should such a man, who quietly ignores such accusations and who probably must ignore them, be your representative in the Reichstag? No! . . . Every honorable man must vote for Professor Virchow."[89]

A short time later, the *Freie Zeitung* followed with another lead article entitled "Court Chaplain, Reichstag Candidate, and Liar." This article repeated many of the previous charges and added a few new ones. Stöcker was now brutally characterized as "a frivolous liar . . . a slanderer who is not worthy of a seat in parliament."[90] The article ended with this explicit challenge to Stöcker's honor:

> The duty [of the Conservative Party] should be to persuade Stöcker to go before a judge to cleanse himself of these charges before he becomes their candidate. We offer an opportunity to do this now. *If Mr. Stöcker would like to sue us . . . for the content of this article, we will produce proof of its accuracy.*[91]

Apparently, Stöcker could not resist taking such a challenge.

The libel trial against the editor of the *Freie Zeitung*, Heinrich Bäcker, began on June 9, 1885.[92] The well-known Berlin attorney August Munckel and his associate, Dr. Hugo Sachs, served as Bäcker's

---

[88] *Freie Zeitung* October 1884 Extra-Blatt, in LAB A Pr. Br. Rep. 030, Polizeipräsidium Berlin Nr. 14754, p. 7. (These issues of the *Freie Zeitung* have been mistakenly attached to the archival file concerning police surveillance of the anti-Semitic agitator Carl Paasch.) According to the *Correspondenzblatt*, the editor of the liberal *Berliner Volks-Zeitung* had the "audacity" to challenge Stöcker to a duel after printing libelous attacks against him. *Christlich-Soziales Correspondenzblatt* 1 October 1884 #40 Beilage.

[89] *Freie Zeitung* October 1884 Extra-Blatt, in LAB A Pr. Br. Rep. 030, Polizeipräsidium Berlin Nr. 14754, p. 7.

[90] Ibid., 8.

[91] Ibid. (Bold in original).

[92] Trial transcripts published in an anonymous pamphlet called *Zeuge Stöcker: Ein Zeitbild aus dem Jahre 1885* (Berlin: Fortschritt, 1885) This pamphlet had a decidedly liberal and anti-Stöcker perspective and included in boldface type any statements which portrayed Stöcker in a negative light. In its basic text, however, it seems to be consistent with other summaries of the trial.

defense counsel. Because of Stöcker's position as Court Chaplain, Bäcker was charged not just with ordinary libel, but with libel of a public official. However, the way the proceedings were conducted, it soon began to seem that Stöcker, not Bäcker, was the one on trial. Because Bäcker's defense was that his charges against Stöcker were factually accurate, he was allowed to present a series of witnesses that would support his accusations. What followed was a steady stream of former associates of the Court Chaplain, many of whom had now become his bitter enemies.[93]

One of these witnesses, Stöcker's former associate Emil Grüneberg, was the original source of the charges that formed the core of the *Freie Zeitung* articles. Grüneberg explained that despite Stöcker's denials, the assassin Hödel had indeed attended several Christian-Social meetings before his attempt to kill Kaiser Wilhelm. Grüneberg claimed that he had later destroyed the attendance lists, with Stöcker's permission, in order to maintain the public impression that Hödel had been a Social Democrat.[94] In addition, Grüneberg and several other former Stöcker associates admitted that they had occupied high positions in the Christian-Social Party despite their own criminal records. Finally, Grüneberg testified that Stöcker had once tried to ruin a rival minister, Pastor Carl Witte, by spreading rumors that he had helped rich Jews receive titles in exchange for personal gifts.[95] Witte, like Grüneberg himself, had once been seen as a rival to Stöcker's power within the Christian-Social Party. Through Grüneberg's testimony, the defense implied that Stöcker had not only surrounded himself with hooligans, but had also behaved like one.[96]

---

[93] The flurry of charges leveled against Stöcker on the first two days of the trial ranged from the most insignificant to the most treasonous of offenses. In addition to the charges listed above, Munckel claimed that Stöcker was guilty of embezzling charitable donations for political purposes, distributing political newspapers in his Berlin Mission, and even of distributing radical republican literature to his congregation. Although the defense did attempt to substantiate some of these charges with witness testimony, most were supported only with innuendo and *ad hominem* attacks. The defendant, Bäcker, even stood up to ask Stöcker if it was true that his school report cards had often included the comment: "lying rascal." The judge dismissed this question as irrelevant. See *Zeuge Stöcker*, 23.

[94] The Hödel and Nobiling assassination attempts in 1878 resulted in the anti-Socialist laws that lasted until 1890.

[95] Witte was a little-known pastor at the St. Golgatha Church in Berlin.

[96] Grüneberg admitted previous convictions for begging, embezzlement, and making false accusations. Stöcker admitted knowing about these criminal offenses, but he argued that his purpose as a pastor was to rehabilitate such lost souls and turn them into responsible individuals.

But the attacks on Stöcker did not stop there. Bäcker's defense attorneys brought out a file of Reichstag speeches, articles, and public addresses to force Stöcker to explain various inaccurate or contradictory statements. Their primary piece of evidence was Stöcker's Reichstag speech in the infamous *Judendebatte* of November 1880. Referring to this speech, Bäcker's defense attorneys accused Stöcker of having mistakenly identified several liberal public figures as Jews, of having falsely accused signers of the "Statement of Berlin Notables" of being disreputable businessmen, and of having lied about whether or not he had actually signed the original Anti-Semitic Petition.[97] Stöcker responded that he had been quick to correct inaccuracies in parts of his speech, but he also claimed that many of these remarks had been taken out of context. As for the Anti-Semitic Petition, Stöcker now claimed that he had only meant that he did not sign the first version presented to him, but had signed a later version designed for dissemination to other priests.

The defense attorneys also accused Stöcker of having committed perjury in a recent court case. As a minor witness in a January 1885 trial, Stöcker had testified that he had never before seen the plaintiff, a Social Democratic leader named Ewald. Bäcker's lawyers, however, now summoned witnesses to show that Stöcker had not only met Ewald repeatedly, but had spoken to him at a political rally and had even mentioned this conversation in a later Reichstag speech. Therefore, according to the defense, although these facts may have been irrelevant to the outcome of the original Ewald trial, they still constituted a case of perjury against Chaplain Stöcker. In response, Stöcker denied that he had had any intention to mislead the Ewald court, and claimed that he honestly did not remember having met Ewald before the trial. Bäcker's attorneys, however, insisted that Ewald was a well-known public figure and asserted that because so many bystanders remembered the meeting clearly, Stöcker's lapse in memory was suspicious at best.

Stöcker tried desperately to answer each of these defense accusations as they arose. But as soon as he finished answering one charge, the defense team would present several others. The attacks on Stöcker

---

[97] These charges came directly from a long list of Stöcker's misstatements and lies which had been printed by the *Berliner Börsen-Courier* in the immediate aftermath of the *Judendebatte*. See the original article in Krieger, ed., *Der "Berliner Antisemitismusstreit,"* Teil 2, 647–655.

were so furious, that on the third day of testimony, the lead judge quite accidentally opened the hearing with the statement: "I hereby reopen the proceedings against Stöcker."[98] This slip was actually a fairly accurate appraisal of the case, since many observers agreed that the verdict would now prove to be as much a judgment of Stöcker's activities as of Bäcker's articles. This fact was made clear in newspapers across the political spectrum. Even Stöcker's *Christlich-Soziales Correspondenzblatt* now portrayed the trial as an event of extraordinary political importance:

> The accused (Bäcker), a completely insignificant man, . . . has stood silently in the background as a 'straw man' since the start of the trial . . . it soon became clear that this was not a case of two individuals fighting with each other over their private interests, but a case where two parties, represented by the lead witness and the defense attorney, were engaged in a life and death struggle. Therefore, it has surpassed any kind of normal libel trial, and has now become a trial of immense historical importance.[99]

The prosecutor's closing argument sounded as if it were a defense argument by Stöcker's personal attorney. He opened by proclaiming that "the much defamed, persecuted, and slandered man, Court Chaplain Stöcker, has emerged from this torrent of slanders completely intact and will retain his spotless reputation."[100] Though the prosecutor was forced to admit that Stöcker had committed many errors in the past, he insisted that these failings only proved that Stöcker was an ordinary human being. Finally, the prosecutor took special care to defend Stöcker from any claim that he had committed perjury in the Ewald case. Although he admitted that Stöcker's testimony had indeed proven to be false, he argued that this was not a grave enough error to constitute perjury. As he put it: "There are false oaths that are not punishable by law, and this is one such case." The prosecutor ended by condemning Bäcker's libelous articles, and asking for a sentence of five months in prison.[101]

Bäcker's two defense attorneys responded by claiming that these "errors" by Stöcker actually constituted a willful dissemination of innuendoes, inaccuracies, and outright lies. The defense attorneys

---

98 *Zeuge Stöcker*, 25.
99 *Christlich-Soziales Correspondenzblatt* 17 June 1885 #25.
100 *Zeuge Stöcker*, 37.
101 Ibid., 38.

reviewed Bäcker's accusations and stressed that they all had been proven both by evidence and by witness testimony. In addition, they suggested that Stöcker's "error" in the Ewald trial was likely a case of willful perjury or at the very least a case of careless perjury (*fahrlässige Meineid*). In his speech, defense attorney Munckel admitted that it was entirely plausible to condemn Bäcker for having gone too far in his rhetoric. But since his articles were part of a vicious election campaign, and since Stöcker had done far worse in his own articles, Munckel suggested that Bäcker deserved at most a small fine.

After eight hours of deliberation, the exhausted judges returned to deliver their verdict.[102] The lead judge, Superior Court Director Lüty, gave a long speech in which he investigated each of the accusations and then laid out all the extenuating and aggravating circumstances regarding the charges against Bäcker. Lüty concluded that although Bäcker was certainly guilty of libel, his articles must be viewed as a response to Stöcker's own polemical speeches. In addition, Lüty targeted Stöcker himself for severe criticism. As he wrote in his decision:

> The claims that the witness Stöcker repeatedly contradicted himself against his own better judgement, knowingly lied, and consciously acted in an unjust manner, are in no way justified. However, through some circumspection, the kind one would expect of someone of his position as the herald of Christian truth, [Stöcker] could have avoided the contradictions and the errors in his comments and his actions that were uncovered here. Therefore, in consideration of the majority of [the evidence presented], the behavior of the witness Stöcker must be described as irresponsible (*leichtfertiges*).[103]

Thus, the court concluded that it was not "in the position to blame Bäcker . . . for reaching the conclusion that the witness stood in conflict

[102] Judge Lüty told the court that he would read the verdict despite an illness. Lüty and the other judges were undoubtedly tired from the long deliberations and the intense media scrutiny. But they were also tired from the repeated attacks by defense attorneys on the integrity of the court. According to many newspaper reports, any attempt by the judge to restrict defense arguments or reject defense motions had been met with angry challenges by the attorneys, and even suggestions that the judges had anti-Semitic leanings. Lüty, however, seemed unfazed by these attacks and repeatedly reminded those present in the court that any legal case should be decided free of emotion.

[103] GStA PK, VI. HA Nachlass Stöcker Abt. III Nr. 6. The original verdict of the Stöcker-Bäcker trial is here included with documents related to the later Stöcker-Witte proceedings.

with the truth."[104] Because of these extenuating circumstances, the court decided on a relatively mild sentence of three weeks in prison for Bäcker—far less than the five months demanded by the prosecutor.

The verdict in this case was a political bombshell. The liberal press jumped at the chance to ridicule Stöcker as the "truth-loving Court Chaplain" and the "Pastor of perjury." The *Berliner Tageblatt* even turned its front page into a fake legal document charging Stöcker with both perjury and embezzlement. In place of the public prosecutor's signature, the document was given the signature "Public Opinion."[105] The *Jüdische Presse* joined in by listing nine separate charges against Stöcker that had been proven in court, each of which was enough to discredit him personally and politically. Even if it did not lead to his dismissal as Court Chaplain, the *Jüdische Presse* concluded, "this case is essentially the death blow to Mr. Stöcker's career as an agitator."[106] Liberal and Jewish newspapers all repeated the slogan made popular by one of Bäcker's defense lawyers, Hugo Sachs: "The defendant (Bäcker) is convicted, but Mr. Stöcker is condemned!"

The Stöckerite and Conservative press, meanwhile, responded to liberal jubilation by bitterly challenging the character of Bäcker and his lawyers. The *Reichsbote*, for example, asserted that Bäcker had once lived on bread-stamps from Stöcker's *Stadtmission* and now lived with his parents in an old-age home despite the fact that he was 30 years old.[107] The *Deutsche Volkszeitung*, meanwhile, told its readers that Bäcker's defense lawyer, Hugo Sachs, had once been beaten by fellow law students for breaking an oath, and added that he had once been slapped by an actor after having criticized a stage performance.[108]

But Stöcker's allies had a more difficult task in trying to explain the court's opinion of Stöcker's behavior. Stöcker's own *Christlich-Soziales Correspondenzblatt* first tried to argue that Stöcker had come untouched out of the "hailstorm" of slanders and lies. However, as the true nature of the verdict became known, the newspaper's atti-

---

[104] *Zeuge Stöcker*, 59–60.

[105] *Berliner Tageblatt* 18 June 1885 #302.

[106] *Jüdische Presse* 18 June 1885 #25.

[107] *Reichsbote* 23 June 1885 #143, in LAB A Pr. Br. Rep. 030, Polizeipräsidium Berlin Nr. 14750, p. 41.

[108] *Deutsche Volks-Zeitung* 16 June 1885 #137 Beiblatt, in LAB A Pr. Br. Rep. 030, Polizeipräsidium Berlin, Nr. 14750, p. 28.

tude changed dramatically.[109] The *Correspondenzblatt* lamented that as a mere witness in a state-run prosecution, Stöcker did not have either an attorney or the right to call witnesses in his own defense.[110] Thus, Stöcker was left with just his own word to refute the mass of charges made against him. Although it vowed to respect the judgment of the court, the *Correspondenzblatt* wondered that a Superior Court could draw such conclusions from only unsubstantiated accusations.[111]

In the immediate aftermath of the trial, Stöcker's supporters tried desperately to rehabilitate his reputation. His friends in the Reichstag quickly circulated a petition in support of his character. Even some of Stöcker's anti-Semitic rivals began to bury their old differences and rush to his defense. They doubtless realized that Stöcker's demise would almost certainly have a negative effect on support for their own anti-Semitic splinter groups. The German Anti-Semites' League (DAB), for example, held several rallies for Stöcker despite the fact that his religious anti-Semitism clashed with their own strict racial views. One of these rallies drew an estimated 4,000 spectators.[112] Nevertheless, support from such radical anti-Semitic politicians could sometimes be a double-edged sword. For instance, Wilhelm Pickenbach, a city councilman and founder of the DAB, made the following statement in one of his rallies:

> The abuse of public court procedures by the Jews and Jew-servants will perhaps have the result that one will no longer seek satisfaction through legal action but through other means. . . . A man might dream

---

[109] *Christlich-Soziales Correspondenzblatt* 17 June 1885 #25. Stöcker, meanwhile, took a three-week leave of absence and left for his country home in Bavaria.

[110] Because the case was a state-run prosecution, Stöcker was considered only a witness and not a plaintiff. In cases prosecuted by the public prosecutor, the libeled party could often participate in the prosecution as an accessory plaintiff (*Nebenkläger*), but Stöcker had apparently chosen not to do so.

[111] *Christlich-Soziales Correspondenzblatt* 24 June 1885 #26. This newspaper, which had praised the judge for his impartiality while the trial was underway, now expressed its disbelief that the lead judge could issue a verdict that was so hostile to Stöcker. The judge's politeness to Stöcker and the fact that the defense attorneys repeatedly suggested that the judge was biased against their client had given the *Correspondenzblatt* the impression that a positive verdict was certain. In a long series of articles on the trial, the paper now criticized the modern courtroom, where "every word spoken by an attorney is designed for reprint in the press, and where a smear campaign in the courtroom is continued with impunity in various newspaper columns . . . and quickly prepared brochures." *Christlich-Soziales Correspondenzblatt* 24 June 1885 #26 Beilage.

[112] Police surveillance report in LAB A Pr. Br. Rep. 030, Polizeipräsidium Berlin, Nr. 14961, p. 213.

> these days that while lying in the Grunewald he might see one man beating another with a whip. Before he could intervene the second man would say, 'It's all right, he's only a lawyer.'[113]

Pickenbach's implication that anti-Semites could resort to violence shocked even those who were sympathetic to Stöcker's plight. The Catholic *Deutsche Reichszeitung*, for example, commented in reference to Pickenbach's remarks that Stöcker would do well to keep his distance from such characters.[114]

The degree to which this trial damaged Stöcker's political credibility is shown not by who came to his defense, but by those traditional supporters who now either criticized him or remained silent. The Free Conservative *Post*, for example, had never been a particularly close ally to the Christian-Socials, but had previously supported Stöcker in his comments on the Jewish Question. In the mid-1880s, however, the Free Conservatives began to see Stöcker more as a threat to a pro-Bismarck *Kartell* than as a guardian against the growth of socialism. Although the *Post* described the entire Bäcker affair as a scurrilous attempt by the left-liberals to ambush Stöcker, it also charged that Stöcker had been damaged badly enough that it would be prudent for him to resign from his political activities. The *Post* concluded: "As unpleasant as this trial has been for most, it can still bear good fruit for the Conservative cause if Mr. Stöcker resigns his prominent position in the party . . . and thus removes the main obstacle for the cooperation of the 'national parties.'"[115]

Moderate Conservatives, many of whom were also anxious to weaken Stöcker's influence on their own party, were only lukewarm in coming to his defense. When Conservatives and anti-Semites circulated a petition expressing full support for Stöcker and complete faith in his honor and integrity, many prominent moderate Conservatives, including Moltke, Helldorf-Bedra, Maltzahn, and Minnigerode failed to sign.[116] While these men were far from friends of the so-

[113] *Deutsche Reichs-Zeitung* (Bonn) 23 June 1885 #171, in BAK ZSg. 113 Sammlung Fechenbach, Nr. 740.

[114] Ibid.

[115] *Die Post* 23 June 1885 #168, in LAB A Pr. Br. Rep. 030, Polizeipräsidium Berlin, Nr. 14750, p. 42.

[116] *Frankfurter Zeitung* 11 July 1885 #192. This liberal paper asserted that only 60 of 160 Conservative deputies had signed the petition.

called Berlin "*Judenpresse*," they probably feared that a spirited defense of Stöcker against liberal attacks might ruin the possibility of an alliance with the more moderate National Liberal party.

Even the Catholic *Germania*, which had in the past defended Stöcker from liberal attacks, was now less than enthusiastic in coming to his defense. In a long series of articles on the Bäcker trial, the *Germania* described the case as a devious plot to ruin Stöcker's reputation and destroy his political career. But, while their anti-liberal and anti-Jewish rhetoric showed that the *Germania* was still bitterly opposed to its enemies in the "*Judenpresse*," the *Germania*, like the Free Conservative *Post*, expressed grave doubts about Stöcker's continued usefulness:

> That Mr. Stöcker has made more of these kinds of errors and unfortunate statements than is permissible, cannot now be denied. And if this is caused by the fact that his varied undertakings prevent him from dedicating the necessary attention to each one, then Mr. Stöcker must give up one portion of his activities in order to conduct the other in a more faultless manner.[117]

Although the *Germania* meant the articles to be a critique of the behavior of Bäcker and the liberal press, excerpts like this one showed Stöcker the degree to which he had become politically isolated.

As it turned out, Stöcker's legal troubles were far from over. Less than a month after the Bäcker verdict, Stöcker found himself embroiled in another court case that served as a sequel to the Stöcker-Bäcker trial. In the same 1884 election campaign that spawned the conflict with Bäcker, a brochure had appeared in Siegen (Stöcker's home district) with many similar accusations to those Bäcker had published. Stöcker assumed that this pamphlet was authored by his election opponent in Siegen, Reinhart Schmidt; so he published his own article, which attacked Schmidt's integrity. Schmidt filed libel charges against Stöcker, and Stöcker responded with a counter-suit.

At the trial in July of 1885, Schmidt claimed that it was well known that he did not write the anti-Stöcker brochure; thus, Stöcker's charges that the brochure proved Schmidt was "a fool and a liar" were made despite the knowledge that he had not been involved. Stöcker responded by claiming that he had used the phrase "*er läßt*

---

[117] *Germania* 19 June 1885 #36 Zweites Blatt.

drucken" not to indicate that Schmidt was the author, but merely to show that he had tolerated those who had printed such lies.[118]

Despite Stöcker's explanation, and despite his complaints that Schmidt's own libels during the election campaign had been far more egregious, the judges were not entirely convinced. Their verdict condemned both parties, but reserved special criticism for the Court Chaplain. The lead judge, Dr. Kronecker, attacked Stöcker for "having hurled similarly harsh libels for many years against members of other religious orientations and opposing political parties without these parties deigning to hold him responsible." In addressing Schmidt, however, the court took the recent Stöcker-Bäcker verdict into consideration: "It has been established in the Stöcker-Bäcker trial that Stöcker has often deviated from the truth in a careless manner; because of this, [Schmidt's] charge of deceitfulness (*Doppelzüngigkeit*), which ordinarily would have brought a stiff sentence, will not be punished as harshly."[119] Schmidt was thus sentenced to only a 50 Mark fine, while Stöcker was ordered to pay 150 Marks.

This verdict was a second crushing defeat for Stöcker. The ultra-conservative and anti-Semitic press continued to defend Stöcker's honor; but now they had to overcome not just a judge's critical words, but an actual conviction for libel. The ultra-Conservative *Kreuzzeitung* reacted with a blistering attack on the liberal legal reforms of the 1870s. These reforms, the *Kreuzzeitung* claimed, had not only severed the courts from the state, but had also severed the courts from justice itself. When one of Stöcker's enemies gleefully cited the old adage "There are still judges in Berlin!", the *Kreuzzeitung* altered this slogan to "There are still Jews in Berlin!" to express its displeasure about the number of Jewish judges and lawyers.[120]

---

[118] "Er läßt drucken" can be interpreted as "he printed it" or "he allowed it to be printed."

[119] *Reichsfreund* 25 July 1885 #30, in BAK ZSg. 113 Sammlung Fechenbach, Nr. 740. This liberal newspaper was founded by the *Freisinnige* politician Eugen Richter.

[120] This adage, which celebrated the independence and fairness of the German courtroom, comes from the time of Frederick the Great. Frederick had traveled to visit a poor miller who had property adjoining Sans Souci which he refused to sell. When Frederick hinted that he could simply take the land if he wished, the miller allegedly responded that he was not afraid because "there are still courts in Berlin". See David Fraser, *Frederick the Great* (New York: Fromm International, 2000), 224. The *Kreuzzeitung* article "The 'Free Judgment' of the Court" was also reprinted in many anti-Semitic and Stöckerite papers. See *Christlich-Soziales Correspondenzblatt* 29 July 1885 #31. The *Correspondenzblatt* also asserted that as a "baptized Jew," the

Weeks after the end of the Schmidt trial, the polemics from each side seemed to be intensifying rather than fading. The Stöckerite *Christlich-Soziales Correspondenzblatt*, which was originally deferential toward the Superior Court, now did not hesitate to attack it directly. The *Correspondenzblatt* wrote that "there are a growing number of people who believe that the Superior Court verdict in the Stöcker-Bäcker trial contains a long series of serious formal and material violations of current constitutional, civil, and penal law, and therefore they demand that this verdict be overturned."[121] This newspaper then brought in several legal experts to support these assertions.

After months of articles that reviewed both the Stöcker-Bäcker and the Stöcker-Schmidt trials in detail, the *Christlich-Soziales Correspondenzblatt* claimed to have fully exonerated Stöcker of all charges. As the *Correspondenzblatt* wrote: "The trial of Stöcker against Bäcker, in which an appeal in the courts was unfortunately denied, has instead had its appeal outside of the courtroom; this battle was led by the Christian-conservative press and won in convincing fashion."[122] But since attaining this "public acquittal" required direct criticism of the original verdicts and of the courts, it brought the Christian-conservative press into conflict with the public prosecutor. Because of their attacks on the fairness of the courts and the impartiality of judges, the public prosecutor filed libel charges against several newspapers, including the *Reichsbote*, the *Kreuzzeitung*, and the *Christlich-Soziales Correspondenzblatt*.[123] These trials would serve to extend the popular debate over the Stöcker trials since they provided additional forums to retry those cases in a court setting.[124]

---

judge in the Schmidt case, Dr. Kronecker, should have recused himself. But the newspaper stopped short of accusing Kronecker of acting in a biased manner. The *Correspondenzblatt*, however, did criticize Kronecker for allowing the Bäcker trial to influence the Schmidt trial verdict since the first case was still under appeal. A few days later, a higher court rejected this appeal.

[121] *Christlich-Soziales Correspondenzblatt* 19 August 1885 #34.

[122] Ibid., 9 September 1885 #37 Beilage.

[123] Ibid. The libel trials that arose out of the Stöcker-Bäcker case also involved liberal newspapers. The *Freie Zeitung*, for example, was charged with libel after criticizing the public prosecutor for allowing Conservative papers to reprint part of a previously banned *Freie Zeitung* article without being punished. *Christlich-Soziales Correspondenzblatt* 26 August 1885 #35 Beilage.

[124] The trial against the *Kreuzzeitung* for libeling Dr. Kronecker ended with a relatively mild fine of 150 Marks for the editor Wilhelm von Hammerstein. The *Kreuzzeitung*, however, declared this case a victory because of the mildness of the sentence, and because Hammerstein had a chance to set the record straight about

As the battle over Stöcker's reputation continued to echo in the Berlin courts and the national press, rumors began to spread that Stöcker would resign his position as Court Chaplain and leave Berlin. One newspaper even reported that he had applied for a clerical position in Kassel.[125] While these rumors were false, Stöcker was indeed in a precarious position. The Kaiser, disgusted with the outcome of the trials, was ready to dismiss Stöcker from his post. Only the energetic intervention of Prince Wilhelm and other influential allies persuaded the Kaiser to allow Stöcker to retain his religious office.[126]

Despite Stöcker's legal defeats and his conflict with the Kaiser, most ultra-Conservatives still remained loyal to him. In fact, as it became clear that Bismarck was committed to a moderate coalition in the Reichstag, Stöcker became an even more important leader for those who opposed such an alliance. In order to launch a public campaign against the new *Kartell*, Wilhelm von Hammerstein and the ultra-Conservatives needed Stöcker's political power and personal magnetism. This was particularly true since Hammerstein's primary weapon in this campaign would be anti-Semitism.[127]

Thus, despite the disasters in the Bäcker and Schmidt trials, Stöcker continued to be politically active. Stöcker's renewed involvement in the Christian-Social Party, however, created even more enemies across

---

the "old legend of Stöcker's untruthfulness." (The *Correspondenzblatt* would later react similarly to a 200 Mark fine in its own trial.) *Christlich-Soziales Correspondenzblatt* 21 October 1885 #43. This entire issue of the *Correspondenz* is dedicated to covering the *Kreuzzeitung* trial—including a stenographic report of the trial proceedings. Ironically, soon after the verdict against the *Kreuzzeitung*, Stöcker's appeal of the Schmidt case was heard in the Berlin Superior Court. Before the new judge could issue a ruling, Schmidt and Stöcker announced that they had reached an agreement to drop the charges and counter-charges as long as Stöcker would pay all the court costs. This settlement allowed Stöcker to clear his record of the libel conviction and permitted the Stöckerite press to claim that Stöcker had been exonerated of all charges. *Christlich-Soziales Correspondenzblatt* 11 November 1885 #46 Beilage.

[125] *Kasseler Journal*, as reported in *Reichsbote* 27 June 1885 #147.

[126] See Hans Engelmann, *Kirche am Abgrund: Adolf Stöcker und seine antijüdische Bewegung*, Studien zu jüdischem Volk und christlicher Gemeinde, Band 5 (Berlin: Selbstverlag Institut Kirche und Judentum, 1984), 146–148; see also Walter Frank, *Hofprediger Adolf Stoecker und die christlichsoziale Bewegung* (Berlin: R. Hobbing, 1928) for a description of the letters exchanged between the Kaiser and his grandson.

[127] Hammerstein and Stöcker hoped to use anti-Semitism as a wedge issue to divide the National Liberals and Conservatives. Presumably, attacks on Jewish wealth and liberal rule in the 1870s would be enough to provoke the National Liberals to attack the *Kreuzzeitung*, and would force moderate Conservatives to choose between the National Liberals and their traditional ultra-Conservative roots.

the political spectrum. Bismarck had never thought highly of Stöcker, but had found him useful in the early 1880s as a tool against socialists and left-liberals. In the late 1880s, however, Stöcker's anti-*Kartell* position brought him into direct conflict with the chancellor. In addition, Stöcker's growing friendship with Prince Wilhelm turned him from a political nuisance into a potential political rival. Wilhelm's presence at an 1887 conference with Stöcker and General Waldersee (who was viewed as a potential successor to Bismarck) convinced Bismarck that Stöcker was part of a conspiracy to oust him as Chancellor. From this point on, Bismarck was determined to reduce Stöcker's influence on the young Prince Wilhelm.

Stöcker had also managed to alienate many Catholic journalists and politicians in the years after the Bäcker and Schmidt trials. Perhaps because of the lukewarm reaction of the Catholic press after those verdicts, Stöcker began to express a growing anti-Catholic rhetoric in his various newspapers. This rhetoric turned several former allies, including Christoph Joseph Cremer and Freiherr Friedrich Karl von Fechenbach, into bitter enemies. Fechenbach, a frequent benefactor of anti-Semitic causes, had formerly tried to foster cooperation between radical Catholics and ultra-Conservatives. But, less than a decade later, he was as committed to forcing Stöcker's removal as he was to spreading anti-Semitism.[128] Cremer, a former Catholic ally of Stöcker in the Berlin Movement and editor of the *Westfälische Merkur*, had also become disillusioned by Stöcker's anti-Catholic rhetoric. Although he had little political support in the Reichstag, Cremer authored an anti-Stöcker pamphlet in 1889 that ignited renewed interest in the Stöcker-Bäcker case.

In his pamphlet, Cremer claimed that Stöcker had attempted to get his old associate, Pastor Carl Witte, to perjure himself in the Bäcker trial. Furthermore, Cremer claimed that Witte still possessed letters that incriminated Stöcker in this regard. Stöcker's angry denunciation

[128] Freiherr Karl Friedrich Fechenbach zu Laudenbach, a wealthy Catholic anti-Semite, repeatedly switched party allegiance between the Conservative and Center Parties before finally being marginalized by both. Although Fechenbach had little political support, he did wield considerable power due to his wealth and his title. Fechenbach's enmity for Stöcker led him to gather an enormous collection of documents and newspaper articles about Stöcker's legal troubles. This existence of this collection, which reached up to 20 volumes of material, was used to intimidate Stöcker. It still exists as part of the Sammlung Fechenbach at the Bundesarchiv Koblenz.

of both Cremer and Witte, and Witte's public response, eventually led to a new series of legal proceedings.[129]

The first battles in the Stöcker-Cremer-Witte affair took place in church disciplinary hearings rather than in the German courts. Stöcker initiated these hearings in early 1889, when he denounced Witte to the Evangelical Consistory (*Konsistorium*) and denied that any incriminating letters existed. After Witte published several letters from Stöcker in the *Norddeutsche Allgemeine Zeitung*, however, the Consistory rejected Stöcker's complaint.[130] Pastor Witte, emboldened by this success, filed his own grievance against Stöcker with the Evangelical Church Council (*Oberkirchenrath*). The Church Council, however, found Witte's public attacks against Stöcker to be objectionable and gave him, not Stöcker, a public censure. Once again, this apparent victory for Stöcker was a hollow one. The Church Council's decision was highly critical of both Witte and Stöcker and asserted that "which of these clergymen was attacked first, and who is the most to blame does not warrant a debate."[131] This meant that the church authorities had made no judgment on the truthfulness of Witte's charges, but had merely condemned both parties for engaging in such a public feud.

---

[129] Cremer had previously signed the petition supporting Stöcker after the Stöcker-Bäcker trial in 1885, but the two parted ways shortly thereafter. Cremer, like Fechenbach, had a very colorful political history. In the mid-1870s, Cremer had served as the chief editor for the Catholic *Germania* and had inspired the vicious series of anti-Semitic articles in 1875. By 1882, however, Cremer had been removed from this post and excluded from the Center Party for his participation in the anti-Semitic Berlin Movement. After a brief flirtation with Conservatives, Cremer then joined the National Liberal Party and eventually repudiated anti-Semitism. Many newspapers suggested that Cremer was a paid agent of Bismarck, and that his attacks on Stöcker were made on Bismarck's orders. But Cremer claimed that he was only responding to Stöcker's anti-Catholic rhetoric. Cremer's 1889 brochure, *The Alleged 10,000 Marks of Mr. von Bleichröder*, was written as a response to Stöcker's charges that Cremer had been bribed by Bismarck's banker Gerson von Bleichröder to withdraw from an election in order to aid a liberal candidate.

[130] According to the *Trierische Landeszeitung* 15 February 1889 #44, in BAK ZSg. 113 Sammlung Fechenbach, Nr. 740. According to the modern historian Hans Engelmann, these letters were forged. However, in 1896, a German court deciding a libel suit between Stöcker and Witte claimed that there was reason to believe such a letter was real. Witte had hired the famous Berlin attorney Erich Sello to handle his case. See Engelmann, *Kirche am Abgrund*, 147.

[131] See *Neue Westfälische Volkszeitung* (Bielefeld) 17 April 1889 #91. The Evangelical Church Council had always been a conservative body, and in 1878 the Council declared that Church officials should refrain from interfering in political matters. It was thus hostile to Stöcker's activities in the Christian-Social Party. Gordon Craig, *Germany 1866–1945* (New York: Oxford Univ. Press, 1978), 184.

This verdict also caused an uproar in the German press. While ultra-Conservative newspapers steadfastly defended Stöcker's reputation, liberal newspapers once again reviewed the Stöcker-Bäcker case and listed Court Chaplain's record of "proven misconduct." Pastor Witte, stung by the censure of the Church Council, printed a new pamphlet that included more charges against Stöcker. This pamphlet was bitterly attacked by many of Stöcker's allies—thus provoking another long series of libel trials.[132] Witte was eventually suspended from his position as Pastor of the St. Golgatha church by the Evangelical Consistory (Konsistorium) for what it called "an addiction to troublemaking" (*Querulantenwahnsinn*) and "simple and hallucinatory paranoia" (*unkomplizirten und hallucinatorischen paranoia*). But, as one might imagine, this act served only to increase his bitterness against Stöcker.[133] Stöcker's public battle with Witte would continue for over a decade more.

As a result of his ongoing public conflict with Pastor Witte, Stöcker again was pressured by government and religious authorities to stop his political agitation. The new Kaiser, Wilhelm II, now gave Stöcker a choice between continuing his political activities or keeping his position as Court Chaplain.[134] At first, Stöcker decided to keep his office and announce a withdrawal from German politics. But avoiding comment on political matters was difficult for a man who saw his political and religious work as inseparable. After months of relative quiet, Stöcker delivered an anti-Semitic speech at the 1890 Conservative Party convention in Baden. Because of public complaints about this speech, the Kaiser finally removed Stöcker from his position as Court Chaplain.

Although Stöcker had lost his religious office and much of his political power due to these legal defeats, he did not disappear quietly from the political scene. In fact, for the indefatigable Stöcker, his dismissal as Court Chaplain proved to be a blessing in disguise. Now freed from restrictions on his political activities, Stöcker plunged

[132] See *Frankfurter Zeitung* 28 January 1890 #28 on the charges filed by Witte against Hans Leuß. As the editor of Stöcker's *Das Volk*, Leuß paid for his attacks on Witte with 15 days in prison.

[133] See Witte's angry reaction to his dismissal in a report on his 1896 libel suit against Stöcker, GStA PK, VI. HA Nachlass Stöcker Abt. III Nr. 5.

[134] Otto Pflanze, *Bismarck and the Development of Germany*, vol. 3, *The Period of Fortification 1880–1898* (Princeton: Princeton Univ. Press, 1990), 318.

once again into the fray in support of his friend Wilhelm von Hammerstein. Although his public appeal had waned along with his credibility, Stöcker still possessed a significant political following among anti-Semites and ultra-Conservatives. His most loyal supporters now adoringly referred to him as the "Chaplain of all Germans" (*Hofprediger aller Deutschen*), a play on his new official title of "Chaplain in retirement" (*Hofprediger außer Dienst*). But Stöcker's political rehabilitation lasted only for a few years. As the ultra-Conservatives began to lose influence after 1893, Stöcker slowly lost his base of support. Continued conflicts with Pastor Witte, and the destruction of Hammerstein's own reputation in a scandalous trial in 1896, further isolated Stöcker from the mainstream of the Conservative Party.[135]

The final blow came with the publication of the "Funeral Pyre Letter" (*Scheiterhaufenbrief*) in the Spring of 1895. In this letter, originally written in 1888, Stöcker had advised his friend Hammerstein to avoid attacking Bismarck directly in the *Kreuzzeitung*, but instead advised him to light a series of "funeral pyres" to illuminate the areas where the ultra-conservatives and the Kaiser both disagreed with Bismarck. When this letter was discovered and published by the socialist *Vorwärts*, it convinced most Germans that Stöcker was a devious and manipulative man. Even for the last of his political followers, Stöcker had now become politically disgraced. In February 1896, the Conservative Party severed all connections to Stöcker.[136] Although he retained his Reichstag seat for more than a decade, Stöcker remained politically isolated until his death in 1909.

---

[135] In 1896, Witte resurfaced and won a civil libel suit against Stöcker after Stöcker once again claimed Witte had falsified evidence against him. The judges in this case sentenced Stöcker to a 600 Mark fine, and declared that Witte's charges had the "appearance of truthfulness". A year later, however, this verdict was overturned on appeal. GStA PK, VI. HA Nachlass Stöcker Abt. III, Nr. 5. Stöcker's Nachlass contains two volumes of letters and legal documents pertaining to his conflict with Witte.

[136] The cause of this final severance of ties with Stöcker was not only the *Scheiterhaufenbrief*, but also Stöcker's failure to condemn his old newspaper, *Das Volk*, which had become increasingly socialist in the late 1890s. See Levy, *The Downfall of the Anti-Semitic Political Parties*, 173.

Hirsch Hildesheimer and Jewish Self-Defense

The Kantorowicz Affair and the Stöcker trials are fairly unique in that they show Jewish citizens publicly resisting or even attacking leading anti-Semitic figures during the height of the Berlin Movement. These incidents seem unusual in light of a perceived reluctance of German Jews to publicly confront anti-Semitism in an organized way. Except for a small committee formed briefly in 1880, there was no organized Jewish group dedicated to resisting German anti-Semitism until more than a decade after the Berlin Movement became active.[137] There are many reasons why Jews were hesitant to form such organizations. Some believed that anti-Semitic agitation was only a reaction to social and economic stresses and would disappear after a few years. Others believed that anti-Semitism needed to be stopped, but they were afraid that a Jewish defense organization would merely create a more prominent target for anti-Semitic attacks rather than stemming their flow. Finally, many wealthier and more conservative Jews such as Gerson von Bleichröder feared that any such organization would be dominated by leftist-liberal elements who stood in opposition to Bismarck and his government.

As the Kantorowicz Affair and the Stöcker-Bäcker trial demonstrate, however, the lack of a Jewish defense organization in this crucial period did not mean that individual Jews and their allies were unwilling to fight publicly against anti-Semitism. During the 1880s, many individual Jewish and liberal Christian journalists took enormous personal and financial risks in order to fight anti-Semitic agitators in court. The Stöcker-Bäcker case was just the first of many instances where a liberal or Jewish journalist provoked a libel trial in order to "prove" that his anti-Semitic opponents were dishonorable or corrupt. One journalist in particular, Hirsch Hildesheimer of the *Jüdische Presse*, became renowned for such tactics.

---

[137] The *Deutsch-Israelitischer Gemeindebund* had been formed in 1869, but was not very active in fighting against anti-Semitic agitators. A defense committee was also formed after the infamous *Judendebatte* in December of 1880, but it lasted only a few months before succumbing to disputes over tactics. See Arnold Pauker, "Zur Problematik einer jüdischen Abwehrstrategie in der deutschen Gesellschaft," in *Juden im Wilhelminischen Deutschland 1890–1914*, ed. Werner E. Mosse, Schriftenreihe Wissenschaftlicher Abhandlungen des Leo Baeck Instituts, no. 33 (Tübingen: J.C.B. Mohr [Paul Siebeck], 1976), 486.

The name Hirsch Hildesheimer was immediately recognizable for most German Jews because his father, Esriel Hildesheimer, was one of the most prominent leaders of Orthodox Jewry in Imperial Germany. Esriel Hildesheimer had founded the Berlin *Rabbinerseminar* in 1873, the first modern Orthodox rabbinical seminary in Germany. Through this institution, the elder Hildesheimer supported the academic study of the Jewish religion and also encouraged compromises between traditional Jewish rituals and the demands of modern European life.[138] Ezriel Hildesheimer also dedicated himself to cooperation among various branches of the Jewish religion where such cooperation did not violate religious precepts. He energetically supported the battle against anti-Semitism, especially against attempts to outlaw the *shehitah*, the ritual slaughter of animals for kosher meat.[139]

In many ways, the career of Hirsch Hildesheimer paralleled that of his father. After receiving his doctorate in 1879, Hildesheimer lectured in his father's *Rabbinerseminar* on Jewish History and the geography of Palestine. Like his father, Hildesheimer also dedicated himself to a fairly moderate and flexible orthodoxy, which would retain traditional religious principles without requiring isolation from other Germans or from Reform Jews. Inspired by the rise of political anti-Semitism after 1880, however, Hirsch Hildesheimer would eventually far surpass his father in the desire to publicly defend Judaism against anti-Semitic attacks.

In 1883, the 28 year-old Hildesheimer began to step out of his father's shadow when he became chief editor of the *Jüdische Presse*, a small but influential newspaper that represented the interests of Orthodox Jews in Berlin. The *Jüdische Presse* reported on a number of cultural, religious, and political topics, but as Hildesheimer became more aggressive in his campaign against anti-Semitism, the newspaper increasingly became a forum for him to attack anti-Semitic agitators and publicize his own struggles to defend Judaism.

Even before Hildesheimer assumed control of the *Jüdische Presse*, it was common for the newspaper to comment on the activities of Stöcker and other anti-Semitic agitators in Germany. But in the

[138] David Ellenson, *Rabbi Esriel Hildesheimer and the Creation of a Modern Jewish Orthodoxy* (Tuscaloosa: University of Alabama, 1990), x. See Ellenson for a discussion of the significant differences between Esriel Hildesheimer and another prominent Orthodox modernist, Samson Hirsch.

[139] Ibid., 105–108.

years after 1883, the pace and intensity of such articles seemed to increase. Hildesheimer frequently wrote lead articles criticizing the activities of Stöcker or rejecting the anti-Semitic Talmud scholarship of August Rohling—occasionally his father even contributed scholarly responses to anti-Semitic propaganda.[140] Hildesheimer also closely monitored various trials involving Jewish or anti-Semitic defendants, and he frequently traded barbs with newspaper editors, regardless of their political affiliation, who dared to employ anti-Semitic rhetoric.

In 1885, the *Jüdische Presse* reacted with glee to the verdict in the Stöcker-Bäcker trial, which seemed to have permanently destroyed the anti-Semitic chaplain's credibility. For Hildesheimer, this was a clear case of an anti-Semitic agitator getting his just desserts:

> As loud and strident as the vile agitation of this court chaplain has become, as often as he has dared to drag the civil honor (*bürgerliche Ehre*) of others through the mud, so much more this judge's verdict must enthusiastically be welcomed—this verdict that has ripped the mask from the countenance of this apostle of hatred, and sent this slanderer to the same pillory that he had once deviously constructed for others.[141]

Although Hildesheimer's hope that this trial would lead to the end of Stöcker's political career went unfulfilled, the trial still served as an important precedent: by libeling Stöcker and forcing him to sue, his opponents had succeeded in getting a judge to publicly impugn his reputation. It would not be long before Hildesheimer himself would use these same tactics to attack other anti-Semitic agitators.[142]

In August of 1887, Dr. Adolf König, a prominent anti-Semitic politician from the small Ruhr Valley town of Witten, published an article that criticized the "educated classes" for embracing Jewish materialism and rejecting anti-Semitism. Soon after, Hildesheimer responded in an angry article in the *Jüdische Presse*, which labeled

---

[140] See for instance Esriel Hildesheimer's lead article "The Oath According to the Bible and the Talmud", which was written at the height of the Hapke incident. *Jüdische Presse* 15 August 1883 #48.

[141] *Jüdische Presse* 25 June 1885 #26.

[142] This sensational humiliation of Stöcker occurred almost simultaneously with the similar public disgrace of the anti-Semitic scholar August Rohling in Vienna. Pressured to sue for libel after a Jewish rabbi insulted him in print, Rohling was eventually discredited by scholarly testimony, and he was forced to withdraw the libel charges before an unfavorable verdict could be rendered. For more on the Rohling-Bloch trial, see chapter 5.

König as a "highway robber" (*Strauchritter*) and a "wretched fellow" (*trauriger Geselle*).[143] König immediately sued Hildesheimer for libel, and the civil suit was heard in December 1887 before the *Schöffengericht* in Berlin-Moabit. At trial, Hildesheimer was accompanied by Hugo Sachs, the famous defense attorney from the Stöcker-Bäcker trial. In a long and detailed opening statement, Sachs pelted Dr. König with accusations of insurance fraud, medical malpractice, previous convictions for libel, false denunciations against Jews, associating with known felons, and operating a bordello in his brother's house. If this wasn't enough, Hildesheimer also filed a counter-suit against König for his affiliation with Theodor Fritsch's *Antisemitische Korrespondenz*. Although Hildesheimer could not prove to the court that König had libeled him personally, he argued that general libels against the Jewish religion in the *Antisemitische Korrespondenz* were personally offensive to him.[144]

Dr. König's lawyer rejected all the assaults on his client's character, but he could present no direct evidence to refute the charges. König's lawyer instead accused Sachs of attempting to repeat the tactics of the infamous Stöcker-Bäcker trial, where he had turned the court's attention away from the libelous statements at issue and instead put the character of the plaintiff on trial. Sachs replied that he fully accepted the comparison with the earlier trial, where a judge ruled that libels were less egregious because of the true nature of the person that was libeled.[145] In his own address to the court, Hirsch Hildesheimer assured the judges that his countersuit was heartfelt since he believed that general attacks on his religion were also personal affronts. As he put it: "I am not only a Jew, but a strict religious Jew. Thus, an attack on the laws of my religion or their sources is even more insulting than an attack on my personal honor as a man and citizen."[146]

Even before the verdict in the trial was delivered, Hildesheimer proudly defended his own conduct in the *Jüdische Presse*. The newspaper devoted two entire issues to printing the trial transcripts, and mocked anti-Semitic editors for not being brave enough to print the

[143] Original article in *Jüdische Presse* 11 August 1887 #22.
[144] *Jüdische Presse* 16 December 1887 #50.
[145] Ibid.
[146] *Jüdische Presse* 22 December 1887 #51.

transcripts in their own newspapers.[147] Hildesheimer also implied that the case, regardless of the verdict, showed that German Jews would not be afraid to fight back when insulted:

> We did not want this fight. But after he threw down the gauntlet . . . After this man abandoned the field of journalistic battle for that of the courts, then 'cowardly thoughts of anxious vacillations' would have been a dishonorable dereliction of duty. It was necessary to demonstrate, *coram iudicio*, before the same court that he had called, that this man has no right to serve as a moral judge over Jews and Judaism.[148]

The *Jüdische Presse* further asserted that the trial would "demonstrate to our opponents, who often accuse Jews of cowardice and timidity, that we Jews do not shy away from battle, and that we stand our ground when weapons are placed in our hands."[149]

After a long delay, the verdict was finally returned. Hildesheimer was found guilty of libel and assessed a moderate fine of 200 Marks. In addition, the court dismissed Hildesheimer's counterclaim since it found he was not personally libeled and thus had no standing to sue.[150]

---

[147] *Antisemitische Correspondenz* January 1888 #21.

[148] Ibid. The reference to "cowardly thoughts of anxious vacillations" is a reference to Goethe's short poem "Beherzigung" (Heartening), included here with a rough translation:

Feiger Gedanken	Cowardly thoughts of
Bängliches Schwanken,	Anxious vacillations,
Weibisches Zagen,	Of womanly wavering,
Aengstliches Klagen	And frightened lamentations
Wendet kein Elend,	Won't end your suffering,
Macht dich nicht frei.	Can't make you free.
Allen Gewalten,	All of the powers
Zum Trutz sich erhalten,	Maintained in defiance
Nimmer sich beugen,	Unwilling to bend
Kräftig sich zeigen,	Will show their reliance,
Rufet die Arme	And with arms will send,
Der Götter herbei.	The Gods to your side.

This reference to Goethe not only reinforces Hildesheimer's claim of masculine bravery, but perhaps also a claim on Germanness as well.

[149] *Antisemitische Correspondenz* January 1888 #21.

[150] Verdict reported in *Reichsgeldmonopol* 19 April 1888 #304 and *Antisemitische Correspondenz* 1 May 1888 #26. This verdict is not altogether surprising. The Supreme Court (Reichsgericht) had already ruled in 1881 that individual Jews had no standing to pursue libel charges if the insults were directed against the religion as a whole. The Reichsgericht made this ruling despite having previously acknowledged the right of soldiers and judges to pursue charges against general slanders of their respective professions. The König case can be seen as a challenge of this inconsistent

After the trial, however, it seemed to be Adolf König, not Hildesheimer, who was most affected by the proceedings. König immediately launched a public speaking tour to clear his name, and he authored a bitter pamphlet on the trial entitled *A Piece of Villainy Designed to Destroy a Man's Honor.*[151] Hildesheimer, on the other hand, was far from deterred by the result. In fact, it was the first of many such episodes.

At the time of the König trial, Hildesheimer was still one of only a few Jewish figures to challenge anti-Semites so openly and directly. There was still no organized Jewish defense against anti-Semitic attacks, and those who wished to "stand their ground" did so of their own volition and at their own risk. By the early 1890s, however, things had begun to change. Faced with a new wave of anti-Semitic sentiment created by the rise of new agitators such as Otto Böckel and Hermann Ahlwardt, German Jews started to move toward organizing a more concentrated defense. The first major step was the founding of the Association for Defense against Anti-Semitism (*Verein zur Abwehr des Antisemitismus*)—better known as the *Abwehrverein.* This organization was formed in November of 1890 under the leadership of two prominent non-Jewish liberals, Heinrich Rickert and Rudolf von Gneist.[152] Although some Jews did join the *Abwehrverein*, and although most Jewish leaders wholeheartedly supported it, this organization was primarily envisioned as a Christian organization dedicated to defending Jews.[153] In addition, the *Abwehrverein* did not fully adopt the aggressive methods of Hirsch Hildesheimer in bringing anti-Semitic activists into court. Apparently, members worried that the courtroom could still serve anti-Semitic agitators by providing another public forum for them to spread their ideas and claim to be victims of a Jewish conspiracy. Instead, the defense against anti-Semitism consisted mostly of educational speakers and literature as well as the support of rival candidates in regions where agitators were active.[154]

---

interpretation of libel law (§185 RStGB). See Johannes Groß, *Ritualmordbeschuldigungen gegen Juden in deuschen Kaiserreich 1871–1914* (Berlin: Metropol, 2002), 217.

[151] Dr. Adolf König, *Ein Bubenstück, ersonnen um eines Mannes Ehre zu vernichten. Aktenmäßige Darstellung s. Prozesses gegen Hirsch Hildesheimer* (Hagen: H. Risel, 1888).

[152] Sanford Ragins, *Jewish Responses to Anti-Semitism in Germany 1870–1914* (Cincinnati: Hebrew Union College Press, 1980), 40.

[153] Ragins, *Jewish Responses to Anti-Semitism*, 40.

[154] Ismar Schorsch, *Jewish Reactions to German Anti-Semitism 1870–1914* (New York: Columbia University Press, 1972), 84.

As anti-Semitic agitation intensified through the early 1890s, other Jews became more vocal in calling for organized Jewish action to fight anti-Semitism. An 1890 article in the Orthodox newspaper *Der Israelit,* for example, called for Jews of all religious orientations to join together in a defense organization. Entitled "Up, Israel, Into the Fray!", this article avowed that "Israel can and will lead and defend its own cause, and it needs no outsiders to fight its battles."[155] In March of 1891, the *Allgemeine Zeitung des Judenthums* (*AZJ*) published a lead story under the headline "The Anti-Semitic Way of Fighting" which mocked the meekness of anti-Semitic agitators but still expressed reticence about the desirability of direct legal challenges:

> If, however, a Jew dares to stand up to them, it is a part of the nature of battle that things can easily get rough or, at times, even aggressive in the heat of combat. Immediately, the drums will begin to beat, the entire anti-Semitic camp will awaken, and with their entire collective might they will—cry out to the district attorney . . . We would never call on the help of the courts against the anti-Semites, since we don't believe that anything would be altered or improved if a slanderer pays a 300 Mark fine or, in the case of an inability to pay, sits in jail for eight days.[156]

Although the *AZJ* had reported regularly on the legal troubles of agitators such as Otto Böckel and Theodor Fritsch in previous years, the editors apparently still felt that direct challenges of anti-Semites in court were beneath their dignity. Instead, the *AZJ* concluded its article with a comparison of their own measured gentlemanly tactics with those of anti-Semitic agitators, who were likened to "wild Indian tribesmen (*Indianerstämme*)".[157] Thus, despite some Jewish support for more aggressive action and efforts of the *Abwehrverein*, Hildesheimer was still alone in confronting anti-Semitism directly in court.

This does not mean that other Jews were not publicly defending Judaism. Jacob Borut has described several organizations both in Berlin and in the countryside that arranged public anti-anti-Semitic

---

[155] *Der Israelit* 9 June 1880, XXXI, No. 45 as quoted in Jacob Borut, "The Rise of Jewish Defence Agitation in Germany, 1890–1895: A Pre-History of the C.V.?" *Leo Baeck Institute Year Book* 36 (1991): 59–96.

[156] *Allgemeine Zeitung des Judenthums* 13 March 1891 #11 in BAK *ZSg. 113* Sammlung Fechenbach #17.

[157] Ibid.

meetings and lectures. The Göttingen Rabbi Benno Jacob, for example, appeared at several anti-Semitic rallies to refute the claims of agitators, and the leader of the briefly active Association for the Struggle Against Race-Baiting (*Vereinigung zur Bekämpfung der Rassenhetze*), Edmund Lichtenstein, was one of the first to unearth and publicly disseminate evidence of Hermann Ahlwardt's unsavory criminal past. But those few who dared to engage in legal actions against anti-Semites, such as Karl Wiesenthal, a Leipzig correspondent with *Der Israelit*, quickly withdrew because of the threat of court fines and personal attacks.[158] Such activists were still the exception, not the rule. Even Abraham Berliner, a colleague of Hildesheimer at the Berlin rabbinical seminary who had published a famous attack against Paul de Lagarde, complained in 1892 about Jewish newspapers that were too obsessed with bringing attention to anti-Semitic incidents instead of working to support religious education and faith.[159]

In May of 1892, however, Hildesheimer returned to action after the anti-Semitic *Staatsbürgerzeitung* printed a special supplement containing what purported to be excerpts from the Talmud and Schulchan Aruch. These excerpts were lifted from the work of three well-known anti-Semitic scholars, Johann Eisenmenger, August Rohling, and Jakob Ecker, and contained passages that supposedly ordered Jews to lie to, steal from, and even murder their innocent Christian neighbors. The printing of the "Talmud Excerpt", which occurred while public attention was focused on a ritual murder allegation in Xanten, was intended to suggest to readers that there was already "scholarly" proof of Jewish criminality and bloodthirstiness. To spread this message, and certainly also to enhance their own profits and visibility, the editors of the *Staatsbürgerzeitung* reprinted the supplement as a pamphlet and distributed as many as 150,000 copies.[160]

Hirsch Hildesheimer's immediate reaction was one of despair that the government seemed to be unable or unwilling to reign in such libels. As the *Jüdische Presse* wrote:

> Are we Jews outside the law? . . . Can our personal, civil, and religious honor really be dragged in the filth, be ridiculed and derided in this

[158] Borut, "The Rise of Jewish Defence Agitation," 73, 76, 84.

[159] Mordechai Breuer, *Jüdische Orthodoxie im Deutschen Reich* (Frankfurt: Jüdische Verlag bei Athanäum, 1986), 463 n. 312.

[160] *Jüdische Presse* 30 June 1892 #26.

> way without hindrance or penalty? Has some law removed us Jews from the protection of those legal paragraphs which bring the disrupters of civil peace and the defilers of religious sanctities to punishment?[161]

A week later, Hildesheimer continued his tirade. But this time his frustrations were directed not only at the government, but also at the perceived passivity of his fellow Jews: "How much longer? To what desperation must conditions come in order to startle the indolent? Has the confidence in the 'protection of the authorities,' the boasting of our so-called 'equal rights' not yet been shaken?"[162] Hildesheimer concluded this article by calling on all Jews to unite in a vigorous self-defense.

Hildesheimer's response to the "Talmud Excerpt" did not stop with this call to action. He quickly published his own pamphlet, called "The True Talmud Excerpt" which contained accurate translations along with derisive comments about the way anti-Semitic scholars had distorted or falsified their version. Although the *Jüdische Presse* expressed doubt that the distribution of this pamphlet could ever match the well-organized network of the anti-Semites, it hoped that this would at least repair some of the damage.[163]

By the end of June, the rhetoric between the *Jüdische Presse* and *Staatsbürgerzeitung* over the "Talmud Excerpt" had escalated into an all-out war. After Hildesheimer described those responsible for writing and printing the anti-Semitic pamphlet as "defamers and libelers (*Ehrabschneider und Verleumder*)," an associate at the *Staatsbürgerzeitung*, Ludwig Schwennhagen, issued a statement that promised immediate legal action. According to Schwennhagen, Hildesheimer's outbursts had done the editors of the *Staatsbürgerzeitung* a great service by allowing them to take the issue to court. A libel trial would force an independent court review of the two Talmud excerpts that would prove once and for all which translations were accurate.[164]

Hildesheimer responded to Schwennhagen with an article in the *Jüdische Presse*, which repeated in detail his evidence that the fraudulent anti-Semitic translations had already been refuted by reputable

---

161 *Jüdische Presse* 12 May 1892 as quoted in Ragins, *Jewish Responses to Anti-Semitism*, 38.

162 *Jüdische Presse* 19 May 1892 as quoted in Ragins, *Jewish Responses to Anti-Semitism*, 38.

163 *Jüdische Presse* 16 June 1892 #24.

164 Schwennhagen's statement as reprinted in *Jüdische Presse* 30 June 1892 #26.

Der wahre Wert des jüdischen Eides.

Seit einigen Tagen verbreiten die Antisemiten ein Schandblatt, in welchem behauptet wird, daß das die Feier des ‹dischen Versöhnungsfestes einleitende **„Gebet Kol Nidre“** den Eidbruch Anderen gegenüber gutheißt. Das ist

infame Lüge und Verleumdung!

Jene Formel hat mit Eiden und Verpflichtungen Anderen gegenüber — seien sie Juden oder ‹hristen — absolut nichts zu thun, sondern erstreckt sich nur auf religiöse Selbstverpflichtungen, mit denen ‹emand sich selbst Entbehrungen und Beschränkungen auferlegt. Das ist in der Formel **ausdrücklich** gesagt. ‹d um das Gegentheil behaupten zu können, wird in dem antisemitischen Schandblatt eine

niederträchtige Fälschung

‹gangen, indem die ausschlaggebenden Worte „al nafschatana“, welche in dem beigegebenen hebräischen Texte stehen, der deutschen Uebertragung unterschlagen werden.

Nach dem jüdischen Religionsgesetze giebt es nämlich Gelübde und verschiedene gelübbeartige Formen, durch welche ‹mand **sich selbst** irgendwelche Verpflichtungen auferlegen kann. Um nun nicht der Sünde zu verfallen, im Laufe des Jahres ‹überlegt eine solche Verpflichtung zu übernehmen und unbewußt oder unüberlegt zu übertreten, ist seit uralter Zeit in ‹m liturgischen Stück Kol Nidre die feierliche Erklärung enthalten, daß alle derartigen unüberlegten Selbstverpflichtungen — und ‹**ur** diese — von vornherein nicht bindend sind. Verpflichtungen, welche man mit vollbewußter Ueberlegung eingeht, und nun ‹r **Verpflichtungen, welche einem Anderen gegenüber eingegangen, und Eide, welche einem Anderen gegenüber geleistet werden, sind dagegen unter allen Umständen bindend.** Daß vollends **Eide, die vor ‹ericht, gleichviel in welcher Form, geschworen werden, absolut bindende, unlösbare Kraft haben und ‹halten**, braucht nach dem Gesagten nicht betont zu werden.“

Um jedem Schimmer eines Mißverständnisses vorzubeugen, wird in den jüdischen Gesetzesschriften und in allen Gebet‹chern, welche das Kol Nidre enthalten, mit nachdrücklichster Entschiedenheit betont, daß die Formel sich auf Verpflichtungen ‹d Eide Anderen gegenüber nicht entfernt bezieht. Dies wird aber nicht etwa bloß von jüdischer Seite behauptet, sondern ‹ch von **christlichen Gelehrten** rückhaltlos bestätigt. So z. B. erklären:

> **Eisenmenger**, einer der grimmigsten Judenfeinde aller Zeiten, in „Entdecktes Judenthum“, Theil II S. 501:
> „Berichteter maßen können die Juden **weder durch die am Versühnungsfest gebrauchliche Entbindung der Eydschwuren durch Col Nidre,** noch sonsten von einem vornehmen Rabbinen oder dreyen schlichten Männern **vom Eyd, den sie einem Christen oder der christlichen Obrigkeit thun, nach ihrer angezogenen Lehr loßgesprochen werden.**“

> Dr. **Franz Delitzsch,** weiland Professor der evangelischen Theologie an der Universität zu Leipzig, in „Rohling's ‹lmudjude“, VII. Auflage (Leipzig 1881) Seite 52:
> „Was aber das Ungeschehenmachen geleisteter Eide betrifft, welche der Jude in dem Kol nidre am Vorabend des Versöhnungsfestes erfleht, so wird dieses Ungeschehenmachen durch den Zusatz daasorna al nafschatana (d. h. durch welche wir uns auf unsere eigene Person verschworen haben) ausdrücklich auf solche Eide beschränkt, welche man aus freiem Willen **vor sich selbst** abgelegt hat, also auf eidlich übernommene und hinterdrein als sündlich oder **unausführbar anerkannte Selbstverpflichtungen, mit Ausschluß gerichtlicher Eide und mit Wissen des Nächsten eidlich übernommener Verpflichtungen gegen diesen.**“

> Dr. **Hermann L. Strack**, Professor der evangelischen Theologie an der Universität zu Berlin, veröffentlichte, als ‹hofprediger Stöcker i. J. 1885 in sattsam bekannter Manier das Kol Nidre zu Angriffen gegen Juden und Judenthum aus‹lachtete, in der „Kreuzzeitung“ eine Erklärung, in welcher er, gleichwie in seinen wissenschaftlichen Ausführungen in ‹erzog's Real-Encyclopädie für protestantische Theologie“ (Leipzig 1881) Band VIII, S. 127 fg., wiederholt bekundet:
> „In der Formel Kol Nidre ist, wie eine Vergleichung von 4. M. 30, 3 (s. auch V. 14) ergibt, **nicht** die Rede von Eiden, die anderen geleistet werden, sondern nur von Gelübden, Verpflichtungen, die man **sich selbst** auferlegt. **Gelübde und Eide, welche einem Andern geleistet sind, sind unlösbar, außer wenn die betheiligte Person anwesend und einverstanden ist.** Das ist die einstimmige Ansicht der maßgebenden jüdischen Autoritäten. Dazu kommt noch, daß in den meisten neueren Ausgaben der Festgebete in einer Anmerkung nachdrücklich erklärt wird, daß durch dieses liturgische Stück die Interessen Anderer nicht berührt werden. **Aus der Formel Kol Nidre kann daher kein Bedenken gegen die Glaubwürdigkeit des von einem Juden geleisteten Eides hergenommen werden.**“

Ebenso urtheilen **ausnahmslos alle christlichen Gelehrten.** Und wegen dieser liturgischen Einrichtung, ‹ doch nur die peinliche Gewissenhaftigkeit bei **Heilighaltung des Wortes**, sogar dessen, das man sich selbst giebt, ‹eugt, erfrecht sich antisemitische Verlogenheit, die Juden als „ein Volk, wie es gemeingefährlicher und verderbter wohl ‹um gedacht werden kann“, zu verunglimpfen. Alle anständig und gerecht gesinnten Christen werden wissen, was ‹n einem derartigen rohen Gebahren, das mit infamen Fälschungen und Verleumdungen die religiöse und bürger‹liche Ehre Anderer besudelt, und was von den antisemitischen Hetzlehren überhaupt zu halten ist, welche Lüge du‹ ‹üge stützen.

Verantwortlich für den Inhalt: Dr. Hirsch Hildesheimer in Berlin. — Verlag der Expedition der „Jüdischen Presse“ Berlin C. 22.
Druck von H. Itzkowski, Berlin, Gr. Hamburgerstr. 18-19.
Preis dieses Flugblattes: 1 Exemplar 5 Pf., 10 Expl. 30 Pf., 100 Expl. 1,50 M., 1000 Expl. 6 M.

Fig. 2. “The Real Value of a Jewish Oath”—A direct response by Hirsch Hildesheimer to the earlier pamphlet on the Kol Nidre disseminated by the Deutsche Antisemitenbund (Fig. 1). Courtesy of the Landesarchiv Berlin.

scholars. Hildesheimer welcomed the challenge in court, but also claimed the need for legal action was regrettable:

> It is a sad sign of the times that we must seek the protection of a judge instead of being able to protect ourselves through scientific refutations and through an appeal to a common love of truth—but the events of the day teach this lesson only too well. Our self-defense is powerless if it is not supported by the weight of a judge's verdict.[165]

Hildesheimer concluded by once again throwing down the gauntlet, repeating in boldface type that those responsible for the text were "defamers and libelers."

Several months later, however, a frustrated Hildesheimer was still waiting for formal charges to be filed. In an October article, he mocked his opponents' hesitance to file a suit:

> After having dared to go too far, it is understandable that Schwennhagen, Baade, and company now make a cowardly retreat to escape the ignominious defeat that they would inevitably have faced before a judge; but these men err if they think that this will quiet us: every accusation shall be hurled in their faces again and again until they can no longer dodge the obligation to make the aforementioned suit a reality . . .[166]

Hildesheimer claimed that over the past several months various anti-Semitic newspapers had been seeking donations for a fund to support a lawsuit; however, since no charges had been filed Hildesheimer suggested that these men must have used these funds for other illicit purposes. Finally, as if to intensify the insult, Hildesheimer once again repeated the same libelous comments about the authors of the pamphlet in boldface print.[167]

It is not clear if Ludwig Schwennhagen ever filed a libel charge against Hirsch Hildesheimer. Several months later, he was still publicly promising to take action.[168] Schwennhagen did, however, eventually get his day in court. After claiming that Chancellor Caprivi and Finance Minister Johannes Miquel were descendants of foreign Jews, Schwennhagen was sentenced to one year in jail for libel.[169]

[165] *Jüdische Presse* 30 June 1892 #26.
[166] *Judische Presse* 5 October 1892 #40/41 Beiblatt.
[167] Idem.
[168] See LAB A Pr. Br. Rep. 030, Polizeipräsidium Berlin, Nr. 8679, pp. 220–221.
[169] *Staatsbürgerzeitung* 18 March 1894 #130 in LAB A Pr. Br. Rep. 030, Polizeipräsidium Berlin, Nr. 12322, p. 74.

Even before this conviction, the *Staatsbürgerzeitung* was forced to back away from Schwennhagen after it was revealed by the *Berliner Tageblatt* that he had previous convictions for property crimes and petty theft.[170]

Unfortunately, Schwennhagen was not the same caliber of leader as Stöcker or König, and his loss did little to slow the rising tide of anti-Semitic agitation. Hildesheimer's own efforts, however, continued without pause. During the 1892 ritual murder trial in the Westphalian town of Xanten, Hildesheimer not only covered the case closely in the *Jüdische Presse*, he also attended the trial proceedings in person, and spoke frequently there about the absurdity of ritual murder charges.[171] Not surprisingly, Hildesheimer's critical speeches and articles led to further libel charges, including those filed by another editor of the *Staatsbürgerzeitung* and by an anti-Semitic publisher in Dresden.[172]

As a result of his activities, Hildesheimer was demonized in the anti-Semitic press, where he gradually began to replace the aging Gerson von Bleichröder as the perceived figurehead of a Jewish world conspiracy. Beginning in 1891, for example, the Glöß Verlag in Dresden printed a series of anti-Semitic cartoons called *Politische Bilderbogen* that portrayed the German government as being under the control of a Jewish conspiracy. Mirroring the extreme pessimism of Wilhelm Marr's infamous pamphlet more than a decade earlier, the sketches were highly critical not only of Jews, but also of the liberals (and Chancellor Caprivi) who were portrayed as their co-conspirators in a plot to ruin Germany. In a cartoon entitled "A *Freisinnige* Future" (*Freisinnige Zukunftsbilder*), Hirsch Hildesheimer is represented as a rabbi alongside several other Jewish and liberal leaders such as Heinrich Rickert, Paul Nathan, and Otto Hermes. In one part of the picture, anti-Semitic agitators such as Hermann Ahlwardt and Adolf Stöcker are drawn and quartered, burned at the stake, or imprisoned, while in the other, Chancellor Caprivi exchanges clothes with the liberal deputy Eugen Richter.[173] In a slightly later issue, entitled "The Jews at Friedrichsruh", Hildesheimer

---

[170] *Berliner Tageblatt* 5 February 1893 #64.

[171] *Hirsch Hildesheimer: Ein Gedenkbuch seinen Manen gewidmet* (Berlin: Itzkowski, 1911), 11.

[172] *Volkszeitung* 18 February 1894 #55 and *Deutsche Reform* 22 July 1894 #17, both in HStA Polizeibehörde, Abteilung IV, Politische Polizei S 576, Teil IIIa.

[173] *Politische Bilderbogen* #3 (Dresden: Gloß, 1892).

is once again front and center, dressed as a rabbi and standing under Bismarck's balcony amidst a band of "Jewish criminals". Nearby, a crying mother holds the body of her ritually-slaughtered child as Hildesheimer gestures mournfully toward the casket of the late Jewish politician Eduard Lasker.[174]

The cartoons of the *Poltische Bilderbogen* and the diatribes of men like König and Schwennhagen are proof that although Hildesheimer's legal challenges did not halt the spread of anti-Semitic propaganda, they at least made the work of individual agitators more difficult. In the aftermath of the Xanten trial, the election of several radical anti-Semites to the Reichstag, and the adoption of specific anti-Jewish rhetoric in the Conservative Party platform, Hildesheimer thundered once again against the continued passivity of his fellow German Jews:

> How much longer? For heaven's sake, how much longer?! When will the spell finally be broken that has held our modern race (*Geschlecht*) in apathetic indifference and spineless timidity? To action! To quick, strong, selfless, and never resting action![175]

Finally, less than a month after this plea, Hildesheimer's calls for an organized Jewish response to anti-Semitic agitation became a reality. In January of 1893, eighty-nine prominent Jews signed a proclamation advocating a more organized response to anti-Semitism. Less than two months later, the *Centralverein deutscher Staatsbürger jüdischen Glaubens* (Central Organization of German Citizens of the Jewish Faith) was born.[176]

Over the next several years, the *Centralverein* followed the example set by Hildesheimer in actively seeking legal action against those who libeled individual Jews or the Jewish religion. The *Centralverein* developed a Legal Defense Commission that served as a clearinghouse for lawsuits and accepted complaints from Jews across the country. Under the leadership of Eugen Fuchs, this commission was very active both in launching libel suits and in protecting the civil rights of German Jews. Like Hildesheimer before him, Fuchs did not measure his success by the number of lawsuits he won, but considered his goal to educate the nation and cultivate civic courage among

---

[174] *Politische Bilderbogen* #10 (Dresden: Gloß, 1893).

[175] *Jüdische Presse* 8 December 1892 #49 as quoted in Borut, "The Rise of Jewish Defence Agitation," 90.

[176] Ragins, *Jewish Responses to Anti-Semitism*, 51.

Fig. 3. "A Liberal (*Freisinnige*) Future"—An 1893 exemplar of *Politische Bilderbogen* that depicts Germany under "Jewish-liberal" control. Among those drawn on the billboard in the foreground are Hirsch Hildesheimer with deer horns (top left), Heinrich Rickert with a "Jewish" mask (top center right), and Otto Hermes portrayed as a frog (bottom right). Elsewhere in the picture, the Bible and Christian symbols are burned (top right) and Otto Hermes lectures students on the "fable of Christ" (bottom right). Persecuted anti-Semites are depicted on the left, while a "Mental Hospital for Anti-Semites" sits at the back horizon next to the Jewish casino. Courtesy of Klau Library at Hebrew Union College.

German Jews.[177] Even the reluctant *AZJ* now supported a more aggressive legal defense. Noting recent successes in battling anti-Semitism, the newspaper asserted: "Now we know that resistance helps. We are permitted to hope that *energetic, systematic defense activity* will succeed in damming up the anti-Semitic stream and—in years of assiduous work—in draining its sources."[178] The defense activity of the *Centralverein* would continue throughout the duration of the *Kaiserreich.*

The existence of an organized forum for legal action against anti-Semites did not mean an end to the activities of Hirsch Hildesheimer. In the following decades, Hildesheimer continued to denounce those that libeled the Jewish religion, and his most famous work came in his energetic defense of the *shehitah*, or Jewish kosher slaughter. When Hildesheimer died of a heart attack in 1910 at the surprisingly young age of 55, German Jews from all walks of life stepped forward to pay tribute to his many achievements. Letters, speeches, and articles praised his charity work for poor Russian Jews, his efforts to maintain unity between diverse Jewish sects, and his presence as a popular teacher at the *Rabbinerseminar*. But in almost every eulogy, special attention was given to Hildesheimer's record of active defense against anti-Semitic attacks. Albert Katz, an editor at the *Allgemeine Zeitung des Judenthums*, wrote with sincerity about the debt that German Jews owed to Hildesheimer:

> What he accomplished in that era in the field of defense can really only be understood by an insider like me, and I would expect to encounter no objections when I assert that most of the defense organizations that exist today would never have been formed if he had not directly or indirectly nudged their sluggish founders into action.[179]

* * *

The case studies discussed in this chapter were selected from hundreds of libel trials that involved anti-Semitism during the 1880s and 1890s. The coverage of such trials was a regular fixture in the

---

[177] Marjorie Lamberti, *Jewish Activism in Imperial Germany* (New Haven: Yale Univ. Press, 1978), 15.
[178] *Allgemeine Zeitung des Judenthums* 16 June 1893 as quoted in Ragins, *Jewish Responses to Anti-Semitism*, 53.
[179] *Hirsch Hildesheimer. Ein Gedenkbuch*, 42.

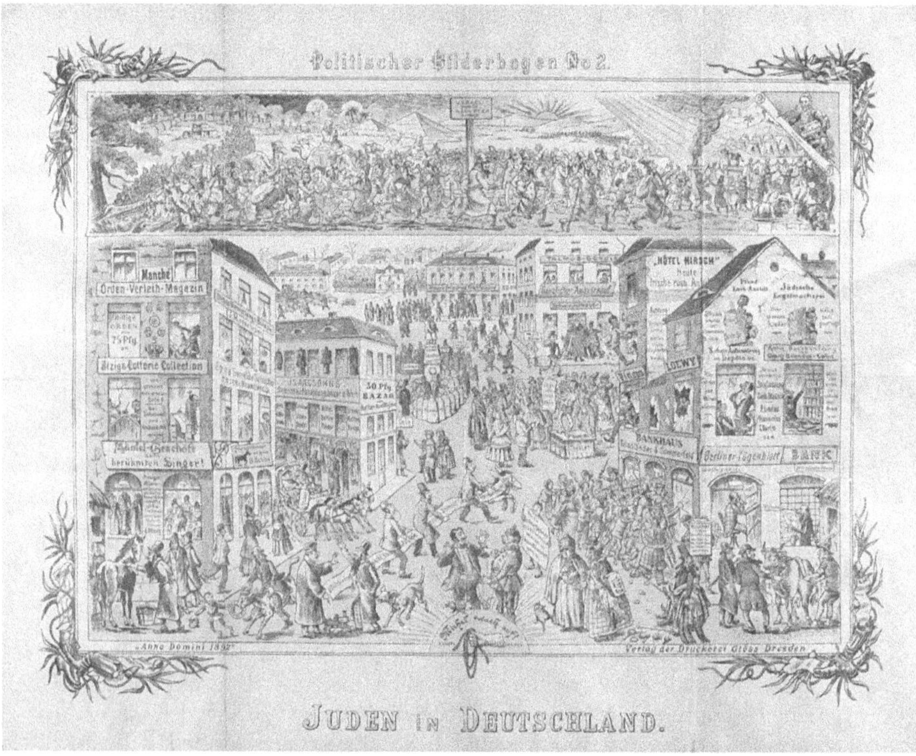

Fig. 4. "Jews in Germany"—An 1892 exemplar of *Politische Bilderbogen* that depicts the alleged immorality and criminality of Jews. On the left, a carriage carries Gerson von Bleichröder, his alleged mistress, and a 70,000 Mark bribe he supposedly paid her to keep quiet. The building in the right foreground houses both the recently bankrupted bank of Friedländer and Sommerfeld and the "Berlin Daily Liar," a play on the liberal *Berliner Tageblatt.* In the building on the back right, a Talmud school is housed directly above the firm of "Schwindelmayer". Courtesy of Klau Library at Hebrew Union College.

political press during this era—especially in anti-Semitic newspapers. Although the participants in these cases varied and the specific issues under debate could shift slightly, most of these trials fit into a common pattern. Such libel trials occurred so frequently not because of a special German litigiousness, but because the courtroom provided the possibility of seeking justice before an impartial authority, because it offered a public forum to spread (or refute) anti-Semitic propaganda, and because it served as a convenient alternative to the duel for defending one's honor.

Both prominent Jews and political anti-Semites were generally unhappy with the performance of the German legal system with regard to libel trials. Hirsch Hildesheimer, for example, complained bitterly when government prosecutors agreed to file libel charges on behalf of anti-Semites such as Bernhard Förster and Adolf Stöcker. His unhappiness was exacerbated by the perception that government attorneys were often unwilling to pursue cases against those who libeled the Jewish religion.[180] However, if Hildesheimer was critical about the number of government prosecutions, individual anti-Semitic agitators were just as loud in their own protests. Radical agitators such as Otto Böckel and Hermann Ahlwardt, who spoke out against both Jews and *Junkers*, were often the target of government attorneys. In fact, in 1892 Otto Böckel complained that he and his newspaper, the *Reichsherold*, were simultaneously fighting fifty-two lawsuits.[181] More moderate agitators who regularly swore their allegiance to Kaiser and country, such as Max Liebermann von Sonnenberg, complained just as bitterly about their repeated prosecution for criticizing government officials.[182] As the anti-Semitic *Deutsche Wacht* reported

---

[180] There are several cases where prosecutors refused to press charges against anti-Semitic agitators since their libels were focused generally against Judaism and not against individual Jews. Various Jewish *Gemeinde*, however, were also rebuffed since it was claimed that even these organizations did not represent Judaism as a whole. See for example, the exchange of letters between the leader of the Berlin *Jüdische Gemeinde*, Meyer-Magnus, and several government officials in LAB A Pr. Br. Rep. 030, Polizeipräsidium Berlin, Nr. 15219, pp. 16–19.

[181] Levy, *The Downfall of the Anti-Semitic Political Parties*, 139–141. Levy explains that the prosecutions against Böckel were largely the result of the Hessian Prime Minister Jacob Finger, who launched a concerted effort to limit Böckel's political activities. Finger issued a decree in 1890 that ordered prosecutors to pay special attention to anti-Semitic propaganda.

[182] In addition to suits involving the Berlin school board and various city councilmen, Liebermann also became involved in a lawsuit filed by Police President of Berlin Guido von Madai. In an 1881 election speech, Liebermann had claimed that

in 1889: "If Mr. Hildesheimer complains that until now too few anti-Semitic convictions have occurred, he is mistaken. Unfortunately, convictions have now occurred that no one could have thought possible!"[183]

Thus, if the courtroom promised an unparalleled opportunity for anti-Semitic agitators to attract public attention and spread propaganda, it also posed serious dangers. The careers of Bernhard Förster, Otto Glagau, Max Liebermann von Sonnenberg, Adolf Stöcker, Adolf König, and many other anti-Semites were seriously damaged by their courtroom experiences. Echoing the sense of frustration that many others must have felt, Otto Böckel's *Reichsherold* warned his anti-Semitic colleagues: "Avoid lawsuits like fire."[184]

---

his liberal opponent was financed by English money. When pressed for a source for this allegation, Liebermann mentioned Madai. When Madai later denied having any contact with Liebermann, Liebermann tried to backtrack and now claimed he had only overheard Madai make this remark. Madai responded by denying ever making such a statement and filing suit for libel. Liebermann was forced to admit in court that he had heard a vague rumor from a friend of a friend, who had claimed to have overheard Madai. While Liebermann was sentenced to a relatively small fine of 50 Marks, he was pilloried relentlessly in the liberal press. See LAB A Pr. Br. Rep. 030, Polizeipräsidium Berlin, Nr. 11453, pp. 8–9, 79.

183 *Deutsche Wacht* (Dresden) 14 April 1889 #15, in BAK *ZSg. 113* Sammlung Fechenbach # 12.

184 As quoted in Levy, *The Downfall of the Anti-Semitic Political Parties*, 140.

CHAPTER THREE

ARSON IN NEUSTETTIN: THE LIMITS OF ANTI-JEWISH VIOLENCE IN THE NEW REICH

On February 18, 1881, the synagogue in the small Pomeranian village of Neustettin burned to the ground.[1] At first, many Germans dismissed the burning of the synagogue as an isolated incident. But during the following summer, a wave of anti-Jewish violence began in Neustettin and spread throughout the Pomeranian and West Prussian countryside. Although this violence was less serious than that of the concurrent Russian pogroms of 1881, the suddenness and ferocity of the riots nevertheless shocked most German observers.

Until recently, this example of German violence against Jews, and the national response that it generated, was overlooked by most German scholars—seemingly with good reason. After all, police intervened swiftly to stop the rioters, and although scattered violence continued for over 4 months, it never amounted to the *Bürgerkrieg* that many in the German government and the Jewish community had feared. In the past few years, however, historians such as Christhard Hoffmann, Gerd Hoffmann, Bernhard Vogt, and Stephen C.J. Nicholls have examined the Pomeranian violence in detail, and argued convincingly that historians need to take this violent episode into account when analyzing the nature and extent of anti-Semitism in the German Empire.[2]

---

[1] Neustettin is the modern Polish town of Szczecinek, ca. 250km northeast of Berlin. At the time, Neustettin had 8064 residents, 455 of them Jewish. Gerd Hoffman, *Der Prozess um den Brand der Synagoge in Neustettin: Antisemitismus in Deutschland ausgangs des 19. Jahrhunderts* (Schifferstadt: Gerd Hoffman Verlag, 1998), 23.

[2] Christhard Hoffmann, "Politische Kultur und Gewalt gegen Minderheiten: Die antisemitischen Ausschreitungen in Pommern und Westpreußen 1881," *Jahrbuch für Antisemitismusforschung* 3 (1994): 93–120; Bernhard Vogt, "Antisemitismus und Justiz in Kaiserreich: Der Synagogenbrand in Neustettin," in *'Halte fern dem ganzen Lande jedes Verderben . . .': Geschichte und Kultur der Juden in Pommern*, ed. Margret Heitmann and Julius Schoeps (Hildesheim, 1995); and Stephen C.J. Nicholls "The Burning of the Synagogue in Neustettin: Ideological Arson in the 1880s," (Research Paper No. 2, Centre for German-Jewish Studies, University of Sussex, Spring 1999).

My interest here is less in the social and cultural forces behind the rioting, and more on a crucial aspect of the Neustettin episode that other historians have seemed to minimize: the two arson trials for the burning of the Neustettin synagogue. These trials should not be overlooked. They received national attention, and they opened a crucial forum both for general debate on the "Jewish Question" and for public discussion on the causes and the meaning of the Pomeranian violence. The Neustettin trials were all the more controversial because of the defendants in the case. Five local *Jewish* men were accused of setting fire to their own synagogue.

Although the original investigators in the Neustettin case failed to agree on whether the fire was caused by arson or accident, many in the Jewish community immediately blamed the supporters of the Berlin anti-Semitic agitator Ernst Henrici. In early 1881, Henrici had embarked on a speaking tour to rally support for the Anti-Semitic Petition in areas outside of Berlin. This tour stopped in Neustettin on February 13, 1881, and Henrici delivered a vicious speech that blamed all of Germany's ills on the Jews.[3] This speech echoed the tone set by the local Neustettin newspaper, the *Norddeutsche Presse*, known for its virulent anti-Semitism, which had only a few months earlier printed an article under the headline "Dr. Martin Luther and the Jewish Question." This article cited Luther's statement that the only way to deal with the Jews was to burn their schools and synagogues. Only five days after Henrici's *Brandrede* (incendiary speech) and this provocative newspaper article, the Neustettin synagogue burned to the ground.

The liberal and Jewish press across Germany reacted immediately to the burning of the synagogue. They argued that the fire was a direct result of Henrici's speech, and they also placed blame on ultra-Conservative and radical-Catholic politicians who had served as Henrici's indirect benefactors. The liberal *Kölnische Zeitung*, for example, angrily attacked Adolf Stöcker, whose powerful position and anti-Jewish rhetoric helped to lend credibility to even the most radical anti-Semitic agitators. One newspaper went even further. The *Berliner Nachrichten* claimed that Bismarck himself had indirectly caused the

[3] The Neustettin *Jüdische Gemeinde* later tried to sue Henrici for criticizing Judaism in his Neustettin speech, but this suit was unsuccessful. At the time, Neustettin had 8500 residents, of which about 500 were Jews. Most Jewish men in the town worked as traders or merchants. Christhard Hoffmann, "Politische Kultur," 96, 104–105.

arson by not condemning the anti-Semitic agitation of the past year or explicitly rejecting the Anti-Semitic Petition. Through his inaction, the newspaper claimed, Bismarck allowed the arsonists to delude themselves that in attacking Jews they had his tacit support.[4]

The *Jüdische Presse* also condemned Stöcker, demanded a thorough investigation of the incident, and asked for government intervention to prevent further anti-Jewish violence.[5] Governmental authorities remained hesitant to intervene, however, and the Ministry of the Interior rejected an appeal by the Neustettin Jewish Community to send a special Criminal Commissar from Berlin to take over the local investigation.[6] Prosecutors in the regional capital of Köslin also rejected efforts by the Neustettin Jewish Community to sue Henrici and his associates for slander, leading to further complaints that the government was cultivating anti-Jewish sentiment and shielding anti-Semitic agitators for political purposes.[7]

Meanwhile, anti-Semitic newspapers like the *Deutsche Landeszeitung* responded to the liberal and Jewish press by suggesting that local Jews had burned the temple themselves in order to collect insurance benefits.[8] It was also suggested that the Jews knew that such a fire would be blamed on Henrici, and they therefore set the blaze in the hopes of turning public opinion against the anti-Semites.

Many Conservative and radical-Catholic newspapers claimed to want to withhold judgment on responsibility for the arson, but several

---

[4] The editor of the *Berliner Nachrichten,* Emil Eppenstein, was charged with libeling Bismarck in this article. However, the Berliner Landgericht acquitted Eppenstein since his article contained no knowingly false claims and fell in the realm of acceptable political criticism. See Vogt, "Antisemitismus und Justiz," 390–391.

[5] *Jüdische Presse* 24 February 1881 #8.

[6] Christhard Hoffmann, "Political Culture and Violence against Minorities: The Antisemitic Violence in Pomerania and West Prussia," in *Exclusionary Violence: Antisemitic Riots in Modern German History*. Christhard Hoffmann et al. (Hg.), (Chicago: University of Michigan Press, 2002), 80. This is a revised and extended version of his German-language article in the *Jahrbuch für Antisemitismusforschung*.

[7] Christhard Hoffmann, "Political Culture," 81. State Prosecutors across Germany were often reluctant to prosecute anti-Semites under either normal slander laws (§185, 186 RStGB) or under the law against insulting an established religion (§166 RStGB). The usual excuses were either that leaders of the Jewish Community did not have legal standing to represent all Jews or that general slanders against Jews could not be prosecuted as a slander against individual members of the Jewish community.

[8] The *Deutsche Landeszeitung* claimed that the local *Jüdische Gemeinde* had insured the aging temple for over 180,000 Marks. Quoted in *Berliner Zeitung* 22 February 1881 #87. See also *Berliner Ostend-Zeitung* 22 February 1881 #44.

took the opportunity to respond to liberal attacks. Some of these newspapers openly argued that the *Deutsche Landeszeitung* story about a Jewish conspiracy behind the arson was the "more probable version" of events.[9] The Catholic *Germania* blasted the "*Juden und Judengenossen*" for turning what should have been a matter for insurance companies and "*die Lokalchronik*" into a political event. While the *Germania* condemned the tactics of Henrici, it also sharply criticized the "Semitic press" for unfairly using the incident in an attempt to taint the entire anti-Semitic movement.[10]

While discussion of the Neustettin arson in the mainstream press decreased in the weeks after the incident, the controversy was kept alive through the rivalry of two local newspapers: the radical anti-Semitic *Norddeutsche Presse* and the recently founded liberal *Neustettiner Zeitung*. These two newspapers continued to battle for public opinion (and local advertisement funds) with pointed editorials on the Jewish Question. In fact, it was a physical altercation between one of the Jewish editors of the *Neustettiner Zeitung* and a leader of the local *Antisemitenliga* that ignited the wave of violence across Pomerania and West Prussia the following summer.[11] On July 17, 1881, after a brief fight between these two men, a crowd of over 1000 townspeople gathered and shattered the windows of Jewish shops while yelling the old anti-Jewish cries of "*Hepp! Hepp!*" and "*Juden raus!*" Although the government quickly realized the danger of such public violence and sent additional police and soldiers to the region, the anti-Jewish rioting soon spread to other towns and villages. Over the next six weeks, violence against Jews or Jewish owned businesses was reported in more than 17 communities. Although these incidents consisted mostly of loud demonstrations and vandalism, they were nevertheless enough to force many local Jewish residents to flee.

The press reaction to the riots was fiercely divided along political lines. The liberal *Berliner Tageblatt*, for example, labeled the wave of violence as the "Pomeranian *Bürgerkrieg*", and placed the blame for

[9] *Germania* 22 February 1881 #42.
[10] Ibid.
[11] The recurrence of violence in Neustettin was also blamed on another Neustettin appearance by Henrici in late May. For a more detailed description of the events leading to the outbreak of violence, as well as a discussion of the social and political factors that contributed to the violence, see Christhard Hoffmann, "Political Culture."

the unrest on the trio of Stöcker-Henrici-Förster. These three were the real arsonists, the paper claimed, and they should all be prosecuted for their incendiary speeches.[12] Naturally, the ultra-Conservative and anti-Semitic press defended their own actions and placed blame on local Jews for having aroused the anger of German peasants through economic exploitation. The anti-Semitic *Der Kulturkämpfer*, for example, claimed that the extent of the violence had been greatly exaggerated by the "*Judenpresse*" and portrayed the riots as a series of regrettable but understandable incidents.[13]

During the first few weeks of the violence, most government officials tended to share the opinion of the Conservative press and attribute the unrest to a pattern of Jewish economic exploitation. But as the violence continued, the attitude of government officials began to change. The Police-President von Madai, for example, was at first quite sympathetic toward the rioters and held the Jews directly responsible for the violence. After rioting continued to spread through the Pomeranian countryside, however, Madai began to criticize anti-Semitic agitators for whipping up anti-Jewish sentiment.[14] Soon after, the government promised to take a hard line against any anti-Semitic agitator whose rhetoric provoked or encouraged violent action.[15] Thus, in the months after the outbreak of violence, the public battle to assign blame for the riots became a matter of self-defense for both the Jewish community and for leading anti-Semitic agitators. It

[12] *Berliner Tageblatt* 28 August 1881 #401 Morgen.

[13] *Der Kulturkämpfer* Heft 41 (1 September 1881): 23–32.

[14] See the changed tone in the reports by *Oberregierungsrat* Graf Clairon D'Haussonville to the *Minister des Innern* von Puttkamer and various police authorities on the causes of the violence: GStA PK, I. HA Rep. 76 Kultusministerium, Nr. 56 Band 1, pp. 230–236, July 21, 1881; GStA PK, I. HA Rep. 76 Kultusministerium, Nr. 56 Band 1, pp. 270–273, August 10, 1881; GStA PK, I. HA Rep. 76 Kultusministerium, Nr. 56 Band 1, p. 275, August 9, 1881. D'Haussonville had very strong anti-Jewish feelings, which he was not afraid to voice publicly. While he still held Jewish exploitation responsible for the social unrest, D'Haussonville gradually called for more aggressive measures against those that spread anti-Semitic rhetoric.

[15] As the semi-official *Provincial Correspondenz* wrote: "The participating authorities are especially instructed to fight any aggravation or exploitation of the present unrest which could be produced by the meetings of well-known anti-Semitic agitators and the public discussion of the current events and their causes that these meetings may engender. All legal means are to be used which are beneficial for protecting against a misuse of the right to assembly that could endanger the rule of law and order." *Provincial Correspondenz* 19 August 1881 #32. In the end, 28 people were arrested for participating in the riots, but most were acquitted or given mild sentences. Vogt, "Antisemitismus und Justiz," 387–389.

was in this atmosphere that the Neustettin arson investigation ran its course.

Unfortunately, it is difficult to analyze the motivations of the local investigators of the Neustettin arson case.[16] Even during the violent summer of 1881, the case took a relatively low profile, and seemed only to make news for the local populace. Under pressure from local residents and the anti-Semitic *Norddeutsche Presse*, local investigators soon began to focus on members of the local Jewish community as suspects.[17] Many local anti-Semites repeated the allegation that the fire must have been started for insurance reasons or as a clever ploy to discredit local anti-Semites. In addition, several local witnesses came forward with eyewitness testimony, and each one denounced local Jews as the culprits. It is unclear if the investigators acted because of popular pressure or out of their own convictions, but eventually they arrested five local Jewish men as suspects. The accused were the 41 year-old merchant Gustav Heidemann and his 76 year-old father Hirsch, the retired furrier Hirsch Lesheim and his teenage son Leo, and the synagogue worker Adolf Löwenberg.[18] Because of the seriousness of the charges, the local Jewish community hired a well-known Berlin lawyer named Dr. Erich Sello as a defense attorney.[19]

Even after the arrest, the Neustettin arson case seemed to draw very little national interest outside of anti-Semitic circles. The inves-

[16] According to the *Berliner Tageblatt*, the eventual prosecutor in the first trial, a man named Pinoff, was a baptized Jew, and according to another newspaper, one member of the three-judge panel in Köslin was also a Jew. See Max Liebermann von Sonnenberg, *Beiträge zur Geschichte der antisemitischen Bewegung vom Jahre 1880–1885* (Berlin: Selbstverlag des Herausgebers, 1885), 219; *Christlich-Soziale Correspondenzblatt* 24 October 1883 #43 Beilage. The course of the investigation was also influenced by the local prefect, Landrat Bogislav von Bonin, who stayed behind the scenes and allegedly encouraged testimony against Jews with promises of money. See below for more on Landrat von Bonin.

[17] According to the anti-Semitic *Berliner Ostend-Zeitung*, Staatsanwalt Pinoff had already started interrogating Jews and searching Jewish houses by the end of February 1881. *Berliner Ostend-Zeitung*, 3 March 1881 #51 Beilage (issue mislabeled as 3 March 1880). In this article, written less than two weeks after the fire, the *Ostend-Zeitung* already boasts of the growing evidence against several (unnamed) Jewish suspects.

[18] Investigators had earlier suspected Löwenberg of having started the fire accidentally while cleaning the temple, but the *Strafkammer* of the *Landesgericht* in Köslin refused to press charges due to a lack of evidence. This according to attorney Erich Sello, as quoted in Gerd Hoffmann, *Der Prozess*, 45.

[19] According to Gerd Hoffmann, Erich Sello was personally asked to take the case by the Crown Prince Friedrich Wilhelm (later Kaiser Friedrich III), who was known to hold anti-Semitic agitators in low regard. Gerd Hoffmann, *Der Prozess*, 42.

tigation had dragged on for more than two and a half years, and public interest had apparently waned soon after the Pomeranian violence passed from the national headlines. So what brought this case back on to the national political stage? The answer is the Tisza-Eszlar ritual murder trial of 1883.[20] This Hungarian trial once again revived the German national debate on the Jewish question, and inspired polemical articles between anti-Semitic, ultra-Conservative, and radical Catholic journalists on one side and liberal and Jewish journalists on the other. The trial ended in a complete acquittal of the Jewish defendants and thus a propaganda defeat for those who had sided against the Jews. However, because the Neustettin arson trial opened just a few months later, this case, which again featured Jewish defendants on trial for a highly publicized crime, could now serve as a logical sequel. The issue of Jewish criminality and immorality, which was supposed to have been decided with the Tisza-Eszlar verdict, was now once again up for discussion. Simply put, a favorable verdict could allow those who had lost out on the Tisza-Eszlar case to claim vindication for their earlier polemical articles. Consequently, the Neustettin trial was covered extensively by the national press, and major newspapers such as the *Germania*, the *Berliner Tageblatt*, and the *Kreuzzeitung* carried edited transcripts of the daily proceedings.

The trial began on October 19, 1883 at the Royal Superior Jury Court (*königliche Landschwurgericht*) in the town of Köslin. Like all German criminal trials, the Neustettin trial would proceed in a logical order. After a reading of the charges and a brief questioning of each defendant, the trial would enter the phase of the *Beweisaufnahme* or "taking of the evidence". During this part of the trial, eyewitnesses and expert witnesses would be interviewed by the judge and (with the judge's permission) by the attorneys from each side. After the evidence had been heard, the prosecutor and defense attorneys would have the opportunity to deliver a closing argument or *Plaidoyer* before the jurors retired to deliberate.[21] While the case progressed according to these general procedures, this did not mean that it always transpired in an orderly fashion. In fact, because the German

---

[20] See Chapter 4 for a description of the Tisza-Eszlar case.

[21] Benjamin Carter Hett, *Death in the Tiergarten: Murder and Criminal Justice in the Kaiser's Berlin* (Cambridge, Mass.: Harvard Press, 2004), 28.

legal code allowed defendants to respond to individual witness testimony, and because witnesses were occasionally allowed to directly challenge one another, the courtroom resounded each day with angry insults and accusations. In addition, because partisan Neustettin townspeople jammed the courthouse, and because everyone knew these proceedings had a national audience, the atmosphere in the courtroom was constantly charged.

There was no physical evidence that the defendants had set the fire. In fact, expert witnesses still could not agree on whether the fire was deliberate, accidental, or the result of negligence. A local building inspector named Kleefeldt, for example, testified that fire was a clear case of arson. The fact that the floor was completely reduced to ashes suggested to him that a strong incendiary fluid had been poured over the floor. But another expert witness, an engineer named Schreiber, claimed that the large amount of smoke meant that the fire smoldered in the furniture without extra incendiary fluids—thus suggesting an accidental fire, not arson. This second expert was bitterly attacked by both the prosecutor and other witnesses for the prosecution. In addition, several witnesses, including Inspector Dahlitz, who as a police sergeant (*Feldwebel*) at the time of the fire was one of the first on the scene, claimed that the fire was concentrated in a pile of material near the temple altar (*Allerheiligsten*). While not entirely consistent with either of the previous experts, Dahlitz's testimony would nonetheless suggest arson. Finally, a few policemen said that books taken from the burned structure smelled like petroleum. Some additional witnesses also claimed to have smelled petroleum, but many others denied that any perceptible odor had been present.[22]

Because of the lingering disputes over the physical evidence, the prosecution's case depended almost entirely on local witnesses to the crime. These witnesses, many of whom came forward only months or years after the crime, all claimed to have seen the Jewish defendants acting suspiciously in and around the synagogue in the hours before the fire. Perhaps the most important witness was a 41 year-old blacksmith named Carl Christlieb Buchholz. Buchholz claimed

[22] Trial summaries taken from several leading newspapers including *Germania* and the *Berliner Tageblatt*. See also Gerd Hoffmann, *Der Prozess* and Hugo Friedländer, *Interessante Kriminal-Prozesse*, vol. 9 (Berlin: Hermann Barsdorf Verlag, 1913), 9–144.

to have seen one of the defendants, Adolf Löwenberg, carrying a petrol can toward the temple at 5 AM. He said he saw the stone-layer Beyer soon after and both discussed what Löwenberg might be doing. Buchholz also testified that two weeks before the fire, Hirsch Heidemann told him to break the fence near the temple to allow quick access from Heidemann's adjacent house.[23]

Buchholz's own behavior on the stand, however, seemed to undermine his credibility. Although he appeared in military dress (including two medals), Buchholz appeared to many in the courtroom to be either drunk or mentally unbalanced. His responses were often unintelligible, and his behavior sometimes seemed bizarre. Buchholz, for example, repeatedly refused to acknowledge the defense attorney's questions until ordered to answer by the judge. Defense attorneys were also quite effective in destroying any of Buchholz's remaining credibility. He was forced to admit that he did not come forward to the investigators, but first told his story to the anti-Semitic *Norddeutsche Presse*. He was also forced to admit that he had worked for one of the accused, Hirsch Heidemann, and was involved in an angry pay dispute with Heidemann at the time of the fire. The defense further alleged that Buchholz had attempted to extort money from Heidemann against the threat of spreading rumors about the origin of the fire.[24]

Another key witness for the prosecution was a 57 year-old school teacher named Pieper, who testified that he was teaching a class at the school across the street from the synagogue when the fire broke out. Pieper claimed to have seen many of the defendants creeping around suspiciously in the temple just as the smell of smoke first became noticeable. Several of Pieper's former students immediately came forward to support their teacher's account. One student in particular, Hermann Denzin, testified that in the moments before the fire he looked through the schoolroom window and observed the defendant Hirsch Lesheim standing on a stool outside a temple window and handing a loose window panel to his son. Denzin also asserted that earlier that day he had watched as Hirsch and Gustav Heidemann moved quickly back and forth between the temple and their nearby home.

[23] Gerd Hoffman, *Der Prozess*, 63.

[24] For the Jewish historian Simon Dubnow, this evidence was enough to suggest Buchholz himself was the likely perpetrator of the arson. See Christhard Hoffmann, "Political Culture," 79 n. 45.

As in the case of Buchholz, however, the defense attorneys once again succeeded in attacking the character and credibility of these witnesses. Erich Sello presented evidence that Pieper had previous anti-Semitic leanings, and had even caused a scandal by slandering Old Testament figures. When asked why he didn't come forward with his testimony until over 18 months after the incident, Pieper responded meekly that his wife had threatened him with physical harm if he involved himself.[25] As for the student, Hermann Denzin, he was forced to change the details of his story when a court-ordered visit to the school demonstrated it would have been impossible for anyone to view the temple from the seat Denzin had occupied. Although Denzin remained adamant that his eyewitness testimony was true, he now claimed not to remember the exact circumstances that allowed him to have a clear view of the scene.[26]

As ridiculous or incredible as the testimony of Buchholz and Pieper may have sounded, it was much harder to dismiss when it was confirmed and supported by dozens of other Neustettin residents. These witnesses often came forward to support Buchholz and Pieper at the trial after previously denying to investigators that they had any knowledge of the crime. Despite their often wildly conflicting versions of events, these witnesses all pointed the finger directly at the Jewish defendants.

After six extremely long days of testimony, the attorneys finally delivered their summations.[27] The prosecutor, *Staatsanwalt* Pinoff, began by expressing dismay at the partisanship and prejudice both inside and outside the courtroom. However, he nonetheless expressed confidence in the credibility of all the major witnesses against the defendants. Although Pinoff admitted that some of the witnesses had changed their stories and had come forward only recently, he argued that this could easily be explained through ordinary lapses in memory or fear of getting involved in such a contentious public affair. The prosecutor suggested that although the individual arsonist might never be identified, the weight of physical evidence and witness tes-

[25] Ibid., 58–59.

[26] Ibid., 93.

[27] The lead judge, *Landgerichtsdirektor* Buhrow, was obsessed with finishing the trial in the shortest amount of time possible. So he insisted on having 14 hour court sessions and once held court in session until almost 2:00 A.M. He did this despite the frigid winter weather and the repeated complaints from witnesses and attorneys.

timony pointed to the five defendants as part of a criminal conspiracy. Pinoff ridiculed the idea that all local Jews had conspired to burn their own synagogue, and he also dismissed the suggestion that the defendants had set the fire to claim insurance money. He was convinced, however, that this small group of defendants did set the fire in the hopes of provoking government action against local anti-Semitic agitators. Therefore, he asked jurors to find the five defendants guilty of arson or at least convict them as being accessories to the arson.[28]

The defense attorney, Erich Sello, responded with an eloquent and detailed critique of the witness testimony. The major witnesses in the case, Buchholz, Pieper, and Denzin were described as having obvious conflicts in their testimony as well as clear ulterior motives for coming forward. Sello argued that because of the active anti-Semitic agitation in Neustettin both before and after the crime, such witness testimony had to be treated with an increased amount of skepticism. Because of their changing stories and conflicting accounts, the entirety of this witness testimony was difficult to believe. Sello then questioned whether it had ever been established that a crime had taken place. He reminded jurors that at least one expert witness had insisted that the cause of the fire was more likely accidental rather than arson. Finally, Sello closed by passionately defending the innocence of the defendants, and by pleading with jurors to restore religious peace and tolerance in Germany with a verdict of not guilty.[29]

After a brief speech by Sello's co-counsel, and after brief responses by both prosecution and defense, the judge dismissed the jury to deliberate. The jurors, almost all of whom were conservative local landowners with anti-Semitic sympathies, deliberated for less than an hour before returning with a verdict: four of the five Jews were convicted on charges of being accessories to arson or of having knowledge of the conspiracy, while the fifth, Adolf Löwenberg, was acquitted of all charges. The four who were convicted received terms ranging from six months to four years in prison.

The local response to the verdict was quite positive. Whipped up by anti-Semitic propaganda, crowds of people gathered at the Neustettin

[28] Gerd Hoffmann, *Der Prozess*, 87.
[29] Ibid., 94–95.

railroad station to welcome home from Köslin those witnesses that had testified against the Jews. Those who testified for the defense or even showed sympathy for the defendants, on the other hand, were shown no mercy.

Outside of Neustettin, anti-Semitic agitators proclaimed their joy that the Jews had finally been held responsible for their actions. The anti-Semitic *Staatsbürger Zeitung* wrote from Berlin:

> The case is decided, and the world now learns through the verdict of the Köslin court that this fire was set by Jewish hands, and that the idea originated in Jewish minds along with the slogan 'That comes from Henrici's Jew-hatred.'[30]

Henrici, the anti-Semitic agitator who first contributed to the anti-Jewish feelings in Neustettin with his "Brandrede," responded to the verdict with a new speech that he published as a popular pamphlet. He claimed to have been a martyr to false Jewish allegations, and he demanded that based on this evidence of Jewish criminality, the Tisza-Eszlar ritual murder case should be reopened. As Henrici concluded:

> If the arson of Neustettin has been proven through powerful circumstantial evidence, the evidence in the Tisza-Eszlar case was even more damning; but in that case Hungarian judges set the defendants free—it is really too bad that the Kingdom of Hungary is so in debt to the Rothschilds. But Prussia still has incorruptible juries; yes, there are still judges in Prussia![31]

Ultra-conservative and radical Catholic papers were almost as jubilant as Henrici. Newspapers like the *Kreuzzeitung* wrote that the verdict was a catastrophic defeat for the "*Judenpresse*," who had tried and failed to influence the justice system in the same way they had previously in the Tisza-Eszlar case. Liberal and Jewish newspapers,

---

[30] *Staatsbürger Zeitung* 24 October 1883 #248A. Other anti-Semites also revisited the issue of who was to blame for the Pomeranian violence. Max Liebermann von Sonnenberg, for example, gave a speech on October 25, 1883 to a crowd of almost 5000 people. As he told his audience: "It is my firm conviction that all anti-Jewish riots in Germany are produced in the same manner; we have learned this out of the Neustettin *Synagogenbrandaffaire*." See Liebermann von Sonnenberg, *Beiträge zur Geschichte*, 230.

[31] Ernst Henrici, introduction to *Der Neustettiner Synagogenbrand vor Gericht* (Berlin: M. Schulze, 1883); quoted in Carl Paasch, *Eine jüdisch-deutsche Gesandtschaft und ihre Helfer. Geheimes Judenthum, Nebenregierungen und jüdische Weltherrschaft*, vol. 2, pt. 4 (Leipzig: Selbstverlag, 1891), 49.

meanwhile, reacted first with shock and sadness, and later with anger. The liberal and Jewish-owned *Berliner Börsen-Courier*, for example, wrote that it was improper to criticize trial verdicts, but then went on to make sarcastic comments about the objectivity of the judges and jury. The editors wrote that they were forced to accept the verdicts for the present, but they expressed the hope that more level heads might eventually exonerate the defendants.[32]

Both the despair and jubilation over this verdict were short-lived. Just a few short months later, the verdict was appealed to the Supreme Court (*Reichsgericht*) in Leipzig. The court rejected almost all the various arguments that defense attorney Erich Sello made for overturning the verdict, including the behavior of the judge and the hostile atmosphere in the courtroom. The appeals court did, however, decide to overturn the trial verdict on a technicality: Gustav Heidemann's nephew, a restaurateur named Engel, was never informed of his right to refuse to testify. Even though Engel's testimony had supported Heidemann's innocence, the court ruled that his testimony could have negatively affected the jury's perception of the other defendants. Therefore, on the basis of this one legal error, the verdict was reversed. Whether this minor technicality was the true reason for the reversal, or whether popular or governmental pressure influenced the decision of the appeals court, is not entirely clear. The court, however, did agree to Sello's suggestion to move the second trial to a new court district farther away from the atmosphere in Neustettin. The Neustettin arson trial would thus begin all over again in February 1884 in the Jury Court (*Schwurgericht*) in the West Prussian town of Konitz.[33]

If public attention had been great for the first trial, for the second it was overwhelming. All public and private lodging in the town of Konitz were full, and two direct telegraph lines were laid all the way to Berlin to aid German and international journalists in relaying the latest trial details. While the first trial had included dozens of witnesses from Neustettin, the second brought over 150 witnesses along with their family and friends.[34]

---

[32] Press reactions as reported by *Germania* 25 October 1883 #245 Zweites Blatt.

[33] See Friedländer, *Interessante Kriminal-Prozesse*, vol. 9, pp. 58–61. The town of Konitz is the present-day Polish city of Chojnice; in 1890, Konitz had a population of 10,107 of which 502 were Jewish. Gerd Hoffmann, *Der Prozess*, 116.

[34] *Germania* 2 March 1884 #52 Erstes Blatt. According to one report, the first trial had 88 witnesses. See Liebermann von Sonnenberg, *Beiträge zur Geschichte*, 219.

Erich Sello again returned to lead the defense, but this time he had enlisted the help of another well-known Berlin defense lawyer, Hermann Makower. A prominent and respected attorney for several decades, Makower was perhaps best known for defending the historian Theodor Mommsen in 1882 against a charge of having libeled Otto von Bismarck. Makower had also earned a reputation as an active member of the Berlin Jewish Community. He did not seek to hide his faith, and spoke out frequently in favor of Jewish activism and against anti-Semitism.[35]

In addition to Makower, there were three other participants in the second trial who exerted an important influence on the proceedings. The first, Criminal Commissar Höft, was a special investigator who had been sent to Neustettin by the Minister of the Interior, Robert von Puttkamer. Although Puttkamer had rejected an earlier request by the Neustettin Jewish Community to send an investigator, he had responded more favorably to a second request soon after the reversal of the Köslin verdict.[36] In the weeks before the second trial, Höft re-interviewed hundreds of witnesses in an attempt to find out the true course of events. He was seated next to the jury throughout the second trial, and was quite vocal in expressing his doubts about witness testimony against the Jewish defendants. Also present in the courtroom was *Landrat* Bogislav von Bonin, a local Conservative official with anti-Semitic leanings who had been active in "uncovering" new witnesses in the months after the first trial.[37] Not surprisingly, Bonin's new witnesses always testified

---

[35] See the biographical essay about Makower in Gerd Hoffmann, *Der Prozess*, 282–292.

[36] According to Johannes Groß, special commissars were occasionally sent to handle special cases in regions that lacked investigative resources or expertise. The second request before the Konitz trial may have been successful due to the influence of Hermann Makower. Johannes Groß, *Ritualmordbeschuldigungen gegen Juden in deuschen Kaiserreich 1871–1914* (Berlin: Metropol, 2002), 38; Gerd Hoffmann, *Der Prozess*, 115.

[37] The Landrat, or Provincial Prefect, still exerted some local police powers despite the *Kreisordnung* legislation of 1872, which was designed to limit Junker control over local affairs. From Gordon Craig, *Germany 1866–1945* (New York: Oxford Univ. Press, 1978), 67. See also Robert Berdahl, "Conservative Politics and Aristocratic Landholders in Bismarckian Germany," *Journal of Modern History* 44 (1972): 1–20. Several newspapers complained about the influence of the Landrat, who they claimed should have sent all witnesses to the Mayor of Neustettin, rather than intervening in the case himself. The *Vossische Zeitung* also complained that von Bonin had no business interfering in the second trial since it was far outside of his jurisdiction. See *Vossische Zeitung* 16 March 1884 #129 Morgen.

for the prosecution and against the Jews. Finally, the new presiding judge, *Landgerichtsrat* Arndt, played a very significant role in the second trial. While the lead judge in the first trial had insisted on finishing the case as quickly as possible, Arndt allowed much more time for the examination of witnesses. Arndt was also very skeptical of those who had changed their testimony or come forward with new evidence years after the crime, and he occasionally threatened a charge of perjury against witnesses he thought were lying or altering their original testimony.

The main prosecution witnesses, Buchholz, Pieper, and Denzin all returned. But this time their testimony was embellished. Buchholz, for example, who earlier testified to seeing one defendant with a petrol can, now also testified that he found incendiary fuses inside another defendant's house a few days after the fire. Buchholz claimed that he did not present these as evidence earlier because he did not know that the cords could be used to set a fire. But this time Buchholz was attacked not only by the defense attorneys, but also by Judge Arndt, who questioned both his truthfulness and his tendency to drink in excess. When the judge pressed Pieper for more information about his previous censure for slandering Old Testament figures, he at first refused to answer, then began to shake, and was finally removed from the courtroom after passing out.[38]

For each witness who was challenged by Arndt, Höft, and the defense attorneys, however, several more came forward claiming to have direct eyewitness accounts. Most of these witnesses had been "discovered" and encouraged to testify by Landrat von Bonin. For instance, 16–year old Emilie Ratzner came forward for the first time to claim that she had seen Gustav Heidemann squeezing through a gap in the fence and the younger Lesheim running out of the burning temple with a petrol can in his hand. Another new witness, the wagon-greaser Gärtner, testified that he heard the wives of two defendants say on a local train that their husbands were just pawns, and that the real mastermind of the scheme was Rabbi Wolff Löwe, the leader of the local *Jüdische Gemeinde*. All of these new prosecution witnesses were attacked by the lead judge, the defense attorneys, and Criminal Commissar Höft, who confronted them with their conflicting statements or ulterior motives. In Gärtner's case, Höft checked the

[38] Gerd Hoffmann, *Der Prozess*, 134–135.

ticket records and proved that neither he nor the defendants' wives could have been on that train. Gärtner was forced to admit that he was "in error" about the conversation.[39] When the defense lawyers complained about the constant stream of new witnesses coming forward with unreliable testimony, the prosecutor, *Staatsanwalt* Schlingmann, asserted that he did not know the subject matter or relevance of all the new witnesses, but he must follow his duty, "otherwise someone could complain that I have not done everything possible to clear up this matter."[40]

Despite the presence of several additional new witnesses who were ready and eager to testify, the prosecutor and defense attorneys finally agreed to end the taking of evidence on the seventh day of the trial. In his closing argument, the prosecutor admitted that many of the witnesses, including Carl Buchholz, were probably not credible. But he nevertheless claimed that all the prosecution witnesses could not have lied, and thus urged the jury to convict the defendants based on the overall weight of the evidence. Erich Sello responded with an impassioned plea for the jurors to reverse the injustice done at the first trial. Hermann Makower, Sello's co-defense counsel, then delivered an attack on the involvement of Landrat von Bonin that was aimed as much at government officials as toward members of the jury:

> It seems disquieting to me that the a police authority functions that is not the local police (*Ortspolizei*), namely the office of the Landrath, which until the last day of the proceedings exercised prosecutorial powers, took sworn statements from witnesses, and so on.... God protect us if such alternate authorities regularly come into being next to the prosecutor and the courts! Then no man would ever be safe from an accusation![41]

After a short rebuttal by the prosecutor and a response from the defense, the jury retired to consider the verdict. This time, after only 45 minutes, all four remaining defendants were acquitted on all charges.[42]

---

[39] Ibid., 171.

[40] As quoted in Ibid., 146.

[41] Quoted in *Berliner Tageblatt* 11 March 1884 #119 Morgen 1st Beiblatt. Ironically, two decades later, local liberals would support von Bonin in the 1903 Reichstag elections against the even more radical anti-Semite Hermann Ahlwardt. Gerd Hoffmann, *Der Prozess*, 42.

[42] Ten of twelve jurors acquitted Lesheim of participation in the arson; otherwise, the verdicts were unanimous.

As one might expect, the second verdict provoked very different public reactions than the first. Rioting and looting of Jewish businesses was reported in Neustettin, and anti-Semitic agitators responded with outrage at the fact that the Jews had been able to corrupt the German legal system. As one Stöckerite newspaper asked rhetorically: "Which vox populi (*Volksstimme*) of the two courts is really the vox dei (*Stimme Gottes*)?"[43] The liberal and Jewish press, however, greeted the verdicts as an exoneration of both the defendants and the German courts. In their opinion, although clearly flawed, the legal system had finally allowed truth and justice to prevail.

The debate over the acquittal of the Jewish defendants did not die out quickly. Liberal newspapers, for example, blamed the Interior Minister von Puttkamer for not taking sufficient precautions to prevent post-trial violence or protect the Neustettin Jews. The *Berliner Tageblatt* suggested that an interpellation in the Reichstag would be an appropriate way of forcing the Minister to respond to these allegations.[44] On March 14, a liberal deputy named Zelle made such an interpellation. Puttkamer, the same man who had originally agreed to send Criminal Commissar Höft to Neustettin, now responded to Zelle's challenge in the Reichstag by attacking liberal journalists for exaggerating the scale of the violence for their own propaganda purposes. This sparked a firestorm of debate. Adolf Stöcker, for instance, jumped at the opportunity to accuse the liberal parties of trying to influence the German justice system in favor of Jewish interests. His tirade was laced with references to previous trials involving anti-Semitism:

> The Minister's statements lead to the conclusion that the first provocation in the Neustettin riots came from the Jews. That doesn't surprise me; The Jews have always provoked first. In Berlin it was a Jew who struck the first blow. (Call from the Left: 'Henrici !') Henrici never hit anyone, Kantorowicz did! In the earlier Neustettin unrest it was also Jews who were responsible for the first acts of violence.[45]

---

[43] *Reichsbote* 11 March 1884 #60. Both Latin phrases and German translations are from the original quotation. This newspaper, which had grown to replace the *Kreuzzeitung* as the largest ultra-conservative newspaper in Germany, was in the midst of a series of articles called "Judaism in the State." These articles, written by the chief editor Heinrich Engel, were later printed as a popular book.

[44] *Berliner Tageblatt* 10 March 1884 #118 Abend. See also the criticism of the *Vossische Zeitung*, 14–15 March 1884.

[45] Quoted in *Reichsbote* 16 March 1884 #65 from BAK ZSg. 113 Sammlung Fechenbach Nr. 19. The Kantorowicz Affair focused on a Jewish businessman who

As expected, Stöcker also made reference to the Tisza-Eszlar case, and he claimed that the "*Judenpresse*" was celebrating their apparent victory in Neustettin in the same arrogant and undignified manner as they did after the Tisza-Eszlar verdict. Of course, Stöcker was in turn attacked by liberal politicians, and the debate raged on for several days.[46]

Eventually, the tensions in Neustettin receded, the parliamentary debate moved on to other issues, and the Neustettin trials faded from the headlines. But the Neustettin episode, and the implication that Jewish defendants had once again evaded punishment for their crimes, would remain an important part of anti-Semitic propaganda over the next several decades.

* * *

So then, what conclusions can we draw from the Neustettin episode? Most historians have tended to focus less on the trials themselves and more on the wave of violence that spread across Pomerania and West Prussia a few months after the synagogue fire. Still, their conclusions are important to understanding the milieu that contributed to accusations of arson against local Jews. Christhard Hoffmann, in particular, has suggested four specific factors that contributed to the outbreak of violence:

1.) Economic dislocation caused by the transition to capitalism and the economic downturn after 1873
2.) Existing social and occupational differences between Jewish and non-Jewish residents
3.) Intense anti-Semitic agitation in the region
4.) Tacit government support of anti-Semitism during the election of 1881 that allowed locals to believe they were acting in the interests of the state and had the support of their leaders[47]

---

was tried for slapping an anti-Semitic agitator who had insulted him. The case caused a scandal in late 1880. For a discussion of this incident, see chapter 2.

[46] See stenographic record of the Zelle interpellation in several newspapers, including *Reichsbote*, 16 March 1884 #65 and *Germania*, 15 March 1884.

[47] Hoffmann claims that the violence was probably an unplanned response to existing social tensions that had been exacerbated by anti-Semitic rhetoric. He also classifies the Pomeranian riots as "loyal pogroms," where the rioters believed that they were following the unstated will of the governing authorities by attacking Jews. This is meant to contrast with so-called "protest pogroms" or "state-supported pogroms" like Kristallnacht in 1938. Christoph Nonn rejects this interpretation, however, in an article on the riots surrounding the Konitz ritual murder accusa-

Hoffman also mentions the concurrent pogroms taking place in Russia, which undoubtedly played an important, if indirect role in inspiring the violence against Jews. It was the culmination of all these factors, mixed with various personal conflicts and the synagogue fire itself that caused relations between Christians and Jews in the region to decline so precipitously.

Perhaps the most controversial of Christhard Hoffmann's arguments is his suggestion that the Pomeranian riots followed the older pattern of "*Hepp Hepp* riots," which were mainly rituals of humiliation and intimidation (*Demütigungs- und Einschüchterungsrituale*) or symbolic expulsions (*symbolische Vertreibungen*).[48] While such rituals were enormously destructive and could occasionally intensify into physical attacks against Jews, they tended to lack the lethal intentions of concurrent pogroms in Russia. According to Hoffmann, rioters were primarily interested in reestablishing their "superiority over a socially rising minority perceived as a threat," and they stopped "when it was somehow determined that all Jews had been 'taught their lesson.'"[49] Regardless of the ritualized nature of the violence, it is clear that both Jews and government officials feared that the riots could, and probably would, continue to intensify. After a lackluster response at the start of the violence, the Prussian government eventually responded with a show of force and a series of statements condemning the rioters and calling for order. Despite this intervention, thousands of Jews fled Pomerania after the riots to escape the continuing physical threats and social isolation.[50]

The violence of 1881, however, also had some negative effects on the overall development of German anti-Semitism. As the violence spread, there was a growing sense in government circles that extreme anti-Semites like Henrici had contributed to the volatile situation in Pomerania. This growing backlash threatened not only Henrici and his followers, but also endangered the Conservative-anti-Semitic alliance that had been formed for the 1881 elections. While most

tion in 1900. Since police and government officials served as targets for violence, and since the public mood was inflamed by rumors that the government would intervene to support local Jews, Nonn argues that these riots were far more oppositional than loyal. See Christhard Hoffmann, "Political Culture," 70–79; Christoph Nonn, "Zwischenfall in Konitz. Antisemitismus und Nationalismus im preußischen Osten um 1900," *Historische Zeitschrift* 266 (1998): 397.

48 Christhard Hoffmann, "Politische Kultur," 110.

49 Christhard Hoffmann, "Political Culture," 86.

50 Christhard Hoffmann, "Politische Kultur," 112–114.

Conservatives had greeted the rise of Stöcker's Christian-Social Party as an opportunity to wean Berlin workers away from socialism, the growing radicalism of the "Berlin Movement" led to fears that anti-Semitism might lead these same workers to a kind of violent populism rather than into the camp of traditional conservatism. The backlash against Henrici did not lead the Conservatives to abandon their anti-Semitic rhetoric, but it did cause them to try to purge their ranks of the most radical anti-Semites. Extremists like Henrici were now seen as a political liability, and the Conservative press gradually tried to distinguish between these "rowdy" anti-Semites (*Radau-Antisemiten*) and more "moderate" anti-Semites. In late 1881, Henrici was forced out of the Conservative Central Committee—a Berlin electoral alliance of right-wing candidates. Without the tacit support of the Conservatives, Henrici's fledgling political party quickly diminished in strength and his private newspaper soon disappeared.[51]

The reaction of government officials to the Pomeranian violence also resulted in what Christhard Hoffmann has called the "domestication" of German anti-Semitism.[52] More "moderate" anti-Semites like Stöcker and Max Liebermann von Sonnenberg tried desperately to separate themselves from men like Ernst Henrici, and to do this they openly denounced violent tactics and proclaimed their own loyalty to the Kaiser and the rule of law. After the violence of 1881, these kinds of assurances became a relatively common part of anti-Semitic propaganda. Whenever anti-Semitic speeches verged on public incitement against the Jews, the agitators would reaffirm their loyalty to the state and explain that they intended to fight only within the bounds of legality.[53] This did not mean that agitators

---

[51] After his political decline, Henrici became interested in German colonialism and trade. He was especially interested in establishing a tobacco farm in the German colony of Togo. However, his company, the *Deutsche Togogesellschaft*, quickly foundered and Henrici was left penniless. Over the next decades, Henrici tried various lines of work in Venezuela, Costa Rica, and even Baltimore—but without much success. See the biographical essay on Henrici in Gerd Hoffmann, *Der Prozess*, 247–281.

[52] Christhard Hoffmann uses the term "*Pazifizierung*." Christhard Hoffmann, "Politische Kultur," 113.

[53] For example, *Die Post* reported that in a meeting of *Deutsche Reformverein*, a letter was anonymously given to the police guard saying that there was a plan after the meeting to smash windows and beat up innocent Jews. On the public reading of the letter, the main speaker, Pickenbach, assured everyone that the *Verein* was against any form of violence against Jews. *Die Post* 21 April 1882 #107.

would work any less furiously to spread anti-Jewish propaganda; they would merely try to do it in a way that would avoid provoking a government response. Largely because of this "domestication," there were relatively few incidents of open violence against Jews until after 1918.[54]

In analyzing the long-term repercussions of the Neustettin episode, however, historians such as Hoffmann have tended to underestimate the importance of the two arson trials and their coverage in the national press. These trials allowed for a more developed public discussion (or public confrontation) on the causes and the meaning of the Pomeranian violence. Trial coverage also gave anti-Semitic, Conservative, radical-Catholic, and liberal journalists across Germany ample opportunity to put forward their own competing interpretations of both the arson case and the Pomeranian riots. Debates about the trials were easily incorporated into existing political discussions, and they provided fodder for both polemical articles and parliamentary speeches.

As with other trials involving anti-Semitism, the Neustettin arson trials were an outstanding business opportunity for anti-Semitic agitators. Ernst Henrici, for example, could use the trials to attract public attention, sell copies of his pamphlets and newspaper, and portray himself to the public as an innocent martyr. Even though Henrici's personal appeal eventually declined after the acquittal of the Jewish defendants, the Neustettin case still served many other agitators as a convenient symbol for rallying public anger against Jewish power and influence. Over the next decades, anti-Semites would often point to Neustettin as a clear example of both Jewish criminality and Jewish ability to corrupt and evade the German justice system.

Finally, the involvement of Criminal Commissar Höft in the Neustettin case is important because it provides an interesting example of government intervention on behalf of Jewish defendants. In fact, this kind of intervention was not an isolated case. Höft himself later interviewed witnesses in the 1885 Skurcz ritual murder trial, which occurred outside of Danzig. There, Höft played a similar role as he had in the Neustettin trial, and his presence aroused popular anger at Berlin interference in local affairs.[55] It is important, however,

---

[54] Christhard Hoffmann, "Politische Kultur," 114. Riots after the Xanten and Konitz ritual murder cases of 1892 and 1900 are notable exceptions.

[55] See chapter 4 for a discussion of Skurcz.

that this interference not be equated with a pro-Jewish attitude on the part of government officials. During the Pomeranian riots, the letters of the *Oberregierungsrat* in nearby Köslin, Clairon D'Haussonville, make clear his sympathy for local rioters and his reluctance to intervene until after the violence had escalated.[56] Many higher government officials, including Robert von Puttkamer, favored intervention in the arson case only because they believed that radical anti-Semites might threaten the functioning of the justice system and the rule of law. Otherwise, as he showed in the parliamentary debates over the post-verdict violence, Puttkamer could be openly hostile to those who defended Jewish interests.

The interference by Criminal Commissar Höft may also be understood as a part of the continuing struggle between local and national authorities. The *Kreisordnung* of 1872 was meant to restrict the power and influence of the *Landrat* in local affairs. But this measure was never as effective as many liberal legislators had hoped. For example, many *Landräte* routinely abused their legal power to support Conservative or anti-Semitic candidates in local elections. The government was often slow to censure such actions since most officials felt that Conservative and anti-Semitic candidates were more appealing than their liberal counterparts. In some instances, however, arbitrary actions by the *Landräte* could provoke a hostile response from the Berlin government. Thus, in the Neustettin case, Puttkamer's decision to send Criminal Commissar Höft may have been designed to prevent men like Landrat von Bonin from exerting an undue influence over local affairs as much as it was meant to protect local Jews or ensure an impartial hearing of the case.[57]

The widespread publicity and controversy surrounding the Neustettin trials made them a significant episode in the history of German anti-Semitism. But it is also important to remember that these tri-

---

[56] See, for example, GStA PK, I. HA Rep. 76 Kultusministerium, Nr. 56 Band 1, pp. 230–236, July 21, 1881; GStA PK, I. HA Rep. 76 Kultusministerium, Nr. 56 Band 1, pp. 270–273, August 10, 1881; GStA PK, I. HA Rep. 76 Kultusministerium, Nr. 56 Band 1, p. 275, August 9, 1881.

[57] Richard Levy, *The Downfall of the Anti-Semitic Political Parties in Germany* (New Haven: Yale Univ. Press, 1975), 137. As Levy also notes, the independent *Landräte* could not always be counted on to support anti-Semitic candidates. Because of their frequent anti-Junker rhetoric, later agitators like Otto Böckel and Hermann Ahlwardt ran into strong opposition among some *Landräte*, including *Landrat* von Bonin.

als were only one battle in an ongoing war in the German courtroom. Far from resolving the question of "Jewish criminality", the acquittal of the Neustettin Jews only left German anti-Semites even more anxious for their next chance to put Jews and their religious beliefs on trial.

CHAPTER FOUR

RITUAL MURDER TRIALS: ANCIENT PREJUDICE AND MODERN PROPAGANDA

In the last two decades of the Nineteenth Century, an old and familiar charge against Jews made a surprising resurgence in Europe—the blood ritual allegation. Accusations of Jewish ritual sacrifice were based on the centuries-old myth that Jews required the blood of Christian children for their Passover services.[1] Although ritual murder accusations had not completely disappeared in Europe during previous centuries, after 1880 a veritable flood of new cases surfaced across the continent.[2] Often arising in small rural villages, nineteenth-century blood ritual allegations, like their medieval counterparts, were usually a spontaneous outgrowth of social friction, economic dislocation, and local traditions of anti-Semitism. Although all of these

[1] According to Helmut Smith, the first officially documented accusation of ritual murder came with Thomas of Monmouth's *The Life and Passion of Saint William the Martyr of Norwich* in 1150. Smith also presents the controversial argument that an epistemic shift occurred in ritual murder allegations after the formal acceptance of the doctrine of transubstantiation by the Catholic Church in the Thirteenth Century. He suggests that thereafter charges of blood rituals and "host desecration" against Jews were partially a projection of subconscious concerns about consuming the body and blood of Christ. See Helmut Walser Smith, *The Butcher's Tale: Murder and Anti-Semitism in a German Town* (New York: Norton, 2002), 95–104. In addition to consecrating the Passover matzo, Christian blood was also alleged during the Middle Ages to be useful for healing circumcision wounds, for difficult births, to get rid of a revolting "Jewish" odor, and to remove the horns that all Jewish children had at birth. Johannes Groß, *Ritualmordbeschuldigungen gegen Juden in deuschen Kaiserreich 1871–1914* (Berlin: Metropol, 2002), 11–12.

[2] Ritual murder allegations were occasionally influential in Europe during the early Nineteenth Century as well. See Jonathan Frankel, *The Damascus Affair: "Ritual Murder," Politics, and the Jews in 1840* (Cambridge: Cambridge Univ. Press, 1997) for an account of the infamous Damascus case and its substantial repercussions in Western Europe. Georg Kalckert counted 128 publicized ritual murder accusations in Europe between 1870 and 1900, of which 120 came after the highly publicized Xanten incident of 1891. Contemporary anti-Semitic sources count well over 300 cases in the same period. Georg Kalckert, *Die Haltung des deutschen Katholizismus zum Judenthum im 19. Jahrhundert* as cited in Stephan Lehr, *Antisemitismus—religiöse Motive im sozialen Vorurteil*, Abhandlungen zum christlich-jüdischen Dialog, Band 5 (München: Chr. Kaiser Verlag, 1974), 238–243.

accusations were unique, they frequently centered on a specific range of anti-Semitic themes and motifs.

Since modern accusations of ritual murder arose from an age-old tradition of anti-Jewish stereotypes and myths, they have often been portrayed as remnants of pre-modern ignorance and superstition intruding into the modern world. Stephen Lehr's 1974 book, *Antisemitismus—religiöse Motive im sozialen Vorurteil*, for example, argued that ritual murder allegations often arose out of religious superstitions and mass hysteria, and that ritual murder trials in the late nineteenth century were often reminiscent of witchcraft trials from centuries before.[3] Certainly, these accusations have what might easily be called "irrational" elements: uneducated witnesses seemingly unable to discern imagination from reality, wild rumors and stories that describe improbable or impossible events, and real or threatened mob violence against both local Jews and those who would defend them. Recent scholarship on crowd behavior and violence, however, has warned historians to look beyond the frenzy of the mob to the internal logic or ritual patterns of these public events.[4]

Helmut Walser Smith's recent book, *The Butcher's Tale*, is a masterful example of this kind of scholarship. Smith's book, which focuses on an alleged ritual murder in the small West Prussian town of Konitz in 1900, pushes beyond the apparent fanaticism of the crowd to examine how a complex web of interpersonal conflicts, a familiarity with old anti-Semitic stories and stereotypes, and the influence of outside agitators could turn a simple murder mystery into sensational allegations of Jewish ritual slaughter. These accusations motivated ordinary townspeople in Konitz to isolate and exclude Jews from daily village life, and also threatened to engulf the regions of West Prussia and Pomerania in anti-Semitic violence. In constructing his microhistory of the Konitz Affair, Smith uses detailed police records and court proceedings both to reconstruct the efforts of investigators and to speculate on the motivations of various accusers. While Smith concludes that some of those who testified against local

[3] Lehr, *Antisemitismus*, 101. To be fair, Lehr provides a complex analysis and recognizes that mixed in with these "pre-modern" characteristics, the power of the modern press was essential in turning such episodes into public spectacles with significant political repercussions.

[4] See, for example, Arlete Farge and Jacques Revel, *The Vanishing Children of Paris* (Cambridge: Harvard University Press, 1991).

Jews in Konitz were consciously lying for ideological or personal reasons, he also suggests that many witnesses truly believed their own imagined or fabricated stories.[5] Instead of attributing this incident to ignorance or fanaticism, Smith describes the Konitz case as part of an elaborate social ritual—both a ritual of exclusion toward local Jews and a ritual that affirmed solidarity among other members of the community.[6] Charges of ritual murder drew support from across social, religious, and ethnic boundaries in Konitz, and focused frustration on a common enemy. These accusations also allowed those Christian citizens who were low on the social ladder to assert power over their Jewish neighbors.[7]

Smith's careful analysis also suggests that while developments in the Konitz case often seemed chaotic and unpredictable, they frequently followed common rules, patterns, or scripts. A cursory comparison of the Konitz case with other nineteenth-century ritual murder accusations reveals a surprising amount of commonality and predictability in the way most modern ritual murder cases unfolded. Such events often centered on a number of key elements, including:

- testimony of Jews carrying suspicious sacks on the night of the murder or sneaking around with lanterns
- testimony of suspicious foreign Jews coming to town before the murder and leaving shortly thereafter
- testimony of overheard conspiracies whispered between local Jews both before and after the crime
- testimony against local Jews that was first offered months after the crime or which seemed to improve dramatically in detail over time
- shoddy autopsies carried out by local doctors that reinforced local views of the crime
- allegations of sexual impropriety or transgression

[5] Smith, *The Butcher's Tale*, 135–136, 156–160.

[6] Ibid., 172–180.

[7] Ibid., 124–125, 136. Christoph Nonn's equally fascinating and useful book on the Konitz case also emphasizes "an anti-Semitism of opportunity" (*Gelegenheitsantisemitismus*) rather than a shared anti-Semitic world view. In an article examining the Xanten ritual murder accusation, Bernd Kölling also claims that "the popular discourse of ritual murder centered primarily around community status rather than ideology, and therefore anti-Semitism should be thought of here as a subordinate or instrumental phenomenon." See Christoph Nonn, *Eine Stadt sucht einen Mörder* (Göttingen: Vandenhoeck und Ruprecht, 2002), 197–198; Bernd Kölling, "Blutige Illusionen. Ritualmorddiskurse und Antisemitismus im niederrheinischen Xanten am Ende des 19. Jahrhunderts," in *Agrarische Verfassung und politische Struktur. Studien zur Gesellschaftsgeschichte Preußens 1700–1918*, ed. Wolfgang Neugebauer and Ralf Pröve (Berlin: A. Spitz, 1998), 378.

- and fears that outside authorities, perhaps corrupted by Jewish influence, might sabotage the local prosecution of Jewish suspects

These and other similarities do not necessarily signal that ritual murder allegations were centrally orchestrated or planned. Differences in each case were substantial, and similarities in developments could at the time be attributed to a common Jewish *modus operandi* rather than to popular anti-Semitic stereotypes.

Although Smith's account of the Konitz Affair is a brilliant study of how local pressures and interpersonal conflicts could degenerate into rituals of social exclusion, Smith at times seems to underestimate the role of outsiders in driving the Konitz case forward. For example, while the first suggestions of a potential ritual murder occurred locally, much of the witness testimony was "uncovered" and publicized by an infamous anti-Semitic editor from Berlin who had rushed to Konitz almost immediately after the crime. Wilhelm Bruhn, editor of the anti-Semitic *Staatsbürgerzeitung*, set up a permanent camp in Konitz where he met regularly with local anti-Semites and cajoled or even bribed local residents to testify against the Jews. Even what Helmut Smith calls the "Butcher's Tale", the key written testimony of the Christian butcher Hoffmann against the Jewish butcher, Lewy, was almost certainly composed not by Hoffmann himself, but by Bruhn and his associates.[8]

In light of this significant outside influence in the Konitz case, it seems prudent when examining modern ritual murder allegations to look beyond a microhistory of local social relations to examine how ritual murder allegations were part of the wider social and political world of Germany as a whole. In the late Nineteenth Century, ritual murder allegations did not simply function as an act of local ritual, they were also exploited as a powerful form of political propaganda. Detailed articles about ritual murder accusations such as those in Konitz could dominate the Berlin political press for weeks at a time, and such articles also frequently appeared in smaller newspapers across the country. Coverage in the press became even more intense when ritual murder allegations led to a court trial—a public forum that promised both sensational revelations and a potentially controversial final outcome. This intense press coverage was not limited to

[8] Smith, *The Butcher's Tale*, 48, 66.

the few ritual murder cases that occurred on German soil; many accusations from outside the borders of Germany also made headlines thanks to a political press already finely attuned to the "Jewish Question".

In the use of ritual murder cases for propaganda purposes, the anti-Semitic press clearly took the lead. But a blood ritual allegation could hardly have become a *cause célèbre* in Germany through the influence of the anti-Semitic press alone. In several cases, the discussion of blood-ritual charges was incorporated into existing debates between the leading political parties, and controversial articles on these allegations helped to fuel angry exchanges between opposing political factions and their representative newspapers. The extreme Conservative and Catholic press, for example, often used the trials as opportunities to ridicule their liberal political opponents for embracing "Jewish values" and protecting Jewish criminals. Liberal and Jewish newspapers, on the other hand, attacked the blood ritual trials as remnants of medieval prejudice, and blamed the Conservative and Catholic press for fanning the flames of anti-Semitism. As the level of debate over ritual murder trials intensified, the anticipated verdict often took on significant political implications. For a newspaper aligned with the "winning side," the verdict would be trumpeted both as a political victory and as a vindication of that newspaper's reputation; the "losers", meanwhile, faced a potential political and public relations defeat.[9] In times of great political tension and rivalry, therefore, these ritual murder trials could have a powerful impact.

Articles on the blood ritual cases were also popular for another reason—sensation sold newspapers. In addition to advertisements for brochures on a particular investigation or trial, anti-Semitic editors sometimes filled their newspapers with oversized headlines and sketches of the major participants. Even mainstream papers that avoided this kind of showy presentation frequently teased their readers with early telegram updates of events that would be reported more fully on the following day. These bulletins promised new sensational revelations or dramatic testimony in further issues of the paper. Thus, for the

[9] In fact, the Conservative, radical-Catholic, and anti-Semitic press were often faced with such "defeats." But by claiming that unfavorable verdicts were a sign of Jewish domination of the justice system, they became quite adept at turning such defeats into rallying points against the Jews, the liberals, and even the German government itself.

press across the political spectrum, blood ritual trials made for both good politics and good business.

Despite this kind of open sensationalism, many newspapers still claimed to be objective observers and commentators on the blood ritual cases. The Catholic *Germania*, for example, often insisted on avoiding comment while trials were underway in the interests of objectivity. But even *Germania* editors would publish sensational articles preceding the trials, and once the verdict had been recorded, their pretense of objectivity quickly disappeared. Also, any efforts by Jewish or liberal newspapers to criticize ritual murder trials were quickly condemned by Conservative and Catholic newspapers as attempts to interfere in the German justice system. Thus, by hiding behind a facade of objectivity, newspapers could portray themselves as reasonable and disinterested observers, while at the same time attacking their rivals as biased and politically extreme.

Just as the local dynamics of ritual murder accusations often revolved around a common script or formula, so did much of the journalistic exploitation of such cases. First of all, each new allegation of ritual murder led to a flood of anti-Semitic brochures and pamphlets. Even before a case came to trial, many anti-Semitic newspapers would already start printing advertisements for future brochures that would provide revelations from the investigation or review the trial proceedings. These pamphlets were often widely available in regions such as West Prussia, Pomerania, and Westphalia, where they were instrumental in laying the foundation for subsequent accusations.[10] Second, while ritual murder trials allowed anti-Semites to portray Orthodox Jews as barbaric and evil, they also provided propaganda for use against their real targets—assimilated Jews and the liberal politicians who supported them. According to many anti-Semites, even if the leading Jews of German society did not approve of blood rituals, they were still responsible for trying to hide these crimes and protect those Jews who were accused. Third, most ritual murder accusations culminated in sensational trials in which the validity of ritual murder charges would be tested in court. For anti-Semites, these trials had two possible outcomes. Either the charge of ritual murder would once and for all be legally substantiated with a conviction, or the German justice system would once again suc-

[10] *Berliner Tageblatt* 22 April 1885 #202 Abend.

cumb to Jewish influence. Thus, in each case, not only the guilt or innocence of the accused was put at issue, but also the guilt or innocence of all Jews. And finally, the heated press debates over these ritual murder cases would often lead to libel trials, which would only prolong the public focus on the issues surrounding each case. For anti-Semitic journalists, whose anger at unfavorable verdicts often provoked prosecution for libel, these post-verdict trials provided both an opportunity to publicly retry the original ritual murder allegations and a chance to portray themselves as brave campaigners for truth and justice.

Although blood ritual trials did follow a general pattern, they were far from predictable. The sensational twists and turns of trial proceedings and the dramatic confrontations between lawyers, judges, witnesses and defendants turned each trial into something resembling a soap opera or a circus. In addition, newspaper editors often spiced up the trial coverage by removing the most pedestrian testimony from the transcripts and supplementing the trial record with their own pointed commentary. This commentary could turn simple and uneducated trial participants into caricatures of evil or paragons of virtue. While these efforts to sensationalize the trials sometimes failed to turn them into national political issues, the trials were at the very least useful as a form of public entertainment, and often helped to reinforce anti-Jewish stereotypes. Thus, although each blood ritual trial had its own unique circumstances and peculiar cast of characters, each case made a general contribution to debate on the "Jewish Question" in German society.

This chapter, then, will focus on press coverage of six major blood ritual allegations that occurred in Europe between 1880 and 1895: Tisza-Eszlar (Austria-Hungary), Skurcz bei Danzig, Lutscha (Austria-Hungary), Breslau, Korfu (Greece), and Xanten.[11] Although only three of these trials occurred on German soil, the others were covered so thoroughly in the German press that they had a very significant

[11] Johannes Groß lists a number of additional ritual murder allegations that arose in late nineteenth-century Germany, including Enniger (Westfalen) in 1873; Kempen (Niederrhein) in 1893; Berent (Westpreussen), Burgkunstadt (Oberfranken), Ulm (Württemburg) in 1894; Berlin in 1896; Issum (Niederrhein), Skaisgirren (Ostpreussen), Schoppinitz, Lengendorf, and Braunsberg (all in Schlesien) in 1898; Oderberg (Vorpommern) in 1900; and Neuss (Niederrhein) in 1910. Groß, *Ritualmordbeschuldigungen*, 28.

impact on popular discussions of ritual murder allegations within Germany. Although not all of these trials dominated the press for long periods of time, each was significant in its own way, and each was part of a running debate in Germany on the political rights of Jews and morality of Jewish teachings. This analysis will be centered less on a microhistory of the local social conflicts which first produced each ritual murder allegation, and will focus instead on the exploitation of these cases by a national political press that was fixated on the "Jewish Question".

Tisza-Eszlar (1882–1883)

Just before noon on April 1, 1882, a young peasant girl named Eszter Solymosi disappeared while running an errand in the small Hungarian farming village of Tisza-Eszlar.[12] Although members of the local synagogue had volunteered to help in the search for the child, the girl's hysterical mother soon became convinced that the Jews had been involved in Eszter's disappearance. Rumors and accusations against local Jews spread rapidly through the countryside, and the story quickly came to the attention of Hungarian anti-Semites who exploited it for their own political benefit. With the aid of anti-Semitic journalists, these hysterical accusations from an obscure Hungarian village eventually led to one of the most celebrated trials of the Nineteenth Century.

Although usually discussed in the framework of Hungarian or Eastern European anti-Semitism, the Tisza-Eszlar case also had a dramatic influence in Germany.[13] Almost as soon as the incident was reported in the Hungarian press, the story began to dominate German anti-Semitic newspapers as well. For German anti-Semites, the facts of the Tisza-Eszlar case were clear. Young Eszter had disappeared while walking on a path that passed the village synagogue. Furthermore, the girl's disappearance coincided both with the Passover festival and

[12] Transliterations of the names of Hungarian cities and individuals differed widely in German newspapers. Except for the city Tisza-Eszlar, all Hungarian spellings come from Andrew Handler, *Blood Libel at Tiszaeszlar* (New York: Columbia Univ. Press, 1980).

[13] See Lehr, *Antisemitismus*, 88–108.

the appearance of several foreign Jews in town who were vying for the vacant position of village *schochet* (kosher slaughterer).

The most convincing evidence against the Jews, however, came from two young Jewish boys, Samu and Móric Scharf, who testified that they had personal knowledge of Eszter's murder. Although only four years old, Samu allegedly told the Court Investigator that he had gathered Eszter's blood from the synagogue floor as the candidates for *schochet* held her down and made the ritual incision. Móric, a boy of 14 years, first denied his brother's statements, but over two long days of interrogation and intimidation he began to change his story. Móric eventually claimed that he had not taken part in the killing, but had witnessed Eszter's slaughter through a keyhole in the synagogue door. As a result of Móric's testimony, the three visiting *schochet* were arrested for murder, and several other members of the local Jewish community, including Móric's father, József Scharf, were charged with complicity.[14]

Public fascination with the Tisza-Eszlar case continued to grow in the months after the incident, fueled by the steady stream of revelations coming out of the investigation. The local Court Investigator, Jószef Bary, had been convinced from the beginning that this was a case of ritual murder; therefore, he conducted his investigation in a manner that considered any new evidence only as it related to proving the guilt of the Jewish defendants.[15] For example, several months after Eszter's disappearance, the body of a young girl dressed in Eszter's clothing was found in the Tisza River. The girl's body had no signs of ritual incisions or the draining of blood—thus suggesting that she was not the victim of a ritual killing. Eszter's mother, however, steadfastly claimed that the corpse was not that of her daughter, and Investigator Bary proceeded on the assumption that a "phony" corpse was planted as part of a Jewish conspiracy to mislead the investigators.[16] A riverside autopsy conducted by local

---

[14] When possible, this trial summary has been based on trial transcripts and commentary published in various German newspapers. Additional information comes from Handler's useful and detailed account.

[15] Bary was accused of taking counsel from two of the most active anti-Semitic agitators in Hungary: Géza Ónody and Gyula Verhovay. Although Bary denied the charges, he also openly stated his admiration for Ónody. Handler, *Blood Libel at Tiszaeszlar*, 75.

[16] In the initial viewing of the corpse, four friends of Eszter made a positive identification and two others said that the body was possibly that of Eszter—but

doctors under Bary's supervision seemed to support many of his claims. The corpse was said to have been that of an 18–20 year old woman, with a shaved head and evidence of sexual experience. Also, the local doctors claimed that the body could not have been dead more than ten days, and could not have been floating in the river for more than three or four days—all facts that seemed to exclude the possibility that the corpse was Eszter's. When Bary found out that the leader of the group of raftsmen who had found the body was a Jew, it reinforced his certainty about the Jewish plot, and the entire group of raftsmen was arrested for complicity. Under repeated interrogation (and allegedly also torture), several of the raftsmen "confessed" to complicity in transporting the "phony" body and hiding it on the riverbank. One of the visiting *schochet*, Salamon Schwarcz, also confessed under torture to complicity in Eszter's murder. Although Schwarcz and the raftsmen recanted their confessions soon after they were offered, Bary felt that he had more than enough evidence to proceed to trial.

Throughout the next year, sensational reports on the investigation filled the Hungarian press, including stories about the discovery of new witnesses, new conspirators, and even rumors of Eszter being discovered alive. These stories proved to be fertile ground for anti-Semitic newspapers, and the spread of provocative anti-Semitic propaganda led to anti-Jewish riots throughout Hungary in October and November 1882. While the liberal Hungarian government openly criticized the anti-Semites and pleaded for public calm, its official policy was one of non-interference in matters of the law. Liberal and Jewish newspapers in Hungary, therefore, were on their own in fighting for the innocence of the defendants. Many liberals feared that a rapid spread of anti-Semitism might lead to a loss of votes to the political right, and they therefore attacked both the trial and the blatant electioneering of anti-Semitic politicians that surrounded it.[17] Thus, despite government neutrality, the Tisza-Eszlar case quickly became a focal point in the battle between Hungarian liberals and

---

Eszter's mother firmly denied that the body was that of her daughter. In a second viewing a few days later, after rumors had spread that the Jews had substituted the body of a Jewish girl for Eszter, all 12 people viewing the body denied that it was Eszter. Ibid., 70–71.

[17] Ibid., 82, 84.

conservatives. The case also attracted the direct involvement of some of the country's most prominent public figures. One of Hungary's leading politicians, Károly Eötvös, for example, accepted the post as chief defense attorney, and Károly Szalay, an aspiring politician and editor of the anti-Semitic newspaper *Népjog* was hired as Mrs. Solymosi's personal attorney. The Tisza-Eszlar affair, therefore, had become a political battleground, with each side using the case to attack political opponents and seek public support.

As in Hungary, the controversy about the Tisza-Eszlar accusations was important in Germany both as anti-Jewish propaganda and as general political propaganda. German anti-Semitic newspapers such as the *Berliner-Ostend Zeitung*, the *Patriotische Zeitung*, and the *Deutsche Reform* printed sensational stories about the case that were accompanied by portraits of major participants, including sketches that demonized the accused and portrayed Eszter as an innocent and saintly young girl. Most of these newspapers claimed that Móric's "confession" meant that the accusations of ritual murder were all but proven. Several newspapers even included detailed sketches of the crime scene and descriptions of how the ritual slaughter had taken place.[18] In fact, the Tisza-Eszlar case became such a crucial part of anti-Semitic agitation that when the German anti-Semites hosted the first International Anti-Semitic Congress in Dresden during mid-September 1882, the meeting was held under a portrait of Eszter Solymosi. The highlights of this convention were the speeches by the Hungarian delegates, Győző Istóczy and Iván Simonyi, on the state of the proceedings.[19]

Although the first reports of the investigation to reach Germany appeared only in the anti-Semitic press, the discussion of the Tisza-Eszlar incident did not stay confined to anti-Semitic newspapers for

[18] See, for instance, *Wucherpille*, 16 June 1883 #24 in BAK *ZSg. 113* Sammlung Fechenbach #22.

[19] Peter Pulzer, *The Rise of Political Anti-Semitism in Germany and Austria* (New York: John Wiley & Sons, 1964), 103–105. The Congress included representatives from Russia, Austria-Hungary, France and the Balkans, but was clearly dominated by the German delegates like Adolf Stöcker and Max Liebermann von Sonnenberg. Győző Istóczy (called Victor von Istoczy in Germany) was known as the founder of Hungarian political anti-Semitism and edited one of the leading anti-Semitic journals, *12 Röpirat.* Simonyi was a close associate to Istóczy, and published the *Westungarischer Grenzbote*, which was the most important source of articles on Tisza-Eszlar for the German anti-Semitic press. See Handler, *Blood Libel at Tiszaeszlar*, 31–32.

long. As early as June 1882, the radical Catholic daily *Germania* printed a story that examined the possibility that Jewish law required the blood of Christian children for ritual purposes. The article related the Tisza-Eszlar incident to the Damascus Affair of 1840, which had allegedly produced testimony from rabbis about the role of ritual murder in the Jewish religion. According to the *Germania*, this testimony proved that the accusations from Tisza-Eszlar were not entirely out of the realm of possibility.[20] When this article met with bitter criticism in the liberal and Jewish press, the *Germania* and other Catholic newspapers responded by printing vicious anti-liberal and anti-Semitic attacks reminiscent of the peak of the *Kulturkampf* in 1875.[21] The debates between the Catholic press and newspapers such as the *Jüdische Presse* and the liberal *Berliner Börsen-Courier* grew more heated over time, and their greatly contrasting commentary on the Tisza-Eszlar investigation often gave way to political criticism or even personal attacks on opposing editors.[22]

Meanwhile, the proceedings against the Jewish *schochet* and their alleged accomplices proceeded slowly. The trial did not begin until June 19, 1883—more than fourteen months after Eszter's disappearance. However, the fourteen months of waiting had not dampened public interest in the case in either Hungary or Germany. In fact, in early June, the libel trial of the Hungarian anti-Semite Győző Istóczy for a vicious article about Hungarian Jewry had provided a perfect vehicle for Istóczy to whip up pre-trial emotions. His acquittal only a few days before the opening of the Tisza-Eszlar trial gave

---

[20] *Germania* 24 June 1882 #281 Morgen.

[21] See, for example, *Fränkisches Volksblatt* 7 June 1882 #129. Although the two *Germania* editors responsible for the 1875 articles, Paul Majunke and Christoph Joseph Cremer, were forced out of the Center party in the early 1880s, *Germania* still returned to anti-Semitic rhetoric to attack liberal opponents. It is important to remember that although the tenuous détente of the early 1880s signaled an end to the most radical phase of the *Kulturkampf*, contemporary observers believed that the struggle was far from over.

[22] *Germania* 28 June 1882 #287 Morgen. Throughout 1882, *Germania* printed frequent updates on the investigation and critiques of the "Jewish-liberal" press under the title "The Secret of Tisza-Eszlar". Although the *Germania* articles rejected the idea that blood rituals were an established part of Jewish religious practices, the *Germania* soon became one of the most avid defenders of the murder charges against the Hungarian Jews. The editors reasoned that while a murder might not have been a traditional ritual practice, it could have been committed because of Jewish superstitions or the anti-Christian feelings of individual Jews.

Extra-Blatt.

Der Mord von Tisza-Eszlar.

Als vor Jahresfrist die Nachricht zu uns drang, daß in dem Dorfe Tisza-Eszlar in Ungarn **das Christen-Mädchen Esther Solymossi von jüdischen Schächtern zu rituellen Zwecken geschlachtet worden sei,** erhob die ganze liberale Presse ein Zetergeschrei über diese „mittelalterliche Anklage," welcher jeder vernünftige Grund fehlt. Nachdem es der Judenschaft gelungen war, die Untersuchung ein Jahr zu verschleppen, ist dieselbe nun doch soweit gediehen, daß die Gerichte sich veranlaßt gefunden haben, die Anklage wegen rituellen Mordes zu erheben. Wir lassen die Motivirung des bereits bekannten Anklagebeschlusses im wesentlichen nach der „N. Fr. Pr." hier folgen:

Am 1. April v. J., dem Tage vor dem jüdischen Passahfeste, hatte Esther Solymossi von der Frau Andreas Huri's, bei dem sie in Dienst stand, den Auftrag erhalten, aus dem Laden des Josef Kohlmayer Farbe und Ruß zu bringen. Dieselbe war auch in dem Laden, machte die Einkäufe, wie ihr aufgetragen und entfernte sich nach wenigen Minuten wieder. Sowohl auf dem Hin- als auf dem Rückwege traf sie mit ihrer Schwester Sophie zusammen, auch sah sie, wie sich Esther eilig nach Hause zurückbegab. Das war gegen 11½ Uhr, trotzdem aber war Esther um 2 Uhr noch nicht nach Hause zurückgekehrt. Die Schwester suchte sie bei ihrer Mutter; aber auch da war das Mädchen nicht und nun begann letztere ebenfalls nach der Verschwundenen zu suchen, ohne aber eine Spur von derselben entdecken. Als die Mutter abends am jüdischen Tempel vorüberging, kamen ihr der Tempeldiener Josef Scharf und dessen Gattin entgegen, trösteten sie, das Mädchen werde sich schon finden, auch in Nanas habe sich ein ähnlicher Fall ereignet, auch dort habe man die Juden beschuldigt, und dennoch sei das Kind später auf einer Wiese gefunden worden. Anfangs legte die Wittwe Solymossi diesen Worten der Eheleute Scharf garkeine Bedeutung bei. Als jedoch am nächsten Tage eine andere Person denselben Verdacht in ihr rege machte, begab sie sich am 4. April zum Stuhlrichter von Bencsello, um demselben das Verschwinden ihrer Tochter anzuzeigen und zugleich ihren Verdacht gegen die Juden auszusprechen; sie bat den Stuhlrichter sogar, er möge den jüdischen Tempel untersuchen lassen. Der Stuhlrichter hielt die Anzeige für so unsinnig, daß er blos die Notiznahme des Fehlens der Esther Solymossi anordnete. Als jedoch später infolge einiger Aeußerungen des 5jährigen Samuel Scharf, Sohnes des mehrfach erwähnten Tempeldieners, der Verdacht der Wittwe Solymossi neue Nahrung erhielt, suchte letztere am 4. Mai neuerdings den Stuhlrichter auf und berichtete diesem, daß nunmehr auch schon einige Ortsbewohner den von ihr gehegten Verdacht theilen. Der Stuhlrichter verhörte an diesem Tage 6 Weiber. Dieselben erzählten, sie hätten von dem 5jährigen Samuel Scharf gehört, daß sein Vater und die am 1. April zu einem Probegebet versammelten Schächter die Esther Solymossi ermordet hätten. Auf Grund dieses Ergebnisses der Voruntersuchung wurde die gerichtliche Untersuchung angeordnet, in deren Verlauf durch die gravirende Aussagen des 14 jährigen Moritz Scharf, welche durch die Aussagen der Frau Stephan Lenayel und Wittwe Johann Fekete bekräftigt wurden, der Verdacht immer begründeter erschien, daß Salomon Schwarz, Abraham Buxbaum, Leopold Braun und Hermann Wollner die Esther Solymossi in der Synagoge zu Eßlar des Lebens beraubten, daß Josef Scharf, Adolf Junger, Abraham Braun, Samuel Lustig, Lazar Weißstein und Emanuel Taub die That der früher genannten bewußt unterstützten.

Salomon Schwarz, der Schächter von Tisza-Eszlar.

Die Synagoge von Tißa-Eßlar.

1. Synagoge.
2. Wohnhaus des Tempeldieners.
   a) Die Wohnung des Tempeldieners.
   b) Das rituelle Bad der Jüdinnen.
   c) Das Fenster, welches den Ausblick gegen den Theißdamm gestattet, aus welcher Richtung Esther Solymossi kam, als sie den Heimweg mit den gekauften Farben angetreten hatte.
3. Eingang zur Synagoge.

Fig. 5. "Extra!—The Murder of Tizsa-Eszlar"—From the small anti-Semitic *Ostend-Zeitung* in Berlin. On the back in large bold letters was the announcement "Trial Proceedings begin on June 4th!" Courtesy of the Landesarchiv Berlin.

the anti-Semitic press in Hungary free-reign to print the most sensational libels with little fear of punishment. On the opening day of the trial, the small town of Nyíregyháza, which hosted the trial as the local county seat, was crowded with foreign correspondents, Hungarian politicians, and tourists just eager to catch a glimpse of the proceedings. To accommodate more spectators, the trial was moved from the courthouse to the county council chamber. But the building still had to be roped off and heavily guarded to keep those without tickets from pushing their way into the courtroom.[23]

Most of the anti-Semitic newspapers in Germany had guaranteed their readers a quick trial and a certain conviction. These predictions, however, suffered a serious blow on the opening day of the trial. The prosecutor, Ede Szeyffert, delivered an opening speech that was filled with ironic references to the absurdity of the charges, and direct criticism of the illegal methods of Court Investigator Bary. The anti-Semites, stunned at first, quickly became enraged at the prosecutor who seemed to be an active supporter of the defendants.[24] As the correspondent for the anti-Semitic *Patriotische Zeitung* commented:

> Today the local residents are unanimous in their indignation toward the prosecutor, who treats the young witness Moritz Scharf as if he were a criminal defendant while he views the accused Jews as his own personal charges. If justice is allowed to run its course, this will certainly happen not through, but in spite of the prosecutor. This truly dreadful conclusion is expressed unanimously here . . .[25]

Szeyffert was soon faced by numerous death threats, and was challenged to a duel by the anti-Semitic politician Géza Ónody. But the prosecutor remained unfazed. His critical attitude toward his own witnesses and his overt skepticism toward the charges of ritual murder made Szeyffert a target for anti-Semitic attacks throughout the duration of the trial.[26]

---

[23] Handler, *Blood Libel at Tiszaeszlar*, 117.

[24] Ibid., 121–122. Szeyffert was not responsible for the decision to go to trial, and he and many of his superiors found the case embarrassing and the charges ridiculous. Although he did not have the power to end the trial, Szeyffert could present the case as he saw fit, and could even call for an acquittal—which he later did.

[25] *Patriotische Zeitung* (Liegnitz) 6 July 1883 #27 in BAK *ZSg. 113* Sammlung Fechenbach #12. In this same collection, Freiherr von Fechenbach, a noted benefactor and collector of all things anti-Semitic, scribbled "Mr. Szeiffert, lawyer for the Jews" in the margins of a *Frankfurter Zeitung* article on the opening statements in the trial.

[26] *Germania* 22 July 1883 Zweites Blatt. Ónody faced prosecution for threatening

Robbed of the public champion they had hoped to find in the prosecutor, the anti-Semites began to focus instead on the crucial testimony of the young witness Móric Scharf. Separated from his family for more than a year and sent to live with a local constable of known anti-Semitic tendencies, Móric appeared in court as a changed figure. Clean-cut, and wearing traditional Hungarian peasant clothing, Móric bore little resemblance to his father and the other Jewish defendants. He testified that he had heard a commotion in the synagogue on that fateful day, and then had watched through a keyhole in the front door as Salamon Schwarcz slit Eszter's throat while the other *schochet* held her down. Although he testified in a calm and controlled manner, when challenged by the defense attorney or encouraged by the spectators, Móric responded with emotional outbursts toward his father and disrespectful comments about Judaism as a whole.[27] Press reactions to Móric's testimony were varied. Anti-Semitic newspapers claimed that Móric had bravely resisted attempts by both the prosecutor and defense attorney to confuse him. Liberal and Jewish papers, on the other hand, claimed that Móric's testimony was clearly rehearsed and even produced psychological experts to explain how the young boy could have turned so completely against his own father.[28] With both sides claiming that Móric's testimony was beneficial to their own point of view, the trial turned next to the matter of the riverside autopsy on the "phony" corpse.

Soon after Károly Eötvös had taken the job of lead defense attorney, he had realized that the inexperience and incompetence of the local doctors would leave their conclusions about the "phony" corpse vulnerable to attack. Eötvös had demanded a new autopsy on the body, and in December 1882 he invited three of the most respected

---

a public official, but action was hindered by Ónody's parliamentary immunity. Szeyffert was frightened by the incident and asked to be replaced as prosecutor, but after his request was denied, he continued to openly voice his doubt about the credibility of prosecution witnesses and the believability of ritual murder accusations.

[27] See Handler, *Blood Libel at Tiszaeszlar*, 123–130. The courtroom exchanges were heated, with Móric calling his father a liar and repeatedly libeling the Jewish religion. One of the defendants responded by yelling at Móric and spitting in his face.

[28] The *Jüdische Presse*, for example cited an article by a Viennese psychiatrist in the *Wiener Medicinischen Wochenschrift* in which "moral insanity" is suggested as a possible psychiatric diagnosis for Móric. The article then goes on to cite Krafft-Ebing to support this diagnosis and asserts that once the trial had ended, Móric should probably be sent to a mental institution. *Jüdische Presse* 12 July 1883 #28.

Hungarian pathologists to Tisza-Eszlar for a new examination. Despite rudimentary conditions and a hostile local atmosphere, the experts calmly proceeded in proving that many of the major conclusions of the first autopsy had been erroneous.[29] The experts claimed that there was strong evidence that the body was that of a pre-pubescent girl, and that she had been floating in the water for several weeks (not the 3 or 4 days claimed in the first exam). In addition, other details from the first autopsy, such as the shaved head and evidence of sexual experience, were explained as the effects of the body's long submersion in water. In the end, the panel of experts argued that the girl bore strong similarities to Eszter, and they added that it was unrealistic to conclude that the raftsmen had planted a "phony" corpse to mislead authorities. To supplement these findings, Eötvös solicited the opinions of the world-renowned Professors Eduard Hoffman of Vienna and Rudolph Virchow of Berlin.[30] While this expert testimony was impressive when presented in the courtroom, it did not shake the faith of the anti-Semitic press in the guilt of the Tisza-Eszlar Jews. The anti-Semites suggested that the outside experts were clearly biased, and they instructed their readers to instead place their faith in the conclusions offered by the simple country doctors at the first autopsy.[31]

After the unconvincing testimony of Móric and the two conflicting autopsy reports, the lead judge ordered one final test of the charges: a visit to the murder scene to test the details of Móric's story. While some anti-Semitic newspapers proudly claimed that the visit corroborated Móric's testimony, most others were less enthusiastic about the results of the visit—with good reason. The keyhole in the synagogue door was extremely low, and Móric was forced into a very uncomfortable position in order to look through it. In addition, the keyhole offered a very limited view of the synagogue, and much of the alleged crime scene was well out of the field of vision. After this visit, the court decided that Móric's testimony was not credible and that he should therefore not be sworn in as a witness.[32]

[29] See Handler, *Blood Libel at Tiszaeszlar*, 96–98.

[30] Ibid., 100–101.

[31] See, for example, *Der Kulturkämpfer* Heft 86 (July 1883): 1–10 and a speech by Adolf Stöcker in *Patriotische Zeitung* (Liegnitz) 14 September 1883 #37 in BAK *ZSg. 113* Sammlung Fechenbach #12.

[32] Handler, *Blood Libel at Tiszaeszlar*, 153–156. In the Hungarian legal system, a witness could only be sworn after the court ruled his or her testimony valid. Many

After the decision not to swear in the lead prosecution witness, the verdict was all but decided. Both the prosecutor and the defense attorney delivered summations that demanded that the defendants be acquitted, and only Mrs. Solymosi's personal attorney, Károly Szalay, was left to plead for a conviction. Faced with evidence that was inconclusive and unconvincing, the judges had no choice but to acquit the defendants on all charges.[33]

In many cities of the Austro-Hungarian Empire, news of the verdict in the Tisza-Eszlar trial was followed by serious rioting. Budapest and Bratislava (then Preßburg) were hit especially hard. While the anti-Semitic press in Germany generally advised their readers to avoid violence, they also made it clear that the violence was usually deserved and often provoked by arrogant Jewish celebrations of their "victory". These anti-Jewish riots did not spread to cities in Germany, but small altercations and limited vandalism were reported by the Berlin press.

German anti-Semitic newspapers, many of which had portrayed the trial as a series of defeats for the Jewish defendants, reacted with shock and disbelief to the verdict. The *Patriotische Zeitung* gave this angry summary of the trial and its lessons:

> A mother who supposedly cannot recognize the corpse of her own daughter.—
>
> A body that was not photographed even once upon its discovery, but was immediately dismembered and sent to the Professors.—
>
> A 15 year old boy who accuses his own father of murder.—
>
> A prosecutor who believes the defendants are innocent from the start, but who instead of simply dismissing the case, leads the defense team himself.—
>
> In essence, everywhere inconceivabilities, monstrosities, and stupidities . . .
>
> The trial may be formally ended, but morally it is just beginning . . .
>
> The best advice that we could give to Christians in Hungary would be—to *emigrate* . . .[34]

anti-Semitic newspapers like the *Wucherpille*, a weekly from Mainz, seemed oblivious to the situation and reported that the experiment of looking through the keyhole had worked perfectly to the consternation of the defense. (*Wucherpille* 28 July 1883 #30). Others simply claimed that the experiment did not work because the door had been tampered with by local Jews.

[33] According to Handler, the lead judge had anti-Semitic leanings and would have gladly voted for a conviction, but confronted by the flawed evidence and under pressure from the other two judges on the panel, he reluctantly agreed to acquit. Handler, *Blood Libel at Tiszaeszlar*, 155–156.

[34] *Patriotische Zeitung* (Liegnitz) 3 August 1883 #31 in BAK *ZSg. 113* Sammlung Fechenbach #12.

Other anti-Semitic newspapers claimed that the verdict was a result of Jewish bribes and threats that had succeeded in corrupting the prosecutor and forcing the judges to acquit despite the "overwhelming evidence". Allegedly, the *Alliance Israélite* and the Rothschild family had used their influence with the Hungarian government to assure that the guilty Jews would remain unpunished.[35]

Many anti-Semitic newspapers continued to spread sensational rumors about the Tisza-Eszlar case long after the trial had ended. The *Neue Deutsche Volkszeitung* for example, printed a rumor that the defendant József Scharf and his family had been secretly brought to Berlin by the *Alliance Israélite.* The article warned that riots could result from this action and begged the city authorities to make sure that Scharf was sent out of the country.[36] In addition, anti-Semitic journals such as *Der Kulturkämpfer* charged that in the period before the trial several investigating officers had been hounded into committing suicide by powerful Jews who were attempting to blackmail them.[37] These kinds of stories had a dual purpose. First of all, the anti-Semitic press wanted to keep up public interest in the case because it was an excellent source of propaganda for attracting people to the anti-Semitic cause. Second, sensational "revelations" were also good for business—that is, they would aid newspaper sales and also publicize post-trial brochures that were being offered to the public.

While the scandal surrounding Tisza-Eszlar was good business for the anti-Semites, it also provided a new battleground for members of the mainstream political press to attack their rivals. Just as in the pre-trial discussion of the case, the Tisza-Eszlar verdict led to a renewed war of words between Catholic and Conservative newspapers and their liberal counterparts. At first, commentary on the

---

[35] *Wucherpille* (Mainz) 1 September 1883 #35 in BAK *ZSg. 113* Sammlung Fechenbach #22.

[36] *Neue Deutsche Volkszeitung* 21 August 1883 #193 Beilage. New rumors about the case were often accompanied by advertisements for brochures or invitations to anti-Semitic political meetings. These newspapers hoped that an appeal would bring renewed public attention. But the appeal was quickly denied, and related law suits, like the one against Ónody for his assault on Szeyffert, did not bring the anticipated public response. Still, the rumors about the case did not stop. As late as 1891, a rumor spread that Eszter had been discovered living under the name of Kohlmeyer in New York City. The report was denied by the New York Police Department. *Allgemeine Zeitung des Judenthums* 20 March 1891 #12 Beilage.

[37] *Der Kulturkämpfer* Heft 86 (July 1883): 1–10.

Fig. 6. "Our Tisza-Eszlar"—The two pictured Jews, labeled "Open Competition" and "Usury" are slaughtering a young girl labeled "Honesty" on the cutting block of "Liberal Legislation, Freedom of Occupation, and Free Trade" while under the sign "Stock Market". On back of this illustration is a subscription form for the newspaper *Die Wahrheit*. Courtesy of the Landesarchiv Berlin.

verdict in the Catholic press was relatively mild, with newspapers like *Germania* claiming that they were impartial observers, and would not be moved by the biased propaganda of either the anti-Semitic or the "Jewish-liberal" press. While admitting that neither the charge of ritual murder nor the charge of planting evidence had been completely proven in the trial, *Germania* still blamed the agitation of the Jewish-liberal press for making any impartial verdict in the trial impossible.[38] These comments, of course, drew a quick response from liberal newspapers, and the post-trial commentary in the competing papers again quickly descended into political attacks. The *Germania* condemned the "*Jubelhymnen*" of liberal newspapers like the *Frankfurter Zeitung* and the *Berliner Tageblatt*, and dismissed the idea that the acquittal had been a total vindication for the Jews. The verdict had spoken only of insufficient evidence, they pointed out, not of proven innocence.[39]

As the polemical exchanges with the liberal newspapers continued, the *Germania* began to adopt much of the rhetoric and arguments being advanced by the anti-Semitic press. The Catholic paper, for instance, now wrote of the "feverish action of all international Jewry" who "worked with customary passion, often with recklessness in the choice of method."[40] Articles also appeared in the *Germania* that claimed that Rothschild and the "Jewish Golden International" had held international finances hostage to pressure Hungarian politicians into influencing the Tisza-Eszlar verdict.[41]

The rhetoric of the ultra-Conservative press generally matched that of *Germania*. The ultra-Conservative *Reichsbote*, for example, claimed that while the accusations of a "ritual" killing had not been proven absolutely, significant evidence still pointed to the Jewish *schochet* as the guilty parties.[42] Adolf Stöcker's *Christlich-soziales Correspondenzblatt* agreed with this assessment. Conservative newspapers had been objective in their analysis of the trial, the *Correspondenzblatt* argued, and had separated themselves from the partisanship of both the Jewish and the anti-Semitic press. This "objectivity" was meant to contrast with the actions of the "Jewish-liberal" editors, who had allegedly

[38] *Germania* 4 August 1883 #175 Zweites Blatt.
[39] Ibid.
[40] *Germania* 7 August 1883 #177 Zweites Blatt.
[41] *Germania* 9 September 1883.
[42] *Reichsbote* 5 August 1883 #180.

interfered in the proceedings and behaved in a partisan manner. The *Correspondenzblatt* even chided other newspapers for not taking a stronger critical stand against the *Judenpresse*:

> We want to comment . . . that if the entire non-Jewish press had taken a similar bearing toward the Tisza-Eszlar trial as we had, in spite of the successful "acquittal" of the accused, today all Israel would have stood condemned before the entire morally educated world (*sittlich gebildeten Welt*) because of their behavior in this strange case! The last word has not been spoken; there is justice in world history, and this must eventually come for Israel![43]

As in the case of *Germania*, when faced with the hostile responses of the Jewish and liberal press, Conservative newspapers like the *C-S Correspondenzblatt* and the *Reichsbote* intensified their anti-Jewish rhetoric. Stöcker's newspaper, for example, responded to liberal criticism by attacking the Berlin "*Judenpresse*" for making "statements that border on insanity". After the verdict, the "*Judenpresse*" allegedly "was sent into convulsions of joy and anger, and celebrated in an ecstasy comparable only to true orgies."[44] Stöcker not only singled out the editors of Germany's leading liberal newspapers for criticism, but also claimed that the "the whole of degenerate Jewry has made itself an accessory to the crime through its behavior, regardless of who actually committed the deed. . . ."[45] The *Kreuzzeitung*, the leading Conservative daily newspaper, concluded a response to liberal criticism with the statement: "International, cosmopolitan Judaism is a danger for the stability of nations and peoples . . . that its power must be broken, that is the lesson from the Tisza-Eszlar episode that princes and peoples should draw and take to heart."[46]

The polemical articles in the German press on the Tisza-Eszlar case continued almost unabated until the end of October 1883, when the Neustettin arson trials began to replace it in the headlines. But even decades later, the name Tisza-Eszlar continued to provoke many of the same emotions that it had in 1883.[47] In the hands of the anti-

[43] *Christlich-soziales Correspondenblatt* 8 August 1883 #32.

[44] *Christlich-soziales Correspondenblatt* 15 August 1883 #33.

[45] Ibid. For Stöcker, the Tisza-Eszlar trial also provided a business opportunity. His speeches and articles on the affair, like those of other anti-Semitic journalists, were printed and sold as brochures.

[46] As quoted in *Christlich-soziales Correspondenblatt* 15 August 1883 #33.

[47] The Tisza-Eszlar case was eventually turned into a drama "Ritualmord in Ungarn" by Arnold Zweig (1914) and later served as the basis for two films: "The

Semitic press, the Tisza-Eszlar case quickly became the stuff of myth. With every future accusation of Jewish wrongdoing, the story of Tisza-Eszlar could be revived and embellished with new details. Thus, while the case resulted in acquittal for the Jewish defendants, it opened up a promising new source of propaganda against Jews in general. Soon after the verdict, the liberal *National Zeitung* had optimistically claimed that "the end of this trial will make a future criminal accusation on grounds of ritual murder both legally and scientifically impossible."[48] This kind of optimism did not last long.

Skurcz (1885)

The hysteria surrounding the Tisza-Eszlar trial inspired a series of other ritual murder accusations throughout the 1880s, most of which were never publicized outside of regional newspapers or the anti-Semitic press. Some of these cases, however, became the subject of polemics between anti-Semitic and Jewish newspapers, and a few caught the attention of the mainstream political press. The next ritual murder accusation to attract significant public attention in Germany took place less than a year after the end of the Tisza-Eszlar trial. But, unlike Tisza-Eszlar, this case took place on German soil.

On January 22, 1884, the dismembered body of the young boy Onophirius Cybulla was found in a marsh outside the small town of Skurcz near Danzig.[49] An autopsy fixed the cause of death as loss of blood, reported seven long wounds on the neck, and claimed that the body had been dismembered by someone with experience in such things. As these details became public, talk of a possible Jewish ritual murder spread throughout the region.[50]

Trial," directed by G.W. Pabst in 1948, and "Memories of a River," directed by Judit Elek in 1989. See Lehr, *Antisemitismus*, 101.

[48] *National Zeitung* 5 August 1883 #363 as quoted in *Der Kulturkämpfer* Band 10 (1885): 383.

[49] Skurcz is the modern Polish town of Skórz, ca. 70 km. east of Konitz and south of Gdansk.

[50] *Berliner Tageblatt*, 22 April 1885 Abend claimed that ritual murder charges had been made more likely by anti-Semitic brochures on Tisza-Eszlar that had recently been distributed.

Two witnesses soon came forward to support the theory of ritual murder. One, a local worker named Sprada,[51] told police that he had witnessed a Jewish businessman named Heymann Boss invite the young boy into his home on the night of his disappearance. A second witness, a local worker named Johann Mankowski, claimed to have seen another Jewish merchant, Hermann Josephson, carrying a sack the next morning with what could have been a young boy's body. The local investigators soon turned up more evidence that seemed to point to Boss and Josephson. Several neighbors told police that they had heard loud noises in Boss's house on that night, and a search of his animal stall revealed copious amounts of blood thought to be of recent origin. The investigators also found what seemed to be bloodstains on clothes owned by both Boss and Josephson.

In addition to this impressive physical and circumstantial evidence, the alibis offered by the two Jewish suspects were shaky at best. Boss claimed to have been at home all evening with his family and said that the blood in his stall was from a recently slaughtered animal. Josephson, meanwhile, told investigators that he had returned home at 7:30 PM and had dinner with his family and a guest, *Rätherin* Kroll. But Kroll claimed to have been at the Josephson house until 11 PM, and she told police that Josephson was not present during that time. Several other witnesses told police that they had seen Josephson on the street late in the evening, and some had noticed a cut on Josephson's hand—a cut that he claimed had been the result of a work accident a few days before. The seemingly damning witness testimony and the mounting physical evidence soon led to the arrest of Hermann Josephson, Heymann Boss, and his father Rochem in early February 1884.[52]

The case against the Jewish merchants took a dramatic turn a month later, however, when the Interior Minister sent a top justice official, Criminal Commissar Höft, to look into the matter. After reviewing the case with local investigators, Höft decided to re-interview several witnesses. He started with the worker Mankowski, who, after several stern warnings to tell the truth, suddenly changed his

---

[51] Once again, transliterations of Polish names vary in different newspapers. I have used those from Otto Glagau's journal *Der Kulturkämpfer*.

[52] *Der Kulturkämpfer* Heft 118 (May 1885): 28.

story. Mankowski now said that he had not seen the Jewish defendant Josephson with the sack that morning, but a local Christian butcher named Joseph Behrendt. Allegedly, Behrendt had come to Mankowski after the body was discovered, and had promised him money to give a false story to police. Now convinced that the accusations against the Jewish men were unfounded, Criminal Commissar Höft began to re-focus the investigation. He soon learned that Behrendt had behaved strangely on the day that the body was found, and was later overeager to blame the incident on local Jews. Höft also discovered that Behrendt was a convinced anti-Semite who had a previous criminal history, and as a butcher, Behrendt would have also been an expert in anatomy. Under interrogation, Behrendt claimed to have returned home early that evening in a drunken stupor—his wife told the investigators that she had personally undressed him and put him to bed. Although there was strong local pressure to continue the case against the Jewish defendants, Höft was unmoved. In early April 1884, the Jewish suspects were released, and less than a month later Joseph Behrendt was taken into custody.[53]

The trial of Joseph Behrendt began on April 22, 1885 before a packed house in the Danzig Superior Court (*Landgericht*). Behrendt would be represented by a local attorney, *Rechtsanwalt* Thurau, while the prosecution would be led by the local prosecutor, *Staatsanwalt* Preuss. The judge in this case was the same figure involved in the retrial of the Neustettin arson case, *Landgerichtsrat* Arndt. Although Behrendt entered the court as the defendant, it was generally assumed that that the verdict of the trial would affect the fate of the Jews as well. The popular perception was that either Behrendt was guilty of trying to frame Boss and Josephson of the murder, or the Jews themselves were the guilty parties. Either way, the issue of guilt or innocence would be resolved by the verdict in this trial.

The trial began ominously for the Jewish former defendants. The first two days were filled with witness testimony that seemed to implicate Boss and Josephson instead of Behrendt. A local doctor named Lindenau testified that the wound on Josephson's finger appeared to be a bite mark—a wound that could easily have come during a struggle with the victim. Although Lindenau's testimony was quickly contradicted by another medical expert, it still gave the impression

[53] Ibid., 27.

that Josephson was a possible suspect. *Rätherin* Kroll again insisted that Josephson could not have returned home until well after 11 PM. The local investigating officer also told of the physical evidence found behind Boss's house—including the copious amounts of fresh blood. The testimony against Boss and Josephson continued to mount, with several local residents alleging that the murdered boy had provoked Boss's anger by selling goatskins in direct competition to him. According to these witnesses, Boss and his wife had been overheard while threatening to do the boy harm.[54]

This kind of damaging testimony continued uninterrupted, until a chemist and blood expert, Dr. Bischoff, was called to the stand.[55] Dr. Bischoff explained that he had used the most modern scientific techniques to analyze the blood evidence in the trial. He claimed that the blood from Boss's house could not be identified as either human or animal blood since it was so thoroughly mixed with dung. The blood stains on the clothing, however, were all animal blood—except for a stain of human blood on the right sleeve of a jacket worn by Hermann Josephson (matching the cut on his finger). Despite this possibly exculpatory evidence, the momentum of the trial seemed to be running against Boss and Josephson. After two full days of testimony, Behrendt's name had hardly been mentioned.[56]

Finally, late on the third day of the trial, witnesses were called to testify to Behrendt's strange behavior on the day before and after the murder. However, even these witnesses did not provide convincing evidence of the defendant's guilt. Some witnesses testified that Behrendt was drinking on the night of the killing, but added that he was not too drunk to have committed murder. These witnesses were opposed by others who claimed Behrendt had been so drunk that he was unable to walk. Then, after more conflicting testimony, the key witness in the case, Mankowski, was called to testify. Mankowski repeated the story that he had seen Behrendt, not Josephson, with a sack on the morning of the murder. Under

[54] *Berliner Tageblatt* 24 April 1885 #206 Abend.

[55] The same Dr. Bischoff would later be called as an expert witness on blood and sperm evidence in the Konitz ritual murder investigation. See Bernhard Vogt, "Die 'Atmosphäre eines Narrenhauses'. Eine Ritualmordlegende um die Ermordung des Schülers Ernst Winter in Konitz," in *Zur Geschichte und Kultur der Juden in Ost- und Westpreußen*, ed. Michael Brocke et al. (Hildesheim, 2000), 555.

[56] *Berliner Tageblatt* 24 April 1885 #206 Abend.

questioning from the judge, however, Mankowski admitted that he never had a close view of the man with the sack, and he couldn't be absolutely sure that the man was indeed Behrendt. Then came another stunning twist in the trial. Two former associates of Mankowski testified that it was Criminal Commissar Höft, not Behrendt, who had been guilty of bribing witnesses to change their testimony. Although Höft fervently denied the accusations, and claimed he had only offered a customary stipend for travel expenses, Behrendt's defense lawyer would use this testimony to suggest the presence of a powerful conspiracy behind Mankowski's change of heart.[57]

With all the eyewitness and expert testimony finished, it was now up to the prosecutor and defense attorney to convince the jury of guilt or innocence. The two trial summations could not have been more contrasting. The prosecutor, Dr. Preuss, claimed Behrendt had been moved to murder the child by personal grievances against the boy's family, and was motivated by anti-Semitism to blame the murder on the local Jews. He also dismissed much of the testimony against Boss and Josephson as the products of either mistaken identity or of outright prejudice. Preuss assured the jurors that officials had first investigated the Jewish defendants, not because they gave the charges of ritual murder any credence, but because they were just following the available evidence. This evidence led them to Behrendt as the killer, not Boss and Josephson.[58] Preuss argued that the multitude of brochures about the recent trials in Tisza-Eszlar and Neustettin had been the inspiration behind Behrendt's plot.

Behrendt's defense attorney, Thurau, claimed that the prosecution had failed to provide a single piece of convincing physical or circumstantial evidence in the case. Although Thurau admitted that the defendant was an anti-Semite and a rival to Josephson, he argued that these facts alone did not prove he was the murder. After the end of the defense arguments, the jury deliberated for less than a half-hour before acquitting Behrendt of all charges.[59]

The anti-Semitic press reacted to the verdict with a mix of jubilation and indignation. The trial had cleared a known anti-Semite and placed suspicion back on the Jewish suspects—all as the anti-

---

[57] *Der Kulturkämpfer* Heft 118 (May 1885): 28–29.
[58] Groß, *Ritualmordbeschuldigungen*, 48.
[59] *Der Kulturkämpfer* Heft 118 (May 1885): 31.

Semitic press had hoped. But the anti-Semitic press had only half a "victory". That is, there still were still no Jews in prison, and there was no legal precedent for the conviction of Jews on charges of ritual murder. The most prominent anti-Semitic journalist to attack the trial was Otto Glagau, editor of the journal *Der Kulturkämpfer.*[60] Like much of the Conservative and Catholic press after the Tisza-Eszlar case, Glagau stated that he was unsure whether the evidence pointed conclusively to a "ritual killing" or not. However, he claimed that all of the evidence in the case pointed to the guilt of the Jewish suspects. Glagau's main focus, therefore, was not on proving the existence of ritual murder, but on condemning the outside interference by the Berlin authorities who, he claimed, had made an impartial investigation of the charges impossible. Glagau reminded his readers that Criminal Commissar Höft and Judge Arndt were previously involved in forcing a retrial of the Neustettin arson case, and he asserted that they had also done everything possible in that case to assure the acquittal of the Jewish defendants.[61] In an angry article, Glagau demanded that the government continue its investigations:

> The bestial murder at Skurz cries out to heaven, and it must be redressed. Otherwise it will result in a deep shock to public perceptions of the justice system . . . The murder at Skurz should also be a warning to the government that it must employ native German scholars to thoroughly examine rabbinical texts in order to gauge if these teachings pose a danger to the general public.[62]

The real victim of the trial, Glagau added, was the innocent Christian butcher Behrendt. Poor Behrendt had not only been held in prison for almost a year for a crime he did not commit, he had also lost his livelihood. Glagau urged his readers and members of the *Deutsche*

---

[60] Glagau was responsible for the series of articles in the journal *Gartenlaube* from 1875 that had set off the first wave of political anti-Semitism in the *Kaiserreich*. Although he never ran for public office, Glagau nonetheless established himself as one of the leading figures of German anti-Semitism. He served as chairman of the first International Anti-Semitic Congress in Dresden in mid-September 1882, and his *Kulturkämpfer* was one of the few anti-Semitic journals to function uninterrupted through the 1880s.

[61] Other papers like Stöcker's *Christlich-soziales Correspondenzblatt* were quick to point out a growing pattern in all legal procedures involving Jews: "The crime at Skurz is similar to those in Tisza-Eszlar and Neustettin; the criminals are not to be found and—the rest is silence." *Christlich-soziales Correspondenzblatt* 6 May 1885 #19 Beilage.

[62] *Der Kulturkämpfer* Heft 118 (May 1885): 36.

Antisemitenbund to take up a collection to aid this poor martyr of a Jewish conspiracy.[63]

The *Christlich-Soziales Correspondenzblatt* echoed Glagau's concerns and also expressed its incredulity that government officials still refused to consider any Jews as suspects in the murder. When nothing came of their complaints about the behavior of investigators, prosecutors, and the judge in the Skurcz trial, the *Correspondenzblatt* concluded in frustration: "Beyond a fallible earthly justice there is still an infallible eternal justice; that is our consolation."[64]

Lutscha (1881–1886)

A third case of alleged ritual-murder, this time in Galicia, attracted the attention of the German press in late 1885 and early 1886. Based on a murder committed in 1881, this case was still winding its way through the courts of the Austrian Empire several years later when it finally became a topic of debate in Germany. Although not a traditional case of ritual murder, this trial touched off a debate about Jewish fanaticism and led to more polemics between anti-Semitic newspapers and their Jewish and liberal counterparts.

The decomposed body of a middle-aged woman was found in late 1881 in a canyon outside the small town of Lutscha in Galicia. The woman had been five months pregnant, and her abdomen had been cut open and the fetus removed. In addition, the woman's hair had been completely shorn. The body was assumed to be that of a 40 year-old Polish woman named Franciska Mnich, who had been missing from town for several months. Suspicion quickly focused on the Jewish tavern-keeper, Moses Ritter, who had employed Franciska and was allegedly the father of her child. The Christian farmer Marcell Stochlinski was also suspected by local residents of having participated in the crime. Under interrogation, Stochlinski confessed that he had helped the Ritters murder Franciska, and he claimed that the murder had followed Jewish rituals. This time, the alleged

[63] *Der Kulturkämpfer* Heft 118 (May 1885): 31–32. Glagau also took the opportunity to plead for government compensation for those who were unfairly imprisoned or convicted. His own unfortunate court experiences undoubtedly spurred this demand.

[64] *Christlich-Soziales Correspondenzblatt* 6 May 1885 Beilage.

murder had not been committed for the purpose of gaining Christian blood, but in order to rectify the sin of the illicit union of Moses Ritter and Franciska. Stochlinski claimed that Moses and his wife Gittel decided to remove the fetus so it wouldn't be buried along with Franciska in Christian holy ground. As a result of Stochlinski's testimony, both Moses and Gittel Ritter were charged with murder.

The trial against the Ritters took place in the local Jury Court (*Schwurgericht*) of the small Polish town of Rzeszow in December 1883 (only a few months after Tisza-Eszlar). The jury quickly convicted both defendants of murder and sentenced them to death. The guilty verdict against the Ritters was soon reversed, however, by the Supreme Court (*Oberstegerichtshof*) in Vienna. The Vienna court ordered a new trial—this time in Krakow—and forbade the use of a Jewish ritual murder charge. Despite this ruling, the second trial in Krakow resulted in another unanimous verdict of guilty. The verdict in this second trial received attention in Austrian newspapers, but relatively few German newspapers took notice. One of the few that did, Adolf Stöcker's *Christlich-soziales Correspondenzblatt*, took the opportunity to attack the "*Judenpresse*" for trying first to influence the trial and then trying to suppress any public discussion of the guilty verdicts.[65] Soon after the article in the *Correspondenzblatt*, however, defense lawyers appealed this second conviction to the same Supreme Court in Vienna, and it too was reversed. Once more a new trial was ordered in Krakow, and this third trial began in September 1885.

By the time the third trial had started, many obstacles had arisen for the prosecution. Banned from using a ritual murder allegation, the prosecutors were now also unable to rely on the testimony of their main witness, the farmer Stochlinski, who had decided to withdraw his confession. As it turned out, the prosecution did not need Stochlinski's testimony for a conviction. First of all, even though testimony about Jewish "rituals" was not supposed to be permitted, a priest from Lutscha was allowed to testify that he had read in a book that Jews must kill those girls they seduce in order to allow

[65] *Christlich-soziales Correspondenzblatt* 29 October 1884 #44 Beilage. Stöcker was still angry about the liberal charge that Dr. Karl Nobiling, who had made an assassination attempt on Kaiser Wilhelm I in 1878, was a former member of the Christian-Social Party. This article made explicit reference to the Nobiling case and attacked the *Judenpresse* for distorting the truth in order to mislead the German people.

their own legitimate children to marry.[66] In addition, the prosecutor summoned witnesses who testified that a recently deceased farmer had previously spoken of seeing Moses Ritter with a corpse on the day of Franciska's disappearance. Even though this farmer had publicly sworn before his death to having no knowledge of the crime, the prosecutor insisted that the hearsay testimony of his neighbors was trustworthy. Apparently swayed by the priest's testimony and the scanty hearsay evidence, the jury in this third trial once again found Moses and Gittel Ritter guilty, and the Krakow court ordered them to be hanged.[67]

It was at this point that the case was reviewed in Germany by Hirsch Hildesheimer in his newspaper *Die Jüdische Presse.* Hildesheimer wrote sympathetically about the defendants, and he condemned the legal system in Austria for allowing such a spurious case to continue. According to Hildesheimer, there were multiple flaws in the case that should have led to an acquittal, if not an outright dismissal. First of all, since the woman's body had been exposed for more than six months, pathology experts could never conclusively identify it as that of Franciska. Second, the confession of Stochlinski was obtained only after torture, and his own previous murder conviction made him a more likely suspect than the Ritters themselves. Finally, the local prosecutors, like those in the Skurcz case and the Tisza-Eszlar case, had considered evidence only as it led to the guilt of the accused. The local prosecutors had attempted in three successive trials to load the jury with anti-Semites, and only the honesty of the Vienna Supreme Court had prevented them from succeeding. To counter the image of the fanatical Jew described in the anti-Semitic press, Hildesheimer portrayed Moses Ritter as a generous man who had taken Franciska into his home after she had been rejected by everyone in town, including her own family.[68]

Hildesheimer's *Jüdische Presse,* however, was not the only German newspaper to adopt the Lutscha case as a personal crusade. In May

[66] This book was allegedly *Der Talmudjude* by August Rohling. The priest had claimed to have read a Polish translation of Rohling's book. According to the *Jüdische Presse,* although the defense attorney proved that Rohling's work had never been translated into Polish, the jury was nonetheless swayed by the priest's "authoritative" testimony. *Jüdische Presse* 8 October 1885 #41.

[67] Summary of the third Lutscha trial based on *Jüdische Presse* 8 October 1885 #41.

[68] Ibid.

1885, Otto Glagau's anti-Semitic journal, the *Kulturkämpfer*, devoted an extensive article to various ritual murder charges in an attempt to demand government investigation of the Jewish scriptures. In this article, Glagau placed the Lutscha case on the same plane as previous cases from Tisza-Eszlar, Neustettin, and Skurcz. The conviction in the Lutscha case was further proof both of the truth of blood ritual charges against the Jews and of the complicity of the "*Judenpresse*" in trying to protect Jewish criminals.[69] However, when Glagau returned to the topic of the Lutscha trials in another article several months later, the case had taken another dramatic turn. It was appealed a third time to the *Oberstegerichtshof* in Vienna, and once again the Supreme Court found the verdict flawed. This time, instead of ordering a fourth new trial, the Vienna court ordered the accused to be summarily acquitted and freed from prison.

In an angry second article, Glagau claimed that these new developments were the work of the "Jewish newspaper hegemony from across Europe" and "all of Israel's blood and election relatives."[70] For Glagau, the case that once provided legal proof that ritual killings existed was now another powerful symbol of how influential Jews could pervert European legal systems. As he wrote:

> The Lutscha case is more significant than Tisza-Eszlar, Neustettin and Skurz put together. It has no comparison in the annals of history. After this case, one can justly claim that for today's Jews nothing is impossible. The predominance that Jews have assumed, and the enormous influence that they now exert must fill the hearts of the native-born with fear and dread.[71]

Despite the efforts of Glagau and other anti-Semitic agitators, the acquittal in the Lutscha case did not excite widespread popular outrage in Germany. Like the Skurcz case before it, the story of Lutscha received only moderate mention in the mainstream German press. But while the story of Lutscha disappeared rather quickly from the public eye, it lived on in the annals of anti-Semitic literature, and its legacy waited to be reawakened with the next ritual murder allegation.

---

[69] *Der Kulturkämpfer* Heft 118 (May 1885): 21.
[70] *Der Kulturkämpfer* Heft 128 (February 1886): 5–6.
[71] Ibid., 6.

Breslau (1889)

Although it also did not generate the international attention or popular unrest of Tisza-Eszlar, the trial of a young rabbinical candidate in Breslau turned out to be one of the most controversial cases of its kind. Unlike the other blood ritual allegations, this incident did not involve an alleged murder, but only a ritual assault. Also, unlike Tisza-Eszlar, Skurcz, or Lutscha, this incident did not involve a long public investigation or a complex and controversial trial. All of these were over in short order and made few waves. But the verdict in this case did draw attention: a Jewish rabbinical candidate was convicted of assaulting and drawing blood from a young Christian boy.

In July 1888, the rabbinical candidate Max Bernstein allegedly lured a Catholic boy named Severin Hacke to his apartment with the promise of cherries, and persuaded him to remove his clothes. Bernstein then gave him a slight wound on the genitals and collected a little blood on a blotter. The boy at first told no one about the incident, but he later told his father, who reported it immediately to police. Bernstein admitted some kind of involvement with the boy, but his testimony to the investigators was confused and contradictory. Nonetheless, the prosecutor believed there was enough evidence to charge Bernstein, and he was eventually brought to trial in February 1889. The court found that there was compelling proof of Bernstein's guilt; but because the injuries inflicted on the boy were slight, the court sentenced Bernstein to only three months in prison.[72]

This verdict brought a loud but mixed reaction from the anti-Semitic press. While the Breslau court had refused to accept Jewish rituals as a motive for the assault, it had also failed to assign any other motive to the crime. Thus, the anti-Semitic press called for an immediate re-investigation to determine whether Bernstein had followed religious precepts. The anti-Semitic press also complained about the relatively light sentence for the defendant, and suggested that the presence of Jews among the judges may have played a role.[73] Overall, however, the reaction of the anti-Semitic press was joyous.

[72] *Das Volk* 23 February 1889 #46.

[73] Carl Paasch, *Ein Jüdisch-deutsche Gesandtschaft und ihre Helfer. Geheimes Judenthum, Nebenregierungen und jüdische Weltherrschaft*, vol. 2, pt. 4 (Leipzig: Selbstverlag, 1891), 81. Paasch provides a long history of anti-Semitic trials including libel trials and blood ritual trials. Most of his material is reprinted from other anti-Semitic brochures.

For the first time, they claimed to have proof that Jews collected blood for religious rituals. As the *Antisemitische Korrespondenz* wrote:

> Now we have a legally substantiated case in which an apprentice Rabbi used Christian blood, and we can now justifiably expect that the State will intervene to investigate the motives in the case that the court deemed irrelevant.[74]

Other anti-Semitic newspapers proclaimed that this new verdict provided ample grounds to re-open old ritual murder cases, and they called for a thorough government investigation of Jewish religious practices. After rebuttals by several Jewish and liberal newspapers, the coverage of this case quickly degenerated into a long and heated debate over the nature of the Purim holiday and other "barbaric" Jewish rituals.[75]

The liberal press, however, claimed that the Bernstein case was an example of psychological and sexual deviance, and was not related in any way to Jewish religious teachings. Also, several of Bernstein's family members reported that he and at least seven other family members had histories of mental instability. To substantiate their claims, liberal newspapers cited the newly discovered fact that Bernstein had assaulted several Jewish children in a similar way before attacking the Christian boy.[76] In the weeks after the trial, the parents of several young Jewish boys that Bernstein had tutored over the previous year came forward to report incidents of sexual abuse. These boys claimed that Bernstein had asked if they were circumcised, and then convinced them he needed to draw blood from their genitals to ensure they would never convert to Christianity. A distant cousin, George Bernstein, claimed that Max Bernstein had molested him more than 25 times before drawing blood in a similar way. Many of the parents of these victims claimed that they knew what Max Bernstein had done, but didn't report the incidents out of embarrassment.[77] Of course, anti-Semitic journalists (and some government

---

[74] *Antisemitische Korrespondenz* 17 März 1889 #47.

[75] See, for example, *Das Volk* 8 March 1889 #57 and 27 March 1889 #73; *Deutsche Wacht* 10 March 1889 #10 and 14 April 1889 #15; and *Reichsbote* 9 March 1889 #58.

[76] *Berliner Tageblatt* 24 July 1891 #361.

[77] See the letter from the Erste Staatsanwalt Rosenberg in Breslau to Justice Minister Schelling (April 7, 1889) GStA PK, I. HA Rep. 84a Justizministerium, Nr. 56464, p. 61.

officials) found it suspicious that liberal newspapers reported the existence of Jewish victims before these new charges had been made public by the government. But the lead investigator (*Erste Staatsanwalt*) Rosenberg reported to Justice Minister von Schelling that leaks to the press were undoubtedly due to the fact that the families had gone first to relatives and then to Jewish community leaders before going to police.[78]

The report of the other incidents involving Bernstein and Jewish children did not end the public debate about ritual murder. In fact, the debate among the anti-Semitic, liberal, and Jewish press became even more heated with the involvement of a leading Conservative paper, the *Conservative Correspondenz*. This Conservative newspaper printed an editorial that claimed that the Breslau trial not only proved the existence of Jewish ritual murder, but also that such rituals were based on explicit precepts of the Talmud. These comments brought a quick answer from an enraged Jewish press. The *Israelit und Jeschurun*, for example, demanded that government officials bring charges against the *Correspondenz* for libeling the Jewish religion. The *Israelit* called the article "a shameless slander" and an "insidious and brazen lie," and dared the *Conservative Correspondenz* to sue it for libel so that the issue could be resolved in court. The editor of the *Israelit*, Dr. Adolf Blumenthal, even offered a million Marks for anyone who could prove that passages about ritual murder actually exist in the Talmud. Despite the "proof" immediately offered by the anti-Semitic press, this reward remained unclaimed.[79]

The polemics between the *Conservative Correspondenz* and the *Israelit und Jeschurun* soon spread to other Conservative, Catholic, liberal, and Jewish newspapers. As the debates continued, the polemical articles focused less on the trial itself, and more on personal attacks and general criticism of the Jewish religion. For example, the phrase "Remember what Amalek has done to you!" became the center of controversy after it was used in an article in the *Israelit und Jeschurun* and was adopted by several liberal papers like *Berliner Börsen-Courier* and the *Berliner Tageblatt*.[80] This biblical reference had been meant

[78] Ibid.

[79] On this debate, see for example: *Deutsche Wacht* 10 March 1889 #10 and *Antisemitische Korrespondenz* 17 March 1889 #47.

[80] *Berliner Börsen Zeitung* 16 February 1889 #85; *Reichsbote* 9 March 1889 #58 Beilage. In German, the phrase was "Gedenke was Amalek dir gethan hat!" It

to symbolize the repression of Jews by other peoples, but the ultra-Conservative press gave this phrase an entirely different meaning. Conservatives claimed that the comment exposed the kind of Jewish wrath against Christianity that was evident in both the blood rituals and in the Purim festival. According to stories printed in the *Kreuzzeitung*, *Reichsbote*, and several other ultra-Conservative papers, the Purim holiday was not a commemoration of escape from persecution, but a celebration of the extermination of thousands of political enemies. This kind of barbaric festival allegedly painted a true picture of what Jews had in mind for the Christian world. As the Stöckerite paper, *Das Volk*, responded to an article in the *Israelit*:

> Such a Purim celebration, in which the Jews 'do according to their will to those who are their enemies,' . . . that would certainly be appropriate to their tastes . . . And the bloodthirsty article from the Jewish paper that is presented above, with its threat against the ghosts of Haman, is also not unsuspicious. A cruel and bloodthirsty trait is often evident in Jews . . .[81]

Thus, what for the Jewish and liberal newspapers was a tragic case of a deranged young man, became proof for the Conservative and anti-Semitic press of the dangers posed by Judaism.

Concern over the Bernstein case reached all the way to the new Kaiser, Wilhelm II. Undoubtedly spurred by the uproar in the press, the Kaiser asked his Prussian Justice Minister, Hermann von Schelling, to further investigate the matter of Jewish blood-rituals, especially as they pertained to the Bernstein case. Wilhelm's interest in the Bernstein case is not at all surprising. As his biographers have demonstrated, the Kaiser had an extensive history of anti-Jewish statements and writings, both before and after his ascent to the throne. His prejudice was a by-product of his aristocratic and military upbringing, and his anti-Jewish attitudes were cultivated by an entourage that also harbored such sentiments.[82] Like many Germans, however,

---

appears in Deuteronomy 25:17 and relates to God's demand for vengeance against the Amalekites, who had attacked the Israelites in the Sinai desert. This phrase arose independently of the Breslau trial, but it soon became associated with the post-trial debate.

[81] *Das Volk* 8 March 1889 #57.

[82] See Lamar Cecil, *William II*, 2 vols. (Chapel Hill: University of North Carolina Press, 1989–96); Christopher Clark, *Kaiser Wilhelm II* (New York: Pearson Education, 2000); Giles MacDonough, *The Last Kaiser: The Life of Wilhelm II* (New York: St. Martin's Press, 2000); and John C.G. Röhl, *Kaiser and His Court: Wilhelm II and the*

Wilhelm was capable of voicing the ugliest of anti-Semitic statements and at the same time fostering alliances or even close friendships with prominent Jews.[83] Wilhelm's verbal attacks on Jews were also rarely translated into action or into direct support for anti-Semitic organizations, and those anti-Semites who celebrated his rise to the throne in 1888 were soon disappointed by his lack of open support.[84] Like many of his contemporaries, Wilhelm could represent himself as "neutral" on the Jewish Question simply because he generally held both Jews and most radical anti-Semites in contempt.

Acting on the Kaiser's request, Schelling urgently wrote to the *Kultusminister*, Dr. Goßler, asking him to seek information on the Bernstein case or about the existence of ritual murder in the Jewish religion. Schelling made a specific request that Goßler consult with non-Jewish experts.[85] Goßler responded by providing testimony from three renowned experts on Jewish religious texts: Franz Delitzsch, Hermann Strack, and Paul de Lagarde. Delitzsch was a professor of Theology at the University of Leipzig, and was recognized as one of the most prominent Old Testament scholars in the world. In addition to being a Lutheran pastor and a prominent member of the *Judenmission*, Delitzsch had been actively involved in attempts to publicly refute the conclusions of the infamous anti-Semitic scholar August Rohling in the early 1880s. Hermann Lebrecht Strack was a professor of the Old Testament at the University of Berlin. Like Delitzsch, Strack was also involved in Christian missionary activity among the Jews and founded an *Institutum Judaicum* for the study of the Jewish religion. He later battled against anti-Semitic agitators such as Adolf Stöcker and Theodor Fritsch both in literary debates and in court. Paul de Lagarde, on the other hand, had a reputation for being much less sympathetic to Judaism. Known in scholarly circles for his expert exegesis of the Old Testament, Lagarde had also achieved

---

Government of Germany, trans. Terence F. Cole (Cambridge: Cambridge University Press, 1994).

[83] See Werner Mosse, "Wilhelm II and the Kaiserjuden: a Problematical Encounter," in *The Jewish Response to German Culture: From the Enlightenment to the Second World War*, ed. Jehuda Reinharz and Walter Schatzberg (Hanover: University Press of New England, 1985).

[84] Richard Levy, *The Downfall of the Anti-Semitic Political Parties in Imperial Germany* (New Haven: Yale University Press, 1975), 136.

[85] See letter from Schelling to the Königlichen Staatsminister der geistlichen, Unterrichts und Medizinal Angelegenheiten Herrn D. Dr. Dr. von Goßler (March 8, 1889) GStA PK, I. HA Rep. 84a Justizministerium, Nr. 56464, p. 25.

public notoriety because of his collected essays called *Deutsche Schriften*, in which he rejected Judaism and traditional Christian faiths and called instead for a new Germanic religion.[86]

Kultusminister von Goßler forwarded the testimony of these experts to the Kaiser and the Justice Minister, along with his own opinions on the subject.[87] According to Goßler, the three expert witnesses represented a range of opinions. Delitzsch, a converted Jew, was described as the most sympathetic to Judaism. Lagarde, on the other hand, was assumed to have anti-Semitic leanings. Goßler concluded, therefore, that the most objective viewpoint belonged to Strack who seemed to occupy a middle ground. Although all three scholars disagreed in their speculation about the motivations for Bernstein's attacks, they all agreed that Jewish rituals and teachings were not to blame. Lagarde did discuss blood superstitions that had come indirectly from Judaism; however, even he did not conclude that the Jewish scriptures would condone such an act. Unfortunately, there is no record of Wilhelm's response to these expert opinions. Goßler, however, was firm in relaying his own opinion to the Kaiser that "the acts of Bernstein cannot be traced back to any existing Jewish rituals."[88]

In the meantime, local prosecutors continued to keep Justice Minister Schelling informed of the progress of the Bernstein investigation. But the further proceedings turned out to be rather anticlimactic. Bernstein's lawyers repeatedly attempted to overturn the original conviction (as well as several new charges) on grounds that Bernstein was insane. The case dragged on for almost two years while medical experts debated Bernstein's mental stability. Eventually, in early 1891, long after the political press had moved on to other matters, the Royal Scientific Deputation gave a final opinion that Bernstein suffered from *paranoia chronica religiosa*. The proceedings were immediately halted and Kaiser Wilhelm II was informed that the criminal prosecution of Max Bernstein had reached an end.[89]

---

[86] For more on Lagarde's anti-Semitism, see Fritz Stern, *The Politics of Cultural Despair* (Berkeley: Univ. of California Press, 1961).

[87] Unfortunately, the original testimony of the three expert witnesses is not present in the case file, only the reflections of Goßler. See GStA PK, I. Rep. 84a Nr. 56464.

[88] Letter from Goßler to Justizminister Dr. von Schelling (Berlin May 4, 1889).GStA PK, I. Rep. 84a Nr. 56464, p. 70.

[89] Letter to Kaiser Wilhelm II (Berlin February 12, 1891). GStA PK, I. Rep. 84a Nr. 56464, p. 115.

The Bernstein case soon vanished from the headlines, but not from public memory. In the future, both the anti-Semitic press and the Conservative press could cite this episode whenever the liberal or Jewish press spoke of ritual murder as a medieval fantasy. Even though the case did not result in a conviction on explicitly ritual grounds or a legal substantiation of Jewish blood murder allegations, it produced a conviction nonetheless. And for the anti-Semitic movement, this verdict breathed new life into the old blood ritual myths.

Korfu (1891)

The ritual murder accusation on the Greek island of Korfu in 1891 caused some of the most serious anti-Semitic violence of all the ritual murder cases in this period. It also caused fierce press debates in Germany thanks primarily to the provocative coverage offered by the ultra-Conservative *Kreuzzeitung.* On April 12, 1891, an eight year old *Jewish* girl, Rubina Sarda, disappeared from a small town on the island. Her anguished father, a local tailor named Vita Sarda, enlisted the help of the Jewish community and the local police force to find her. That night, Rubina's father found her body hidden in a passage near the local synagogue. Her corpse showed multiple wounds and was reported by local doctors to be almost completely drained of blood. As this news spread around the island, a rumor quickly developed that the corpse was not really that of a Jewish girl, but instead a Christian girl named Maria Desilla. According to these stories, young Maria had been kidnapped as a baby by Vita Sarda, who then disguised her as his daughter in order to save her for later use in ritual slaughter. A local anti-Semitic official apparently was convinced by these rumors and focused his investigation on a group of local Jews—including Sarda himself. Although the charges against the Jews were soon dropped, local anger had risen to such a level that an armed mob invaded the Jewish quarter and attacked any Jews they could find. Seven kosher butchers were rounded up for a lynching, and only the intervention of the Greek military prevented the executions from taking place. Even with this military intervention, the anti-Jewish rioting raged on for over a month, and Jews were blockaded in a small Jewish ghetto under guard.[90] Fearing the

[90] *Allgemeine Zeitung des Judenthums* 29 May 1891 #22.

spread of violence to the Greek mainland or a repeat of the Russian pogroms of 1881, several European countries demanded that the Greek leader Delyannis tighten his control of the situation and even sent warships to the area to pressure him into acting.[91]

The extended rioting on Korfu and the foreign intervention in the affair brought international publicity to the accusations of ritual murder. These circumstances also led to the usual polemics in Germany between the anti-Semitic, Conservative, and Catholic press on the one side and the liberal and Jewish press on the other. The polemics followed the familiar pattern of the other ritual murder allegations, but this time the most vicious exchanges about the Korfu case came to be centered on one ultra-Conservative newspaper—the *Kreuzzeitung*. According to this newspaper, the Greek Jews had incited the riots in order to hurt the reputation of Greek Prime Minister Delyannis—and the local Jews had called for international intervention in the hope of toppling his government. The *Kreuzzeitung* also claimed that the proof of a Jewish ritual murder was overwhelming, and that the delay in the trial proceedings was merely an attempt by "international Jewry . . . to hide from public opinion the crimes committed on that island by their fanatical tribesmen and fellow-believers."[92]

Without its own correspondent in Greece, however, the *Kreuzzeitung* was dependent on other newspapers for updates on the Korfu investigation. On May 14, 1891, for example, it printed an anonymous telegram that claimed that Minister Delyannis had told a group of European ambassadors that the investigation "has found proof that lends credibility to the supposition of the Christian populace about a ritual murder."[93] The paper also reprinted the reports of the anti-Semitic *Staatsbürgerzeitung*, whose correspondent, Georgios Zerros, claimed to be a member of the Greek parliament who had inside information on the case. Zerros wrote that he had absolute proof that the murdered girl actually was a Christian girl who had been

[91] This according to the ultra-Conservative *Kreuzzeitung*, which claimed that Minister Delyannis had two choices. Either he could suppress the accusations against the Jews and face a popular revolt, or stand up against international Jewry and prosecute those responsible. In either case, the *Kreuzzeitung* claimed, he would probably forced out of office by popular or international pressure. *Kreuzzeitung* 14 May 1891 #220 Abend.

[92] *Kreuzzeitung* 14 May 1891 #220 Abend.

[93] Ibid.

kidnapped as a baby. Allegedly there were several nuns ready to testify to the girl's Christian identity, and the birth certificate bearing the girl's Jewish name had already been proven to be a forgery. Also, Zerros reported that a watchman named Charlampis actually saw three Jews carrying a large sack late on the night of the murder. Based on this evidence, the *Kreuzzeitung* confidently claimed that the proof against the accused Jews was irrefutable.[94]

It was not long, however, before the *Kreuzzeitung*'s reports on the Korfu case came under fierce attack from both liberal and Jewish newspapers. Through its own correspondent in Korfu, the liberal *Berliner Tageblatt* asserted that there was no Greek parliamentarian by the name of Zerros, and although there was one named Zervos, he denied being the source for the *Kreuzzeitung* articles. The *Tageblatt* further claimed that the so-called key witness to the crime, the watchman Charlampis, was a known criminal who had been in jail at the time of the incident, and was thus lying about his involvement in the case. The *Tageblatt* also happily printed a statement from Minister Delyannis that condemned the *Kreuzzeitung* articles and denied there was evidence for a charge of ritual murder. Thus, the *Tageblatt* claimed, the coverage of the trial in the *Kreuzzeitung* was fraudulent and dishonest, and the entire Conservative and anti-Semitic press had exposed itself as nothing less than a "widespread band of swindlers" with the *Kreuzzeitung* at its head.[95]

These attacks on the *Kreuzzeitung* were repeated throughout the liberal and Jewish press. The *Allgemeine Zeitung des Judenthums*, for example, criticized the "decay in morality" of "that newspaper which still dares to place a religious symbol on its front page..."[96] The *Jüdische Presse* also expressed its contempt for the newspaper that "always shamelessly publishes the most brutal and most obvious lies, despite the fact that they are fervently refuted by the most qualified sources."[97]

---

[94] This evidence was also repeated by conservative Catholic newspapers like the *Deutsche Reichszeitung* (Bonn), which in a correspondence from "a friend" in Korfu, confirmed much of the *Kreuzzeitung* reports. In fact, the correspondent claimed that "anti-Jewish riots" were really a misnomer since more Christians were killed in the suppression of the riots than Jews in the riots themselves. *Deutsche Reichszeitung* 2 June 1891 #149.

[95] *Berliner Tageblatt* 22 May 1891 #251 Morgen.

[96] *Allgemeine Zeitung des Judenthums* 22 Mai 1891 #21 Beilage.

[97] *Jüdische Presse* 4 June 1891 #23.

Angered by these insults and challenges, the *Kreuzzeitung* editors responded to this criticism with even more aggressive articles on the case. Now writing under headlines like "On the Concealment of the Jewish Crime in Korfu", the paper continued to claim that there was overwhelming evidence against the Jewish defendants and also irrefutable proof that the girl had been Christian. The *Kreuzzeitung* explained that the reports from Zerros had simply been the result of a misunderstanding, and blasted the "*Judenpresse*" for daring to challenge the paper's credibility. The Korfu case had now become a matter of honor for the *Kreuzzeitung*, and the paper's editors did everything possible to attack the *Berliner Tageblatt* and to defend their own position on the charges of ritual murder.[98]

The *Kreuzzeitung*'s hopes for a sensational trial in Korfu never materialized. The presiding judge ended his investigation against the local Jews and issued a list of nine possible murder scenarios. Because of all the rumors and false witnesses, the judge argued that the truth about the murder would probably never be discovered. Several months later, the Greek authorities reportedly opened the investigation again, this time against several local Christian residents, many of whom had previous criminal records.[99] Faced with the collapse of the ritual murder allegations, the *Kreuzzeitung* finally began to back away from its claims that overwhelming evidence supported a charge of ritual murder. As in the other ritual murder cases, however, the Conservative and Catholic press continued to use the case to attack the German Jews and their liberal allies. As Adolf Stöcker's *Deutsche Evangelische Kirchenzeitung* claimed, even if the ritual allegations were untrue, they were "doubtless reflections of what the Jews in many regions actually do. They suck out the blood of prosperity from the populace and take away their spiritual life (*geistiges Leben*)."[100] Once again, it was claimed, international Jewry had intervened to assure that Jewish defendants would never come to justice.

---

[98] The *Kreuzzeitung* now claimed that as the "official Berlin organ of the *Alliance Israélite*," the *Berliner Tageblatt* and its correspondent Hans Barth "were the chief conspirators in a system of falsification." See *Kreuzzeitung* 30 May 1891 #245 Morgen; 5 June 1891 #255 Morgen.

[99] *Jüdische Presse* 16 October 1891 #42–43. In a later parliament speech, Heinrich Rickert mentioned that these Christian defendants had been convicted of the crime. Other conservative sources disputed that a conviction occurred. See *Jüdische Presse* 11 February 1892 #6. See also the speech by Freiherr von Wackerbarth in the *Preußischen Abgeordnetenhaus* on March 19, 1892.

[100] *Deutsche Evangelische Kirchenzeitung* 29 August 1891 #35.

Xanten (1892)

The debacle of Korfu did not mean an end to the use of ritual murder accusations as propaganda. On the contrary, the Korfu Affair was merely a prelude to what was perhaps the most significant ritual murder incident in German history: the Xanten Affair. On June 29, 1891, only days after the Korfu incident had begun to fade from the headlines, five-year old Johann Hegemann was found murdered in the small town of Xanten in Westphalia.[101] Hegemann, the son of a local cabinetmaker, had been reported missing by his family that morning, and his body was found several hours later in the barn of a local city councilman named Wilhelm Küppers. The boy had bled to death, and a local doctor, Joseph Steiner, reported that his throat had been cut almost to the spine.[102] Several local witnesses, including a laborer named Hermann Mölders and several young children, immediately came forward to say that they had seen the wife of the local Jewish butcher, Wolf Buschhoff, lead the boy into her home earlier in the day. This, apparently, was the last time young Johann had been seen alive. Because the Buschhoffs lived next door to where the body was found, and because of rapidly spreading rumors that the case was a Jewish ritual murder, local pressure mounted for an arrest of the Buschhoff family. In early July 1891, sporadic violence erupted in and around Xanten. Jewish citizens were attacked, and their houses and businesses were vandalized. The house of Wolf Buschhoff had the word "Mörderhaus" painted on it.[103]

---

[101] Xanten am Niederrhein is a small town near the Dutch border. At the time of the trial, it had a population of about 4000. Groß, *Ritualmordbeschuldigungen*, 51. Ritual murder accusations were not new to this region. In fact, Stephan Rohrbacher and Michael Schmidt discuss cases of ritual murder accusations in 1808, 1819, 1834, 1835, 1840, 1862—all of which occurred within a 40 kilometer radius northwest of Cologne. Rohrbacher and Schmidt use this pattern to argue that it was not social or economic tensions that served as the primary motive for such accusations, but instead a local and regional tradition of ritual murder stereotypes. See Stephan Rohrbacher and Michael Schmidt, *Judenbilder: Kulturgeschichte antijüdischer Mythen und antisemitischer Vorurteile* (Reinbek bei Hamburg: Rowohlt Taschenbuch Verlag, 1991). Hillel Kieval, on the other hand, describes a relatively stable Jewish-Gentile social equilibrium both in Xanten and in many other locations where ritual murder accusations would eventually emerge. See Hillel J. Kieval, "The Importance of Place: Comparative Aspects of the Ritual Murder Trial in Modern Central Europe," in *Comparing Jewish Societies*, ed. Todd M. Endelman (Ann Arbor: 1997), 135–165.

[102] As in Tisza-Eszlar and Skurcz, local doctors played an important role in giving credibility to initial popular suspicions of ritual murder. See Kölling, "Blutige Illusionen," 361–364.

[103] Groß, *Ritualmordbeschuldigungen*, 55–56.

Fearful of the growing unrest, local Jewish community leaders immediately brought the case to the attention of government officials in Berlin. The leader of the local Jewish community even offered to pay the cost for a special investigator to come to Xanten to take over the case.[104] The local prosecutor in the nearby town of Kleve, named Baumgard, sympathized with the fears of the Jewish community, and recommended to Justice Minister von Schelling that investigators from outside the region be sent in to help since "local police officials may not be up to the task".[105] Baumgard described the population of Xanten as "very agitated and singularly focused on the delusion that this is a case of Jewish ritual murder." He also complained to the Justice Minister that "so far, *all* the significant witness testimony has been directed against the Jews, namely against the Buschhoff family, and has proven to be fabricated and untrue, and I must confess that in my long years of criminal practice, I have never experienced something so sad and disturbing."[106] In response to this information, the Police Commissar of the nearby town of Crefeld, named Verhülsdonk, was immediately sent to assist the local Xanten officials in their investigation.

In the following months, Baumgard attempted to calm public outrage and reduce anti-Jewish sentiment by publishing an anonymous story in a local newspaper which claimed that investigators doubted the guilt of Buschhoff and believed there was no evidence of a ritual murder. Unfortunately, the editor of this newspaper, Bresser, agreed to publish only a partial version of the statement since he still believed that this was a case of ritual murder.[107] Baumgard then asked Justice Minister von Schelling if he could print an official statement about the investigation. But this request was refused because "instead of calming emotions, it would more likely arouse anger and incite protest."[108]

In September of 1891, almost three months after the murder, a special investigator named Criminal Commissar Wolff was finally sent from Berlin to supervise the case. As word spread that the Jewish

---

[104] Letter from Erste Staatsanwalt Baumgard to Justizminister Dr. von Schelling (Cleve Juli 7, 1891). GStA PK, I. HA Rep. 84a Justizministerium, Nr. 57459, p. 3.

[105] Ibid.

[106] Letter from Erste Staatsanwalt Baumgard to Justizminister Dr. von Schelling (Cleve Juli 16, 1891). GStA PK, I. HA Rep. 84a Justizministerium, Nr. 57459, p. 10.

[107] Groß, *Ritualmordbeschuldigungen*, 58–59.

[108] Groß, *Ritualmordbeschuldigungen*, 59.

community had offered to pay for outside government investigators, several anti-Semitic newspapers began to suggest that this case would have a similar outcome to the Neustettin and Skurcz trials, where Criminal Commissar Höft was allegedly sent from Berlin to secure an acquittal. However, after interviews with local residents and visits to the scene of the crime, Criminal Commissar Wolff unexpectedly concluded that there was significant evidence that Wolf Buschhoff had indeed committed murder. Although Criminal Commissar Wolff doubted whether such a crime had been based on Jewish rituals, he nonetheless concluded that the witness evidence was substantial enough to warrant an arrest. Baumgard, while not convinced of Buschhoff's guilt, agreed that an arrest might be the prudent course despite the potential risk of adding to local anti-Semitic feeling. As Baumgard explained in a letter to the Justice Minister: "Even if there is a fear that a criminal prosecution of Buschhoff—on completely different grounds—will give nourishment to the legend of ritual murder, I am still of the opinion that the path of justice should not be impeded for this reason alone."[109] Thus, in October of 1891, police officials took Wolf Buschhoff, his wife Sibilla, and their daughter Hermine into "investigative custody."[110]

To many observers, the formal filing of murder charges against the Jewish couple seemed imminent. But then, on Christmas Eve 1891, without public comment or justification, Prosecutor Baumgard ordered that the Buschhoff family be released from jail. What had happened? After the arrest of the Buschhoff family, the case had passed from the jurisdiction of Commissar Wolff to the local investigating judge, *Untersuchungsrichter* Brixius. After interviewing with the same witnesses who had presented evidence before Wolff, speaking with the accused, and visiting the crime scene, Brixius became convinced that the murder charges were unfounded. Brixius quickly petitioned Baumgard for permission to free the Buschhoff family.[111] The quick decision to release the accused did not sit well with Justice Minister Schelling, however, who urged an immediate re-arrest of the Buschhoffs if any new evidence appeared.[112]

---

[109] Letter from Erste Staasanwalt Baumgard to Justizminister Dr. von Schelling (Cleve October 7, 1891) GStA PK, I. HA Rep. 84a Justizministerium, Nr. 57459, p. 33.

[110] Rohrbacher and Schmidt, *Judenbilder*, 337.

[111] Groß, *Ritualmordbeschuldigungen*, 61–2.

[112] Ibid., 62.

The reaction to the Buschhoffs' release was immediate and widespread. After sporadic violence in the region, Buschhoff and his family fled to Cologne.[113] Anti-Semitic journalists once more alleged that various public officials were actively aiding the Jewish defendants and interfering in the administration of justice. These allegations were accompanied by frequent comparisons with the Skurcz incident, where a government official was also alleged to have interfered in a case and freed Jewish defendants.[114] The *Staatsbürger Zeitung*, for example, printed an angry front page article called "Who Then is Guilty?" which examined the ritual murder allegations in Tisza-Eszlar, Skurcz, Lutscha, and Korfu and described the "miscarriages of justice" that had allowed guilty Jewish defendants to go free in each case.[115] While this newspaper's editors were careful not to slander German justice officials directly, they demanded that these officials reinstate the charges against the Buschhoff family.

The anti-Semitic *Neue Deutsche Zeitung*, however, went even further in its commentary on the investigation. In a long series of articles on the case, this newspaper suggested that after finding irrefutable evidence of the Buschhoffs' guilt, Royal Criminal Commissar Wolff was forced from the case by the local prosecutor Baumgard, who was friendlier to the Jews. The paper then accused Baumgard of working for Jewish interests, intimidating witnesses, and mishandling the investigation. Finally, the *Neue Deutsche Zeitung* reviewed the "overwhelming" evidence against Buschhoff and demanded that Justice Minister von Schelling and Minister of the Interior Herrfurth, both of whom had in recent times been accused of being pawns of the Jews, now prove themselves to be unbiased by intervening in the affair and re-arresting the Buschhoffs.[116] The articles in the *Neue*

[113] Rohrbacher and Schmidt, *Judenbilder*, 337.

[114] *Der Fall Buschhoff. Die Untersuchung über den Xantener Knabenmord. Von einem Eingeweihten* (Berlin: Verlag der Vaterländischen Verlags-Anstalt, 1892). The *Staatsbürgerzeitung* made an even more direct comparison with Skurcz. They alleged that the Jewish Community of Xanten paid 700 Marks to get Commissar Höft, the investigator who "helped to dismiss" the charges in Neustettin and Skurcz, sent from Berlin. Unfortunately for the Jews, the paper claimed, they got Commissar Wolff instead. See *Staatsbürgerzeitung* 20 January 1892 #32 Abend.

[115] *Staatsbürgerzeitung* 10 January 1892 #15A Morgen. In addition to comparisons with the Skurcz case, comparisons were also made between this case and a libel case against Gerson von Bleichröder that was a hot political topic at this time. In the Bleichröder case, police officials were publicly accused of aiding von Bleichröder in covering up evidence that he had previously committed perjury.

[116] Reprinted in *Staatsbürgerzeitung* 14 January 1892 #21B; see also *Der Fall Buschhoff*, 7–16.

Deutsche Zeitung were so critical of the conduct of government officials that libel charges were filed by government prosecutors against the paper's publisher, Erwin Bauer.[117]

The articles in the *Neue Deutsche Zeitung* were reprinted in several national newspapers, including the *Kreuzzeitung* and the *Germania*. The *Germania*, however, responded to the articles rather coolly, writing that "we no more want to claim the case is a ritual murder than we would want to accuse any one person of committing the crime. What we demand is only a *clarification* of this affair, a *prompt* clarification, in the interest of calming the public." Their advocacy of an objective analysis, however, did not stop the paper from remarking that "powers seem to be at play in this affair, which the Prussian justice system must confront in order to maintain its unimpeachability and decisiveness."[118]

The reaction of the ultra-Conservative *Kreuzzeitung* was less noncommittal. Still angry over the debacle of the Korfu affair, the *Kreuzzeitung* repeated many of the accusations of the *Neue Deutsche Zeitung* and then demanded an investigation by the Justice Minister:

> Our German people have a right to demand that full clarity be brought by officials to this shameful murder... As long as this does not happen, no one can blame us if we place ourselves on the side of popular opinion and believe in the guilt of Buschhoff, just as we still consider the perpetration of a ritual murder in Korfu as a proven fact.[119]

The public clamor over the case reached its height when the Progressive deputy Heinrich Rickert gave a long speech on the issue in the Prussian Assembly (*Preußische Abgeordnetenhaus*) on January 9, 1892.[120]

---

[117] Charges were also brought against many newspapers for reprinting articles that were critical of the prosecutors. These libel cases often became minor sensational episodes in their own right, and offered free publicity to the editors of anti-Semitic newspapers. See *Reichsbote* 14 April 1893 for detailed treatment of the Bauer trial, which included testimony of witnesses from the actual Xanten case.

[118] Quoted in *Der Fall Buschhoff*, 16–17. This brochure was published by Heinrich Oberwinder.

[119] Quoted in Ibid., 18.

[120] Parliamentary debates on ritual murder accusations were also common in Austria-Hungary, especially in 1883 (Tisza-Eszlar), 1890, and 1899 (Polna). Because of the tremendous growth of the Austrian Christian-Social Party under the leadership of Lueger, the later parliamentary debates were more heated and involved many more delegates who gave credence to ritual murder allegations. See Albert Lichtblau, "Die Debatten über die Ritualmordbeschuldigungen im österreichischen Abgeordnetenhaus am Ende des 19. Jahrhunderts," in *Die Legende vom Ritualmord: Zur Geschichte der Blutbeschuldigung gegen Juden*, ed. Rainer Erb (Berlin: Metropol-Verlag, 1993), 267–292.

In this speech, Rickert denounced the anti-Semitic press, the *Kreuzzeitung*, and especially Adolf Stöcker for spreading religious hatred and attempting to manipulate the court system for propaganda purposes. Stöcker immediately replied that it was not he, but the liberal press that had attempted to make a mockery of the justice system. While claiming that he had never asserted that "ritual murder" existed in the Jewish religion, Stöcker insisted that there was overwhelming evidence that Jews often had killed Christians out of fanaticism or superstition:

> I remind Mr. Rickert of the Bernstein case, which was tried in Breslau. There it was clearly proven that an apprentice Rabbi did in fact draw blood several times from Christian children, and as he was being interrogated he said that he had done it to soothe religious concerns . . . Here is a case along the same lines as the Buschhoff case.[121]

Stöcker proceeded to review the state of the Xanten investigation, and he repeated accusations from the latest issues of the *Neue Deutsche Zeitung*, including claims that a high Jewish religious official was present at the search and the interrogation of witnesses.[122] In addition to commenting on the Xanten case itself, Stöcker went on to list the names of several other ritual murder trials and suggest that it was strange that in each case the "real" culprit was never found. Stöcker also cited other contemporary trials related to the Jews, in which the government had chosen to file charges only after the exertion of public pressure in public meetings, protests, and petitions.[123]

While Stöcker's comments were framed with faint praise for the German justice system, they were a clear attack on the Justice Ministry for its bias toward Jews. Minister of Justice Schelling offered an immediate response that was deeply critical of Stöcker, and which

---

[121] Printed in *Jüdische Presse* 11 February 1892 #6.

[122] *Untersuchungsrichter* Brixius had indeed invited the leader of the local Jewish community, a merchant named Oster, to watch the investigation of the scene since Buschhoff, who had the right to attend, was in Cologne at the time. Brixius believed this act was completely justified.

[123] Specifically, Stöcker mentions the Ahlwardt-Bleichröder case, as well as the cases of Liebmann and Morris de Jonge. See Chapter 6 for a discussion of these cases. (See also *Staatsbürgerzeitung* 9 February 1892 #65A for comparisons with other cases.) Such comparisons were a common part of anti-Semitic rhetoric during this time, which suggested that the proceedings in such cases were creating a crisis of public confidence in the justice system (*Erschütterung des Rechtsbewustseins*). This particular parliamentary *Judendebatte* continued sporadically over several weeks, and anti-Semitic politicians often compared the Xanten case to other sensational cases involving anti-Semitism that were still underway.

defended the objectivity and sanctity of the German justice system.[124] But Schelling's speech did contain an official announcement on the Xanten case that boosted the spirits of the anti-Semites: after the appearance of new evidence in the case (a knife that matched the boy's wounds), both Wolf Buschhoff and his wife had once again been taken into investigative custody.

In the light of this latest news, the anti-Semitic and right-wing Conservative press ignored the treatment of Stöcker by the Justice Minister and claimed that the latest *Judendebatte* was a complete victory. The *Staatsbürgerzeitung*, for example, gave a detailed report on a speech given by the anti-Semitic agitator Hermann Ahlwardt entitled "The Victory of Anti-Semitism in the Prussian Assembly" and added that the interpellation by Rickert had "done the anti-Semitic cause a great service."[125] The response by the liberal and Jewish press was, of course, quite the opposite. The *Jüdische Presse*, for example, congratulated Rickert for being a champion of truth and justice, and then discussed case by case the ritual murder incidents that Stöcker had mentioned in his parliamentary speech.[126] The paper argued that Stöcker had distorted the details of each incident to suggest both Jewish guilt and government interference.

While the *Kreuzzeitung* and the Stöckerite papers remained critical of government handling of the Xanten case and aggressive in their attacks on Jews and liberals, the reaction in Conservative circles was far from unified. By this time, the great split between ultra-Conservative

[124] Schelling vigorously defended the independence and objectivity of the judiciary and the legal process: "There is therefore no reason for any kind of anxiety in the public perception of law and order (*öffentlichen Rechtsbewußtseins*); the verdict, whatever it may be, will be decided by Prussian judges with the same impartiality and lack of bias which has been an innate trait of theirs for centuries." Report from *Haus der Abgeordneten* February 9, 1892 in GStA PK, I. HA Rep. 84a Nr. 57459, pp. 177 ff. A week later, Schelling ordered prosecutors to begin legal actions against anyone who went too far in criticizing justice officials. GStA PK, I. HA Rep. 84a Nr. 57459, p. 226a.

[125] *Staatsbürgerzeitung* 10 February 1892 #68 Abend; *Staatsbürgerzeitung* 11 February 1892 #69A Morgen.

[126] *Jüdische Presse* 18 February 1892 #7. After the speech of Justice Minister Schelling, several liberal speakers, including the attorney August Munckel, defended Minister Schelling and expressed their gratitude that the pressure of anti-Semitic politicians and public rallies had little to no effect on the progress of the case. They said this despite the suspicion that Schelling had pushed for the re-arrest of Buschhoff, in part, to counter rhetoric that the justice system was too friendly to Jews. Groß, *Ritualmordbeschuldigungen*, 152–153, 157.

and moderate Conservative politicians had become almost irreconcilable.[127] While the moderate leader, Count von Helldorf-Bedra, remained loyal to the government and the old electoral alliance with the National Liberals, the ultra-Conservative leader, Wilhelm von Hammerstein, was intent on destroying the old *Kartell* and was determined to use anti-Semitism to attack the liberal parties. Thus, after the *Judendebatte* in the Prussian Assembly, the moderate *Conservative Wochenblatt* threw its support behind the Justice Minister, condemned the anti-Semitic newspapers, and criticized the *Kreuzzeitung* and Stöckerite papers that reprinted their accusations.

The Center Party seemed at first to be equally split on how to react to the anti-Semitic furor. The *Germania*, which, while condemning anti-Semitic agitators, had often lent its tacit approval to charges of ritual murder against Jews, took a similar attitude to the Xanten case. But more moderate Catholic papers like the *Kölnische Völkszeitung* would normally be expected to condemn the excesses of anti-Semitic attacks. The conflict over the *Volksschulgesetz* in early 1892, however, led to a significant change in political alliances and an increase in anti-Semitic rhetoric throughout the Catholic press. In early April 1892, a few months after the *Judendebatte*, the *Kölnische Volkszeitung* printed a list of "Seven Theses" on the Jewish Question. While beginning with a condemnation of the anti-Semitic parties, these theses then went on to explicitly adopt many of their demands and much of their vicious anti-Jewish rhetoric. These "theses" were quickly attacked in the liberal and Jewish press, which criticized the growing anti-Semitism of moderate Catholic newspapers.[128] Thus, political conflicts in the early 1890s helped to create the perfect atmosphere for the journalistic exploitation of the Xanten trial.

Many of the prosecutors, meanwhile, were still not convinced that the charges against Buschhoff could, or should, be sustained. Brixius, the investigative judge who had previously ordered the release of the

---

[127] See Chapter 6 for a further discussion of this conflict.

[128] The "theses" of the *Kölnische Volkszeitung* were actually sent in by a reader who claimed to be tired of the paper's weak position on anti-Semitism. The *Volkszeitung* accepted many of the reader's criticisms of the Jews, but rejected any mention of disenfranchisement or restriction of Jewish rights. Thus, the moderate Catholic journalists of the *Volkszeitung* and moderate Catholic politicians like Lieber tried to take advantage of the growth of popular anti-Semitism in the Catholic readership to focus resentment on the liberal parties, while at the same time making sure public anger was channeled away from the explicitly anti-Semitic parties.

accused, had vigorously resisted any reopening of the case. However, Brixius was removed from his position after it was publicly reported that his son-in-law was working as a lawyer for the defendants. Although Brixius claimed that his son-in-law's participation in the case came against his advice and did not have any effect on his own actions, Justice Minister Schelling demanded his removal.[129] Meanwhile, Prosecutor Baumgard still remained highly skeptical of the charges, and in a letter to Schelling he dismissed the earlier conclusions of Criminal Commissar Wolff:

> The alleged findings of Criminal Commissar Wolff need to be viewed with the greatest caution; this official seems to have acted in a biased and superficial manner . . . If Criminal Commissar Wolff has repeatedly claimed that Buschhoff's testimony of his whereabouts on June 29th of last year has been 'demolished, annihilated, and completely disproved', these accusations are not at all supported by the latest investigations, which in many respects contradict Wolff's conclusions.[130]

Baumgard was equally suspicious of the medical expert who had provided the new evidence that led to Buschhoff's re-arrest. The district medical officer (*Kreisphysikus*), Dr. Bauer, had conducted the autopsy on the boy and had concluded that a knife found at Buschhoff's house seemed especially likely to have caused the boy's wounds. But when Baumgard consulted other medical experts, they all concluded that there was no reason to believe this knife was the likely murder weapon. Although Baumgard did believe a trial might be the best way to resolve the affair, he warned the Justice Minister that it might be best to first allow public pressure to subside: ". . . it seems espe-

---

[129] Letter from Justice Minister von Schelling to the Präsident des königlischen Oberlandesgericht Köln (January 28, 1892) GStA PK, I. HA Rep. 84a Nr. 57459, p. 136. Johannes Groß suggests that it was much more than a simple conflict of interest that resulted in the removal of Brixius. Schelling and Brixius had clashed since the start of 1892 about whether Buschhoff should be taken into custody again. Because Schelling controlled prosecutors and not judges, however, he could not directly order Brixius to reopen the case. Instead, Schelling used his influence to provoke a court hearing on the matter of judicial bias, and at this hearing a panel of judges officially removed Brixius from the case. Groß suggests that Schelling worked so hard to dismiss Brixius and re-open the case because of the pressure exerted by the press and public opinion. He wanted to counter frequent claims by Conservative, Catholic, and Anti-Semitic politicians that the justice system was under the control of Jews. See Groß, *Ritualmordbeschuldigungen*, 64–69.

[130] Letter from Erste Staasanwalt Baumgard to Justizminister Dr. von Schelling (Cleve March 17, 1892) GStA PK, I. HA Rep. 84a Justizministerium, Nr. 57459, pp. 263–264.

cially important not to rush this important and difficult case, but instead to let a public trial begin only when the proceedings can assure that the possibility of convicting an innocent man is precluded."[131]

Baumgard's hope that the public furor about the Xanten case would diminish over time was soon dashed. In the spring of 1892, the spirited debate about the Xanten case continued in the press as new "revelations" emerged from the investigation. In addition, the trial of the anti-Semitic demagogue Hermann Ahlwardt in February, Ahlwardt's arrest for his sensational *Judenflinten* brochure, and several other highly-publicized trials involving Jewish defendants all helped to focus public attention on the "Jewish Question" in the weeks before the start of the Xanten trial.[132] By the time the trial against Wolf Buschhoff finally opened on July 4, 1892 in the small town of Kleve, the entire nation was transfixed.[133]

Like previous ritual murder trials, this case was plagued by interruptions, angry confrontations between witnesses, sensational new revelations, and blatant pandering to the public by both witnesses and lawyers. The witness testimony provided the biggest spectacle of all. The witness list against Buschhoff was comprised mostly of townspeople who claimed to have seen Buschhoff behaving strangely on the day of the murder. But other "witnesses" continued to come forward, even during the trial itself, to testify to having heard Buschhoff or other local Jews whispering to each other about their own guilt. One woman, for example, suddenly remembered seeing a suspicious Jew entering Buschhoff's house on the day of the murder with a black bag, while another claimed to have walked under Wolf Buschhoff's window a week after the murder and heard him telling his son that they would certainly get away with the crime. Heinrich Junkermann, a former butcher, claimed to have been convinced that Buschhoff was the killer because of the early autopsy report of Dr. Steiner and Buschhoff's strange behavior in the days after the

[131] Letter from Erste Staasanwalt Baumgard to Justizminister Dr. von Schelling (Cleve February 15, 1892) GStA PK, I. HA Rep. 84a Nr. 57459, p. 218.

[132] See Chapter 6 for more on Ahlwardt and *Judenflinten*.

[133] The court found sufficient evidence to open the trial against Wolf Buschhoff, but rejected the prosecution's case against his wife and daughter because of a lack of evidence. A prosecution appeal of this dismissal was also rejected. Groß, *Ritualmordbeschuldigungen*, 74. The defense, meanwhile, had petitioned to move case further away from Xanten to Köln or Düsseldorf. This petition was also rejected. Telegram from the Oberstaatsanwalt GStA PK, I. HA Rep. 84a Nr. 57460, p. 88.

crime. He claimed his suspicions were proven when both Jewish friends of Buschhoff and other Jewish outsiders threatened him with harm if he testified.[134]

In addition to these hearsay witnesses, however, there were also witnesses who claimed to have first hand knowledge of the case. Hermann Mölders testified that he saw the young Hegemann being pulled into the Buschhoff's home at about 10 AM, and a boy named Stephan Kernder claimed to have been playing with the boy when Mrs. Buschhoff lured him into her house with the promise of cherries. But the most damaging testimony came from a neighbor named Johann Mallmann, who claimed to have seen Wolf Buschhoff's daughter carrying a heavy sack toward the barn on the morning of the murder. Mallmann's testimony was supported by the fact that a sack had been found in Buschhoff's house with what appeared to be blood stains inside it.[135]

The testimony of many of these witnesses was immediately attacked by both defense attorneys and the prosecutors. The Chief Prosecutor (*Oberstaatsanwalt*) Hamm, for example, suggested that Mallmann was an avowed anti-Semite who had spread anti-Buschhoff and anti-Semitic flyers in the months before the trial. In addition, Hamm pointed out that Mallmann had earlier testified to only having heard and not seen someone in the garden; thus, Hamm suggested that his "improved memory" made him a suspicious witness.[136]

There were also a few witnesses who provided strong exculpatory testimony for Buschhoff. A neighbor named Wilhelm Ullenboom, for instance, testified that he had been with Buschhoff for a substantial part of the day in question, and that for the rest of the day Buschhoff had been out with friends. Ullenboom also claimed that Mrs. Buschhoff had spent most of the day in bed recovering from a severe headache. These exculpatory witnesses were supported by many of the local officials who were involved in the investigation. The investigative

[134] *Kreuzzeitung* 8 July 1892 Morgen in GStA PK, I. HA Rep. 84a Nr. 57463, p. 10; Groß, *Ritualmordbeschuldigungen*, 78–79.

[135] *Kreuzzeitung* 5 July 1892; 7 July 1892; 9 July 1892 Morgen in GStA PK, I. HA Rep. 84a Nr. 57463, pp. 3–12.

[136] This earlier deposition was taken as part of a libel charge filed against Mallmann by Buschhoff for his anti-Semitic activities. Hamm suggested that the change in testimony was a clear case of perjury, but the judge declined to press the matter further.

judge, Brixius, for example, who had worked on the case in its early stages, testified that he felt both the charge of ritual murder and the general suspicion against Buschhoff were a popular fiction. As far as he was concerned, Buschhoff was not guilty and should never have been brought to trial.[137] However, as soon as a witness came forward to testify in support of Buschhoff, a host of additional witnesses would come forward and claim to have information that would discredit him. Ullenboom, for example, was called a liar and a thief by several townspeople, and even the mayor of Xanten came forward to question his credibility. Brixius, of course, was criticized as untrustworthy since his son-in-law was one of Buschhoff's defense attorneys.

In addition to ordinary witness testimony, seven different medical or chemical experts testified on the crime scene and the autopsy results. In addition to Dr. Steiner, the first doctor at the crime scene, and Dr. Bauer, who had conducted the autopsy, several medical experts from the *Medizinalkollegium* in Koblenz were also brought in as expert witnesses. The testimony of the new experts reversed many of the conclusions reported by local physicians immediately after the incident, and contradicted the version of events that had been reported in anti-Semitic newspapers. For example, Dr. Steiner had claimed that the lack of blood at the crime scene or in the boy's body suggested one of two conclusions: either the boy had been murdered elsewhere or blood had been collected by the attacker. But medical experts at the trial claimed that the blood could have easily evaporated or soaked into the ground; thus, they insisted that the child was murdered where he was found, and declared that there was no evidence of missing blood. This testimony not only ruled out ritual murder, but also suggested Mallmann's testimony about Buschhoff's daughter and the sack was invented.[138]

The same medical experts testified that the killer's method was completely inconsistent with a kosher slaughter since it violated many important religious rules. As for the "bloody" sack found in Buschhoff's

---

137 *Antisemitische Correspondenz* 11 Sept. 1892 #213 in BAK *ZSg. 113* Sammlung Fechenbach #23.

138 Dr. Steiner, who had originally argued that the boy had been murdered in another location and his body transported to the barn, and who had given a letter to the anti-Semitic *Neue Deutsche Zeitung* that reaffirmed these conclusions, decided to change his mind after the testimony of the other experts.

house, the doctors testified that although tests could not be completely conclusive, the suspicious stains suggested residue from the smoking of meat and were probably not comprised of blood. Finally, the "momentous" evidence that had served as the justification for reviving charges against Buschhoff, a knife owned by Buschhoff that supposedly matched the boy's wounds, was also dismissed by the experts. Almost all of the experts now agreed that Buschhoff's knife was no more suited to the crime than any other knife.[139] By the end of the expert testimony, almost all of the "evidence" of ritual murder had been completely debunked.

The expert medical testimony was followed by expert testimony on the Jewish religion. In this case, a veteran of such trial testimony, Professor Nöldecke from the University of Straßburg, claimed that the blood ritual was not a part of the Jewish religion and that Jewish law would forbid such an act.[140] Nöldecke also ridiculed anti-Semitic "scholars" such as August Rohling, who used mistranslations and outright falsification to incite public anger against the Jews. Since the prosecution in this case had no desire to consult any of these anti-Semitic scholars, Nöldecke's testimony went unchallenged. The court did, however, receive a flood of letters from laymen claiming to have knowledge of Jewish blood rituals, but most of these letters were disregarded by the prosecution. In fact, the prosecutors even read some of these letters in open court and offered sarcastic comments about their reliability.

Most newspapers refrained from direct comments about the case during the trial proceedings, and offered only a set of edited trial transcripts that were provided by a shared correspondent. But these trial reports were often far from objective—especially in the anti-Semitic press. In anti-Semitic newspapers the reporting of testimony was often selective, and statements that seemed especially damning to Buschhoff were often highlighted with special character spacing.[141] The correspondent of the anti-Semitic *Staatsbürgerzeitung* even went as far as to add his own personal comments on the testimony, includ-

[139] Even Dr. Bauer, who first identified the knife as especially suited to the boy's wounds, eventually bowed to the superior expertise of the other physicians.

[140] Professor Nöldecke had previously testified in the infamous Rohling-Bloch trial in Austria.

[141] The liberal press was not immune from such methods. See the *Kölnische Volkszeitung* 15 July 1892 #386 Zweites Blatt (Abend) for a criticism of such methods in the "philosemitic Berlin press."

ing disparaging comments about many of the witnesses, defense attorneys, and Jewish members of the audience. While this correspondent repeatedly asserted his own objectivity, by the end of the trial he was much less reserved in rendering opinions about the case. When, on the last day of the trial, the entire court moved to Xanten to view the crime scene, the correspondent commented that "we can only say that the visit itself gave observers the impression that the facts alleged in the charges against Buschhoff are in no way impossible; rather, the credibility of the charges has increased dramatically."[142]

Some anti-Semitic newspapers may have even tried to influence the proceedings themselves—such as when copies of the anti-Semitic *Westfälische Reform* were mysteriously sent to the jurors. In any case, the trial provided exciting material for the anti-Semitic press, and even as closing statements were being offered, the *Staatsbürgerzeitung* still was busy reporting that new witnesses had come forward and new revelations were imminent. The paper almost gleefully ended one article with the words: "Who knows what else lies ahead!"[143]

The Xanten trial lasted a total of ten days, the last of which was dominated by the closing statements of the attorneys. As in the Tisza-Eszlar case a decade before, both the prosecutors and the defense attorneys delivered passionate speeches urging the jurors to acquit the accused. Prosecutor Hamm argued that "even if the real killers have not been found, this trial was successful in that it provided an opportunity to publicly demonstrate to every impartial observer that Buschhoff was not the killer."[144] The defense agreed, of course, that Buschhoff was innocent and added their regret that the myth of ritual murder had so clouded the investigation. In light of these presentations, the jurors deliberated only 45 minutes before returning their verdict: Buschhoff was acquitted on all counts.

Like the verdicts from earlier cases of ritual murder, the Xanten verdict brought angry reactions from anti-Semitic newspapers.[145] Most

---

[142] *Staatsbürgerzeitung* 14 July 1892 #324 Abend.

[143] Ibid. Editors of several major newspapers were present in the courtroom on a daily basis, including two bitter rivals: Dr. Otto Bachler, editor of the *Staatsbürger Zeitung*, and Hirsch Hildesheimer, editor of the *Jüdische Presse*. A derisive article on the latter's presence by Bachler's *Staatsbürgerzeitung* brought an angry response by several liberal papers, including the *Berliner Tageblatt*. See *Berliner Tageblatt* 8 July 1892 #341 Abend.

[144] As quoted in Groß, *Ritualmordbeschuldigungen*, 85.

[145] The verdict also caused substantial anti-Jewish unrest in the Xanten area and

of this anger, however, was not directed at the judges or the jurors, but at the prosecution. According to the anti-Semites, the prosecutors had abandoned the interests of the German people and the rights of the young murder victim, and instead accepted the task of shielding the Jews from prosecution for their crimes.[146] As one would expect, vicious attacks were also leveled against the Jews and their liberal supporters, who had apparently conspired to pervert the German justice system. But newspapers like the *Staatsbürgerzeitung* placed much of the blame on the shoulders of government officials in Berlin. The *Staatsbürgerzeitung* demanded immediate reform of the German justice system and criticized what it saw as a bias toward Jews in the highest levels of the Justice Ministry.[147] Motivated by their anger at the Caprivi government and their desire for publicity, several anti-Semitic newspapers launched attacks on the government and especially on the actions of Baumgard and Brixius; predictably, these articles provoked a series of libel cases filed by the government. In fact, one of these libel trials turned Heinrich Oberwinder, the editor of the Stöckerite paper, *Das Volk*, into a minor celebrity. To defend himself against charges of libel, Oberwinder called witnesses from the original Xanten trial in the hope of showing that the charge of ritual murder was true and the Xanten prosecutors had indeed handled the case incompetently.[148]

in the vicinity of Neuss and Grevenbroich. Anti-Jewish riots had also occurred in these areas after ritual murder allegations in 1834. Because of the continued unrest, the Buschhoff family never returned to Xanten and settled instead in the larger Jewish community in Köln. See Rohrbacher and Schmidt, *Judenbilder*, 339–340; Groß, *Ritualmordbeschuldigungen*, 88.

[146] During the trial, the anti-Semitic *Neue Deutsche Zeitung* went as far as to claim that Baumgard's actions were explained by his Jewish-looking face, as was the testimony of the Jewish and half-Jewish medical experts and that of the Jewish-looking Nöldecke. See excerpt (marked July 17) in GStA PK, I. HA Rep. 84a Justizministerium, Nr. 57462, p. 94.

[147] See the angry articles in the *Staatsbürgerzeitung* beginning with 17 July 1892 #329A Morgen, and continuing through October 1892. See also a series of articles on an alleged "Jewish press and justice privilege" in *Germania* beginning with 14 August 1892 #184 Erstes Blatt.

[148] Oberwinder was convicted and sentenced to two months in jail. Soon after the Oberwinder trial, Stöcker's *Das Volk* carried this ad for a new pamphlet: "*The Oberwinder Trial*, a comprehensive stenographic report, which, in contrast to the short and quickly assembled newspaper accounts, gives a true and complete picture of the trial that has justifiably been ascribed with great cultural-historical importance . . . In consideration of the size of the brochure (it is more than three times the size of our brochure on the Buschhoff case) we can set the price no lower than

The contentious political climate of 1892 also helped to intensify the press debate about the legacy of the Xanten trial. Catholic newspapers, like the *Germania* and the *Kölnische Volkszeitung*, and ultra-conservative newspapers like the *Kreuzzeitung* used the Xanten case to voice their enduring bitterness toward the Caprivi government. Although all of these newspapers tried to distance themselves from the most radical of anti-Semitic attacks, they nonetheless adopted much of the anti-Semitic propaganda that described the Caprivi government as under the control of liberals and Jews.[149] The Catholic press also reacted with particular anger to attacks by liberal newspapers on the anti-Semitic tendencies of Rhineland Catholics. When the Jewish *Allgemeine Zeitung des Judenthums* proposed a special libel law for newspapers that spread or supported charges of ritual murder (a law that might be used to intimidate ultra-Conservative and radical Catholic newspapers), the *Germania* rushed to condemn it as a demand for nothing less than a special "Jewish press and justice privilege."[150]

Predictably, the liberal press responded by blaming newspapers like *Germania* and the *Kreuzzeitung* for spreading anti-Semitism and allowing such a spectacle as the Xanten trial to take place. But the anti-Semites and the right-wing press were not the only targets for liberal criticism. The *Berliner Tageblatt* also criticized the Caprivi government for allowing anti-Semitism to thrive. According to the *Tageblatt*, government officials acted irresponsibly in continuing the prosecution

60 Pfennigs per copy. . . ." *Das Volk* 21 December 1892 #299. The editor of *Das Volk*, Otto Balla, was soon also convicted of libeling Baumgard and Brixius and sentenced to 3 months. Balla, like other anti-Semitic editors, saw his own case as an opportunity to retry the Xanten case (with court officials and eyewitnesses from Xanten included). See *Die Post* 7 April 1893 in GStA PK, I. HA Rep. 84a Justizministerium, Nr. 57460, p. 376.

[149] *Germania*, the *Kreuzzeitung* and other radical newspapers were somewhat afraid of being associated too closely with the anti-Semitic agitator Hermann Ahlwardt, who was at his height during this period. Nevertheless, the *Germania* still resorted to common racial stereotypes. Articles accused the expert witness Nöldecke of having been bribed by Jews for his testimony, and also claimed that "it is not just 'possible', but proven by criminal statistics that Jews represent an overwhelming relative proportion of those guilty of perjury, fraud, simple and fraudulent bankruptcy, etc., while they are less well represented in other crimes only because of their better average social standing, their lack of employment in certain professions, and their less developed physical strength and energy." *Germania* 17 July 1892 #160; 30 July 1892 # 171.

[150] *Germania* 14 August 1892 #184 Erstes Blatt.

against Buschhoff even though they knew that no solid evidence existed. The paper also accused the government of buckling to public pressure, and claimed that officials in the Justice Ministry had chosen to appease public anti-Semitic furor rather than protect the rights of an innocent man and the integrity of the justice system.[151] Thus, both the political left and the political right used the outcome of the trial to attack the Caprivi government for not intervening more forcefully in the affair on one side or another.

In the midst of this criticism, Baumgard and other prosecutors continued to investigate the Xanten case. A number of other suspects emerged, including an old and mentally unstable neighbor, a neighbor who later bragged of the murder while drunk, and several other neighbors and strangers in town. As late as September 1893, prosecutors convinced the Minister of the Interior to send another Criminal Commissar from Berlin in the hope of developing new leads in the case. By the following year, however, the investigation had effectively ground to a halt.[152]

The Xanten trial was not the last ritual murder trial in Europe, or even in Germany. In fact, the Xanten case was only the beginning. Inspired by the publicity of the Xanten trial, over 120 ritual murder accusations were reported around Europe in the next decade, and several resulted in highly publicized trials. Most noteworthy among these cases would be the trials in Polna (Bohemia) and Konitz at the turn of the century, and the infamous Beilis case in Russia a decade later. Although all of these cases would provide their unique contributions to the enduring myth of ritual murder, each in its own way was an extension and elaboration of the precedents for ritual murder cases set in the last decades of the Nineteenth Century.

* * *

Of the six ritual murder cases presented here, five resulted in acquittals (or dropped charges) for Jewish defendants, and the sixth, the

---

[151] See *Berliner Tageblatt* 23 July 1892 #368 Morgen.

[152] See reports in GStA PK, I. HA Rep. 84a Nr. 57461, pp. 57–76. The historian Bernd Kölling lays out an interesting case for the guilt of two of these suspects: the cattle-dealer and former butcher Heinrich Junkermann and his relative, the quarryman Wesendrup. Although he acknowledges the impossibility of proving their involvement conclusively, Kölling suggests that the failure of officials to vigorously investigate the pair is telling. Kölling, "Blutige Illusionen," 358–360.

Bernstein case, resulted in only a short sentence on non-ritual grounds. However, far from being propaganda defeats for anti-Semitic agitators, these trials were significant in keeping the "Jewish Question"—and thus the anti-Semites—in the public eye. While it would be difficult to tie any of these trials directly to a marked increase in votes for any one anti-Semitic political candidate, it is clear that these trials as a whole provided a wealth of propaganda for the fringe anti-Semitic parties. They served not only as potent weapons against the "Jewish-liberal" enemy, but also as powerful tools to rally support for the anti-Semitic cause. In addition, the sensational newspaper articles and brochures provided additional income for these fringe parties, which often struggled to stay financially solvent. Most importantly, these ritual murder incidents built a record of "Jewish crimes" that could be resurrected and cited with each new ritual murder allegation. The legacy of these cases, therefore, lasted far longer than the individual politicians and journalists that sought to exploit them.

The most powerful legacy of these blood-ritual trials, however, came not from the anti-Semitic agitators themselves, but from the mainstream political press that incorporated these cases into contemporary political debate. Most Germans learned of the trial proceedings through these mainstream newspapers, and their own opinions were no doubt influenced by the stand taken by the paper to which they subscribed. Motivated less by belief in the actual charges and more by a fierce hatred of the liberal press, newspapers like the *Kreuzzeitung* and *Germania* took a radical line and adopted much of the rhetoric of the anti-Semitic press. Because of their influence, thousands of Germans were exposed to ritual murder cases and were persuaded to lend some measure of credibility to even the wildest of allegations.

CHAPTER FIVE

A MATTER OF DEBATE: SCHOLARS AND PSEUDO-SCHOLARS TESTIFY ON THE NATURE OF JUDAISM

Ancient allegations of Jewish blood rituals were revived in the late Nineteenth Century for various social, economic, and political reasons. Undoubtedly, local rivalries and social pressures were strong contributing factors, as were pre-existing currents of anti-Semitism and the work of individual agitators. But the prominent reappearance of such allegations cannot simply be attributed to the ignorant and poor, or to a few agitators with extremist political agendas. Ritual murder allegations, as well as many other kinds of accusations against the Jews, were part of an ongoing national discussion about the nature of Judaism and the content of Jewish rabbinical texts. This discussion involved agitators, journalists, and politicians, and it frequently occupied both the regional and national press. But discussions of the "Jewish Question" also drew the participation of many of the most noted biblical scholars and "Orientalists" in the German-speaking world. During the 1880s and 1890s, these scholars frequently debated the true contents of Jewish teachings both in newspaper articles and in polemical pamphlets—and occasionally as expert witnesses in court. While many noted scholars would try to defend Judaism against what they believed were irrational and ignorant attacks, there were always some prominent scholars or self-proclaimed experts ready to support anti-Semitic myths and stereotypes.[1] Thus, throughout the last decade of the Nineteenth Century, a scholarly debate raged alongside the public debate over the contents of the Talmud and the moral teachings of Judaism.

[1] The term "anti-Semitic scholars" in this chapter is used for all those who believed that ancient Jewish religious texts contained commands for Jews to abuse, rob, or even murder Christians. But all of these "anti-Semitic scholars" were not the same. Many of these so-called scholars were imposters who lacked any academic training. But some of these men did hold respected university positions, and a few were recognized for their scholarly abilities. These few professionals lent credibility both to anti-Jewish stereotypes and to those pseudo-scholars that supported them.

Because the German courtroom maintained an image as a relatively impartial institution, agitators and scholars from both sides of this debate were often inclined to look to the courtroom to resolve their disputes. When ordinary anti-Semitic agitators were charged with libeling the Jewish religion, scholars from across Germany would often be invited (or would volunteer) to participate in the trial as expert witnesses. For anti-Semitic scholars, these cases were valuable opportunities to gain publicity and respectability for their controversial Talmudic scholarship. For their opponents, the courtroom seemed to be the only forum in which anti-Semitic "scholarship" could be confronted and refuted in front of impartial arbiters. Thus, both anti-Semites and their opponents looked to the German courtroom to show the public the true nature of the Jewish religion.

August Rohling and his Opponents

The most infamous anti-Semitic scholar in the late Nineteenth Century was August Rohling. Rohling was born in 1839 in Neukirchen bei Rheine, a small town in the northernmost part of Nordrhein-Westfalen. In 1865, a few years after taking his vows as a Catholic priest, Rohling finished his habilitation on the Old and New Testament at the Royal Academy in Münster. Shortly thereafter, he was accepted as a lecturer on the Münster theological faculty. However, despite his quick advancement to the rank of professor, Rohling soon found himself short of money. In order to pay his debts, he worked briefly as a vicar and also published several anonymous pamphlets.[2] In 1870 he authored a short book called *The Talmud Jew*, which would eventually become one of the most infamous texts of modern anti-Semitism. At the time it was written, however, this book did not provide a substantial income, and Rohling quickly found himself in the throes of a financial crisis. In May of 1874, Rohling suddenly disappeared from his post in Münster and sent a letter to the dean claiming to have found a more lucrative position in French Canada. A short time later, Rohling sent a second letter asking for reinstatement and

[2] I.A. Hellwing, *Der konfessionelle Antisemitismus im 19. Jahrhundert in Österreich* (Vienna: Herder, 1972), 71–72. Rohling claimed that his financial problems were the result of *Betrügerei* (swindle).

permission for a short leave. The Münster faculty denied Rohling's request and instead started a disciplinary proceeding against him for his unauthorized absence. Dismissed by the Münster Academy and pursued by creditors, Rohling sought refuge in the United States. After a short stay in Memphis, Rohling worked as a professor for Moral Theology at the St. Francis of Sales Seminary in Milwaukee, Wisconsin.[3] But Rohling's fortunes soon changed for the better. In 1876, with the help of influential friends and colleagues in Vienna, Rohling was named as a professor in Bible Studies at the Karl-Ferdinand University in Prague. This prestigious position afforded Rohling a great deal of respect and gave his writings, including *The Talmud Jew*, a much greater degree of credibility.

The Talmud Jew itself was largely a rehashing of Johann Eisenmenger's infamous *Entdecktes Judenthum* (Judaism Uncovered), which had been published in 1710. Eisenmenger's book was a detailed multi-volume analysis of the Talmud that claimed to show that Jews were permitted (or even obligated) to lie, cheat, and steal from their Christian neighbors. Quotes from the Talmud were also provided to substantiate other myths about Jews, including that of ritual murder. According to the modern historian Jacob Katz, Eisenmenger's "evidence" for these charges was distorted, but his translations were not entirely falsified. In fact, Katz argues that many of his translations were quite accurate and equal to those of advanced biblical scholars of the time. Eisenmenger reached his vicious conclusions about Judaism because he searched only for evidence that matched his prior assumptions about Jews. He also failed to recognize that certain passages were contradicted elsewhere, were no longer considered binding, or were not to be interpreted literally.[4] Over a century and a half after Eisenmenger's famous work, August Rohling adopted many of Eisenmenger's conclusions and provided his own distorted or falsified "evidence" to support Eisenmenger's theories.

Like Eisenmenger, Rohling believed that Jews should follow Mosaic teachings if they were unwilling to accept Jesus and convert to Christianity. However, because modern Jews had abandoned the

---

[3] Ibid., 73–76.

[4] For a more thorough analysis of Eisenmenger's methods and motives, see chapter 1 of Jacob Katz, *From Prejudice to Destruction* (Cambridge: Harvard Univ. Press, 1980).

teachings of Moses for those of the corrupted Talmud, Judaism had lost its moral compass. Rohling originally stated that the *Talmud Jew* was designed to encourage Jews to convert, but successive editions of the book showed an increasing viciousness toward both individual Jews and toward the religion as a whole.[5]

Several years after publication of the *Talmud Jew* in 1870, an increase in political anti-Semitism in both Germany and Austria created a high public demand for Rohling's theories about Judaism and the Talmud. Rohling's book provided a "scientific" basis for all sorts of allegations against Jews and served as a "scholarly" resource for those who argued for a reversal of Jewish emancipation. In the first concentrated press battles on the Jewish question in 1875, Otto Glagau cited Rohling's *Talmud Jew* in the introduction to his controversial anti-Semitic articles in the popular journal *Gartenlaube*. These articles reached a broad public audience and set off a public debate on the Jewish Question that lasted for several months. In his 1876 book *Die "goldene" Internationale und die Nothwendigkeit einer sozialen Reformpartei*, C. Wilmanns also cited Rohling extensively to support his argument that Jewish immorality was the source of German financial troubles. Rohling's "scholarship" allowed Wilmanns to claim that no Jew, regardless of his degree of faith, could ever cleanse the Talmudic influence from his own behavior.[6] Especially after Rohling's appointment at the university in Prague, excerpts from *The Talmud Jew* were increasingly cited as "scientific fact," and sales of the book soared. By the early 1880s, references to *The Talmud Jew* became a staple of anti-Semitic speeches, articles, and pamphlets.[7]

The growth of Rohling's reputation and the spread of his anti-Jewish polemics led to hostile responses from both Jewish and Christian theologians. Even during his early years in Münster, Rohling was already a very controversial figure. Soon after *The Talmud Jew* appeared,

---

[5] Katz, *From Prejudice to Destruction*, 219–220.

[6] Ibid., 256.

[7] Hellwing claims that hundreds of thousands of copies were sold, and many distributed free by Catholic or anti-Semitic groups. By 1922, seventeen editions had been published and several more were later printed by Theodor Fritsch's Hammer Press. Not surprisingly, Rohling's work played an even more key role in the Austro-Hungarian anti-Semitic movement. In a country already ravaged by the anti-Semitic propaganda of Schönerer and Lueger, Ónody and Istóczy, Rohling's "scientific proof" of Jewish criminality fell on fertile ground. Even major religious figures, such as the Cardinal-Archbishop Schwarzenberg in Prague, gave Rohling their personal and financial support. See Hellwing, *Der konfessionelle Antisemitismus*, 81–82, 90.

the head of the Münster Theological Academy, Dr. Theodor Kroner, exchanged angry articles with Rohling in the local paper, and the two continued their feud in a flurry of pamphlets.[8] Although this conflict remained primarily a local matter in Münster, it was not long before the *Talmud Jew* provoked a national debate. When anti-Semitism reached a peak in Austria and Germany during the early 1880s, many prominent scholars emerged to challenge the validity of Rohling's work. In Vienna, a critical letter from two leading rabbis, Dr. Adolf Jellinek and Dr. Moritz Güdemann, led to a protracted debate in the Viennese press and provoked two of Rohling's most viciously anti-Semitic pamphlets: *Die Polemik und das Menschenopfer des Rabbinismus* and *Meine Antworten an die Rabbiner*.[9]

Because of his own professorship in Prague, Rohling could dismiss Jellinek and Güdemann's lesser scholarly credentials and declare them to be biased due to their religious confession. But Rohling was unable to use these arguments to dismiss another of his critics, the renowned professor of Theology at the University of Leipzig, Franz Delitzsch. In addition to being recognized as one of the most prominent Old Testament scholars in the world, Delitzsch was also known for being a Lutheran pastor and a prominent member of the *Judenmission*.[10] Although Delitzsch professed his deep love for "Israel,"

---

[8] Katz, *From Prejudice to Destruction*, 219. These pamphlets were *Entstelltes Unwahres und Erfundenes in dem "Talmudjuden Prof. Dr. August Rohlings nachgewiesen von Rabbiner Dr. Kroner* (Münster, 1871) and *Offener Brief an . . . August Rohling als Antwort auf sein Pamphlet "Der Talmudjude" von einem Münsterischen Juden im Namen Vieler* (Münster, 1871). Rohling answered Kroner's polemics in the introductions of the first few editions of the *Talmudjude*.

[9] August Rohling, *Die Polemik und das Menschenopfer des Rabbinismus. Eine Wissenschaftliche Antwort ohne Polemik für die Rabbiner und ihre Genossen* (Paderborn: Bonifatius-Druckerei, 1883); idem, *Meine Antworten an die Rabbiner oder Fünf Briefe über den Talmudismus und das Blutritual des Juden* (Prague: Cyrillo-Method'sche Buchhandlung, 1883).

[10] The *Judenmission* was the Protestant mission to encourage conversions in the Jewish community. Most missionaries viewed themselves as neutral parties between the anti-Semites and the Jews, but individual missionaries often varied in their reaction to political anti-Semitism. Missionary publications frequently denounced radical anti-Semites, but they also commonly reproached Jews for their materialism. Even activists such as Franz Delitzsch, who were outspoken in attacking anti-Semites, often criticized Judaism as an inferior religion. For more on the complex and ambivalent reaction of the *Judenmission* to anti-Semitism, see Christopher Clark, *The Politics of Conversion: Missionary Protestantism and the Jews in Prussia 1728–1941* (Oxford: Clarendon Press, 1995) and Alan Levenson, *Between Philosemitism and Antisemitism: Defenses of Jews and Judaism in Germany, 1871–1932* (Lincoln: Univ. of Nebraska Press, 2004).

as a missionary he was committed to the eventual conversion of all Jews to Christianity. Thus, while Delitzsch was one of the most vocal defenders of the Jews against anti-Semitic attacks, he also asserted that the Jewish Question "would only be solved when Jews exchange the national principle of their religion for an international Christian one."[11] Despite his professed love for the Jews, Delitzsch also did not hesitate to criticize individual Jews who, he believed, were too critical of Christianity or of Jesus. In his 1882 book *Christentum und jüdische Presse*, Delitzsch attacked some of these enemies, including the recently deceased Dr. Abraham Geiger.[12] In addition, Delitzsch agreed with the charge that the radical anti-Semitism of the early 1880s had been provoked by Jewish usury and attacks on Christianity. Thus, although many Jews respected his scholarly work on the Hebrew Bible and his public opposition to anti-Semitism, many others viewed him as an outsider bent on the destruction of the Jewish religion.

Delitzsch's conflict with Jewish scholars like Geiger did not cause him to hesitate in defending Judaism against the "scholarship" of August Rohling. Both as a scholar and as a religious missionary, Delitzsch found Rohling's *Talmud Jew* to be offensive. Faced with growing popular acceptance for Rohling's work, Delitzsch printed a pamphlet of his own in 1881 called *Rohling's Talmud Jew*. In this pamphlet, he denounced Rohling's book as a poor plagiarism of Eisenmenger's *Entdecktes Judenthum*, filled with distorted translations and falsified Talmudic text. Rohling immediately answered with a pamphlet of his own, *Franz Delitzsch und die Judenfrage*, in which he dismissed Delitzsch's interpretation and boasted of his own willingness to swear in court that his translations were accurate.

Over the next several years, Delitzsch and Rohling exchanged a series of polemical brochures that questioned each other's scholarly methods and personal motives.[13] Delitzsch also repeatedly gave expert testimony in cases where Rohling's work was being cited in support

---

[11] Franz Delitzsch, *Christentum und jüdische Presse* (Erlangen: Andreas Deichert, 1882), 42.

[12] Delitzsch disagreed with Geiger, who had claimed that Hillel was the most significant religious reformer of the Roman age, and that Jesus was only a second or third-rank figure. Delitzsch's letter to Geiger was polite but firm in asking Geiger to refrain from attacking Christianity. Geiger's reply was less polite in refusing to censor his own opinions. Levenson, *Between Philosemitism and Antisemitism*, 71–72.

[13] See Franz Delitzsch, *Was D. August Rohling beschworen hat und beschwören will. Zweite Streitschrift in Sachen des Antisemitismus* (Leipzig: 1883).

of anti-Semitic agitators. However, after a few years, Delitzsch began to feel that his literary exchange with Rohling had become useless. Even after Delitzsch repeatedly presented what he believed was irrefutable proof of Rohling's dishonesty, Rohling simply ignored these arguments and attacked him personally. Thus, Delitzsch claimed that any attempts to use logic or engage in scholarly debates with Rohling were futile: "This man, who rushes with fanatical delusion into courtrooms in order to swear that lies are truth, is indefatigable. When checkmated, he sweeps the pieces from the chess board and denounces his opponent as a cheater."[14]

Rohling in the Courtroom

There were several reasons why Rohling was so eager to swear to the accuracy of his scholarship in a court of law. First of all, while *The Talmud Jew* could be dismissed as a piece of polemical literature motivated by religious hatred, a statement made under oath by an expert witness would necessarily be given more credibility. Thus, Rohling could taunt his critics with the fact that his arguments had been given under oath and accepted as expert testimony by a court. Second, if Rohling's own testimony led to a "favorable" verdict for an anti-Semitic agitator, Rohling could claim this legal victory as a triumph over his scholarly critics. In other words, he could claim that judges and jurors had acted as impartial arbiters of truth and had recognized the validity of his arguments. Third, Rohling could use the public proceedings to advance his own demands for a repeal of Jewish emancipation and for restrictions on Jews in German and Austrian society. Finally, by participating in well-publicized libel trials and other court proceedings, Rohling could take advantage of the publicity and enhance his own public reputation as a Talmud scholar.

Rohling's court activities began as early as 1879, when isolated Jewish groups began to sue anti-Semitic agitators for libel. In late 1879, the *Deutsch-Israelitischer Gemeindebund* sent a letter to the Minister of Justice in Saxony about a pamphlet by a local agitator named

---

[14] Franz Delitzsch, *Neueste Traumgeschichte des antisemitischen Propheten. Sendschreiben an Prof. Böckler in Greifswald* (Erlangen: Verlag von Andreas Deichert, 1883), 3.

Egon Waldegg (Alexander Pinkert).[15] Waldegg's pamphlet, *A Manifesto to the German Nation: The Jewish Question in View of German Trade and Business*, had been distributed throughout Dresden in an attempt to support the fledgling local branches of the *Antisemitenliga* and the *Deutsche Reform Verein*. In order to lend credibility to his own observations about Judaism, Waldegg filled his book with quotations from Rohling's *Talmud Jew*.

The *Gemeindebund*, like later organizations that battled anti-Semitism in the German courtroom, believed it had the law squarely on its side. Several sections of the German Penal Code (RStGB) seemed to apply to the excesses of anti-Semitic propaganda, including traditional slander and libel laws (§185, §186) and laws against insulting an established religion (§166). In extreme cases, prosecutors could also rely on laws against the inciting of class violence (§130) and those against disorderly conduct or "*grober Unfug*" (§360 Nr. 11).[16] Although the legal framework existed for the prosecution of anti-Semitic propaganda, convincing prosecutors to intervene was often a difficult and frustrating proposition.

The *Gemeindebund*'s attempts to convince Dresden authorities to prosecute Waldegg met with immediate difficulties. Waldegg's publisher, Grumbkow, who was also under investigation, wrote a letter to the prosecutor defending the pamphlet. Grumbkow claimed that Waldegg had not designed the work to incite violence and had intentionally filled it with quotations from such learned Germans as Schopenhauer, Kant, Fichte, and Herder. According to Grumbkow, all of the alleged libels against Judaism had not come from the author himself, but from the work of scholars such as August Rohling—who, Grumbkow claimed, had never been successfully refuted by his opponents.

Rohling himself also wrote a long letter to the Dresden prosecutor, which he intended as expert testimony on behalf of Waldegg and Grumbkow. In addition to his positive review of Waldegg's pam-

[15] The *Deutsch-Israelitischer Gemeindebund*, founded in 1869, was a loose organization that bound individual Jewish communities. Weakened by the refusal to of most Orthodox Jews to participate, and restricted primarily to educational and philanthropic activities, the *Gemeindebund* was responsible for only scattered attempts to combat anti-Semitism directly. See Sanford Ragins, *Jewish Responses to Anti-Semitism in Germany* (Cincinnati: Hebrew Union College Press, 1980), 28–29.

[16] Johannes Groß, *Ritualmordbeschuldigungen gegen Juden in deuschen Kaiserreich 1871–1914* (Berlin: Metropol, 2002), 213.

phlet, Rohling also used this opportunity to defend his own controversial scholarship. In his letter to the court, Rohling boasted that a 10,000 Thaler reward for disproving his own conclusions had been set by the *Deutsche-Morgenländische Gesellschaft*, but had remained unclaimed. He also reviewed his public debate with Dr. Kroner in Münster, which he claimed to have won convincingly. As Rohling concluded: "According to Talmudic sources recognized by Dr. Kroner himself, these Mosaic principles are only valid in dealing with other Jews, not for relations with all people . . . There is no reasonable doubt, therefore, that Waldegg has portrayed Judaism accurately."[17]

After weighing the arguments on both sides, the public prosecutor at the Dresden Superior Court informed the *Gemeindebund* that he would not file any charges against Grumbkow or Waldegg. The prosecutor claimed that Waldegg's brochure did not intend to libel Judaism as a whole or to incite public violence against Jews, but merely attempted to attract public interest to local anti-Semitic clubs. According to the prosecutor, the fact that the pamphlet was part of an already contentious political campaign may not have justified, but could at least explain its polemical nature. Also, because Waldegg and Grumbkow had accepted many of their quotations in good conscience from more celebrated authors like Rohling, Konrad Martin, and Heinrich von Treitschke, they could not be held fully responsible for their truthfulness. Although the prosecutor argued that the actual validity of the Talmud translations was not an issue in the case, he concluded his letter to the *Gemeindebund* with this comment: "It cannot be denied, however, that teachings of the Talmud as they appear [in the work of Rohling, Rebbert, and Waldegg] cannot be criticized harshly enough, and must be fought against with the greatest determination in order to maintain the State and proper morality."[18]

Despite this setback, the *Gemeindebund* refused to give up. In June of 1881, they filed a new complaint against Waldegg and Grumbkow with the Dresden public prosecutor. Grumbkow once again responded with a long letter of defense. This time, the prosecutor agreed to

[17] R. von. Grumbkow, *Die Judenfrage vor Gericht* (Dresden: R. von Grumbkow, 1883), 9–10. Grumbkow printed this book in 1883, allegedly to provide political, legal, and intellectual authorities a record of the testimony and legal arguments involved in this case. The book is a collection of many court documents, letters, and expert testimony.

[18] Ibid., 10–11.

refer the matter to the Superior Court, although he advised the court that any potential punishment for Waldegg and Grumbkow should be mitigated by the fact that their pamphlet was based on the work of scholars.[19] Grumbkow then wrote a letter to the court, asking that the charges be dismissed. He denied that there was anything in the work that could incite violence against individual Jews, and he even claimed that the pamphlet could not legally be considered an attack on the Jewish religion. According to Grumbkow, since the Talmud was not a common institution or custom of the Jewish religion, criticism of the Talmud did not meet the legal definition of being an insult against Judaism. Finally, Grumbkow asserted that Waldegg's statements were not part of some mere newspaper article, but part of a larger scientific debate on the nature of Judaism. Thus, he suggested, any censorship would amount to a restriction on free scholarly inquiry.

Grumbkow's new letter of defense also included more expert testimony, including a new contribution from August Rohling. This time, Rohling was even more vigorous in his defense of Waldegg. Rohling now asserted that "it is a conclusive truth of science that the holy books of the Jews confirm the contents of [Waldegg's] citations."[20] However, Rohling's letter was not only a defense of Waldegg, but also another attempt to defend his own work. After suggesting that the Talmud allowed Jews to rob, cheat, and even murder Christians, Rohling argued that there was a scholarly consensus on these matters:

> The famous professor from Göttingen, Paul de Layarde (sic) joins me in the demand that we must act to legally reverse the emancipation of the Jews since Judaism contains elements that are not acceptable in a Christian political system, and which entail great dangers for the state, encourage revolution, and promote the destruction of the Christian monarchy for the goal of establishing Jewish world dominance.[21]

---

[19] When complainants thought prosecutors had unfairly refused to pursue their case, German criminal law allowed them to appeal to the court itself. The court judges could then weigh the evidence and decide whether to force the prosecutor to continue his investigation. Still, the prosecutor was the only one who had the power to raise an indictment. On both the so-called *Legalitätsprinzip* and the *Anklagemonopol*, see Benjamin Carter Hett, *Death in the Tiergarten: Murder and Criminal Justice in the Kaiser's Berlin* (Cambridge, MA: Harvard University Press, 2004), 24–25.

[20] Grumbkow, *Die Judenfrage vor Gericht*, 22–23.

[21] Ibid.

Rohling's letter was accompanied by several other testimonials, including one from Adolf Stöcker. Although Stöcker admitted that he was far from an expert on the Talmud, he stated that in his opinion nothing in the brochure warranted prosecution.[22]

Based on the written statements of Rohling and Stöcker, the judges on the Dresden Superior Court decided to dismiss the case. In its decision, the court cited the fact that the allegedly offensive citations originally came from "critical scientific debates." The court also took the word of Court Chaplain Stöcker that such criticism of the Talmud should not be construed as an insult to the Jewish religion.[23]

Rohling continued to make himself available as an expert witness in many similar trials, including one in Habelschwert (Silesia) and one in Vienna.[24] Although his written testimony was sometimes ruled irrelevant by court authorities, Rohling could still claim that his declarations had been certified by legal oath. In fact, Rohling frequently advertised his eagerness to serve as an expert witness in future cases. In his brochure on Jewish ritual murder, for instance, Rohling proclaimed: "I am willing to swear a legal oath on these matters on demand."[25] The Tisza-Eszlar ritual murder case in the summer of 1883 provided a special opportunity for Rohling to publicize his ideas to an international audience. In an open letter to the anti-Semitic journalist and politician Géza Onody, Rohling offered his services to the Hungarian court:

[22] Stöcker criticized a few excerpts from Waldegg's pamphlet that seemed to attack the Old Testament along with the Talmud. However, other than these passages, he found nothing objectionable. In his own "expert testimony," Chaplain Dr. Rüling, went even further in separating the Talmud from the Old Testament: "If both the offending phrases . . . were only used to describe spirit of the Talmud, which was compiled by Rabbis, then I must agree with them; the God of the Talmud is not the God of Abraham, Isaac and Jacob or the God of Moses and the Prophets, but a self-made imaginary God (*Gedankengott*) created by the scribes after the rejection of the Messiah—similar to that of the Koran." Ibid., 20–21.

[23] Faced with such legal setbacks and with the general reluctance of many prosecutors to file charges against anti-Semitic agitators, many Jewish groups became hesitant to rely on legal remedies to fight anti-Semitism.

[24] The Vienna case was the Holubek trial, a well-publicized libel trial of an anti-Semitic agitator named Franz Holubek. After citing Professor Rohling as the source for his attacks on the Talmud, Holubek was acquitted on all charges. This case was seen at the time as the first great political or legal victory for the Austrian anti-Semitic movement. See Hellwing, *Der konfessionelle Antisemitismus*, 43–45, 91.

[25] As quoted in Dr. Josef Kopp, *Zur Judenfrage nach den Akten des Prozesses Rohling-Bloch* (Leipzig: Klinkhardt, 1886), 15.

> Wherever such a case is brought in front of a court, I see it as my duty to inform your eminence . . . that I came into the possession of a work from . . . Moses Montefiore, which states on page 156a that the shedding of blood from a non-Jewish virgin is a holy act for Jews and that such blood is very pleasing in heaven and makes God merciful . . . If it is necessary, I am willing to take an oath in a court of law in order to verify the truth of this passage.[26]

Unfortunately for Rohling, the court in the Tisza-Eszlar case refused to call him as an expert witness. Nevertheless, the case brought Rohling and his theories an immense amount of public attention. Rohling had become a famous man, and his *Talmud Jew* was now available at many inns and restaurants and was even assigned in some schools.[27]

Faced with the ineffectiveness of refutations by Delitzsch, Jellinek, and several other scholars, some of Rohling's opponents decided that the only way to defeat him would be to confront him in court. This courtroom challenge eventually came from one of Rohling's most vocal opponents, Dr. Joseph Bloch, a Rabbi in Floridsdorf (a suburb of Vienna) and a member of the Austrian parliament. In 1882, after the first appearance of Rohling's pamphlet *Meine Antworten an die Rabbiner*, Bloch printed a series of articles in the *Wiener Allgemeine Zeitung* that claimed to provide a scholarly refutation of Rohling's argument. In these articles, Bloch openly labeled Rohling as a liar, forger, libeler, and perjurer in the explicit hope of provoking him to sue for libel. At first, Rohling ignored Bloch's attacks. However, after Bloch published even more vicious personal attacks a year later in the *Morgenpost*, Rohling responded by pressing charges.[28]

The Rohling-Bloch trial promised to be a crucial event in the public (and scholarly) debate on the nature of Judaism. The liberal Austrian deputy, Dr. Joseph Kopp, had agreed to represent Joseph Bloch in court, and a leading anti-Semitic politician named Robert

---

[26] Hellwing, *Der konfessionelle Antisemitismus*, 107–108. Rohling later offered similar testimony to the courts in the Lutscha and Xanten ritual murder cases.

[27] See Hellwing, *Der konfessionelle Antisemitismus*, 92.

[28] One of Bloch's charges was that Rohling's testimony in the Grumbkow case was perjured. See Kopp, *Zur Judenfrage*, 64. It should also be noted that the press played a key role in these scholarly conflicts, providing space for scholars to argue their case and supplying publicity for scholarly pamphlets. The *Jüdische Presse*, for example, regularly covered the debates about *The Talmud Jew*, and even promised to pay Rohling 1000 Marks if he could point to one passage in the Talmud that commanded Jews to use Christian blood. See *Jüdische Presse* 15 March 1883 #11.

Pattai was hired as counsel for Rohling.[29] This long-awaited challenge, however, met with repeated delays. Because Bloch's defense was that his own accusations against Rohling were factually true, the court felt compelled to invite experts to testify on the validity of Rohling's work. The process of finding qualified experts that both sides could agree on and who would be willing to participate in the trial lasted for over eighteen months. First, Rohling suggested his friends, Dr. Justus and Dr. Jakob Ecker; however, Bloch rejected these suggestions because of the well-known anti-Semitic bias of these men. Bloch also objected to having each side call its own experts since he feared that the result would be inconclusive.[30] Finally, both sides agreed to consult the *Deutsch-Morgenländische Gesellschaft*, which referred them to six of the most respected Orientalists in the German speaking world: Franz Delitzsch, Theodor Nöldecke, Gustav Bickell, August Dillmann, Paul de Lagarde, and Johann Gildemeister.[31]

---

[29] Pattai was later the leader of the Lower House of the Austrian parliament. Ironically, one of the leading candidates to serve as Bloch's lawyer was the young liberal politician, Dr. Karl Lueger. However, several friends warned Bloch that Lueger's political sympathies were not to be trusted, and Bloch chose to hire Kopp instead. See Bloch, 87.

[30] Bloch's attorney, Josef Kopp, later wrote that he avoided seeking Jewish experts since Rohling would invariably have challenged them. But Kopp was also reluctant to rely on those that had converted from Judaism, not because of Rohling's potential objections, but because Kopp feared that converts were often the most vocal opponents of their former faith. In fact, many Talmud "scholars" that were sympathetic to Rohling were converts from Judaism, including Dr. Justus and Elias Cohn. See Kopp, *Zur Judenfrage*, 22. Interestingly enough, there is a long history of individual converts leading public campaigns to ban or censor the Talmud. Johann Joseph Pfefferkorn (1469), Peter (1399), Antonius Margaritha (1490), and Christian Gershon (1600) are a few notable German examples.

[31] *Theodor Nöldecke* was a professor in Strassburg and the author of the influential *Die alttestamentliche Literatur* (1868). *Gustav Bickell* (1838–1906) was on the theological faculty in Innsbruck at the time of the Rohling-Bloch controversy. He later became Professor of Syrian and Hebrew in Vienna. Bickell was also a Catholic priest who had converted from Protestantism at the age of 26. *August Dillmann* (1823–1894) was an accomplished Professor of Theology in Berlin. His works on the Old Testament, most compiled in the *Kurzgefaßtes Exegetisches Handbuch zum Alten Testament*, are still consulted by contemporary biblical scholars. *Johann Gildemeister* was a respected professor of Oriental Languages at the University of Bonn. *Paul de Lagarde* (1827–1891) became famous because of his collected essays called *Deutsche Schriften*, in which he rejected Judaism and traditional Christian faiths and called instead for a new Germanic religion. Lagarde was known in scholarly circles for his expert exegesis of the Old Testament, which influenced the development of Biblical scholarship. For more on Lagarde's anti-Semitism, see Fritz Stern *The Politics of Cultural Despair* (Berkeley: Univ. of California Press, 1961). Both Lagarde and Gildemeister later agreed to testify in support of anti-Semitic agitators in other trials (see below), and Nöldecke was a decisive witness in the Xanten ritual murder trial.

Rohling immediately ruled out Delitzsch because of their long-running feud, and Rohling's friend, Dr. Bickell, asked to be dismissed because of his own personal bias.[32] Two other experts, Dillmann and Gildemeister refused the request outright, and Paul de Lagarde agreed as long as the case would not interfere with his research trip to Rome. However, because the case promised to drag on for many more months, Lagarde was also removed from consideration. This left only Dr. Nöldecke, a professor from Straßburg, to serve as an expert witness. Since the Vienna court required two experts, another long delay followed before August Wünsche, a professor of Theology from Dresden, was confirmed as the second expert witness.[33]

The defense attorneys presented Nöldecke and Wünsche with a 42-page questionnaire that covered over 300 Jewish texts ranging from the second to the eighteenth century. Because of the magnitude this task, the court continued to postpone the Rohling-Bloch trial. The work of the experts was finally completed in June of 1885, and the Vienna court scheduled the trial proceedings to begin the following November. However, no trial ever took place. Doubtless disappointed in the conclusions of these Talmud experts, Rohling withdrew his libel charges against Bloch before the case could come to trial. Rohling defended this decision by claiming that the Austrian government had ordered him to refrain from contributing to the growing anti-Semitic furor. But this government order did not stop Rohling from publicly attacking Bloch and the entire trial process. Rohling claimed the proceedings had become biased through the appointment of "the Protestant scholar Nöldecke and the Jew Wünsche, who has converted to Protestantism."[34] He added that the majority

[32] Bickell sent a letter to the court saying that it would be embarrassing to testify in the case since his testimony would so sharply disagree with the conclusions of his longtime friend, August Rohling. He also admitted to having contributed to an open attack on Rohling written by Delitzsch. Kopp, *Zur Judenfrage*, 25–26.

[33] August Wünsche (1839–1919) was a student of Delitzsch and translator of rabbinical texts into German. He later collaborated with Jewish scholars to study Jewish literature. Levenson, *Between Philosemitism and Antisemitism*, 89.

[34] As quoted in Kopp, *Zur Judenfrage*, 188. Strong anti-Protestant rhetoric was fairly typical of Rohling's work. This did not discourage many Protestant anti-Semites—such as Adolf Stöcker—from citing him. Both Wünsche and Nöldecke had previously criticized Rohling for his comments on ritual murder during the Tisza-Eszlar case. Wünsche sent a statement denying any Jewish heritage to several newspapers, including *the Jüdische Presse*. See *Jüdische Presse* 5 November 1885 #45.

of unbiased scholarly opinion was on his side, and cited Eisenmenger and his friends Justus and Ecker as examples.

By withdrawing from the case, Rohling tried to avoid the possibility of a verdict that would damage his public credibility. This public retreat, however, also had serious consequences. Rohling's enemies loudly proclaimed his withdrawal as a humiliating defeat and proof that his work was fraudulent. Both Bloch and his lawyer, Dr. Josef Kopp, took the opportunity to publish the written report of the Talmud experts along with their own commentary.[35] They proudly repeated their claim that Rohling was a liar and perjurer—and now a coward as well. Thus, although Rohling could still claim that his scholarship had never been challenged by any legal authority, his credibility and his standing as a scholar were now tarnished. As a result of Rohling's actions, the Karl-Ferdinand University in Prague decided to dismiss him from his teaching position. Although Rohling continued to write anti-Semitic pamphlets, and although he continued to be a favorite source for "scientific proof" of Jewish criminality, August Rohling's personal credibility never recovered from this legal setback.

After his legal encounter with Rohling, Joseph Bloch quickly gained a reputation as an active defender of Judaism in the courts. He willingly involved himself in many libel trials against prominent anti-Semitic agitators at considerable risk to his own reputation and financial resources.[36] Bloch also played a key role in the legal defeat of Dr. Josef Deckert, a Viennese parish priest and prominent anti-Semitic agitator. According to Bloch, financial misfortunes motivated Deckert to make speeches on the Jewish Question and author an 1892 pamphlet on ritual murder. After a long debate between Bloch and Deckert in the Viennese press, Deckert boasted in the newspaper *Das Vaterland* that he would prove his case with the assistance of a Talmud scholar and converted Jew named Paulus Meyer. In an open letter, Meyer not only testified to the existence of incriminating

---

[35] See Kopp, *Zur Judenfrage; Akten und Gutachten in dem Prozesse Rohling contra Bloch* (New York: Arno Press, 1973); Joseph Bloch, *My Reminiscences*, 2 vols. (New York: Arno Press, 1973); and Peter Pulzer, *The Rise of Political Anti-Semitism in Germany and Austria* (New York: John Wiley & Sons, 1964), 180–181.

[36] See Chapter 2 for more on Bloch's counterpart in Berlin, Hirsch Hildesheimer, who also actively challenged anti-Semitic scholarship and individual agitators in court. Bloch was sometimes referred to as the "Hirsch Hildesheimer of Vienna".

passages in the Talmud, but he also described having witnessed such murders himself. Bloch and his attorney Dr. Kopp quickly searched in Warsaw to find out if any of those people mentioned in Meyer's story actually existed. Although most were long dead, Kopp and Bloch nevertheless filed a libel suit against Meyer and Deckert on behalf of their families.[37]

At the trial, Paulus Meyer, the self-proclaimed Talmud expert, was exposed as a wanderer who had a history of conflicts with Russian, German, and Austrian police. Faced with this evidence, he publicly recanted his assertions about ritual-murder and blamed Deckert for perpetrating the fraud. Meyer was sentenced to four months in prison and both Deckert and Franz Doll, editor of the newspaper *Das Vaterland*, were fined for their own participation in the libel. In the face of such courtroom defeats, the Austrian Emperor sought to intervene to force Deckert out of the priesthood.[38]

Justus and Ecker

While August Rohling was by far the most famous anti-Semitic professor to give expert testimony in a courtroom, there was no shortage of others to follow in his footsteps. One of Rohling's most trusted allies was August (Aron Isidor) Briman, who was born to a Jewish family in Romania and later converted to Protestantism and then to Catholicism. According to some of his critics, Briman had converted to Christianity and started to write anti-Jewish pamphlets only after his own published research on the Talmud had been exposed as a forgery.[39] By the early 1880s, Briman had become a close confidant of August Rohling, and, according to some sources, he had even served as a tutor to Rohling in translating Talmudic texts.[40] In 1883,

---

[37] See Josef Bloch, *My Reminiscences* (New York: Arno Press, 1973).

[38] Just how significant these legal victories were for Bloch can be seen in the fact that despite his long experience as a rabbi and a member of the Austrian *Reichsrat*, Bloch's memoirs are dominated by a detailed record of both the Rohling-Bloch and Deckert-Bloch affairs.

[39] A brief biography of Briman is presented in Hellwing, *Der konfessionelle Antisemitismus*, 137–139. The source for these biographical details, however, is Joseph Bloch and his attorney Kopp, both avowed enemies of Rohling and Briman.

[40] According to Joseph Bloch, Rohling could hardly translate Hebrew texts and was dependent on Briman for assistance. Briman himself later confirmed Bloch's assertions. See Hellwing, *Der konfessionelle Antisemitismus*, 137.

the 25 year-old Briman decided to publish a pamphlet of his own. This pamphlet, called the *Judenspiegel*, or the "Jewish mirror," was written under the pen name of Dr. Justus.[41] The work was comprised of 100 Jewish "laws" that were collected from various rabbinical texts including the Schulchan Aruch.[42] Written just a few months before the Tisza-Eszlar ritual murder trial, the *Judenspiegel* was a clear attempt both to influence and to profit from this highly publicized incident. Both Justus (Briman) and his allies in the anti-Semitic press boasted about his "discovery" of passages that described the murder of Christian virgins as a duty for all Jews, and as an act that was pleasing to God.

The *Judenspiegel* provoked a similar scholarly reaction as Rohling's *Talmud Jew* had years before. Franz Delitzsch wrote a pamphlet called *Schachmatt den Blutlügnern Rohling und Justus*, which not only attacked the *Judenspiegel*, but also blasted the Catholic *Bonifacius-Verein* for printing and distributing such a work.[43] Delitzsch provided his own "true" translation of the passages in question and argued that the only reference to blood had to do with the difference in cleanliness between menstrual blood and the blood shed on the first night of marriage. Delitzsch claimed that there was no mention of murder or of maltreatment of non-Jewish women, and he suggested that Justus' translation had been purposely falsified. Delitzsch also referred readers to the supporting statements of several other scholars, including August Rohling's personal friend, Gustav Bickell. In response, Rohling came

---

[41] The full title was *Judenspiegel oder 100 neuenthüllte, heutzutage noch geltende, den Verkehr der Juden mit den Christen betreffende Gesetzen der Juden: mit einer die Entstehung und Weiterentwicklung der jüdischen Gesetze darstellenden, höchst interessanten Einleitung* (Paderborn: Bonifacius Druckerei, 1892).

[42] See Dr. D. Hoffmann, *Der Schulchan-Aruch und die Rabbinen über das Verhältnis der Juden zu Andersgläubigen* (Berlin: Verlag der Expedition der "Jüdischen Presse," 1894), 37. The Schulchan Aruch (Prepared Table) was a short synopsis of important laws and rabbinical decisions in the Talmud since the destruction of the Second Temple. It was compiled between 1565 and 1598 by Rabbi Joseph Caro in an attempt to make rabbinical laws more understandable and applicable to everyday life. A short time later, Rabbi Mosche Isserles added the Mappah, which included his own commentary on earlier Rabbinical laws along with a summary of German customs and opinions that contradicted those of Caro. Thus, Isserles adapted the Caro's Sephardic code to an Askenazic way of life. The work of Caro and Isserles, along with other minor additions is now generally referred to as the Schulchan Aruch. Rabbi Abraham Scheinberg, *What is the Halacha?* (New York: Schulsinger Brothers, 1974), 9–10.

[43] Hellwing, *Der konfessionelle Antisemitismus*, 101–105. The Bonifacius-Verein responded with a letter defending the work of Dr. Justus.

to the defense of Dr. Justus (who had maintained his anonymity) by lavishing praise on his friend's work. As he wrote in a review of the *Judenspiegel*: "Every word in the book is as good as gold and will convince any doubters. My *Talmud Jew* may disappear now from the stage, and even if a new edition appears by public demand, the *Judenspiegel* is clearly the lion of the day."[44]

Not surprisingly, the dispute over the validity of Justus-Briman's interpretations ultimately led to a showdown in court. On January 16, 1883, the Catholic *Westfälische Merkur* printed an article that described the *Judenspiegel* pamphlet and included several original excerpts. Despite the fact that the *Judenspiegel* had never been censored or banned, the issue of the *Westfälische Merkur* was confiscated and its editor, Dr. Hoffman, was charged with incitement of class hatred (§130). The so-called "Judenspiegel trial" occurred on December 10, 1883, just a few months after the Tisza-Eszlar case and the first Neustettin arson trial. In his own defense, Hoffman claimed that the *Westfälische Merkur* had in the past stayed away from discussion of the Jewish Question, and had no interest in attacking Jews. Hoffman claimed the analysis of the *Judenspiegel* pamphlet was done as a matter of scientific interest, and without any intention of encouraging religious violence.

In order to investigate the accuracy of the *Judenspiegel* brochure, the court summoned two expert witnesses. The court asked both witnesses to consider three questions:

1) Does the Schulchan Aruch have the force of religious law?
2) Does the word "Akum" in that text refer to Christians?[45]
3) Are the quotations of Dr. Justus in agreement with the original text?

The first expert witness was a man named Dr. Treu, a local teacher in the Münster Jewish seminary. Treu asserted that Dr. Justus had falsified or distorted many of his translations in the *Judenspiegel*, and he claimed that the word "Akum" was in no way a reference to

[44] This review, written in 1883, was reprinted in the anti-Semitic *Reichsgeldmonopol* (Cassel) 8 January 1887 #237.

[45] Akum is usually translated by modern Talmud scholars as "idolaters" or "worshippers of the stars," although there are many scholars who suggest this word refers to all Gentiles. The "Akum" are vilified and scorned in several passages in the Schulchan Aruch.

modern Christians. But much to the chagrin of Orthodox Jewish observers, Treu also asserted that neither the Talmud nor the Schulchan Aruch were valid religious texts or law books because most modern Jews could not conform to them.[46] Although this testimony did tend to discredit the *Judenspiegel* pamphlet, it also opened a loophole to allow defense lawyers to argue that attacks on the Talmud and Schulchan Aruch did not constitute attacks on Judaism itself.[47]

The second expert witness was a lecturer at the Royal Academy in Münster, Dr. Jakob Ecker. A Catholic scholar who claimed to have studied "Semitica" for more than 10 years, Ecker worked at the same academy where Rohling began his academic career. Ecker told the court that the Schulchan Aruch had superceded the Talmud in importance, and was now a primary source for modern Jewish law. Ecker also told the court that the word "Akum" in the Schulchan Aruch referred to all non-Jews and thus included modern-day Christians. In Ecker's opinion, therefore, modern Jewish desires to destroy Christianity had their roots in passages from the Schulchan Aruch. On the accuracy of Justus's work, Ecker admitted that some quotes in the book were not translated verbatim and many others were distorted to seem more anti-Christian. However, Ecker concluded that these changes were minor and that the spirit of Justus's work was consistent with the original text.

In his closing arguments, the public prosecutor condemned the anti-Semitic movement for spreading hatred against the Jews. He told the court: "There were once laws that forbade Jews from earning money and that placed them under the authority of Christians. We do not hold these opinions now, and none of us would wish to return to those barbaric times."[48] The prosecutor claimed that it had not been proven that anti-Christian laws were in the Schulchan

---

[46] *Jüdische Presse* 13 December 1883 #52.

[47] This was apparently a common occurrence when liberal or Reform rabbis were called to testify on the meaning and the binding nature of the Talmud and Schulchan Aruch. The irony here, of course, is that anti-Semites who couldn't read or understand these books were using mistranslations to attack Jews, many of whom also had no ability or desire to read the books, and then going unpunished because of it! See Mordechai Breuer, *Jüdische Orthodoxie im Deutschen Reich* (Frankfurt: Jüdische Verlag bei Athanäum, 1986), 307.

[48] *Deutsches Tageblatt* 14 December 1883 #340 Beilage in BAK *ZSg. 113* Sammlung Fechenbach Nr. 19.

Aruch or that this book was currently valid for all Jews. He complained that the *Westfälische Merkur* article had the potential to incite anti-Jewish violence and thus asked the court to sentence the paper's editor to 14 days in prison.

The defense attorney responded that the *Merkur* had intended its article to be a scientific inquiry and not mere anti-Semitic propaganda. According to the defense, the testimony of Dr. Ecker not only proved that such scholarly debate was legitimate, but also suggested that these issues were serious enough to warrant a discussion in the press. The defendant, Hoffman, also rose to argue that the readers of the *Westfälische Merkur* were far too educated to respond to such an article with violence—even if that had been his intention. In the end, the judges agreed with the prosecutor that it had not been proven that Justus's quotes were accurate or that the Schulchan Aruch was valid for all Jews. But the judges also believed that Hoffman had accepted the article in good conscience and did not anticipate such a public reaction. Therefore, the court acquitted Hoffman of all charges.[49]

For the anti-Semitic press, this verdict was viewed as a significant victory in the fight against Jewish influence. The *Geldmonopol* from Kassel, for example, argued that "the Judenspiegel trial in Münster was more important for every Christian than both the Neustettin arson trial and the Tisza-Eszlar trial since here the danger posed to Christians by Jewish religious books has been exposed."[50] But liberal newspapers reacted to the verdict by attacking the credibility of Dr. Ecker, and by questioning his relationship to anti-Semitic leaders. Also, noted Talmud scholars like Dr. Gustav Bickell suggested that Ecker was not qualified to do research on the Talmud and had depended on the help of other anti-Semites to aid him in getting a professorship in Münster.[51] In March of 1884, Ecker responded to these attacks by publishing his own pamphlet on the matter: *Der Judenspiegel im Lichte der Wahrheit. Eine wissenschaftliche Untersuchung von Dr. Jakob Ecker.* Ecker's brochure was quickly followed by several

[49] Ibid.

[50] *Geldmonopol* (Kassel) 30 December 1883 #52 in BAK *ZSg. 113* Sammlung Fechenbach Nr. 22.

[51] Later, August Briman (Dr. Justus) was accused of helping Dr. Ecker prepare his expert testimony in the Judenspiegel trial. In other words, Briman secretly helped Ecker to prepare expert testimony to validate his own anonymous writings.

other books that argued on either side of the issue. Thus, far from ending the debate on the nature of the Talmud and Schulchan Aruch, the verdict in the Judenspiegel trial only further inflamed popular (and scholarly) passions.[52]

In June of 1884, a sequel to the Judenspiegel trial took place in Bonn. This trial, the so-called Isaakiade trial, centered on the 1883 brochure *The Isaakiade, or the Eternal Jew of the Nineteenth Century*, by a local brush-maker named August Maaß. This brochure had been confiscated before it could be widely distributed, and Maaß was charged with inciting class violence (§130) and insulting an established religion (§166). The prosecutor summoned Dr. Johann Gildemeister, a professor of Oriental Languages at the University of Bonn, as an expert witness on Jewish scriptures, and the defense called Dr. Jakob Ecker as their own expert. Gildemeister testified that the Schulchan Aruch was popular among Jewish communities and was openly taught in Jewish schools. Gildemeister also concluded that the passages in the Maaß brochure had been accurately translated. These passages included the assertion that the possessions of non-Jews were to be considered as unclaimed, and the command that Jews should kill any converts to Christianity. Because Dr. Gildemeister's testimony was so favorable to their own case, the defense decided that the testimony of Dr. Ecker was unnecessary. Since both expert witnesses supported the defense, the trial ended in a quick acquittal.

Once again, anti-Semitic scholars could claim that their theories were legitimized by the verdict, and political anti-Semites could point to a legal judgment that confirmed their own statements about the danger posed by Jewish influence. Of course, the Isaakiade verdict led to a new flurry of pamphlets from defenders of Judaism that attacked the proceedings and now criticized Gildemeister as well as Ecker, Justus, and Rohling.[53]

---

[52] See especially Dr. Adolf Lewin, *Der Judenspiegel des Dr. Justus, ins Licht der Wahrheit gerückt* (Magdeburg, 1884) and also M.L. Rodkinsohn, *Der Schulchan Aruch und seine Beziehungen zu den Juden und Nichtjuden* (Vienna: D. Löwy, 1884). Lewin was a rabbi from Koblenz and Rodkinsohn was a converted Jew who later caused a controversy of his own. See below for more on Rodkinsohn.

[53] See Hoffmann. The subtitile of Hoffmann's book is *Zur Berichtigung des von Prof. Gildemeister in dem "Isaakiade" Prozesse abgegebenen gerichtlichen Gutachtens.* Dr. Hoffmann was a lecturer at the Rabbinical Seminary in Berlin, whose comments were originally published in the *Jüdische Presse.* His book was a thorough refutation of the testimony

Despite their "victories" in both the Judenspiegel and Isaakiade trials, anti-Semitic scholars soon found themselves on the defensive. It was only a year after the Isaakiade trial that Rohling was finally discredited at the hands of Joseph Bloch. At the same time, new revelations were beginning to emerge about the record and reputation of Dr. Justus. These revelations came to light when Aaron Briman (Justus) was sentenced to two months in prison and exile for falsifying a certificate that had secured his admission as a medical student at the University of Würzburg.

A few years later, another scholar named Michael Rodkinsohn was discredited under similar circumstances. The editor of the Hebrew-language journal *Hakol* in Preßburg (Bratislava), Rodkinsohn wrote his own book in 1884 called *Der Schulchan Aruch und seine Beziehungen zu den Juden und Nichtjuden.* Although this book was highly critical of Ecker and Rohling, and although Rodkinsohn found some support among Vienna's Jewish community, Joseph Bloch and editors of the *Österreichische Wochenschrift* claimed that he was a wolf in sheep's clothing. Bloch argued that Rodkinsohn pretended to be an apologist for the Jews, while presenting evidence in a way that suggested that there was a kernel of truth in anti-Semitic criticisms. According to Bloch, Rodkinsohn was a con man who had successfully elicited financial support from anti-Semites, Protestant missionaries, and local Jews all at the same time.[54]

Rodkinsohn and Bloch exchanged a series of accusations and threats of legal action with no practical result. In early 1887, how-

---

of Gildemeister, who he accused of having no knowledge of the Talmud. Hoffmann supported this charge with a letter from Gildemeister to the Vienna court in the Rohling-Bloch trial in which Gildemeister refused to serve as an expert witness due to lack of expertise. See also Dr. J. Goldschmidt, *Offener Brief an Herrn Prof. J. Gildemeister in Bonn*; Gustaf Marx, *Jüdisches Fremdenrecht, antisemitische Polemik und jüdische Apologetik. Kritische Blätter für Antisemiten und Juden* (Leipzig: H. Reuther's Verlag, February 1886). Goldschmidt was a local Rabbi from Weilburg in Hessen whose comments on the trial in the *Israelitische Wochenschrift* were published as a brochure. Gustaf Marx was a lecturer in theology at the Evangelical Seminary in Gnadenfeld (Upper Silesia). A prominent participant in the *Judenmission*, Marx first formulated his comments on the field of Talmudic scholarship in Hermann Strack's *Nathaniel: Zeitschrift für die Arbeit der evangelischen Kirche an Israel.* Like Franz Delitzsch, Marx strongly criticized the work of men like Rohling, Justus, and Ecker. However, he also warned his readers against accepting the "false defense" of Jewish scholars, and he suggested that the controversy should lead Jews to act in a more brotherly way toward their Christian neighbors. A collection of many of these pamphlets is available in BABL R 43 Alte Reichskanzlei (Stammakten) #679.

[54] Hellwing, *Der konfessionelle Antisemitismus*, 145.

ever, Rodkinsohn was arrested in Vienna on charges of fraud. The police reported that his real name was Michael Schmiederow-Frumkin, and that he had been born to a Jewish family in Russia. After several conflicts with legal authorities there, Frumkin (Rodkinsohn) migrated to Vienna, where he adopted a new identity and a new religious confession.[55] Rodkinsohn-Frumkin's arrest and public disgrace ended his attempt to become a respected German Talmud scholar.[56] Thus, despite the relative "success" of anti-Semitic scholarship in the courtroom, many anti-Semitic scholars and pseudo-scholars suffered personal defeats far greater than any of their legal victories.

Stöcker and Strack

Even after the public humiliation of Rohling, Justus, and Rodkinsohn, champions for their cause were easy to find. Even Adolf Stöcker, who had once questioned the truthfulness of ritual murder charges, soon became a vocal supporter of a government investigation into the true meaning of Jewish religious texts. After the Tizsa-Eszlar ritual-murder case in 1883, Stöcker had coyly suggested that he could not talk authoritatively about the existence of ritual murders because the matter was still an object of scientific debate. But just a few years later, Stöcker began to make comments that put him squarely in the center of such debates. After his own humiliation in the Bäcker trial of 1885, Stöcker asserted in several public speeches that Jewish texts and songs such as the *Kol Nidre* advocated cruelty toward Christians and allowed duplicity and even perjury when dealing with non-Jewish neighbors.[57] These public statements provoked angry

[55] Ibid., 143–148. Hellwing accepts Bloch's argument that Rodkinsohn was the real intellectual force behind the work of Rohling and Justus.

[56] Rodkinsohn soon fled Vienna for New York, where he sought to forge a new scholarly reputation through a translation of the entire Talmud into English. Even 20 years later, Rodkinsohn was still bitter toward Bloch, who he described as a despicable man who nonetheless performed a useful service in exposing Rohling. See Rodkinsohn's *The History of the Talmud*, Vol. 1 (New York: New Talmud Publishing, 1903), 126.

[57] The *Kol Nidre* (All our Vows) is the song that begins the evening service on Yom Kippur or the "Day of Atonement." According to Albert Schulman, the Kol Nidre is not really a prayer, but a declaration that voids all vows that were made under duress or without time for careful consideration during the previous year.

responses from several biblical scholars—the most prominent being Professor Hermann Strack of Berlin.

Hermann Lebrecht Strack was a professor of the Old Testament at the University of Berlin. He was a former student of Franz Delitzsch and, like his mentor, was also involved in Christian missionary activity among the Jews and founded an *Institutum Judaicum* for the study of the Jewish religion.[58] In 1887, Strack published an *Introduction to the Talmud*, which is still considered a classic source for contemporary Talmud scholars. Strack was motivated to study Judaism both out of scholarly interest and out of a desire to convert Jews to Christianity. In the 1909 English edition of his book, *The Jew and Human Sacrifice*, Strack described his motives in this way: "I am not a 'Philo-semite' in the now generally accepted sense of the word. I have even been slandered as an 'Anti-semite.' As a Christian theologian, I wish simply to serve the truth, for the sake of my Lord, who is 'the way, the truth, and the life.'"[59] In any case, Strack was recognized at the time as one of the foremost opponents of anti-Semitic attacks on the Jewish religion. He had publicly attacked August Rohling in the *Evangelische Kirchenzeitung* during the Tisza-Eszlar trial, and he continued to make public statements following the Breslau and Korfu ritual murder controversies. When Adolf Stöcker delivered his attacks on the Talmud and the Kol Nidre, Strack immediately sent a reply to the ultra-Conservative *Kreuzzeitung*. As in so many other cases, the polemical disputes between these two men could not be "resolved" without the assistance of a court of law.

Some scholars argue that the development of this custom was associated with the Marranos in Spain, who were forced to convert to Catholicism but maintained their Jewish faith in private. Albert Schulman, *Gateway to Judaism* (New York: Thomas Yoseloff, 1971), 363.

[58] Delitzsch had founded the Leipzig *Institutum Judaicum*, which was named the Delitzschianum after his death.

[59] Hermann L. Strack, *The Jew and Human Sacrifice: Human Blood and Jewish Ritual*, trans. Henry Blanchamp (New York: Benjamin Blom, 1971), 17. According to Hans Engelmann, Strack and many others in the *Judenmission* had originally supported Stöcker. However, after Stöcker began to affiliate with more radical anti-Semites, Strack became one of Stöcker's staunchest opponents. In Strack's obituary in *Jeschurun*, however, Josef Wohlgemuth praised his close relationship to the Berlin Orthodox Rabbinical Seminary and to Hirsch Hildesheimer in particular. See Hans Engelmann, *Kirche am Abgrund: Adolf Stöcker und seine antijüdische Bewegung*, Studien zu jüdischem Volk und christlicher Gemeinde, Band 5 (Berlin: Selbstverlag Institut Kirche und Judentum, 1984), 136–137; Levenson, *Between Philosemitism and Antisemitism*, 66.

After Strack's rebuttal in the *Kreuzzeitung*, Stöcker quickly reaffirmed his earlier statements and called on Dr. Simon May, an alleged Talmud scholar and an editor of the Stöckerite *Reichsbote*, to support his own assertions. Strack, along with several liberal and Jewish newspapers, publicly claimed that May was incompetent as a Talmud scholar, and suggested that his degree had been fraudulently obtained. A further debate between Strack and May continued over several months before culminating in a suit and counter-suit for libel.[60] When the trial opened in October of 1885, Strack wasted no time in challenging May's credibility. May was forced to admit a previous conviction for embezzlement, and he told the court that his doctorate was obtained from a Philadelphia university even though he had never visited Philadelphia.[61] As part of the closing arguments in the case, Strack made a speech that denounced May as a tool of Adolf Stöcker, and referred to Stöcker's previous disgrace in the Stöcker-Bäcker trial. Given May's criminal record and his shaky testimony, the court eventually acquitted Strack of libel and convicted May on the cross-complaint. May was fined 100 Marks, while the court left Strack's attacks on the credibility of May and Stöcker unpunished.[62]

After the trial, Stöcker tried to send his friend Freiherr von Hammerstein to arrange a truce with Strack. According to the *Jüdische Presse*, Strack agreed to withdraw his accusations against Stöcker if Stöcker ceased his public attacks and if Simon May was fired from the *Reichsbote*. Apparently, Stöcker had second thoughts about this arrangement, and he soon published another attack on Strack in the *Kreuzzeitung*. Strack responded with a pamphlet called *Herr Adolf Stöcker. Christliche Liebe und Wahrhaftigkeit*, which reminded readers of Stöcker's "careless perjury" (*Fahrlässigkeit*) in the Bäcker case, and suggested that his trust in a man like Simon May proved that he was incapable

[60] When asked in court why he chose to file charges against Strack instead of against even more severe articles in the *Jüdische Presse*, May responded that he would never face someone in court who is not *satisfaktionsfähig* (referring to the Jewish editors). *Jüdische Presse* 22 October 1885 #43.

[61] These revelations about "Dr." Simon May were published in the *Jüdische Presse* several months before the trial. See *Jüdische Presse* 4 June 1885 #23.

[62] May was convicted for having suggested that Strack was a slave of the Jews. The original verdict called for a 30 Mark fine, but this was raised to 100 Mark fine in a January 1886 appeal. A few weeks earlier May was also convicted for libeling a Jewish lawyer and sentenced to an additional 300 Mark fine. See *Jüdische Presse* 14 January 1886 #2; 28 January 1886 #4.

of telling truth form falsehood. Although Simon May quickly disappeared from Stöcker's side, and although Stöcker was discredited even further by this fiasco, Strack's attacks did not stem the flow of Stöcker's anti-Jewish rhetoric.

Ordinary Agitators and Talmud Scholarship

While national figures like Adolf Stöcker could incite debates and provoke responses from prominent biblical scholars, even the most obscure anti-Semitic agitator could use expert testimony in his own defense. In 1886, for example, Hans Leuß, the editor of the *Schaumburg-Lippeschen Landeszeitung*, caused a stir when he authored an article that attacked the Talmud.[63] Leuß's article lamented the de-Christianization of the legal oath and claimed that Jews believe they can receive religious dispensation for lying under oath. Leuß was denounced by the directors of the local synagogue, and was charged with insulting a legally established religion. His trial began in April of 1886 in the small town of Bückeburg near Hanover.

The prosecution immediately tried to enter written expert testimony by Hermann Strack, but the judges refused to accept the testimony because of technical errors in the affidavit. The judges also refused to accept defense requests to allow written testimony from Justus and Ecker. The lead judge in this case decided that the important issue was not so much the truth of Leuß's comments, but whether or not those comments rose to the level of libel. After spirited arguments by both the prosecution and defense, the judges ruled that the article did not rise to the level of libel and thus the issue of the truth of these allegations was irrelevant.[64]

A year later, a similar case arose in Marburg with slightly different results. This time the charges were filed against a local teacher named Ferdinand Fenner for critical comments he made at an 1886 rally

[63] Leuß went on to achieve notoriety as a close associate of Adolf Stöcker and lead editor of *Das Volk* before his eventual conversion to Social Democracy. In this case, the Senior Public Prosecutor (*Oberstaatsanwalt*) agreed to press charges after the public prosecutor (*Staatsanwalt*) had originally refused. *Staatsbürgerzeitung* 4 April 1886 #80 Beiblatt.

[64] Ibid.; *Jüdische Presse* 8 April 1886 #14.

led by Otto Böckel.[65] In addition to allowing the testimony of Böckel and the leader of the local *Jüdische Gemeinde*, the court agreed to allow expert witnesses to testify on Jewish religious teachings. The court accepted two professors as expert witnesses: the respected Jewish philosophy professor Hermann Cohen and the famous professor Paul de Lagarde.[66] The court put two questions to these witnesses:

1) Is the Talmud valid for all Jews (and is an insult against the Talmud an insult against Judaism)?
2) Does the Talmud say that Jews may deceive Christians?

Lagarde, whose testimony was admitted in written form, argued that the Talmud was not considered law for all Jews; therefore, disparaging remarks about the Talmud would not necessarily constitute a slander of all Jews. Although Lagarde acknowledged that Fenner's remarks were not taken verbatim from any part of the Talmud, he claimed that Fenner's comments were consistent with the Talmud in form and content. Then, citing both August Rohling and popular opinion, Lagarde argued that most Jews tend to follow the teachings of the Talmud about their superiority, their own system of morality, and their state of war with non-Jews—even if they have no direct knowledge of the Talmud itself. Professor Cohen responded by attempting to refute each of these points, and criticizing Lagarde for being both unscientific and anti-Semitic.[67]

---

[65] The public prosecutor had originally raised charges in 1886, but the Superior Court in Marburg refused to hear the case. The prosecutor appealed to the High Superior Court (*Oberlandesgericht*) in Kassel, which overturned the objections of the Marburg court and ordered the case to be heard.

[66] Hermann Cohen (1842–1918) was a Neo-Kantian philosopher at the University of Marburg. He had drawn angry criticism in 1880, when his essay response to Heinrich von Treitschke, "Bekenntnis in der Judenfrage," included a denunciation of Orthodox Jews for a lack of patriotism and a suggestion that they abandon the rules of the Talmud. Breuer, *Jüdische Orthodoxie*, 310. Cohen's essay and two responses from the *Allgemeine Zeitung des Judenthums* are reprinted in Karsten Krieger, ed., *Der "Berliner Antisemitismusstreit," 1879–1881* (München: K.G. Saur, 2004), 337–360, 431–441.

[67] *Antisemitische Correspondenz* 15 Mai 1888 #27 in BAK *ZSg. 113* Sammlung Fechenbach Nr. 19. Hermann Cohen's testimony was later published as the pamphlet "Die Nächstenliebe im Talmud". Despite his liberal leanings and his earlier criticism of the orthodoxy, Cohen's testimony earned hearty congratulations and thanks from Ezriel Hildesheimer, the prominent Orthodox leader and founder of the Berlin Rabbinical Seminary. See David Ellenson, *Rabbi Ezriel Hildesheimer and the Creation of a Modern Jewish Orthodoxy* (Tuscaloosa: Univ. of Alabama, 1990), 104–105.

After the end of the expert testimony, Fenner rose to claim that he had no intention of slandering either the Jewish religion or any individual Jews. His attorney added that since the Jews should be considered a race, not a religion, the law against libeling established religions should not apply to this case. After a short deliberation, the judges convicted Fenner and sentenced him to two weeks in prison. The judges claimed that scientific opinion of the teachings of the Talmud was inconclusive. But because Fenner used the Talmud to characterize all Jews as scoundrels, the judges claimed that his remarks were clearly slanderous.[68]

Thus, both the Leuß case and the Fenner case sent a confusing message about the contents of Jewish religious texts and the validity of anti-Semitic scholarship. While Leuß had been acquitted, he could not attribute this victory to the truth of his anti-Semitic sources; and although Fenner had been convicted, his opponents could not rightfully claim this as a refutation of anti-Semitic attacks on the Talmud.

* * *

The record of the German courts on the issue of anti-Semitic scholarship is mixed. While the court could sometimes be used to bring credibility and publicity to men like August Rohling, trial proceedings could also lead to professional condemnation and public humiliation for anti-Semitic scholars. Many of those anti-Semitic "experts" who entered a courtroom did not emerge with their reputation or their dignity intact.

However, those who sought to defend the Talmud against anti-Semitic attacks were often equally frustrated with their inability to end these debates. While men like Bloch, Strack, and Delitzsch were able to discredit pseudo-scholars like Rohling, Justus, and May in the courtroom, they were often frustrated by government reluctance to support their attempts to prosecute those that libeled Judaism. For example, in early 1892, in the midst of the hype over the Xanten

---

[68] Fenner's slanderous comment had been: "A Jew that follows the Talmud and deceives Christians is a scoundrel in our eyes, any Jew who doesn't follow the Talmud is a scoundrel in Jewish eyes; so Jews are scoundrels no matter what they do." Quoted in *Antisemitische Correspondenz* 15 May 1888 #27 in BAK *ZSg. 113* Sammlung Fechenbach Nr. 23.

ritual murder trial, Hermann Strack spoke out repeatedly against those that claimed there was scholarly evidence that the Talmud approved of ritual murder.[69] In May of 1892, Strack sent letters to various government officials demanding that the editor of the *Staatsbürgerzeitung* be prosecuted for publishing a special "Talmud Excerpt" based on the "scholarly court testimony" of Rohling and Ecker. Strack was disappointed when the government declined to prosecute the newspaper, but he was stunned by the reason given by the local prosecutor for the rejection: "The opinions of scholars on the matter vary quite widely, and the opinions of respected scholars stand on both sides. This is after all a matter of theoretical debate, of scientific discussion. And science (*Wissenschaft*) and its doctrines are free."[70] Strack angrily complained to the Justice Minister, von Schelling, that he and many other experts had repeatedly refuted "scholars" such as Rohling and Ecker; however, he met with little success. The Justice Minister gave a curt reply, in which he refused to intervene.[71] Despite years of work by men like Strack, Delitzsch, and Josef Bloch, many prominent Germans still believed that the true nature of the Talmud (and Judaism) was a matter of scholarly debate.[72]

Long after Rohling and Justus had ceased their public activities, anti-Semitic agitators would continue to speak of such works as *The Talmud Jew* and the *Judenspiegel* as if they were scientific truth. Indeed,

---

[69] This included a very public feud with the Italian *Osservatore Cattolico*, which had printed a series of articles that defended ritual murder allegations.

[70] Letter to Strack from the Erste Staatswalt at the Berlin Kammergericht I, published in Hermann Strack, *Die Juden—Dürfen sie als 'Verbrecher von Religions wegen' bezeichnet werden?*, 3 available in GStA PK, I. HA Rep. 84a Justizministerium, Nr. 55746.

[71] *Berliner Tageblatt* (January 25, 1893) in GStA PK, I. HA Rep. 84a Justizministerium, Nr. 55746, p. 22. This despite the fact that a few years earlier, Strack had submitted expert testimony (along with Paul de Lagarde and Franz Delitzsch) for Kaiser Wilhelm II. This testimony was submitted after the Kaiser expressed concern over the Breslau ritual murder case. Of the three submissions, *Kultusminister* von Goßler considered Strack the most believable, since Delitzsch was friendly to the Jews and Lagarde too anti-Semitic. See Letter from Dr. von Goßler to Schelling (Berlin May 4, 1889) in GStA PK, I. HA Rep. 84a Justizministerium, Nr. 55746, p. 70.

[72] Finally, in frustration, Strack published his entire correspondence with government officials as a pamphlet called *Die Juden—Dürfen sie als 'Verbrecher von Religions wegen' bezeichnet werden?*, in the hope of stirring public outrage about the government's intransigence. Even years later, Strack was still challenging the anti-Semitic agitator Theodor Fritsch (both in and out of court) over the existence of ritual murder as a Jewish custom.

each new ritual murder accusation, each new financial scandal, and each new political election would provide renewed opportunities to trot out this "scientific evidence" about Jewish criminality. Unfortunately, just a few decades later, when the Nazis sought to exploit anti-Semitic "scholarship" for their own propaganda purposes, the works of men like Rohling and Justus enjoyed a popular rebirth. This time, there would be no open courtroom in which other scholars could make a public challenge.[73]

[73] Not surprisingly, the works of Rohling, Justus, and Ecker continue to be cited by present-day anti-Semitic groups. Examples include the web-site of Radio Islam, founded by the Moroccan rebel Ahmed Rami in Stockholm, and various Christian Identity Movement sites in the United States. See, for example, Radio Islam, "The Talmud: Judaism's holiest book," http://www.radioislam.net/talmud.

CHAPTER SIX

THE NEW DEMAGOGUES: HERMANN AHLWARDT AND THE RISE OF FANATICAL ANTI-SEMITISM

Despite the fact that anti-Semitic trials and scandals continued to attract public attention to the Jewish Question throughout the 1880s, the fortunes of individual anti-Semitic agitators generally suffered during that time. Partially as a result of the personal and financial toll of participating in libel trials, many anti-Semitic newspapers had already failed or were in a very fragile financial state. Not surprisingly, by the mid-1880s most political anti-Semites were thoroughly discouraged. No anti-Jewish legislation had been passed since the start of the movement, and, other than Adolf Stöcker, no anti-Semitic politician had ever been elected to a national office. The number of votes for anti-Semitic parties was stagnant by mid-decade, and instead of acting as a unified group, individual anti-Semitic leaders often bitterly attacked one another in a desperate attempt to find political (and financial) support.

Although the anti-Semitic movement stagnated in the mid-1880s, it found renewed vigor later in the decade due the success of an agitator named Otto Böckel. A librarian in Marburg and an occasional contributor of anti-Semitic articles under the pen name of Dr. Capistrano, Böckel decided in 1887 to form his own independent political party. However, unlike many of his colleagues in the anti-Semitic centers of Berlin, Leipzig, and Dresden, Böckel decided to aim his propaganda at the primarily peasant population of rural Central Germany. With his demagogic rhetoric and his slogan "Against Junkers and Jews!", Böckel tapped a hitherto unexplored populist and anti-elitist current within the peasantry.[1] By linking local hatred for Prussian landowners with fears and stereotypes of Jewish bankers and money-lenders, Böckel successfully exploited peasant anger in a region that was one of the poorest and most backward in Germany.[2]

---

[1] See David Blackbourn, *Populists and Patricians* (London: Allen & Unwin, 1987), 125.

[2] Peter Pulzer, *The Rise of Anti-Semitism in Germany and Austria* (New York: John

In the 1887 national elections, Böckel won a stunning victory in Marburg, and soon entered the Reichstag as the only non Christian-Social anti-Semitic delegate.

Although Böckel's radical anti-*Junker* rhetoric alarmed many Conservatives and some anti-Semites, Böckel's success caused a general upsurge in the fortunes of all anti-Semitic political parties. Böckel's success in Hessen would eventually be limited, however, as he ran into many of the same difficulties that plagued other anti-Semitic leaders. Because his radical anti-*Junker* rhetoric alarmed many government officials, and because many of his proposals hinted at a socialist agenda, local prosecutors were quite eager to pursue libel charges against him. In addition, Böckel's involvement in a paternity suit with a former housekeeper made him vulnerable to charges of immorality and corruption.[3]

While Böckel's demagogical style helped the anti-Semitic parties to achieve greater electoral success, it also opened the door to a cohort of even more fanatical anti-Semitic demagogues. The most prominent of these new agitators, such as Hermann Ahlwardt and Karl Paasch, focused their attacks not simply on Germany's financial or aristocratic elites, but on almost every part of the German government. While Otto Böckel tended to focus his attacks on specific targets (partially out of the desire to avoid libel proceedings), men like Ahlwardt tended to publish broad-ranging allegations of a Jewish conspiracy that even involved the Chancellor and his ministers.[4] The rhetoric of these new demagogic anti-Semites reminded many government officials of Joachim Gehlsen, who had used anti-Semitism to libel "*Das System Bismarck*" in the 1870s. The memory of Gehlsen's libelous attacks led many to fear that the new demagogical anti-

Wiley and Sons, 1964), 180–189. David Peal suggests that anti-Semitism for Böckel was "as much a creed as a device to hold together disparate social groups and to lend coherence to a patchwork of programs." He also argues that while Böckel was a part of the general development of anti-Semitism in Imperial Germany, his movement was both "transient and regional" in nature. David Peal, "Jewish Responses to German Antisemitism: The Case of the Böckel Movement, 1887–1894," *Jewish Social Studies* 48, Nr. 3–4 (Summer-Fall 1986): 269–270.

[3] Richard S. Levy, *The Downfall of the Anti-Semitic Political Parties in Imperial Germany* (New Haven: Yale Univ. Press, 1975), 103.

[4] As Peter Pulzer put it: "Böckel was an intelligent man who knew when to roar and when to smile . . . Ahlwardt had only one accomplishment, the ability to rant." Pulzer, *The Rise of Anti-Semitism*, 116.

Semitism was only a cover for a general goal of overturning the German government and fomenting a social revolution.

In addition to the extreme nature of their anti-government propaganda, the demagogical anti-Semites were also unique for the degree of viciousness and fanaticism in their accusations against the Jews. While the rhetoric of more "traditional" anti-Semites like Otto Glagau and Max Liebermann von Sonnenberg was filled with accusations of conspiracies that often verged on the paranoid, even these men were shocked by the outrageousness and the irrational nature of many of the new conspiracy theories. For many observers, these demagogues had gone far beyond political fanaticism into the realm of mental illness. In addition, while most "traditional" anti-Semites had sought to use the courtroom as a public forum to spread their ideas and defend their reputations, they never pursued legal confrontations with as much reckless abandon as the demagogical anti-Semites. Agitators like Hermann Ahlwardt voiced their charges seemingly without regard to any potential punishment, and sought court intervention not to prove some truth about the Jews, but simply to turn themselves into public martyrs.

Despite widespread questions about their sanity and their radical political programs, these demagogues had an extraordinary impact on the political course of Imperial Germany and on the development of German anti-Semitism. While they never formed effective political organizations or attracted significant percentages of the electorate, demagogic anti-Semites generated enough publicity with their outlandish claims to influence the German political scene for several years.

The Madness of Morris De Jonge

Morris De Jonge was never a prominent anti-Semitic leader. But with the help of several anti-Semitic and ultra-Conservative newspapers, he became a *cause célèbre* for the anti-Semitic movement during the early 1890s. De Jonge grew up the son of a rich Jewish banker in Cologne. He studied law, and after finding work as a legal clerk (*Referendar*), he seemed well on his way to a career as a successful attorney. However, according to his family, De Jonge's behavior had begun to deteriorate over a period of several years. Not only did he quarrel frequently with other family members, but he also constantly libeled them, denounced them to the police, and threatened them with physical harm. In the late 1880s, De Jonge left the legal profession and moved to Berlin, where he hoped to find work as a freelance author. He also left the Jewish faith and converted to Christianity. However, while in Berlin, De Jonge continued to send letters to his father and brother that denounced them in the strongest terms.[5]

Morris's brother, alarmed by what he saw as a continuing psychological deterioration, went to the Berlin police to report that Morris might be a danger to himself and to others. The police sought the advice of a psychologist named Dr. Abraham Bär. Initially, Dr. Bär consulted with the De Jonge family doctor, who described a long history of bizarre behavior by Morris, and diagnosed him with both paranoid delusions and delusions of grandeur. Dr. Bär then held a brief interview with Morris De Jonge himself to confirm this diagnosis. Based on this evidence, Dr. Bär declared Morris De Jonge to be a public danger and sent him against his will to the *Maison de Santé*. Despite his own protests, including a letter to the Kaiser, De Jonge would remain in this institution for eight long months. However, Morris De Jonge's delusions of grandeur would not remain delusions for long. Just a few months after his release, De Jonge would become a national figure, and a martyr for the anti-Semitic cause.

After his release from the mental hospital in the summer of 1890, De Jonge took his story directly to the ultra-Conservative *Kreuzzeitung*. He claimed that the reason his family had conspired to have him committed was not his own dementia, but his recent conversion from Judaism to Christianity. His "fanatically" Jewish family could not allow him to convert, so they found several corrupt Jewish doctors to fabricate a diagnosis of mental illness. The editors of the *Kreuzzeitung*, apparently impressed by De Jonge's story of Jewish fanaticism, allowed him to write an article called "*Offene Anfrage an den Geheime Sanitätsrat Bär*" (An Open Inquiry to the Senior Public Health Official Bär). This article denounced Dr. Bär on the grounds of medical fraud and corruption.[6] Because of this article, both De Jonge and Wilhelm

[5] De Jonge's account printed in *Kreuzzeitung* 24 June 1891 #342.

[6] Ibid. Ironically, just over a decade later Dr. Bär would be publicly attacked by newspapers from the opposite end of the political spectrum. In 1904, the Social Democratic *Vörwarts* accused Dr. Bär and his colleagues of negligence and outright cruelty for their treatment of mentally ill prisoners. Dr. Bär responded with a libel suit, but after bitter recriminations by both sides in court, the case was eventually settled quietly. Benjamin Carter Hett, *Death in the Tiergarten* (Cambridge Mass.: Harvard Press, 2004), 38, 197–198.

von Hammerstein, the editor of the *Kreuzzeitung*, were charged with libel. For De Jonge, the case promised to be a public forum where he could reclaim his honor and dignity. For Hammerstein, the case would serve as another opportunity to denounce publicly the barbarity and criminality of German Jews.

The De Jonge trial occurred on January 4, 1892, and was covered in many national newspapers. The prosecution's case consisted mainly of several expert psychiatrists who volunteered to testify on Morris De Jonge's state of mind and the validity of Dr. Bär's original diagnosis. One of these experts, Dr. Mendel, had briefly interviewed De Jonge before the trial. According to Dr. Mendel, he listened patiently as the defendant spoke of his great scientific importance, his connection to the high aristocracy, and his personal similarity to Goethe. Based on this interview, Mendel told the court that there was no doubt that the defendant suffered from an acute case of *Paranoia Simplex Chronica*.[7] Two other expert witnesses also testified that they supported Dr. Bär's conclusions and had no reason to question his professional judgment.

At the end of this expert testimony, the prosecutor made a surprising announcement. Because many of the doctors had suggested that Morris De Jonge was still mentally ill, the prosecutor now argued that he should be acquitted from the libel charges due to his defective mental state. The *Kreuzzeitung*, on the other hand, should still pay dearly for accepting and publishing De Jonge's accusations. This announcement was a blow to Morris De Jonge's chances of rehabilitating his name. Because even a stiff jail sentence for libel was preferable to being certified by a court as mentally ill, both the defendant and his attorney were put into the awkward position of having to argue against the prosecutor's demand for an acquittal. In his closing arguments, De Jonge's attorney did his best to portray his client as a reasonable man, and he denounced the entire affair as the result of De Jonge's conflict with the "reform-jewish-atheist-mammonistic" beliefs of his family. In the end, however, the court accepted the prosecutor's recommendation and dismissed the charges against De Jonge due to mental incompetence.[8]

---

[7] *Staatsbürgerzeitung* 4 January 1892 #4 Abend.

[8] *Staatsbürgerzeitung* 5 January 1892 #5A Morgen. Ironically, Hammerstein, who had helped De Jonge launch his libelous attacks, was also acquitted by the court. The court ruled that since Hammerstein had only provided space for De Jonge to

In the wake of this verdict, the anti-Semitic press attempted to turn Morris De Jonge into a martyr. The *Staatsbürgerzeitung*, for instance, followed the trial with several front-page articles that defended De Jonge and criticized the verdict. Citing the Talmud "scholar" August Rohling, the newspaper informed the judges that since "this case deals with a man who leaves Judaism and converts to Christianity, it should not be forgotten by the [Court] President that the Talmud commands Jews to use any means necessary to kill an Israelite who becomes an idolater or a heretic."[9] The *Staatsbürgerzeitung* argued that since it had become difficult to kill converts in such a civilized country as Germany, many Jews viewed a mental institution as the most effective alternative. The newspaper also lamented that doctors had too much power to order ordinary citizens into a mental hospital against their will. If laws dealing with mental health were not changed, the *Staatsbürgerzeitung* warned, every German would be in danger of being committed.[10] In the next several months, the De Jonge case was a very popular topic for anti-Semitic and ultra-Conservative speakers. In a speech on the Xanten ritual murder trial, for instance, Paul Förster told his audience: "The (liberal) *Berlin Börsen Courier* once wrote: 'All who would incite debates on the Jewish Question should be shut up in prison or in a mental hospital.' This demand has recently been turned into reality in the Xanten case and the De Jonge trial."[11]

A few months after his trial, De Jonge received support from another man who claimed to have suffered the same treatment by Jewish doctors. Friedrich Draak, a former businessman from Hamburg, claimed that a local doctor had conspired to have him committed in the hope of ruining his honor and taking over his business. After a long search, Draak found four other psychiatrists to pronounce him sane and prevent him from being committed. Shortly after the De Jonge case came to light, Draak published a book called *Schwarze Banden unter Juristen und Aerzten* (Evil Conspirators among Lawyers and Doctors), a 200 page tome that described his struggle to recover his

---

print his views, it was not clear that Hammerstein himself had the intention of libeling Dr. Bär.

[9] *Staatsbürgerzeitung* 7 January 1892 #9A Morgen.

[10] *Staatsbürgerzeitung* 13 January 1892 #19A Morgen.

[11] *Staatsbürgerzeitung* 21 January 1892 #33 in LAB A Pr. Br. Rep. 030, Nr. 8679, p. 115.

reputation both in and out of the courtroom. Although Draak claimed that a Berlin court agreed that his original committal had been fraudulent, he lamented in his book that no action against the plotters was ever taken.[12] The *Kreuzzeitung*, buoyed by these new "revelations," helped Draak and De Jonge draft a petition to the Reichstag demanding that the laws regarding mental illness be changed. Although this petition produced no practical results, it did allow the anti-Semitic press to continue to cite the laws on mental illness as an example of corrupt Jewish science and an illustration of the danger posed by Jews to ordinary Germans.[13]

Karl Paasch and the Foreign Office

While Morris De Jonge and Friedrich Draak found fleeting celebrity as anti-Semitic martyrs, another German businessman named Karl Paasch achieved even greater notoriety for his long struggle against Jewish corruption in the German Foreign Service. Paasch, the son of a High Government Councilor (*Oberregierungsrath*) in Minden, was originally trained as a civil engineer. By the early 1880s, however, Paasch had moved to China in the hope of making a fortune in this promising new economic market. At first, Paasch developed a friendship with the German ambassador to China, the High Privy Councilor (*Wirklich Geheimen Rath*) von Brandt. However, the two men soon developed serious personal differences and financial conflicts. Paasch blamed Brandt for stealing his plans to finance the creation of a Chinese rail system, and he accused Brandt of trying to discredit him in the eyes of the Chinese government.

---

[12] *Staatsbürgerzeitung* 5 March 1892 #109A Morgen.

[13] Reports on De Jonge's fate are sketchy. Soon after the controversy faded, De Jonge was made the editor of the ultra-Conservative *Hannoverische Post*. In January of 1893, the *General Anzeiger* reported that De Jonge wrote a letter to the *Verein zur Abwehr des Antisemitismus*, a defense group *against* anti-Semitism, asking to become a member. Although De Jonge still claimed that a religious, economic, and moral struggle against Jews was necessary, he now asserted that political anti-Semitism was morally reprehensible. Later that year, the *Berliner Volkszeitung* reported that De Jonge had fled to Switzerland after rumors spread that authorities would send him to a mental institution for six weeks of observation after he publicly slandered the Justice Minister. See *General Anzeiger* 10 January 1893 #8 in HStA Polizeibehörde, Abteilung IV, Politische Polizei, S 576 Teil I, Bd. 2; and *Berliner Volkszeitung* 3 August 1893 #180 in HStA Polizeibehörde, Abteilung IV, Politische Polizei S 576 Teil III a.

In late 1889, Paasch returned to Germany to complain personally about Brandt's misdeeds. He wrote letters to several high government officials, including the Chancellor and members of the Foreign Office. After his complaints were ignored, Paasch became convinced that the conspiracy to ruin him extended to the highest levels of the German government and was being controlled behind the scenes by Jewish bankers and the *Alliance Israélite*.

Faced with this huge conspiracy, Paasch decided to take his case directly to the German people. In April 1891, he wrote *Eine jüdisch-deutsche Gesandtschaft und ihre Helfer. Geheimes Judenthum, Nebenregierungen und jüdische Weltherrschaft* (A Jewish-German Legation and its Helpers: Secret Judaism, Secondary Governments, and Jewish World Dominance). The first section of this several hundred-page work was a thorough review of Paasch's feud with Ambassador Brandt. Paasch asserted that Brandt secretly worked for a rich Austrian Jew named Mandl, who himself was an agent of the *Alliance Israélite*. Allegedly, in addition to ordering Brandt to ruin Paasch, Mandl also ordered him to poison other business rivals and embezzle large sums of money. Furthermore, Paasch accused corrupt members of the Foreign Office of helping to cover up Brandt's crimes.[14] In the second part of his book, entitled "The Jewish Demon," Paasch gave a detailed portrait of alleged Jewish criminality, including a list of ritual murder trials and a description of other legal proceedings that exposed the extent of the Jewish conspiracy.[15]

Paasch sent copies of his book to many prominent government officials in the hope that they would take action against Brandt. Not surprisingly, the book brought the opposite result. On April 27, 1891 the official *Reichsanzeiger* published an announcement that libel charges would be filed against Paasch. However, while Paasch might have been happy about getting his day in court, he was doubtless disturbed by the way in which this announcement was phrased. The government would pursue charges against Paasch, the *Reichsanzeiger* reported, despite the fact that his allegations suggested mental illness.[16]

---

[14] Karl Paasch, *Eine jüdisch-Deutsche Gesandtschaft und ihre Helfer* (Selbstverlag, 1891) in LAB A Pr. Br. Rep. 030, Nr. 14754, p. 28.

[15] This second volume of Paasch's book was largely pilfered from sources such as Otto Glagau's journal *Der Kulturkämpfer* and Osman Bey's *Die Eroberung der Welt durch die Juden* (Bern: H. Koeber, 1888).

[16] Reprinted in Armin Graf, *Herrenhaus redivivus: Der Fall Paasch im preußischen Herrenhaus am 1. April 1892* (Berlin: Dewald, 1892), 10.

Despite the public notice in the *Reichsanzeiger*, several months passed without any movement on the case. In July 1891, Paasch wrote a new pamphlet called *Offener Brief an Se. Excellenz den Herrn Reichskanzler von Caprivi* (Open Letter to His Excellency Reich Chancellor Caprivi). A few days after this pamphlet appeared, Paasch was arrested and the pamphlet was confiscated. Although Paasch told his jailers that he would welcome his day in court and posed no flight risk, the police did not offer him bail. Instead, Paasch was visited by the prison psychiatrist, Dr. Levin. Having read about the experiences of Morris De Jonge (who was at this time still awaiting trial), Paasch refused to speak to a psychiatrist who he presumed to be Jewish.[17] Paasch also claimed to have rejected the services of the "infamous" Dr. Mendel of the Morris de Jonge trial, and he told his friends that the Jews had formed a plot to discredit his accusations by having him committed.

While Paasch was being held in "investigative custody", the anti-Semitic press began a public campaign calling for his release from prison. Like De Jonge and Draak before him, Paasch was proclaimed as a hero and a martyr for the anti-Semitic cause. Erwin Bauer, for instance, the editor of the anti-Semitic *Leipziger Tages-Anzeiger*, gave a well-attended speech on the Paasch Affair in Leipzig and then published this speech as a pamphlet.[18] Bauer celebrated Paasch as a pioneering businessman, who had personally forged close German-Chinese relations and helped to facilitate an official trade agreement. Bauer also gave Paasch personal credit for a Chinese contract to buy German-made warships and a plan for German companies to build railroads in China. Other anti-Semitic agitators followed Bauer's example and portrayed Paasch as a hero while denouncing the government's mistreatment of him. In Berlin, Paul Förster "designated [his] rally as a kind of People's Court (*Volksgericht*), as a portion of the battle for justice that begins when someone is unable to find justice himself." Thus, Förster claimed that as a question of human rights, "the case now stands far above the *niveau* of a simple political question."[19]

---

[17] This may have been Geheim Medizinalrath and außerordentlicher Professor Lewin, Medical Director and Clinical Instructor at the Ward for Syphilitic and Sick Prisoners in Berlin.

[18] Dr. Erwin Bauer, *Der Sensationsfall Carl Paasch* (Leipzig: W. Wauer, 1891).

[19] *Staatsbürgerzeitung* 24 August 1891 #390.

Anti-Semitic agitators informed the public that Paasch had been denied his legal right to bail and was instead being held in isolation—as opposed to prominent "Jewish criminals" who were always treated like royalty. In anti-Semitic rallies all over Germany, ordinary citizens were asked to direct petitions to Chancellor Caprivi demanding that Paasch be freed and his allegations against the Foreign Office be thoroughly investigated. As Erwin Bauer told his audience: "The case of Carl Paasch is perfectly suited to serve as a battering ram against the domination of the Jews."[20]

Eventually, Paasch was released from prison on 10,000 Marks bail. Upon regaining his freedom, Paasch immediately returned to his public campaign against Brandt and the Foreign Office. In early 1892, Paasch wrote a series of new pamphlets—each one containing more bizarre allegations against an ever-widening conspiratorial ring.[21] Paasch, for instance, now accused Justice Minister Schelling of being the *spiritus rector* of the Jewish conspiracy. Although Paasch claimed not to know if Schelling was of Jewish ancestry (he was not), he claimed that Schelling's friendship with the Hildesheimer family and his behavior in the Graef trial proved that he worked for Jewish interests.[22] Paasch also asserted that Schelling had been involved in many scandalous love affairs, and he suggested that he had other information about Schelling's moral fitness that was too disgusting to air publicly. After receiving no reply to his protest letters to Chancellor Caprivi, Paasch began to charge that Caprivi was also biased

[20] Bauer, *Der Sensationsfall Carl Paasch*, 22.

[21] These pamphlets included: *Ein deutscher Pentateuch: Rüstzeug zum Kämpfe gegen das Judenthum für Politiker und Abgeordnete aller Parteien* (Leipzig: Verlag von Carl Minde, 1892); and *Eine Protest-Eingabe an Se. Exellenz dem Reichskanzler von Caprivi* (Leipzig, Selbstverlag, 1892).

[22] The sensational 1885 trial of the well-known Berlin artist Gustav Graef centered on accusations that he had illicit relationships with young girls who he had hired to pose nude. Graef was charged with immoral behavior and several counts of perjury for lying about the affairs. The trial, which occurred only a few months after the courtroom humiliation of Adolf Stöcker, turned into a national political event. While prominent witnesses such as the writer Paul Lindau testified in Graef's defense, anti-Semites called this case a clear demonstration of Jewish immorality and the decadence of Jewish art. When Graef proved that he was the son of a pastor and not a Jew, the anti-Semites simply reminded their readers that his daughter was engaged to a Jew and pointed to the primarily Jewish list of defense witnesses. After Graef was acquitted, some anti-Semites accused justice officials of conspiring to protect Graef from a conviction. For more on the anti-Semitic use of the Graef trial, see *Der Kulturkämpfer* Heft 123 (October 1885): 13–35.

because of an illicit relationship with Ambassador Brandt's niece, who happened to be the widow of a wealthy Jew.[23] Many of Paasch's pamphlets were immediately confiscated by the police, but the allegations contained therein nevertheless leaked out into the public domain.

In addition to propagating these new charges against German government officials, Paasch also used these pamphlets to construct an image of himself as a heroic figure who fought against overwhelming odds:

> I allege that of 100 people subjected to the kind of mistreatment that Schelling has given me, probably 90 would have been driven to suicide or would have been sent to prison because of their insubordination and loud protests, where with the help of Jewish psychologists, who always lurk inside the gates, they would be forced into a straight-jacket and carried to an asylum."[24]

Paasch assured his readers that he would be tireless in seeking justice since this would not only be in his own interests, but also in the interests of the German people.

In the meantime, Paasch was still awaiting a court date for his libel trial. His attorney, Dr. Ivers, petitioned the Berlin Superior Court to subpoena a series of exculpatory witnesses. In addition to prominent government officials, Ivers included a Miss Bird, who would allegedly testify that Ambassador von Brandt had threatened her and attempted to rape her. Ivers also asked the court to invite several prominent Biblical scholars, including Jacob Ecker, August Dillmann, Johann Gildemeister, and Paul de Lagarde to testify to the true contents of Jewish religious teachings. Ivers argued that this question was relevant because it touched on the believability of Paasch's conspiracy charges. The court, however, ruled that since Brandt and his colleagues were not Jewish, the entire issue of Jewish religious teachings was irrelevant. In addition, the court refused to issue all of the other subpoenas because Paasch's accusations "are

---

[23] Sexual innuendoes were a common part of Paasch's accusations. In his original book, *Eine jüdisch-Deutsche Gesandtschaft und ihre Helfer* (Selbstverlag, 1891), Paasch claimed that Jews had used thousands of the prettiest German virgins to sire over 100,000 illegitimate children over the last six years.

[24] Quoted in Karl Paasch, *Die kaiserlich deutsche Gesandtschaft in China. Eine Denkschrift über den Fall Carl Paasch, für die deutschen Landesvertretungen, insbesondere den Reichstag* (n.p.: Selbstverlag, 1892).

so absolutely unbelievable, that there is ample reason to suspect they are false and thus unprovable."[25] This court ruling provoked even greater outrage in anti-Semitic circles. Not only had the judges refused to allow any of Paasch's requested witnesses, they also passed judgment on his charges before the proceedings had started. Petitions of protest sent by Paasch to the Prussian Assembly and *Herrenhaus* received support from anti-Semitic deputies, but achieved no practical success.

Because of repeated delays and postponements, Paasch would have to wait until May of 1893 for a resumption of the Paasch-Brandt libel trial. Paasch continued to send petitions and letters of protest to various parliamentary bodies, and even attempted in January of 1893 to run for a Reichstag seat for the region of Stargard. If he had been elected, Paasch would have received parliamentary immunity for the duration of the legislative calendar. But when Paasch lost this election, he also lost any hope of avoiding punishment.

In May 1893, Paasch was finally brought to trial. His new attorney, Dr. Hertwig, tried to defend him on the grounds that all of his charges were true. However, several of those officials who had been targeted by Paasch came forward to offer proof that his charges were ludicrous. In his closing statement to the court, Paasch was forced to admit that many of his accusations had turned out to be untrue. Despite this admission, he claimed to have acted in good faith and pleaded with the court to show him mercy. The judges saw little grounds for leniency, however, and sentenced Paasch to 15 months in prison.[26] After this verdict, Karl Paasch quickly disappeared from the political scene. He publicly maintained his innocence, but after filing an unsuccessful appeal, he fled the country for Zurich in an attempt to avoid his jail sentence.[27]

The Rise of Hermann Ahlwardt

While Karl Paasch was successful in reaching a national audience with his accusations, he was soon dwarfed in stature by another,

---

[25] Court documents printed in Graf, *Herrenhaus redivivus*, 8–10.

[26] Original court verdict in LAB A Pr. Br. Rep. 030, Nr. 14754, pp. 110–139.

[27] This according to a 1901 letter from the Prosecutor's Office to the Police President in LAB A Pr. Br. Rep. 030, Nr. 14754, p. 147.

even more extreme anti-Semitic agitator: Hermann Ahlwardt. Born in Pomerania in 1848, Ahlwardt moved to Oranienburg as an adolescent and was eventually trained there as a schoolteacher. In 1881, he accepted the post of headmaster (*Rektor*) at a Berlin primary school.[28] After only a few years in Berlin, however, Ahlwardt began to suffer from severe financial problems. In a desperate attempt to raise money, he became involved in several shady financial schemes and was even accused of stealing from the Christmas fund of his school.[29] In 1889, Ahlwardt's name was also mentioned in the sensational Manché trial, in which a Privy Councilor was accused of influence peddling and the selling of titles. Although Ahlwardt was never charged as an accomplice in the case, his involvement signaled the end of his academic career. Less than a year later, Ahlwardt was suspended from his position as headmaster and placed on half-pay. Faced with the loss of his public reputation and his only source of income, Ahlwardt turned away from academia and toward a career as a freelance anti-Semitic agitator.[30] Fueled by a fanatical anti-Semitism and by a desire to rehabilitate his reputation at any cost, Ahlwardt's career as an agitator would be successful beyond his wildest dreams. Within two years, he was a national political figure who his supporters greeted as the "second Luther."

Ahlwardt's first effort as an anti-Semitic author was an 1890 pamphlet called *Der Verzweiflungskampf der arischen Völker mit dem Judentum* (The Desperate Battle of the Aryan Peoples with the Jews). In this pamphlet, Ahlwardt described his innocent involvement in the Manché case, attacked his old superiors in the Berlin school system, and claimed that the Berlin city government was controlled by Jews. With the exception of the Manché material, there was little new in Ahlwardt's allegations. Many of his corruption charges against city councilmen were clearly based on the speeches of Adolf Stöcker a decade earlier, and his complaints about the Berlin school board could easily have been mistaken for the speeches of Bernhard Förster during the

---

[28] Levy, *The Downfall of the Anti-Semitic Political Parties*, 77.

[29] In May of 1891, Ahlwardt was acquitted of embezzling the pay of one of his teachers. Ahlwardt later claimed that these charges along with the allegations about the Christmas fund were created by Jews to discredit him. See *Kreuzzeitung* 6 May 1891 #207 Morgen Erste Beilage.

[30] Ahlwardt had written articles for the anti-Semitic *Staatsbürgerzeitung* as early as 1886. When he embarked on a full-time career as an agitator in 1890, the *Staatsbürgerzeitung* was his most loyal ally.

1881 Kantorowicz Affair. Ironically, some of the same targets for Stöcker and Förster's attacks were also featured in Ahlwardt's brochure, including the Jewish city councilmen Otto Hermes and Joseph Horowitz. The pamphlet's vicious anti-Jewish rhetoric and direct personal attacks on government officials brought attention from newspapers across the political spectrum. It also brought the attention of Berlin prosecutors, who eventually filed libel charges against Ahlwardt on behalf of several former teaching colleagues, the Municipal Executive Council (*Magistrat*), members of the school administration, and a local Jewish doctor.

Far from discouraging Ahlwardt from launching his public attacks, however, these libel charges seemed to inspire him. Ahlwardt quickly delivered a sequel to his *Verzweiflungskampf* brochure called *Der Eid eines Juden* [The Oath of a Jew], which claimed that Bismarck's Jewish banker, Gerson von Bleichröder, had committed perjury in an 1881 lawsuit involving an alleged former mistress.[31] According to Ahlwardt, the former Police-President of Berlin, Guido von Madai, and former Justice Minister Friedberg were instrumental in silencing the mistress and helping Bleichröder to escape prosecution.[32] In subsequent anti-Semitic rallies, Ahlwardt demanded that the government launch a formal investigation of the Bleichröder scandal. When these demands were left unanswered, Ahlwardt produced two new attacks on Bleichröder in *Jüdische Taktik* (Jewish Tactics) and *Die Prozesse Manché und Bleichröder* (The Trials of Manché and Bleichröder). Ahlwardt

[31] Bleichröder had allegedly been involved in an affair with a woman named Dorthee Croner, who later attempted to blackmail him. After she filed a civil suit against him, Bleichröder denied under oath that he had promised to support her and her children (by a previous marriage) for the rest of their lives. Although the law suit was dismissed, the scandal surrounding the alleged affair continued to grow. A former police officer, Hugo von Schwerin later joined Croner in perpetuating this scandal, and it was Schwerin that provided Ahlwardt with information on the case. Allegations of adultery and perjury continued to plague Bleichröder until his death in 1893. For more on this scandal see Fritz Stern, *Gold and Iron: Bismarck, Bleichröder and the Building of the German Empire* (New York: Vintage Books, 1977), 532–540.

[32] Madai and Friedberg were common targets of attack for the anti-Semites. Friedberg was a baptized Jew and Madai was known to be on friendly terms with Bleichröder. Ironically, despite his apparent friendliness with prominent Jews, Madai expressed much admiration for Adolf Stöcker and sympathy for his anti-Semitic message. Thus, both anti-Semites and their liberal or Jewish opponents thought they had an enemy in Madai. See Stern, *Gold and Iron,* 532–540 for more detail on Madai and his involvement with Bleichröder.

hoped that these attacks would either provoke a government investigation or would force Bleichröder to take him to court. Although the Berlin prosecutors considered Ahlwardt's "evidence", they soon sent him a letter stating that there was not enough evidence to support a criminal charge. Bleichröder himself, wary of being a part of a sensational trial, also refused Ahlwardt the satisfaction of filing a libel complaint.

In the meantime, Ahlwardt waited to face libel charges stemming from the original *Verzweiflungskampf* brochure. This trial, eagerly awaited by both Ahlwardt's friends and foes, finally began on February 15, 1892. Since Ahlwardt claimed that all of his allegations were true, he demanded a number of city councilmen and school administrators be forced to appear as witnesses. Ahlwardt even insisted that one of the opposing lawyers, Joseph Horowitz, be called as a witness because of his position on both the city council and the school board. By making wild allegations against these witnesses, Ahlwardt tried his best to shift attention away from his own libels on to the issue of a Jewish conspiracy. He accused Horowitz, for example, of leading a conspiracy to falsify embezzlement charges against him in order to ruin his reputation. This conspiracy had allegedly been instituted because of Ahlwardt's well-known anti-Semitic sympathies. Horowitz answered these charges by assuring the court that the school board had been as patient as possible with Ahlwardt despite his continual financial problems. As his actions continued to bring disrepute on the school system, however, Horowitz claimed that the administration had no choice but to start disciplinary action.

Ahlwardt also accused another Jewish city official, Otto Hermes, of creating a special political exam to prevent the hiring of anti-Semitic teachers. Ahlwardt claimed that Hermes was well known for asking each candidate if he "still believed in the fable of Christ." Hermes responded that he never made the political leanings of a candidate an issue unless political activities might interfere with the duties of a teacher. Although Hermes also denied that there was any sort of special political exam, he did admit that on a few occasions he told of his own belief that the divine origin of Christ was a fable.[33]

Ahlwardt also revived Stöcker's old accusation that Hermes, Horowitz, and the recently deceased council president, Wolfgang

---

[33] *Berliner Tageblatt* 17 February 1892 #87 Abend.

Strassmann, had used city purchases of land to line their own pockets. Ahlwardt asked the court to subpoena a large number of documents and bank records that he argued would support his charges. However, because this "evidence" seemed irrelevant to the charges, and because this request threatened to delay the trial for weeks, the court refused Ahlwardt's demands.[34] In the end, Ahlwardt was unable to prove any of his allegations or seriously harm the credibility of city officials. In his closing statement to the court, Ahlwardt lamented: "I believed that although all the people who were invited as witnesses were also my arch-enemies, under the weight of the German oath they would still be forced to tell the truth. I admit that this trust was my biggest cardinal error, and because of this error I have been left in the lurch."[35]

After four full days of testimony by school officials and city councilmen, the judges finally retired to consider a verdict. Following three hours of deliberation, the judges decided that Ahlwardt was guilty of all of the various libel charges and sentenced him to four months in prison. Although the court was lenient because it was his first conviction, it decided that a firm punishment was necessary because of the seriousness of his allegations and the fact that nearly all were proven to be without merit.

Berlin newspapers, many of which had printed stenographic reports of the trial testimony, greeted the verdict differently along political lines. The liberal *Berliner Tageblatt*, for instance, condemned Ahlwardt as being typical of the morally poisoned atmosphere (*Moralische Brunnenvergiftung*) of the previous decade. Despite the scandalousness of the whole affair, the *Tageblatt* believed that the trial would have at least some positive repercussions "since it will undoubtedly lead to a kind of moral disinfection."[36]

The ultra-Conservative *Kreuzzeitung* had a much different perspective on the *Verzweiflungskampf* trial. Although ultra-Conservative politicians were reluctant to link themselves directly with someone as unpredictable as Ahlwardt, many believed that his accusations against Jews and liberals could be used as political capital. Thus, after the verdict, the *Kreuzzeitung* commented:

---

[34] *Berliner Tageblatt* 22 February 1892 #96 Abend.

[35] Quoted in *Der Prozeß Ahlwardt. Ein Zeichen der Zeit und eine lehrreiche Studie. von *** einem Deutsch-Nationalen* (Berlin: Paul Heichen's Verlag, 1892).

[36] *Berliner Tageblatt* 23 February 1892 #98 Abend.

> Although the accused was generally unsuccessful in providing proof for his allegations, a series of improprieties in the Berlin city administration have surfaced in this trial that fill us with deep concern . . . Unfortunately, we do not expect that the driving forces in city hall—and as such we don't mean the real city officials, but the Progressive party leaders and agitators who are responsible for their election—will behave any differently in the future.[37]

Of course, Ahlwardt and many anti-Semitic newspapers viewed the *Verzweiflungskampf* trial as a victory despite the guilty verdict. In addition to portraying Ahlwardt as an innocent patriot and martyr, anti-Semitic newspapers continued to repeat his allegations against the city government as if they had been proven true. The anti-Semitic *Staatsbürgerzeitung* also expressed its contempt for the remark of Otto Hermes that the divine origin of Christ was a fable. This statement, the newspaper asserted, was proof that the Jews were destroying the moral fabric of Germany.[38] Thus, despite his conviction and his condemnation in the liberal press, Ahlwardt believed his courtroom experience had been quite successful. His outrageous charges and sensational trial had brought him national attention and a growing band of loyal followers. This increased popularity gave him the confidence to launch further attacks on the "Jewish conspiracy," and he produced more sensational accusations in public speeches and brochures throughout the year 1892.[39]

The Judenflinten *Affair*

Inspired by the impact of the *Verzweiflungskampf* trial on the public and the press, and undeterred by his own impending prison sentence, Ahlwardt launched even more outrageous accusations in April and May 1892 with two brochures called *Judenflinten* (Jewish Rifles) and *Neue Enthüllungen. Judenflinten* (New Revelations: Jewish Rifles). Ahlwardt's "new revelations" consisted of a charge of treason against the prominent Jewish businessman Isidor Löwe, and charges of bribery

[37] *Kreuzzeitung* 24 February 1892 #92.

[38] *Staatsbürgerzeitung* 20 February 1892 #85A.

[39] Ahlwardt wrote at least a dozen brochures during 1892, most fashioned after his public speeches in anti-Semitic clubs or party meetings. There were also a multitude of brochures published about Ahlwardt, both critical and supportive of his various allegations.

and incompetence against high government and army officials. Ahlwardt claimed that the munitions factory owned by Löwe had delivered 425,000 weapons to the German army that were seriously defective and even dangerous to their users. The damaged weapons were supposedly part of a conspiracy by the *Alliance Israélite* to make sure Germany would be defenseless in the next European war. The *Alliance*, along with the governments of France and Russia, which Ahlwardt claimed were both already controlled by Jews, apparently hoped to topple the German government and bring the Germans completely under Jewish domination.

While these new charges caused a scandal across Germany, there was much about the "revelations" that fell into a familiar pattern of anti-Semitic propaganda. The charges of a conspiracy run by the *Alliance Israélite* were not new, and neither was the choice of Isidor Löwe as a target. Isidor Löwe was the brother of the recently deceased Ludwig Löwe, who had been a leading industrialist, a long-time Progressive politician, and an active fighter against anti-Semitism.[40] Isidor had followed his brother's example, and was a prominent figure in the inter-confessional *Verein zur Abwehr des Antisemitismus*. Therefore, because of his family's prominence, Isidor Löwe had become a common target for anti-Semitic conspiracy theories, just as the recently deceased Jewish banker Gerson von Bleichröder had a decade earlier.

However, while Ahlwardt's charges were focused on a traditional target, they were unique in the magnitude and nature of the allegations, as well as the degree of self-aggrandizement present in the literature. Ahlwardt, for example, claimed to be ready to martyr himself in a dangerous one-man battle against the great Jewish conspiracy:

> If, as in the Manché case, I must be resigned to the fact that the investigation will proceed not against Löwe for the most despicable crime ever committed, but instead against me, this will still not halt me from fulfilling my duty. Cruel and difficult is the task that fate,

[40] Ludwig Löwe had been a favorite target of attack for the *Berliner Bewegung* and the Conservative Press. He was an outspoken opponent of anti-Semitism, and had a history of battling the anti-Semites in court. After defeating an anti-Semitic candidate, Liebermann von Sonnenberg, in the 1881 Reichstag elections, Löwe was the subject of an accusation by Liebermann that he had paid the Social Democrats not to run a candidate against him—an attack that resulted in Liebermann's conviction for slander.

> not my own will, has laid before me . . . Since Jewish money is all-powerful today, I must resign myself to suffer in prison or to being sent to an asylum.[41]

As with many of his other accusations, Ahlwardt claimed that he had irrefutable evidence of the faulty Löwe weapons, but added that many of his key witnesses were too intimidated to speak out, or had died under mysterious circumstances.[42] He also portrayed the *Judenflinten* issue as the crucial last stand for Germany against the Jewish world conspiracy, and regretted the degree to which "Germanness" had already succumbed to Jewish corruption:

> The decline of religiosity, the rise in a thirst for pleasure, as well as the extinction of patriotic feeling for the Fatherland, the waning of old-German loyalty, and the disappearance of idealistic outlooks on life are undoubtedly the cause of many regrettable recent developments. But who do we have to thank for all of this? Solely the Jews . . . The Mephistopheles of world history."[43]

A few months after publication of the *Judenflinten* allegations, Ahlwardt was once again charged with libel, and government authorities confiscated his brochures. However, these actions only served to increase the public attention that Ahlwardt received. News of the affair continued to reach a wide audience both through Ahlwardt's public speeches and through reviews in the mainstream press. As the months passed, the public and the press waited eagerly for Ahlwardt's return to the courtroom to defend his charges against Löwe.[44]

---

[41] Hermann Ahlwardt, *Neue Enthüllungen. Judenflinten* (Dresden: Verlag der Druckerei Glöß, 1892), 7.

[42] Ahlwardt had made the same claim about his witnesses in previous cases. He explained in a public speech in 1892 that his most important witness in the Manché case, Dr. von Kalckstein, mysteriously fell off a cliff, and that Gerson von Bleichröder's doorman, who was a major source of information in the Bleichröder perjury allegations, died suddenly after ingesting a suspicious powder. See *Staatsbürgerzeitung* 24 August 1891 #390.

[43] Ahlwardt, *Neue Enthüllungen. Judenflinten*, 34. Directly after the appearance of the Judenflinten brochure, Ahlwardt gave speeches like "Judenflinten—Deutschlands letzter Hilferuf" (Germany's last cry for help) to stress the importance of the Affair and the desperateness of the situation. See *Staatsbürger Zeitung* 25 April 1892 #192 Abend.

[44] Although too early for comparisons with the Dreyfus case, the Judenflinten trial was occasionally compared to the Panama Scandal that was beginning to develop in France. Reverse comparisons also took place. When Edouard Drumont was put on trial in France in the summer of 1892, for example, the *Berliner Tageblatt* referred to him as the "French Ahlwardt" (See *Staatsbürger Zeitung* 18 June 1892 #279B).

Throughout the summer of 1892, Hermann Ahlwardt did his best to keep himself in the headlines. His task was made easier by the occurrence of several other trials with anti-Semitic overtones, including the Xanten ritual murder trial and the Polke corruption trial. Ahlwardt gave frequent public speeches on these other trials and their relation to the *Judenflinten* scandal, and he promised that more revelations on *Judenflinten* would be uncovered during his upcoming trial proceedings. Ahlwardt's brief arrest during the summer (because of fears he would flee the country) allowed him to play the martyr, and supporters from many anti-Semitic groups collected money to help pay his bail.[45] When the trial finally opened in December of 1892, it produced a sensation throughout Berlin. The courtroom was packed with spectators every day, and almost every Berlin newspaper printed daily stenographic trial transcripts along with their own trial commentary.

From the first day of the trial onward, Ahlwardt and his lawyer, Dr. Hertwig, did their best to sidetrack or postpone the proceedings. Since the trial had started only a week before the Reichstag elections in which he was a candidate, Ahlwardt hoped that by winning a mandate before the trial was over, he could receive parliamentary immunity, and thus negate any possible conviction. Even these attempts at postponement were highly theatrical. Ahlwardt, for instance, claimed that a Jewish newspaper editor had come to the prison under false pretenses and had given him two cigars that were designed to make him ill, apparently on orders from an "Action Committee" headed by prominent Berlin Jews.[46] This committee, according to Ahlwardt, was apparently also responsible for shepherding most of the witnesses against Löwe out of the city.

In the days that followed, Ahlwardt used every opportunity to extend and sensationalize the trial by shifting its focus onto the topic of an alleged Jewish conspiracy. First, he demanded a full investigation into the existence of the so-called "Action Committee" that

[45] Hermann Ahlwardt, *Meine Verhaftung* (Dresden: Glöß, 1892), 8.

[46] *Der "Judenflinten"-Proceß. Sonderabdr. d. stenogr. Bericht d. "Neuen Deutschen Zeitung"* (Leipzig: Verlag d. "Neuen deutschen Zeitung," 1892), 15. An editor from the liberal *Das Kleine Journal* named Saling actually did lie to Ahlwardt (and prison officials) in order to get a prison interview, and when the writer was called during the trial to testify about the content of the interview, Ahlwardt used the opportunity to charge that Saling was working for the Jewish "Action Committee".

Fig. 7. "The Parade of Degenerates Before Headmaster Ahlwardt"—An illustration from the March 5, 1893 issue of *Feuerfunken: Illustrierte antisemitische Blätter.* Lined up in front of Ahlwardt are various Jews who were involved in sensational scandals at the time, including the Berlin councilman Pinkussohn (corruption), the banker Paul Polke (fraud), the businessman Isidor Löwe (Judenflinten Affair), the Socialist leader Paul Singer, and the butcher Wolf Buschhoff (suspect in the Xanten case). On the far right, the Jewish "army" is led by the drums of the "Jewish press" from in front of the stock market. Courtesy of the Landesarchiv Berlin.

was supposedly supported by the Jewish notables of Berlin. Ahlwardt was allowed to call the chief representative (*Generalbevollmächtiger*) of Gerson von Bleichröder as a witness, and Ahlwardt accused him of being the benefactor of the "Action Committee" and of bribing witnesses not to testify against Löwe. Ahlwardt then called a former member of the criminal police, Hugo von Schwerin, to testify that agents of Bleichröder had tried to pay him 10,000 Marks for material that the *Alliance Israélite* could use in discrediting Ahlwardt.[47]

Once this line of investigation ran out of steam, Ahlwardt tried to prove charges of a Jewish conspiracy by calling several well-known anti-Semitic agitators as "expert" witnesses on the *Alliance Israélite*, including Osman Bey, Karl Paasch, and Professor August Rohling.[48] When these witnesses were rejected by the court, Ahlwardt instead called Professor Moritz Lazarus, a prominent Jewish intellectual and former leader of the German branch of the *Alliance Israélite*.[49] Lazarus, however, could not be pressured or intimidated, and the judge finally insisted that the trial return to the issue of the dysfunctional weapons.

Although Ahlwardt did produce several witnesses who testified to knowing about irregularities at the munitions factory, it was revealed that many of these witnesses had been involved in a long-running labor dispute with Löwe or had been fired for unacceptable behavior on the job. Two of the witnesses even admitted on the stand that they had attempted to extort money from Löwe against the threat of revealing problems at the factory (although they still claimed the stories of irregularities were true). The lead judge's scornful attitude toward these witnesses caused Ahlwardt to claim unfair treatment, and led to heated exchanges between the attorneys.

---

[47] This is the same Schwerin who had been Ahlwardt's source for his anti-Bleichröder pamphlets, including *Der Eid eines Juden*. Schwerin had earlier been dismissed from his position in the police for his association with gamblers.

[48] Bey, whose real name was Frederick Millingen, was the author of an old anti-Semitic classic, *Die Eroberung der Welt durch die Juden*. August Rohling was an infamous former professor at the University of Prague who achieved notoriety through his book *Der Talmudjude*, his public debates with other scholars on the nature of the Talmud, and his "expert" testimony on Judaism in several scandalous trials (See Chapter 5). Karl Paasch, as mentioned above, was a celebrity because of his impending trial for libeling the Foreign Office by claiming that corrupt officials were working for the *Alliance Israélite*.

[49] Lazarus had long been a prominent figure in the Jewish community and an active opponent of anti-Semitism. He was the author of several well-known essays, including *Was heißt National?*, and he was an instrumental figure in forming organizations to fight against anti-Semitism.

Despite the judges' best attempts to keep the trial on track, Ahlwardt succeeded in turning the proceedings into a circus through repeated introduction of new sensational "evidence" that he claimed would prove his accusations. On December 3, for instance, Ahlwardt and his lawyer introduced secret military reports into evidence that he said would make further trial proceedings unnecessary. This surprise introduction of secret government papers caused a sensation both inside and outside the courtroom. Because the documents were thought to have been stolen from the War Ministry, a secret court session was ordered to examine the papers and investigate how they came into Ahlwardt's hands. Journalists and politicians speculated wildly about the contents of the documents, and at least one newspaper reported that the Kaiser and the Minister of War were being kept informed of the secret proceedings by telegraph.[50] By the next day, however, the War Ministry claimed that the papers were not of a dangerous nature, and need not be withheld from the public. The documents were eventually read to the court, with the most prominent statement being that in a recent training exercise, 520 of 939 weapons from the Löwe factory had to be returned for repairs. Although the military expert witnesses claimed that this was normal, and that most of the repairs would have been extremely minor, Ahlwardt dismissed their testimony, and claimed to have proven his allegations.

Two days later, Ahlwardt tried again to bring the anti-Semitic author Karl Paasch to the stand by claiming that he and a conservative politician, Konrad Freiherr von Wackerbarth, had overheard a damaging conversation between Löwe and other conspirators at a Berlin restaurant. Paasch was allowed to testify, but had little to say about the alleged conversation. He did use the opportunity, however, to testify that the *Alliance Israélite* was a kind of insurance group, in that anyone who paid 10 Marks would be protected against prosecution for any crime committed against Christians. Paasch claimed that this group was led by the Rabbi Isidor Hildesheimer and his brother Hirsch, who, as the editor of the *Jüdische Presse*, was present as a journalist in the courtroom. However, when Paasch asserted that the former *Kultusminister*, von Goßler, was a Jew, and that Jews were behind the murder of the Russian Czar Alexander II, the judge finally interrupted and declared this line of testimony irrelevant.[51]

---

[50] *Der "Judenflinten"-Proceß*, 70.

[51] Ibid., pp. 103–4. This charge against von Goßler was an old one, and was the

Ahlwardt continued daily to provide new twists and turns in the trial, and succeeded in his efforts to force some of the most powerful men in Germany to testify as witnesses. The Police-President of Berlin, von Richthofen, for example, was called to testify about accusations that he had been informed of Ahlwardt's charges long before the *Judenflinten* brochure was printed, but had failed to investigate the allegations. Although Richthofen denied any wrongdoing, Ahlwardt and his defense attorney implied that his lack of action was a clear dereliction of duty.[52]

Then, on December 6 and 7, as the trial seemed to be reaching an end, the proceedings took another improbable turn. Ahlwardt entered a wide-ranging motion that called for the acceptance of six new pieces of evidence and demanded several additional prominent witnesses, including the Minister of War, the former *Kultusminister* von Goßler, and *Landrat* Otto von Diest-Daber. When this motion was rejected by the court as being irrelevant and an obvious attempt to confuse the proceedings, Ahlwardt's lawyer, Dr. Hertwig, suddenly stood up and proclaimed:

> I for one, can only state that I must decline to further lead the defense of a man who had already been convicted before the proceedings began, and for whom the court denies any attempt to enter exculpatory evidence. However the verdict may fall, we fear not, and leave the judgment of these proceedings to the court of public opinion.[53]

---

source of an 1886 lawsuit by Goßler against the anti-Semite Bernhard Förster. Despite the fact that the charges were disproved, Goßler nevertheless felt the need to send a letter to the Judenflinten court insisting that his Christian ancestry could be traced back several generations. Ahlwardt later challenged the Christian ancestry of other political opponents, including the Finance Minister and National Liberal leader, Johannes Miquel.

[52] Ibid., 98.

[53] Ibid., 118. The lead judge in the case, Georg Robert Brausewetter, was well-known to Ahlwardt, having previously presided over his *Verzweiflungskampf* trial and a separate hearing on an embezzlement charge. Accusations of bias against Brausewetter were not new; he had already become infamous in Berlin for repeatedly cutting off defendants, attacking defense attorneys, and suggesting guilt to jurors before deliberations had started. As Benjamin Hett points out, however, Brausewetter had been equally rude, abrasive, and prejudiced toward liberal and socialist defendants. His courtroom antics brought repeated complaints by journalists across the political spectrum, from lawyers' associations, and from the Minister of Justice himself. Despite his open antagonism toward Ahlwardt in the Judenflinten case, Brausewetter also drew ire from the liberal and Jewish press for his comment during the trial: "I consider anti-Semitism in a certain sense not unjustified." Liberal critics claimed that far from being prejudiced against Ahlwardt, Brausewetter had given him far too much latitude. For more on Brausewetter and his controversial career, see Hett, *Death in the Tiergarten*, 112–123.

With these words, Hertwig packed his papers and stormed out of the courtroom. After a few moments of shock and disbelief, the judge decided to fine the defense attorney 100 Marks for his behavior. But Hertwig had accomplished his purpose: he had achieved his own martyrdom for the anti-Semitic cause, and his client, Ahlwardt, could now ask for a delay to find a new lawyer or prepare himself to proceed alone.[54] That night, the Berlin press featured detailed discussions of what the *Berliner Tageblatt* called "a scandal . . . the likes of which has not been seen in Prussian courts for quite some time."[55]

As the public was soon to discover, however, the sensational twists and turns in the trial had not quite reached an end. The next day, Ahlwardt did not show up to court and was reported to be seriously ill. A doctor was sent to examine him, and it was recommended that the proceedings be delayed until he had fully recovered. During the delay, however, the prosecutor decided to search Ahlwardt's clothes and found several containers of morphine powder in his coat pocket, along with instructions on how to use the powder to deceive doctors with fake symptoms. Ahlwardt denied any responsibility for the medicine, and claimed that an enemy from the "Action Committee" must have planted it during his trip from the court to the prison. The frustrated lead judge declined to investigate the matter any further, and instead ordered the closing arguments to begin immediately.[56]

Ahlwardt's closing speech was full of sensational new allegations and further claims of a Jewish conspiracy. Ahlwardt spoke, for example, of having read the minutes of a secret meeting of the so-called "*Hauptjuden*" in Frankfurt am Main. This meeting had supposedly included Ludwig Löwe and Professor Lazarus, along with Jewish

---

[54] Hertwig later achieved success as a speaker in anti-Semitic gatherings, and he used his credentials as Ahlwardt's defender as propaganda in an unsuccessful candidacy for the Reichstag.

[55] *Berliner Tageblatt* 7 December 1892 #623 Abend. Such a dramatic withdrawal was shocking to observers in the 1890s, but within a few decades well-known lawyers would make a habit of withdrawing from cases for tactical reasons. See Hett, *Death in the Tiergarten*, 142.

[56] *Freisinnige Zeitung* 10 December 1892 #290. There was almost certainly an ulterior motive for Ahlwardt and Hertwig's tactics and for the judge's insistence on continuing without delay. According to Benjamin Hett, it was relatively common for defense lawyers to enter new evidence or produce a slate of new witnesses at the very end of a trial that was proceeding badly for the defendant. According to §245 of the criminal code, judges could not dismiss evidence simply because it was offered too late but should instead offer time for the prosecution to respond. However, the criminal code also stated that adjournments which lasted over four days would require the trial to start over again. See Hett, *Death in the Tiergarten*, 25.

representatives from other European countries. According to Ahlwardt, Professor Lazarus was given 20,000 Marks to begin a program "to transform the moral life of Europe to fit the interests of Judaism."[57] Despite all of his accusations of dishonesty, immorality, and outright treason against Isidor Löwe, Ahlwardt also asserted that he had nothing against Löwe personally. He claimed to have acted merely out of patriotism, and he insisted that causing such a political scandal had been the farthest thing from his mind.

After more than five hours of deliberation, the judges returned and found Ahlwardt guilty, not of defamatory libel (*verleumderische Beleidigung*), but of simple libel. Although the prosecutor had asked for a sentence of 18 months in prison, the court decided on only a five-month sentence. Their spirits boosted by the relatively mild sentence, Ahlwardt's followers gathered in and around the courthouse to hail their martyred hero. Undaunted by the guilty verdict and basking in the glow of his publicity, Ahlwardt proclaimed that he was ready to carry the fight against the Jews to a new level.

Ahlwardt's immediate reward for his *Judenflinten* agitation was a seat in the Reichstag. Although he was imprisoned for the duration of the *Judenflinten* trial and was unable to campaign personally, Ahlwardt succeeded in crushing his Progressive opponent in Arnswalde-Friedeberg by a margin of 11,206 to 3,306. A rural area in eastern Brandenburg, Arnswalde-Friedeberg had previously been represented by *Junker* politicians. But Ahlwardt's supporters had toured the region giving fiery speeches on the *Judenflinten* Affair and distributing anti-Semitic pamphlets. When the local Conservative leader (who had been defeated in a primary election) rejected calls to ally with the liberals against Ahlwardt's candidacy, Ahlwardt was assured of success.[58] Now granted temporary immunity from punishment for the *Judenflinten* Affair and awarded a Reichstag seat from which he could present his future "revelations" to the nation, Ahlwardt looked forward to what seemed a very promising future.

Another immediate effect of the *Judenflinten* Affair was a general increase in support for the anti-Semitic political parties. These parties were indirectly aided by the propaganda successes of Herman Ahlwardt just as they had benefited from the agitation of Otto Böckel

[57] *Der "Judenflinten"-Proceß*, 145.
[58] Levy, *The Downfall of the Anti-Semitic Political Parties*, 82.

in Hessen after 1887. However, the anti-Semites remained divided in two camps, a pro-conservative wing behind Max Liebermann von Sonnenberg, and a radical wing behind Böckel. The quick rise of Ahlwardt as a popular figure was a double edged-sword for these established anti-Semitic leaders. The dramatic success of Ahlwardt's agitation filled them with hope, but also led them to fear that they would lose their control of the movement. While he had no organized party of his own, Ahlwardt often found support in local anti-Semitic clubs that were run independently from the established anti-Semitic parties.[59] Ahlwardt claimed to be aligned with the anti-Semitic parties, but he did not hesitate to challenge and provoke the party leaders, and he clearly reveled in having the spotlight all to himself. In early 1892, for example, Ahlwardt started a long dispute with Liebermann von Sonnenberg over remarks that Liebermann had been paid by Gerson von Bleichröder to withhold incriminating information. Thus, even after the *Judenflinten* brochure was published to a positive reaction from the anti-Semitic rank and file, Liebermann still expressed grave doubts about the reliability of Ahlwardt and hesitation about the risks of involvement in the *Judenflinten* Affair:

> The question of how one should publicly respond to the newest revelations by Ahlwardt has occupied me incessantly in recent days. I place more worth on these allegations than on all the others that Ahlwardt has produced up to this point. But I have not yet made up my mind as to how one can begin to give public speeches and write newspaper articles on this matter, without placing oneself in danger of committing treason . . .[60]

---

[59] By the end of 1892, Ahlwardt had recruited a group of faithful associates to help spread his message. Many of these men, like Rudolf Plack-Podgorski and Karl Paasch, also published libelous brochures, were involved in long trials, and eventually served time in prison.

[60] BABL 90 Li 1 #12 Nachlass Liebermann von Sonnenberg, 18–22. Letter from Liebermann von Sonnenberg to Hülsen, 21 April 1892. This letter reflects Liebermann's hesitance, as a former army officer, to attack the German military. Liebermann's colleague and rival Otto Böckel was less ambivalent about Ahlwardt. As he wrote in his newspaper, *Reichsherold*, before the trial: "The Judenflinten trial will, without question, end in a conviction because fables such as those that Ahlwardt, this cancer of the German anti-Semitic movement, has concocted in his sensational pamphlet cannot be proven—since they are simply untrue. To the 'Rector of all Germans,' as some of his rabble call him, this fact is of no consequence. He wants to create a sensation at any price." Quoted in *Berliner Tageblatt* 26 November 1892 #602 Morgen. The nickname "Rector of all Germans" (*Rektor aller Deutschen*) was a commonly used play on Ahlwardt's official title as a retired Rector, *Rektor a.D.* (for *Rektor außer Dienst*).

Fig. 8. "Anti-Semitism on the Way to its Goal"—An 1892 illustration from the newspaper *Reichsgeldmonopol* in Kassel. The lion and his army rifle (representing Isidor Löwe from the Judenflinten Affair) and the Berlin Bear (representing the liberal city council and perhaps also Dr. Abraham Bär of the Morris De Jonge case) fail to catch the contemptuous little boy (representing the Anti-Semites). Courtesy of bpk Berlin/Zeitungsabteilung, Staatsbibliothek zu Berlin.

The solution that many anti-Semitic leaders found was to praise Ahlwardt's courage and repeat his allegations, while distancing themselves from him personally. While they refused to take responsibility for Ahlwardt's actions, the party leaders defended him as a patriotic man of principle, if also a naive and over-exuberant one. Liebermann, still a bitter rival of Ahlwardt, even joined other anti-Semites in sponsoring a Reichstag bill to grant Ahlwardt immunity and halt all criminal proceedings in the *Judenflinten* matter.[61] Liebermann, Böckel, and other anti-Semites hoped to take advantage of the groundswell of support for Ahlwardt, while bracing themselves against the eventual conviction that they knew would come, and the disrepute that they feared would follow. Immediately after the *Judenflinten* trial, this tactic seemed to have worked perfectly. In the 1893 elections, the anti-Semitic movement swept into 16 Reichstag seats on Ahlwardt's coattails—the greatest number of seats they had achieved up to that point. Thus, as a result of the *Judenflinten* Affair, it seemed to many anti-Semitic leaders as though their movement had finally found broad public support, and could now become a major factor in German politics.

Ahlwardt's Demise

Ahlwardt's success in gaining public attention was partly a result of the outrageous nature of his attacks on prominent public figures. However, this same quality also helped to cause Ahlwardt's downfall. The kinds of fanatical speeches that worked well in an anti-Semitic rally were much less effective in the Reichstag. This was especially the case because a great majority of Reichstag delegates were either suspicious of him or openly condemned his actions. Thus, almost every parliamentary speech he made was greeted by heckling or derisive laughter from most delegates. Also, because he proved unable or unwilling to unite all the anti-Semitic parties behind him, Ahlwardt's popularity quickly began to wane. Believing that another major scandal was the only way to maintain his popularity, Ahlwardt launched direct attacks against government officials in March 1893

---

[61] BABL 90 Li 1 #12 Nachlass Liebermann von Sonnenberg, 27.

over corruption in the maintenance of the *Invalidenfonds*.[62] These allegations were directed primarily at the powerful National Liberal leader and Prussian State Secretary, Johannes Miquel. In addition to the charges of financial mismanagement, Ahlwardt also accused Miquel of being a co-conspirator with Gerson von Bleichröder in the shady financial deals that had caused the financial crisis of 1873, and he claimed that Miquel had also committed perjury in an 1876 libel trial against Joachim Gehlsen.

Based on Ahlwardt's charges against Miquel, the Reichstag reluctantly agreed to form an investigatory panel. When pressed by this panel for evidence to support his charges, Ahlwardt simply presented them with three infamous books from the 1870s: Rudolf Meyer's *Politische Gründer und die Corruption in Deutschland*, Otto Glagau's *Der Börsen und Gründungsschwindel in Berlin* and Martin Niendorf's *Die Fremdlinge in unserm Heime! Ein Mahnwort an das deutsche Volk von einem Berliner Bürger*.[63] After the panel concluded that these works were irrelevant, Ahlwardt referred to a witness named Meißner, who could have provided direct proof of Miquel's guilt, but who had suddenly disappeared after being bribed by Jews.[64] Once again, when the committee hearing started to turn against him, Ahlwardt sought to turn himself into a martyr. After one commission member suggested that he was not acting honorably, Ahlwardt declared: "Gentlemen, since the judges of this Commission treat me this way even before the case is finished, I refuse to take part in these proceedings any longer. I reject you as judges!" Ahlwardt then stormed out.[65]

This time Ahlwardt's tactics did not work. The Reichstag panel eventually concluded that there was no evidence of wrongdoing, and Ahlwardt was publicly condemned by the government and attacked so viciously in an open Reichstag session that no other deputy dared come to his defense. Ahlwardt's behavior now brought condemnation even from those who had lent him tacit support in the *Judenflinten*

[62] These accusations came directly after the resolution of the French Panama Scandal, and many anti-Semitic newspapers referred to the *Invalidenfonds* accusations as the German Panama Affair.

[63] See Chapter 1 for more on Meyer and Chapter 2 for more on Glagau.

[64] Ahlwardt had made a similar claim in the Judenflinten trial. He claimed that he would have been able to provide more evidence if his main witness, Krähahn, had not disappeared in the days before the trial.

[65] GStA PK, I. HA Rep. 84a Justizministerium, Nr. 55748, p. 19.

Affair—the Conservative, Catholic, and most of the anti-Semitic press. Newspapers from across the political spectrum now claimed that his allegations against Miquel were so outrageous that he deserved to be removed from the Reichstag. Although Ahlwardt remained a Reichstag delegate for many years, the *Invalidenfonds* debacle was effectively the end of his political career.

Ahlwardt and German Politics

Why did Hermann Ahlwardt and his *Judenflinten* Affair attract so much attention? Peter Pulzer, in his classic work on political anti-Semitism in Germany and Austria, attributes Ahlwardt's success primarily to the pre-modern irrational politics of rural Germany. As Pulzer writes:

> It would be a mistake to evaluate the election of men like Ahlwardt in terms of modern parliamentary politics. Its assumptions had not penetrated to areas like Arnswalde . . . where a normally passive and apathetic conservativism is periodically interrupted by brief outbreaks of violent rebellion. Campaigns like those of Ahlwardt or Böckel are more in the nature of a *jacquerie*, reminiscent of those bloody and hopeless uprisings which punctuate the history of medieval and Reformation Germany.[66]

This explanation, however, seems unsatisfactory. While traditional peasant anger at landowners and merchants was certainly a central factor in Ahlwardt's rise, it is clear that he could never have been so successful without the assistance of the mainstream political press. Because Ahlwardt's accusations came at a divisive period in German politics, they were instrumental in making the Jewish Question a part of a national political debate.

The *Judenflinten* Affair occurred during a time of political uncertainty in Germany, in which the relatively stable *Kartellpolitik* of the late *Bismarckzeit* had turned into the chaotic political rivalries of the first years of Caprivi's "New Course". The collapse of old *Kartell* political alliances resulted both in increased tensions between the political parties and in internal struggles within the parties themselves. For example, the *Judenflinten* Affair occurred at the high point

[66] Pulzer, *The Rise of Anti-Semitism*, 113–114.

of a long-brewing split between the moderate wing of the Conservative Party and the so-called *Kreuzzeitungsgruppe*, led by Wilhelm von Hammerstein. This rift was the continuation of long-existing conflicts within the party on whether to join with the National Liberals in a moderate alliance supported by Bismarck, or as the *Kreuzzeitungsgruppe* hoped, to reject the National Liberals in favor of a Conservative-Catholic alliance or even an independent political position. This internal split had become more divisive during the high point of Bismarck's *Kartellpolitik* between 1887 and 1890, when the moderate Conservatives and National Liberals openly cooperated with each other. Over the course of those years, Hammerstein's newspaper, the *Kreuzzeitung*, published open criticism of the moderate leader of the Conservative Party, Count von Helldorf-Bedra, and exchanged increasingly vitriolic articles with moderate and liberal newspapers in the hope of causing friction within the *Kartell*. These articles often used anti-Semitic attacks against the National Liberal "free-traders" in order to make the continuation of a *Kartell* alliance between Conservatives and these "Jewish-liberals" difficult. When the fall of Bismarck in 1890 opened up new possibilities for political realignment, the *Kreuzzeitungsgruppe* used every opportunity—including more vicious anti-Semitic articles—to criticize the liberals and to try to prevent the reestablishment of a *Kartell* coalition.

It is not altogether surprising then that despite Ahlwardt's unpredictability and the outrageousness of many of his charges, the *Kreuzzeitung* would give its tacit approval to Ahlwardt and his methods. Even though many of Ahlwardt's charges verged on paranoid fantasy, the *Kreuzzeitung* did its best to use the issues raised by Ahlwardt for political advantage. Both the anti-Semitic press and the *Kreuzzeitung* took extraordinary glee in Ahlwardt's accusations against figures like Dr. Otto Hermes and Isidor Löwe, who were not only prominent Jews, but also leading liberal politicians.[67] Predictably, the anti-Semitic rhetoric of the *Kreuzzeitung* and its tacit support for Ahlwardt did not find unanimous support within the Conservative Party. Von Helldorf-Bedra and the moderate *gouvernemental* wing of the party were trou-

[67] A decade earlier, Hermes, who was also the director of the Berlin Aquarium, had been the subject of lawsuits filed by the anti-Semites Max Liebermann von Sonnenberg and Bernhard Förster stemming from the Kantorowicz Affair. Förster, like Ahlwardt, had also been dismissed from his teaching position in Berlin and blamed Hermes for this injustice.

bled by Ahlwardt's attacks on government leaders and his suggestions of corruption within the German army. They viewed the escalation in anti-Semitic rhetoric as a strategic attempt by Hammerstein to use popular discontent to drive the Conservative Party into the hands of the *Kreuzzeitungsgruppe*.[68]

The long battle between the *Kreuzzeitungsgruppe* and the moderate wing of the party intensified during 1892 and reached a fever pitch at the Conservative Party convention in the Tivoli Brewery during the 8th and 9th of December—at the most sensational point in the *Judenflinten* trial. This long-awaited convention would focus on one especially contentious issue: whether or not to add a statement to the party platform that explicitly committed the party to fighting the dangerous influence of Jews.

Because of the charged atmosphere produced by the *Judenflinten* trial, the convention was dominated by high emotion and heated exchanges between moderate and radical Conservatives. Ahlwardt's popularity and his recent electoral victory in Arnswalde meant that the moderate Conservatives faced an uphill battle in convincing party members that an anti-Semitic platform would have negative repercussions. The moderates attempted to focus on the ill repute of anti-Semitic party leaders and warned that the party would risk being associated with these "Rowdy-anti-Semites" [*Radau-Antisemiten*] if they approved an explicitly anti-Semitic platform. Moderate leaders like von Helldorf-Bedra instead suggested the adoption of a compromise statement that condemned the excesses of both Jews and anti-Semites. However, this move backfired. Some speakers responded by openly proclaiming their support for Ahlwardt, and the former Conservative candidate from Arnswalde-Friedeberg even announced that "ten Ahlwardt anti-Semites are always better than one Progressive."[69] In the end, the moderate statement was rejected, and the explicitly anti-Semitic platform was approved by a majority of delegates. Seduced by the meteoric rise of Ahlwardt and the success of his demagogy, the Conservatives announced their support for anti-Semitism—and gave a degree of respectability to anti-Semitic agitators.

---

[68] See, for example, commentary about the budding rivalry within the Conservative Party in *Antisemitische Korrespondenz* 15 August 1888 #33, *Berliner Börsen-Courier* 2 June 1889 #274, *Deutsche Reichszeitung* (Bonn) 19 April 1892 #109. See also the *Kreuzzeitung*'s angry response to Helldorf's attacks during the 1892 Tivoli conference in *Kreuzzeitung* 12 December 1892 #582 Abend.

[69] *Kreuzzeitung* 9 December 1892 #577.

Like the Conservative Party, the Catholic Center Party also found itself in a period of crisis in the early 1890s—a crisis that resulted in the increased use of anti-Semitic rhetoric within the party press. In early 1892, the Minister of Education, Count Zedlitz, had proposed a new School Bill in the Reichstag on behalf of the government. This bill, which had been designed to ease restrictions on Catholic education still left over from the *Kulturkampf*, had been favored by both the Center party and the Conservatives. But when the bill was withdrawn by Zedlitz under pressure from the National Liberals and Progressives, it caused great bitterness among Catholics, especially against their liberal opponents. In their anger over the failure of the School Bill, many Catholic papers joined the radical Conservatives in using anti-Semitic rhetoric to attack liberal opponents.

Like the Conservative Party, the Center Party had long contained a split between agrarian-conservative and more liberal-minded politicians. The agrarian-Catholics, led by men like Schorlemer-Alst, had long had sympathy with anti-Semitism, and hoped throughout the 1880s that the Center party would eventually enter a pro-government alliance with the Conservatives rather than join the Progressive Party in opposition. While the Center Party as a whole had often wavered in its position toward the government and toward anti-Semitism in the 1880s, the powerful leadership of Ludwig Windthorst generally led the party in a more liberal direction, away from Conservatives and anti-Semitism, and away from cooperation with the government. After Windthorst's death and the fall of Bismarck, however, radical-Catholic newspapers like the *Germania* began to write anti-liberal and anti-Semitic articles more freely. By the time of the failure of Count Zedlitz's school bill, the Catholic agrarians were eager to use anti-Semitic articles both as a method of attacking liberal politicians and as a way of challenging the liberal wing of their own party.

Thus, while the Catholic press was unified in ridiculing Ahlwardt during the *Judenflinten* Affair, they, like the ultra-Conservatives, were tempted into using Ahlwardt's attacks as propaganda against liberal politicians. Many Catholic newspapers like the *Germania* and the *Deutsche Reichszeitung*, for example, were quick to condemn Ahlwardt as "a symptom of the sickness affecting the body of the people."[70]

[70] *Deutsche Reichs-Zeitung* (Bonn) 19 May 1892 #139.

At the same time, they insisted that the real source of the problem was the irresponsible behavior of Jews and "Jewish-liberals." In a series of articles written during the *Judenflinten* trial, *Germania* proudly traced its "recognition of the Jewish Question" all the way back to a series of anti-Semitic articles in 1875.[71]

Even the *Kölnische Volkszeitung*, which had built a reputation for opposing anti-Semitic articles in more radical Catholic papers like the *Germania*, now took a tougher stand on the Jewish question. In early April 1892, just as the *Judenflinten* accusations were first being publicized (and not long after the withdrawal of the Zedlitz school bill), the *Kölnische Volkszeitung* printed a program of "Seven Theses" on the Jewish question that had been sent by a reader. These Seven Theses included pointed condemnations of the Jews for exploiting Germans economically, corrupting their morals, and encouraging the spread of revolutionary socialism throughout the masses. While the editors took great care in differentiating these Seven Theses from the more radical demands of the anti-Semitic parties, and while they were careful to reject any mention of revoking Jewish civil rights, they concluded in the end that ". . . these theses represent comparatively the best formulation of an anti-Semitic program—if this term is appropriate here—that we have seen up to this point." The program ended with the demand that the Catholic press mount a unified defense against the harmful "endeavors of Judaism."[72]

When liberal newspapers such as the *Berliner Börsen-Courier* and the *Freisinnige Presse* wrote articles during the *Judenflinten* trial that labeled the Catholic press as anti-Semitic and blamed it for aiding Ahlwardt's cause, the Catholic press was quick to respond. In scathing articles against their archenemies in the liberal press, the *Germania* claimed that the excesses of anti-Semitism were the direct result of the overwhelming Jewish support for political radicalism (progressive liberalism and Social Democracy). The paper also denounced Jewish-liberal leaders who allegedly would defend all Jews—even those who were clearly guilty of grievous crimes. In addition, the *Germania* criticized

[71] *Germania* 8 December 1892 #282. While under the editorship of the radical anti-Kulturkämpfer Paul Majunke, the *Germania* was a major source of anti-Semitic attacks in the mid 1870s. Therefore, the *Germania* editors could claim with some justification that they had held a consistent view on anti-Semitism throughout the *Kaiserreich*.

[72] *Kölnische Volkszeitung* 3 April 1892 #186.

Jewish leaders for failing to see the need for reforming themselves, and stated that "... it is self-evident that no peace is possible with such Jewish blindness, which avoids any thorough self-examination and self-improvement and speaks arrogantly about 'compelling' through the 'power of money'. . . ."[73] Therefore, the *Germania* argued, anti-Semitism would continue to grow until "responsible Jewry" disassociated itself from the dangerous elements of German society.

Thus, like the leaders of the anti-Semitic parties, many Conservative and Catholic editors were seduced by the dynamism of Ahlwardt's movement and the immediate successes of his demagogic style. Both ultra-Conservative and radical Catholic editors hoped to disassociate themselves from Ahlwardt personally, while taking advantage of the *Judenflinten* scandal as an opportunity to spread anti-liberal propaganda and to change the direction of their own political parties.[74] Surely a pre-existing anti-Semitic feeling in the populace was necessary to make such propaganda profitable, but the explicit or implicit support of anti-Semitism by the Catholic and ultra-Conservative press did much to give respectability and plausibility to Ahlwardt's cause.[75]

The fact that Ahlwardt influenced national political debate does not necessarily negate what Pulzer suggests is his "pre-modern" appeal for German peasants. However, more recent scholarship has suggested

---

[73] *Germania* 25 December 1892 #296 Erstes Blatt. This quote is actually a response to a post-trial interview of Hirsch Hildesheimer, the editor of the *Jüdische Presse* and a vocal opponent of anti-Semitism. *Germania* had twisted his words to make it appear that he was talking about using Jewish money to quiet dissatisfaction with Jewish abuses of power.

[74] The new attention to anti-Semitism as a political weapon was also inspired by the rural electoral successes of Otto Böckel in the last years of Bismarck's government. By using anti-Semitic rhetoric, therefore, the radical Conservatives and Catholics saw an opportunity not only to fight political battles, but also to broaden their own electoral base.

[75] This brief discussion of the political forces behind the rise in anti-Semitic rhetoric in the early 1890s, does not, of course, constitute a full explanation. Many real economic and social factors also contributed to an increase in anti-Jewish sentiment. In the early 1890s, for example, a series of bank failures throughout Europe led to fears of a repeat of the economic crash of 1873 and resulted in popular resentment against Jewish financiers and public officials. Thus, as James Retallack suggests, the actions of party leaders in this period should be considered partially a result of pressure "from below." See James Retallack, *Notables of the Right: The Conservative Party and Political Mobilization in Germany, 1876–1918* (Boston: Unwin Hyman, 1988), 102. The rise in anti-Semitism was also the result of many regional social and economic tensions. For an analysis of some of these local factors see Levy, *The Downfall of the Anti-Semitic Political Parties.*

that far from being a mere *jacquerie*, the agitation of populist politicians such as Ahlwardt was part of a transformation from the traditional *Honoratiorenpolitik* to modern populist politics. In previous decades, liberal notables and conservative landowners had dominated local politics through institutions such as provincial commissions, district committees, school boards, chambers of commerce, and agricultural associations. Domination of rural politics was so complete that little campaigning was necessary, and some candidates were even elected without visiting their districts.[76] But with agitators like Otto Böckel and Hermann Ahlwardt, this traditional system of politics began to break down. The expansion of the electorate and the rising rate of participation combined with more intense electoral campaigning to challenge all of the traditional political parties.[77] For the Conservative Party, the debate at the 1892 Tivoli conference was essentially a debate about whether the party should embrace this new "demagogical" political style. In this conference, ultra-Conservative delegates like Hammerstein tried to force the party to use anti-Semitism to exploit lower-class anger at the liberal industrial bourgeoisie. Moderate Conservatives like Helldorf-Bedra, on the other hand, were much more hesitant to abandon traditional "gentlemanly" politics.[78]

The dilemmas faced by the Conservatives were equally troublesome to other political parties as well. The Catholic Center Party, which had long sought to attract votes through Catholic peasant organizations, certainly viewed the agitation of Ahlwardt and Böckel as a threat. Thus, when the generally moderate *Kölnische Volkszeitung* published its "Seven Theses" of an anti-Semitic program in April of 1892, it did so primarily as a response to pressure coming from Rhineland peasants. Therefore, while Ahlwardt may indeed have appealed to some "pre-modern" instincts among the German peasantry, he was also a key figure in a growing political revolution.

---

[76] Geoff Eley, *Reshaping the German Right: Radical Nationalism and Political Change after Bismarck* (New Haven: Yale Univ. Press, 1980), 20.

[77] Eley, 22.

[78] For more on the battle over this new "demagogic" politics in the Conservative Party, see Retallack, *Notables of the Right.*

Anti-Semitism and Mental Illness

It would seem appropriate here to say a few words about the possible role of mental illness in the political activities of Morris De Jonge, Karl Paasch, and Hermann Ahlwardt. All three of these men, and many of their lesser-known associates, constantly fought against suggestions that they were mentally unstable. Such suggestions came not only from German Jews and liberals, but also from many moderate Conservatives and government officials. The agitators themselves, of course, believed all suggestions they were mentally ill were part of a grand Jewish conspiracy. In their eyes, Jewish psychiatrists worked alongside Jewish lawyers and journalists to mislead the German people and undermine their values.

Attacks on Jewish doctors were a relatively common part of Hermann Ahlwardt's public rhetoric. Ahlwardt, for example, commonly referred to the old anti-Semitic accusation that a Jewish doctor named Mackenzie had murdered Kaiser Friedrich III to prevent him from acting against German Jews.[79] At the height of his popularity, Ahlwardt also gave a speech in which he claimed that the 1878 assassination attempt on Kaiser Wilhelm I had been part of a Jewish conspiracy.[80] Ahlwardt accused the Jewish prison doctor, Dr. Levin (the nemesis of Karl Paasch), of being an essential conspirator in this attempted regicide. Allegedly, Levin had placed himself at the scene of the crime so he could "heroically" save the Kaiser and then conspired to have a female witness to the plot sent to a mental hospital. According to Ahlwardt, Levin later had himself assigned to examine the assassin so he could make sure that no cross-examination could ever take place (the assassin died before coming to trial). Not surprisingly, when this same Dr. Levin later came to

---

[79] The charge against Mackenzie was not new; anti-Semitic and ultra-Conservative newspapers had suggested since the Kaiser's death from throat cancer in 1889 that Mackenzie was guilty of malpractice or even causing intentional harm to the Kaiser. But the suggestion that Friedrich had been on the verge of dealing a deathblow to the Jewish elite was more than a bit fanciful. Famous for the statement that anti-Semitism was the "disgrace of the century," Friedrich III was known for being considerably more liberal and more hostile to anti-Semitism than either his predecessor Wilhelm I or his successor Wilhelm II.

[80] For suggesting in this speech that a majority of government and army officials were controlled by Jews, Ahlwardt was charged with additional counts of libel. The trial on these separate charges was delayed until June 1893—after the end of the *Judenflinten* affair—but Ahlwardt was eventually sentenced to 3 months in prison.

visit Ahlwardt in prison during the *Judenflinten* Affair, Ahlwardt emphatically refused to see him.[81]

Modern historians seem to be equally split on the issue of Ahlwardt's mental fitness. Some historians have characterized Ahlwardt as a cynical opportunist, while others, like Paul Massing and Richard Levy, have seen in his character "signs of a persecution complex, a penchant for self-exhibition and humiliation, [and] a need to confess, reveal, and expose."[82] It is true that there are several factors that point to Ahlwardt's cynical use of anti-Semitism for financial gain, including his brief attempt to sell "Judenflinten cigars," and his insistence on charging admission to his public rallies.[83] But the fact that many of Ahlwardt's actions were calculated for profit does not necessarily exclude Ahlwardt's true belief in his historical mission, or the possible presence of mental illness.

One reason that it is difficult to evaluate these demagogic anti-Semites is that there is a strong paranoid and conspiratorial element in almost all modern anti-Semitic literature. Thus, at the beginning of his political career, Ahlwardt already had a litany of outrageous accusations and conspiracy theories he could choose from. However, while anti-Semitic propaganda always relied on secret conspiracies and crude stereotypes, the allegations of "traditional anti-Semites" like Max Liebermann von Sonnenberg and Otto Glagau seemed at least to have some potential for plausibility. Ahlwardt and Paasch, however, took these already illogical stereotypes and myths and turned them into the stuff of paranoid fantasy.

Some of Ahlwardt's contemporary opponents condemned him as a clever "*geschäftsantisemit*" (commercial anti-Semite), but a far larger number asserted that his public behavior showed clear signs of madness. Of course, the liberal press had an interest in portraying Ahlwardt as crazy, and they took every possible opportunity to do so. The liberal *Kölnische Zeitung* reported that Ahlwardt granted an interview to the journalist Hermann Bahr, in which his paranoia and megalomania were on full display:

> I am radical, I am far more radical than Böckel, I am the most radical and that is why I am followed by all the nations of Europe; everyone

---

[81] See note 17 above.
[82] Levy, *The Downfall of the Anti-Semitic Political Parties*, 77.
[83] Ibid., 245.

> will follow me, everyone, everyone! . . . I am strong! I am terribly strong! I am now the strongest! I can destroy everyone. I have proof. I can prove everything . . .[84]

Another liberal newspaper reported that Ahlwardt appeared in front of the *Invalidenfonds* investigation committee with a large gash in his pants that exposed his underwear. According to this newspaper, Ahlwardt blamed a Jewish conspiracy among tailors for this mishap.[85]

Such descriptions of Ahlwardt continued in the liberal press long after he had lost his political effectiveness. On an 1896 visit to Hoboken, New Jersey, Ahlwardt was briefly arrested for brandishing a weapon in public. In an account printed in his new English-language newspaper, *The Anti-Jew*, Ahlwardt supposedly wrote of having drawn the revolver after being ambushed by 400 angry Jews.[86] The socialist *Hamburger Echo* gleefully recounted Ahlwardt's ridiculous tale of bravery in Hoboken, and also sarcastically noted Ahlwardt's pride at having created the first anti-Semitic clubs on the Gilbert Islands and Samoa.[87]

Whether or not these kinds of stories about Ahlwardt were completely accurate, it is clear that they were made plausible by Ahlwardt's own outrageous behavior in the public spotlight. During the *Invalidenfonds* controversy, for instance, Ahlwardt and his associates accused the Prussian State Secretary, Johannes Miquel, of being the descendent of Portuguese Jews and thus a secret participant in the Jewish conspiracy. After his unsuccessful scheme to sell *Judenflinten* cigars, Ahlwardt attempted one last comeback with a pamphlet claiming that Schiller, Lessing, and Mozart had all been murdered by a Jewish-Jesuit-Freemason conspiracy.[88] Ahlwardt could still draw audiences with such wild accusations, but in his later years these audiences came to view him more as an oddity than as a serious political force.

---

[84] *Kölnische Zeitung* 5 April 1893 #273.

[85] Ahlwardt bitterly complained about the press exploitation of what he called an embarrassing (and innocent) incident that could happen to anyone. Against the wishes of the *Invalidenfonds* committee, Ahlwardt insisted on a lengthy explanation of the entire episode, which he claimed was being used to suggest his insanity. GStA PK, I. HA Rep. 84a Justizministerium, Nr. 55749, p. 19.

[86] *Hamburger Echo* 25 April 1896 #97.

[87] *Hamburger Echo* 28 February 1897 #50.

[88] Hermann Ahlwardt, *Mehr Licht ! Die Ermordung Friedrich Schillers, Lessings und Mozarts vor dem Forum moderner Literatur- und Weltgeschichte* (Leipzig-Reudnitz: W. Fischer, 1914).

While it does seem clear that men like Morris De Jonge, Karl Paasch, and Hermann Ahlwardt exhibited pathological personality characteristics, any real psychological evaluation would need to be based on far more personal information than is available here. And even if such an analysis was possible, it would certainly not lead to a single diagnosis for all of these agitators. Even those who have assumed that anti-Semitism is a symptom of psychological or emotional disorder agree that anti-Semitism "is not concomitant of any one clinical category of personality disturbance."[89] There is also a danger in making such a diagnosis. Any assumption that men like Ahlwardt were "crazy" should not be used as a substitute for an analysis of their political ideas or as a way to dismiss their political importance. The fact that such outrageous characters as Hermann Ahlwardt, Karl Paasch, and Morris de Jonge were able to have such a significant impact on German politics should instead lead historians to examine their cases even more closely.

---

[89] Nathan Ackerman and Marie Jahoda, *Anti-Semitism and Emotional Disorder: A Psychoanalytic Interpretation* (New York: Harper, 1950), 25.

CONCLUSION

"It is not possible as a German to write about anti-Semitism without thinking of the Shoah. Even for studies of the period before the First World War, questions about continuities with the Third Reich are always in the background."[1] This sentiment, expressed by Christoph Nonn, is true not only for citizens and residents of Germany, but for all historians who choose to focus on anti-Semitism in the years before 1933. Unfortunately, even more than sixty years after fall of the Third Reich, historians still struggle to come to a consensus on even the most basic questions about these continuities: How anti-Semitic was Germany in the Imperial Period? To what degree were Nazi Germany and the Holocaust a culmination of German social and political developments after 1870? And to what degree was Nazi anti-Semitism merely an intensification of prejudices cultivated by ordinary Germans long before the turn of the century?

One of the earliest attempts to answer these questions was Paul Massing's classic 1949 book *Rehearsal for Destruction.* Written as part of a series called "Studies in Prejudice," Massing's work was one part of a five volume set of scholarly investigations designed to uncover the sources of the prejudice that contributed to Nazi genocide.[2] Although Massing presented a balanced and thoughtful analysis of pre-war anti-Semitism in Germany, his work was colored by the circumstances of its creation. As the title of his work suggests, Massing considered the anti-Semitic movement of the late nineteenth and early twentieth centuries as an immediate precursor to Nazi anti-Semitism—as a "rehearsal for destruction." Although he admitted that anti-Semitic agitators were often personally unsuccessful in

[1] Christoph Nonn, "Zwischenfall in Konitz: Antisemitismus und Nationalsozialismus im preußischen Osten um 1900," *Historische Zeitschrift* 266 (1998): 387.

[2] See Paul Massing, *Rehearsal for Destruction: A Study of Political Anti-Semitism in Imperial Germany* (New York: Harper & Bros., 1949). The series was edited by Max Horkheimer and Samuel Flowerman, and it was sponsored by the American Jewish Committee. Other volumes were equally groundbreaking: *The Authoritarian Personality* by T.W. Adorno et al.; *Dynamics of Prejudice* by Bruno Bettelheim and Morris Janowitz; *Anti-Semitism and Emotional Disorder* by Nathan Ackerman and Marie Jahoda; *Prophets of Deceit* by Leo Lowenthal and Norbert Guterman.

the late Nineteenth Century, Massing nonetheless argued that the growth and development of political anti-Semitism during this era eventually culminated in the planned mass murder of European Jews.

Fifteen years after Massing's groundbreaking study, Peter Pulzer published *The Rise of Political Anti-Semitism in Germany and Austria.* Pulzer's work expanded the story of German anti-Semitism to include the roughly parallel, but still independent development of anti-Semitism in Austria. However, Pulzer, like Massing before him, emphasized the high degree of continuity between the Second Reich and the Third. As he wrote:

> The main difference between the political anti-Semitism of the post- and pre-war periods lies not in its content, but in its success. There were some changes in emphasis, a general increase in virulence of tone and unscrupulousness, and a growing acceptance of physical violence; but one would have to go a long way through the anti-Semitic literature of the 1920s and 1930s to discover a point or argument which had not already been used before 1914.[3]

At least to a certain extent, then, the Nazis did little more than exploit existing stereotypes in a more aggressive and, unfortunately, more successful manner.

In *The Downfall of the Anti-Semitic Political Parties in Imperial Germany* (1975), Richard Levy challenged the idea that anti-Semitism in the *Kaiserreich* was merely a "dry run" for later Nazi atrocities. As the title of his book suggests, Levy argued that parliamentary anti-Semitism, which was the most prevalent and most visible form of anti-Semitism at the time, turned out to be a total failure in the pre-war period.[4] Levy pointed out that anti-Semitic leaders during this time had not succeeded in reaching any of their major goals: they failed to pass any significant anti-Jewish legislation, failed to build a grass roots organization, and failed to elect more than a few candidates to the Reichstag. By 1914, Levy argued, the German anti-Semitic movement was in disarray, and most of its leaders were either disgraced or politically irrelevant. For Levy then, Pulzer and Massing are guilty of pre-judging nineteenth-century anti-Semites as

---

[3] Peter Pulzer, *The Rise of Political Anti-Semitism in Germany and Austria* (New York: John Wiley & Sons, 1964), 300.

[4] Richard Levy, *The Downfall of the Anti-Semitic Political Parties in Imperial Germany* (New Haven: Yale Univ. Press, 1975), 1.

"proto-Nazis" and failing to evaluate nineteenth-century anti-Semitism on its own terms.

In a 1985 article, "Kontinuität und Diskontinuität im Deutschen Antisemitismus 1878–1945," Shulamit Volkov further attempted to differentiate anti-Semitism in the Imperial era from anti-Semitism during the Third Reich.[5] Volkov argued that historians must be careful to view the anti-Semitism of pre-war Germany as a *background* for the later development of Nazi *Judenpolitik*, and not as an *explanation* for it. Even the most extreme anti-Semitic agitators of the 1870s and 1880s, much less the "ordinary" German of the time, could not have foreseen nor would have advocated the building of an Auschwitz. While a few of the most radical agitators may have called for the execution of suspected blood-ritual murderers and other Jewish "criminals," relatively few of even these extremists would have advocated the annihilation of an entire people. Volkov also makes a brief comparison between French and German anti-Semitism in the last years of the Nineteenth Century. She concludes that at this time it was France, not Germany, that had a more prevalent and more potentially violent brand of anti-Semitism.

Perhaps the biggest recent challenge to traditional historiography on anti-Semitism in Imperial Germany came from Daniel Goldhagen's 1997 book *Hitler's Willing Executioners*. Although the main focus of Goldhagen's book was on the dynamics of the Holocaust, his first chapters suggested the need for a radical reconsideration of anti-Semitism in Imperial Germany as well. Goldhagen posited several central features of anti-Semitism in nineteenth-century Germany, three of which are especially significant here:

1) From the beginning of the Nineteenth Century, anti-Semitism was ubiquitous in Germany. It was "common sense."
2) This brand of anti-Semitism was unusually violent in its imagery, and it tended towards violence.
3) Its logic was to promote the "elimination" of Jews by whatever means necessary and possible, given the prevailing ethical constraints.[6]

This radical argument of continuity provoked a firestorm of criticism when it was released, but even a decade later many historians

[5] See Shulamit Volkov, "Kontinuität und Diskontinuität im deutschen Anti-Semitismus 1878–1945," *Vierteljahreshefte für Zeitgeschichte* 33, Heft 2 (1985): 221–243.

[6] Daniel Jonah Goldhagen, *Hitler's Willing Executioners: Ordinary Germans and the Holocaust* (New York: Vintage Books, 1996), 77.

of Imperial Germany are still framing their own studies in terms of how they compare and contrast with his polemical arguments.

The works of Massing, Levy, Pulzer, Volkov, and Goldhagen thus leave us with a complex and contradictory picture of anti-Semitism in the *Kaiserreich*. Was anti-Semitism growing or failing? Was it quantitatively and qualitatively different from Nazi anti-Semitism or was it merely less intense and less-successfully marketed? Although this book has focused rather narrowly on anti-Semitic trials during the first half of the German Empire, it can still shed some important light on the nature and development of anti-Semitism during this period.

The Transformation of Political Anti-Semitism

The shocking rise and fall of Hermann Ahlwardt was in some sense the final nail in the coffin of parliamentary anti-Semitism in Imperial Germany. Although other anti-Semitic political leaders were now free of a dangerous figure who had threatened to take over their movement, they also lost the powerful impetus that had led to such astonishing successes during the early 1890s. Without Ahlwardt, the anti-Semitic parties quickly returned to the stagnant and divided state they exhibited throughout most of the 1880s. True, anti-Semitic parties still controlled 15 Reichstag seats; however, in the years after 1893 these delegates rarely worked together. Without Ahlwardt to distract their attention, anti-Semitic leaders quickly began to renew old quarrels and rivalries. Some, such as Max Liebermann von Sonnenberg, gravitated toward the Conservative Party, while others, such as Oswald Zimmerman and Otto Böckel, openly attacked Conservative elites. In addition, Ahlwardt's humiliation on the floor of the Reichstag in the *Invalidenfonds* affair also had a relative "pacifying" effect on the parliamentary anti-Semites in that it convinced them to avoid direct challenges to government authority and to act within parliamentary rules.[7]

Over the next two decades, the ranks of old-guard anti-Semitic political leaders started to thin. In the election of 1898, the number of anti-Semitic delegates in the Reichstag dropped to twelve, and

[7] Levy, *The Downfall of the Anti-Semitic Political Parties*, 172.

then in 1903 to eleven.[8] Otto Böckel retired after his electoral defeat in 1903, as did Paul Förster in 1907. Adolf Stöcker died in 1909, Oswald Zimmerman in 1910, and Max Liebermann von Sonnenberg in 1911. Since these men had developed their political organizations around their own personal authority, and since they were unwilling to train successors, their deaths left the small anti-Semitic parties with few credible leaders.[9]

The demise of Hermann Ahlwardt also had a dramatic influence on the Conservative Party. The victory of Wilhelm von Hammerstein and the *Kreuzzeitungsgruppe* at the 1892 Tivoli conference had promised a decisive change in the nature of the Conservative Party. By taking advantage of Ahlwardt's popularity and the apparent increase in popular anti-Semitism, Hammerstein hoped to turn the Conservative Party into a social-reformist and anti-Semitic *Volkspartei.* Hammerstein's tacit association with Ahlwardt, however, left him vulnerable to criticism once Ahlwardt was politically disgraced. Many powerful party officials, such as Baron Julius von Mirbach, quickly became wary of an association with political anti-Semitism. As Mirbach stated in March of 1893: "We are by no means blind to the good kernel within anti-Semitism . . . however, we regard it as a very difficult task to keep the anti-Semitic stream within the proper bounds."[10]

After Ahlwardt's *Invalidenfonds* Affair in April and May 1893, many Conservatives began to agree with the liberal *Berliner Tageblatt*'s assessment of Ahlwardt and his associates:

> Because the anti-Semites see allies and servants of the Jews (*Judengenossen*) in all branches of the government, the parliament, and the justice system, legal verdicts and decisions of the Reichstag mean nothing to

[8] Ibid., 225. In the 1907 elections, the anti-Semitic parties succeeded in electing seventeen delegates to the Reichstag—an even greater number than in 1893. But both Richard Levy and Peter Pulzer dismiss this achievement as a result of Chancellor Bülow's "Bloc policy." As part of a battle over colonial policies, Bülow sought to form a coalition of pro-government forces against the "internationalist" elements in the socialist and Catholic Center Parties. This political battle created a strange electoral alliance among liberals, Conservatives and anti-Semites who supported German colonial aims. Thus, according to Levy and Pulzer, the electoral gains for anti-Semitic parties in 1907 were the result of temporary political alliances, not increased support for anti-Semitic candidates. See Levy, *The Downfall of the Anti-Semitic Political Parties*, 228–230; Pulzer, *The Rise of Political Anti-Semitism*, 192–195.

[9] Levy, *The Downfall of the Anti-Semitic Political Parties*, 244–245.

[10] Quoted in James Retallack, *Notables of the Right: The Conservative Party and Political Mobilization in Germany, 1876–1918* (Boston: Unwin Hyman, 1988), 97.

> them. Thus, anti-Semitism undermines all state authority while wrapping itself in the mantle of loyalty, and, as the behavior of Ahlwardt has recently shown, the anti-Semitic party does more to encourage a popular revolution than the socialists ever have.[11]

The strains of radical populism inherent in Ahlwardt's speeches and public actions were alarming for many moderate Conservatives. Thus, there was real concern within the party leadership that they had simply gone too far in associating the party directly with anti-Semitism.

To make matters worse, the anticipated electoral gains for the Conservative Party did not materialize in the elections of 1893. In fact, many of the gains made by anti-Semitic candidates in the wake of the Judenflinten Affair came at the expense of moderate Conservative candidates. Thus, while the Conservative adoption of an explicitly anti-Semitic platform may have given a boost to political anti-Semites, it seemed to have resulted in a net loss for the Conservative Party. In addition, the Conservatives now came under direct attack from the government. Soon after the Judenflinten trial, Chancellor Caprivi made a public statement against anti-Semitism and lashed out against the pro-Ahlwardt sentiment that was expressed at the Tivoli conference. Although ultra-Conservatives like Hammerstein dismissed Caprivi's criticism, they were clearly put on the defensive by the strength of the Chancellor's condemnation.[12]

As a result of these setbacks, the power of the *Kreuzzeitungsgruppe* quickly began to decline within the Conservative party. By the end of the century, the major leaders of this faction, Wilhelm von Hammerstein and Adolf Stöcker, had both been removed from the party. In 1896, Hammerstein was charged with embezzlement and fraud for several shady financial deals involving the *Kreuzzeitung*. After his conviction in a very public trial, Hammerstein was forced to give up his editorship of the *Kreuzzeitung* and his powerful position within the party.[13] Soon after, Stöcker was also forced out over a dis-

---

[11] *Berliner Tageblatt* 13 April 1893 #186.

[12] The immediate response by the *Kreuzzeitung* to Caprivi's statement was an article that accused Isidor Löwe of having had treasonous contacts with the French Minister of War, General Boulanger, in the mid-1880s. According to the *Kreuzzeitung*, these new "revelations" showed that even if Ahlwardt's Judenflinten allegations had been unsubstantiated, the anti-Semitic party platform was still entirely justified. *Kreuzzeitung* 16 December 1892 #590 Abend.

[13] For a more detailed account of the Hammerstein scandal, see Alex Hall, *Scandal, Sensation and Social Democracy: The SPD Press an Wilhelmine Germany 1890–1914* (Cambridge: Cambridge Univ. Press, 1977).

agreement on agrarian reforms and a controversy about his so-called "Funeral Pyre Letter," in which he privately expressed interest in sowing discord between the Chancellor and the royal family.[14]

The weakening of anti-Semitic political parties and the collapse of the *Kreuzzeitungsgruppe* led to what some historians have called a "dormant period" in anti-Semitism between 1893 and 1914.[15] However, this "dormancy" should not be confused with a general decline in German anti-Semitism. While the influence of anti-Semitic political parties declined, anti-Jewish rhetoric became an important ideological component for several new quasi-political pressure groups, including the Agrarian League and Pan-German League. Although such pressure groups did not rely on anti-Semitism as their *raison d'être*, they were nonetheless essential in spreading *völkisch* nationalism and racial anti-Semitism to a wider public audience.

The exact nature and importance of these quasi-political organizations has been a frequent source of historical debate over the last thirty years. For historians such as Richard Levy, the rise of these tacitly anti-Semitic organizations signaled a conscious subordination of anti-Semitism to other political and economic goals. Stung by their association with Ahlwardt and the political anti-Semites, leaders of the Conservative Party came to view the Agrarian League as a less controversial and less dangerous way to take advantage of the dynamism of popular anti-Semitism. Levy admits that the Agrarian League contained many "sincere" anti-Semites and periodically supported anti-Semitic parliamentary candidates. However, he argues that anti-Semitism in the Agrarian League was almost always subordinated to the economic and political interests of large-scale agriculture.[16] Through a loose alliance with the Agrarian League, the Conservatives could avoid the pitfalls of being associated with radical anti-Semitic candidates and could exploit rural discontent without

[14] In this letter, originally written in 1888, Stöcker had advised his friend Hammerstein to avoid attacking Bismarck directly in the *Kreuzzeitung*, but instead advised him to light a series of "funeral pyres" to illuminate the areas where the ultra-conservatives and the Kaiser both disagreed with Bismarck. When this letter was discovered and published by the socialist *Vorwärts* in 1896, it convinced most Germans that Stöcker was a devious and manipulative man. Levy, *The Downfall of the Anti-Semitic Political Parties*, 173.

[15] See, for example, Albert Lindemann, *Esau's Tears* (Cambridge: Cambridge Univ. Press, 1997), 334.

[16] Levy, *The Downfall of the Anti-Semitic Political Parties*, 89.

having to press for explicit anti-Jewish legislation in the Reichstag. Thus, according to Levy, in the years after Ahlwardt's demise, "the Agrarian League remained a clearly preferable alternative to a coalition with any of the anti-Semitic political parties."[17]

Richard Levy's conclusions about anti-Semitism in the Agrarian League are not unanimously accepted. Hans-Jürgen Puhle, for instance, has argued that anti-Semitism was not of secondary importance in the Agrarian League, but comprised an essential component of its philosophy and activity. As Puhle wrote: "The *völkisch* anti-Semitism indigenous to the ranks of the Agrarian League comprised an integral element of not only the political and economic ideology of the agrarians, but also their political activity and agitation."[18] As the Agrarian League gained increasing influence in the Conservative Party, it helped to replace traditional conservative prejudices against the Jews with more radical racial forms of anti-Semitism. Thus, according to Puhle, the Agrarian League helped to establish racial anti-Semitism and *völkisch* nationalism as self-evident ideological elements of Conservative party identity. Because the Agrarian League was an accepted and respected political organization, it also succeeded in making a radical anti-Semitic message seem moderate and politically acceptable. Puhle argues, therefore, that the rise of the Agrarian League did not cause a moderation or "dormancy" in anti-Semitism, but merely replaced the ineffective and disgraced anti-Semitic parties with a more effective anti-Semitic mass organization.[19]

A detailed study of anti-Semitism in the Agrarian League lies outside the realm of this work. However, the evidence presented in this book does suggest how the dramatic failure of the anti-Semitic parties before 1895 can be reconciled with the continued appeal of anti-Semitism in later political organizations. In the first decades of the Reich, sensational trials and scandals helped to discredit political anti-Semites while at the same time increasing the political use of anti-Semitic rhetoric and encouraging public debates about the "Jewish Question." Individual agitators suffered, but anti-Semitism continued to be a politically useful and culturally common form of expression.

---

[17] Ibid.

[18] Hans-Jürgen Puhle, *Agrarische Interessenpolitik und Preußischer Konservativismus im wilhelminischen Reich, 1893–1914* (Bonn-Bad Godesberg: Verlag Neue Gesellschaft, 1975), 111.

[19] Ibid., 139–140.

Jewish Self-Defense in the Early Kaiserreich

Before 1890, there were few German Jewish organizations dedicated to actively fighting anti-Semitism. There were several reasons for this. First, prominent Jews had always relied on government officials to safeguard Jewish interests. Thus, leading Jewish figures such as Gerson von Bleichröder preferred to send appeals to Kaiser Wilhelm and Bismarck rather than respond publicly to anti-Semitic attacks. Second, divisions within the Jewish community made any unified Jewish response almost impossible. Since the secession of Orthodox groups in 1876, many Reform and Orthodox Jews still found it difficult to cooperate with one another. Orthodox leaders such as Samson Hirsch believed that Reform Jews had deserted their religious ideals in order to assimilate, and many Reform Jews regarded the Orthodoxy as backward and primitive.[20] Third, since most politically active Jews were associated with left-liberal parties, there was a fear that any Jewish defense organization might be seen as a partisan political group. The left-liberals were in opposition to the government after the mid 1870s, and any such "partisan" organization would not have brought a sympathetic response from government officials. Finally, as the historian Ismar Schorsch has suggested, the formation of an explicitly Jewish defense organization in the post-emancipation era would have required a public affirmation of Jewish identity—precisely what the extended battle for equal rights had conditioned Jews to fear and loathe.[21] Many German Jews believed that a "Jewish response" to anti-Semitic attacks would only reinforce the myth that Jews comprised a separate and distinct population with interests that differed from "ordinary Germans."

Despite this general hesitation, however, there were important attempts by existing Jewish organizations to challenge anti-Semitic agitators long before the founding of the *Centralverein* in 1893. The *Deutsch-Israelitischer Gemeindebund*, for example, had been founded in 1869 to unite Jewish communities in Germany "for the protection of common interests and the pursuit of common objectives."[22] During

[20] Ismar Schorsch, *Jewish Reactions to German Anti-Semitism, 1870–1914* (New York: Columbia Univ. Press, 1972), 20.

[21] Ibid., 1.

[22] Quoted in Ibid., 25. The *Gemeindebund* was formed in part to deal with the problem of Jewish refugees who were fleeing Russia and emigrating to Germany

the 1870s, the *Gemeindebund* tried to take an active role in fighting anti-Semitism, including a willingness to file libel charges against individual anti-Semitic agitators. However, the *Gemeindebund*'s legal efforts met with relatively little success. State prosecutors were often reluctant to bring libel charges against those that criticized Judaism, especially if the charges were associated with a contentious election campaign. Prosecutors cited a variety of excuses for dismissing Jewish complaints, including that anti-Semitic literature did not constitute a public danger, that racial attacks on Jews did not constitute religious persecution, or that general derision of Jews did not constitute individual defamation.[23] In addition, because the *Gemeindebund* officially represented only a fraction of the Jewish communities in Germany, state prosecutors often suggested that the organization was not eligible to sue for general libels against German Jews. Although the *Gemeindebund* was free to pursue civil charges (*Privatklage*) without the approval of prosecutors, these private suits often yielded large legal bills with few practical results.[24]

Internal divisions also hindered the legal efforts of the *Gemeindebund*. Because this organization was originally intended to be apolitical, its leaders were often reluctant to attack political figures such as Adolf Stöcker. One of the original founders of the organization, the Dresden lawyer Emil Lehmann, repeatedly challenged members to take a more active role both in encouraging government prosecution and in filing private suits against anti-Semites. The leaders of the *Gemeindebund*, however, decided to follow a policy of restraint, and they urged members to focus on educational literature rather than directly confronting individual anti-Semites.[25] Thus, following the mixed success of its legal efforts in the 1870s, the *Gemeindebund* eventually abandoned any active legal challenges to anti-Semitism.

---

or through Germany to America. The *Gemeindebund* did cooperate with the predominately French *Alliance Israélite Universelle*, but it frequently portrayed itself as a German counterpart concerned with the particular problems of German Jews.

[23] Ibid., 40. See Chapter 5 for a discussion of the *Gemeindebund*'s frustrations in the Grumbkow case. Although the *Gemeindebund* did successfully prosecute some anti-Semitic agitators, prosecutors often refused to file charges against agitators on behalf of Jewish organizations.

[24] In most civil cases, the plaintiff was forced to pay court fees if his suit was dismissed.

[25] Sanford Ragins, *Jewish Responses to Anti-Semitism in Germany, 1870–1914* (Cincinnati: Hebrew Union College Press, 1980), 28–29.

After the formation of anti-Semitic political parties in 1879 and 1880, many Berlin Jews renewed their calls for an organized Jewish defense against anti-Semitism. Only a few days after the Kantorowicz incident and the Reichstag *Judendebatte* of 1880, Moritz Lazarus, a Jewish professor at the University of Berlin, invited over two hundred Jewish notables to discuss the possibilities for an organized response to anti-Semitic agitation. The new assembly called itself *Das Jüdische Comité*, and a group of 28 members were elected as directors. Although most of those attending the meeting believed in the necessity of a unified Jewish stand against anti-Semitism, they were deeply divided about what kind of action should be taken. Some prominent Jews were convinced that this outbreak of anti-Semitism was a transitory phase that could only be prolonged and worsened by Jewish interference. Thus, they still believed that discreet appeals to the government or educational literature were the most promising methods for fighting anti-Semitism. Other participants in the *Comité* believed that a more aggressive organization should be formed under the leadership of liberal Christian politicians such as Heinrich Rickert and Rudolph Virchow. However, this idea met with disapproval from Lazarus, who feared such an organization would eventually be co-opted by the Progressive Party. Another option, the formation of a specific "Organization for Jewish Interests" (*Verein für jüdische Interessen*) also met with considerable hostility from those attending the meeting.[26] These basic disagreements prevented the *Comité* from taking any meaningful action against anti-Semitic agitators. Although another meeting was held a few weeks later that attracted a crowd of 600, the *Jüdische Comité* soon disappeared without any notable achievements.

For many historians who have investigated Jewish self-defense during the *Kaiserreich*, these false starts were followed by the relative silence of the German Jewish community toward anti-Semitic attacks. As Ismar Schorsch put it:

> Both the Gemeindebund and the committee were undermined by an ambivalence which German Jewry would resolve only when confronted by a yet second unexpected wave of Jew-hatred in the early 1890s. The historical significance of these early unsure countermeasures is the insight they provide into the factors inhibiting a perplexed Jewry from

[26] Police report of the meeting in LAB A Pr. Br. Rep. 030, Polizeipräsidium Berlin, Nr. 15219, p. 23.

> resorting to determined resistance. The records of the Gemeindebund during the first decade and the short-lived Lazarus Committee suggest the communal problems and intellectual reservations which paralyzed German Jewry.[27]

In his work on local Jewish responses to the rise of the Böckel movement in Hessen, David Peal also identified a "Jewish passivity" which resulted both from fears that an overt Jewish response would only further provoke anti-Semites and from a feeling that Böckel's complaints about Jewish exploitation were not entirely unjustified.[28] As in Berlin, communal differences and a general reticence to act publicly made any concerted and organized response to anti-Semitism a very difficult proposition before 1890.

The evidence presented in this book, however, suggests that there were some very important exceptions to this "Jewish passivity," especially among Jewish journalists and lawyers. Although they did not identify themselves in particular articles or bylines, the editors Rudolph Mosse, George Davidsohn, and Leopold Sonneman certainly guided their mainstream liberal newspapers (*Berliner Tageblatt, Berliner Börsen-Courier*, and *Frankfurter Zeitung* respectively) in frequent criticism of anti-Semitic agitation during the 1880s. These newspapers could be counted on to respond forcefully every time anti-Semitism worked its way into political debate. Jewish lawyers such as Hermann Makower also vigorously attacked anti-Semitic myths and stereotypes both inside and outside the courtroom. And, of course, men like Joseph Bloch in Vienna and Hirsch Hildesheimer in Berlin worked tirelessly to challenge prominent anti-Semites in court and to publicly refute stereotypes of Jewish timidity and effeminacy. Hildesheimer's efforts in particular set powerful and visible precedents for future legal campaigns by German Jews against anti-Semitism.

As the agitation of Otto Böckel and Hermann Ahlwardt reached a crescendo in the early 1890s, pressure within the Jewish community for an organized response to anti-Semitism once again began to increase. In November of 1890, after another *Judendebatte* in the

[27] Schorsch as quoted in Bernhard Vogt, "Anti-Semitismus und Justiz in Kaiserreich: Der Synagogenbrand in Neustettin," in *'Halte fern dem ganzen Lande jedes Verderben . . .': Geschichte und Kultur der Juden in Pommern*, ed. Margret Heitmann and Julius Schoeps (Hildesheim, 1995), 393.

[28] David Peal, "Jewish Responses to German Anti-Semitism: The Case of the Böckel Movement, 1887–1894" *Jewish Social Studies* 48, Nos. 3–4 (Summer-Fall 1986): 278.

Reichstag, the election of four new anti-Semitic delegates to the Reichstag, and the public furor over Herman Ahlwardt's *Verzweiflungskampf* brochure, a new attempt was made to form a defense organization. This time, the organization would include both Christians and Jews.[29] A group of twelve influential politicians and intellectuals met to create the *Verein zur Abwehr des Antisemitismus* (Organization for the Defense Against Anti-Semitism), a supra-confessional organization designed to stop the spread of anti-Semitism. Although the "*Abwehrverein*" was allegedly the idea of a Jewish lawyer named Edmund Friedemann, its most vocal leaders were liberal Christians such as Heinrich Rickert and Rudolf von Gneist.[30] The *Abwehrverein* was quite active in combating anti-Semitism both politically and legally in the decades after 1890. However, because the group was dominated by Progressive liberal politicians, it met considerable difficulty in presenting itself as a broad non-political organization.

For many German Jews, the *Abwehrverein* was not a satisfactory response to the growing threat of anti-Semitism. After the Xanten ritual-murder trial and the Judenflinten Affair in 1892, and after the subsequent election of 15 anti-Semitic delegates to the Reichstag, many formerly reluctant Jews began to see a need for an aggressive and organized Jewish response. This change of heart was especially marked in the pages of the *Allgemeine Zeitung des Judenthums*, which had previously warned its readers to remain silent, but now demanded an "energetic, systematic defense activity."[31]

In January of 1893, a Jewish intellectual named Dr. Raphael Löwenfeld circulated a provocative pamphlet called *Schutzjuden oder Staatsbürger?* (Protected Jews or Citizens?). This pamphlet, which passionately argued for an aggressive Jewish self-defense against anti-Semitism, is often considered an important turning point in German Jewish History. It galvanized many prominent Jews into action, and prompted the eventual creation of the *Centralverein deutscher Staatsbürger jüdischen Glaubens* (Central Organization of German Citizens of the

---

[29] Barbara Suchy, "The Verein zur Abwehr des Antisemitismus (I) From its Beginnings to the First World War," *Leo Baeck Institute Year Book* 28 (1983): 208.

[30] Ibid., 207. Suchy claims that Jewish leaders deliberately worked behind the scenes in the *Abwehrverein* to avoid the perception that it was a Jewish organization. Thus, Rickert repeatedly discussed the primarily Christian nature of the organization and avoided any mention of Jewish involvement in its creation.

[31] Ragins, *Jewish Responses*, 53.

Jewish Faith)—a Jewish organization that would pursue a vigorous legal and literary campaign against anti-Semitism.

If not for the response of Hirsch Hildesheimer, however, this incendiary pamphlet could have easily destroyed any chance at turning the new *Centralverein* into a broad-based defense organization. While Löwenfeld had used his pamphlet to criticize the generally timid reactions of Jewish leaders to the growing tide of anti-Semitism, he had also attacked Orthodox Jews and condemned the "dishonorable band of businessmen without a fatherland" who maintained their own "obsolete" Jewish rituals.[32] Löwenfeld went on to demand an aggressive defense organization that would not only combat anti-Semitism, but also discipline Jewish behavior. Several Orthodox leaders such as Samson Hirsch and Solomon Breuer responded to this attack by categorically rejecting cooperation with liberal Jews, whom they regarded as *poshim*, or sinners.[33] Hildesheimer, however, realized the importance of the opportunity that now threatened to slip away. Under the influence of his moderate father, Hildesheimer had always supported liberal Jewish groups in their defense activities, even when those groups espoused versions of Judaism he rejected. Thus, although Hildesheimer responded forcefully to Löwenfeld's criticisms, he still maintained an openness to bridging the gap between Orthodox and Reform Jews. Eventually, Hildesheimer pledged his support for the goals of the *Centralverein*, and by 1895 he was an active member.[34]

In the last decades of the *Kaiserreich*, the *Centralverein* followed the earlier precedents set by men like Hildesheimer and Bloch and took aggressive action to fight anti-Semitism. In addition to printing educational literature on Judaism, it also frequently responded directly to the polemics of individual agitators. More importantly, the *Centralverein* established a Legal Protection Commission (*Rechtsschutzcommission*) to receive complaints from ordinary Jewish citizens who had been libeled, and it established a committee of attorneys to review anti-Semitic literature for objectionable and libelous material that could be challenged in court. Under the leadership of Eugen Fuchs, the *Centralverein* filed many successful lawsuits against anti-Semitic agitators for various offenses. These legal efforts had a significant effect in impeding

---

[32] Ibid., 47–50.

[33] David Ellenson, *Rabbi Esriel Hildesheimer and the Creation of a Modern Jewish Orthodoxy* (Tuscaloosa: University of Alabama, 1990), 102–103.

[34] Schorsch, *Jewish Reactions*, 121.

individual agitators and in forcing anti-Semitic journalists to be more careful and circumspect in their attacks on German Jews.[35]

The German Government and Anti-Semitic Trials

A long record of historical scholarship has left no doubt that anti-Semitism was prevalent throughout the highest levels of the Imperial German government. In addition to Otto von Bismarck's own record of anti-Semitic statements, a variety of Interior Ministers, Justice Ministers, and police officials also openly expressed sympathy for anti-Jewish sentiment. This was especially true of the longtime Interior Minister, Robert von Puttkamer, whom Fritz Stern has characterized as "less fastidious in discriminating among [conservative and liberal] Jews; he liked no variety of them and found license for his prejudice in Treitschke's judgment."[36]

The motives of other high officials involved in prominent legal cases involving anti-Semitism were also less than pure. Kaiser Wilhelm II's desire to commission outside expert testimony about the Bernstein (Breslau) ritual assault case could be interpreted as an impartial inquiry into scholarly opinions about Jewish teachings. But this would be a distortion. His inquiries were evidence that he still found ritual murder accusations potentially credible and Jewish teachings potentially dangerous. And even *Kultusminister* von Goßler (the arbiter of scholarly reports in the Breslau case), who clearly thought ritual murder allegations were nonsense, still cast aspersions on Franz Delitzsch's testimony about the case as "too friendly to the Jews".

It is not surprising, therefore, that the overall reaction of prosecutors, judges, and lesser government authorities to anti-Semitic agitation was inconsistent at best. The decision to file libel charges, for example, was generally dependent not on a federal mandate, but on the attitudes of individual state governments as well as local

---

[35] Levy, *The Downfall of the Anti-Semitic Political Parties*, 157–158. Unfortunately, occasional legal victories over individual anti-Semites did not necessarily mean successfully diminishing the appeal of anti-Semitic rhetoric. Thus, many historians view the legal record of the *Centralverein* as an overall failure. It seems strange, however, to criticize Jewish leaders both for "passivity" and for the fact that their aggressive resistance efforts were not always successful.

[36] Fritz Stern, *Gold and Iron: Bismarck, Bleichröder, and the Building of the German Empire* (New York: Knopf, 1977), 516–517.

prosecutors and judges. This led to a great degree of variation among different states and localities.[37] A few state officials did make systematic legal attempts to curb the influence of particular anti-Semitic agitators. Jacob Finger, for instance, the Prime Minister of the Grand Duchy of Hesse, issued a decree in 1890 that instructed prosecutors to help facilitate legal actions against anyone who slandered Jews. This effort was primarily designed to undermine the popularity of the agitator Otto Böckel, who was active in the region.[38] Many other state and federal authorities, however, asserted a kind of "neutrality" on the Jewish Question, an attitude that permitted them to ignore both pleas for protection by Jews and demands for action by radical anti-Semites.[39]

While state prosecutors were quick to file charges against any literature that libeled government officials or Protestant leaders, they were often hesitant to use the same laws to protect Jewish religious beliefs or institutions. This reluctance was grounded in legal precedent. In 1881, the Supreme Court (*Reichsgericht*) had ruled that individual Jews had no standing to pursue libel charges if the insults were directed against the religion as a whole; the court came to this conclusion despite having previously acknowledged the right of soldiers and judges to pursue charges against general slanders of their respective professions.[40] Even in cases where anti-Semitic propaganda targeted individual Jews, however, German prosecutors often claimed that the rhetoric did not rise to the level of slander or there was no public interest served by pursuing charges.[41] Thus, in cases that were not in the public eye, did not involve criticism of the government, or had no significant concerns about law and order, Berlin government officials were fairly unlikely to intervene.[42]

---

[37] Levy, *The Downfall of the Anti-Semitic Political Parties*, 130–131.

[38] Ibid., 139–141. The Grand Duchy of Hesse was not the only state government to take legal action against anti-Semitic politicians or organizations. Levy also describes concentrated opposition efforts in Baden led by Grand Duke Friedrich I, and more sporadic efforts in parts of Prussia. Anti-Semitic agitators were generally less active in the Catholic south of Germany.

[39] Ibid., 137.

[40] Johannes Groß, *Ritualmordbeschuldigungen gegen Juden in deuschen Kaiserreich 1871–1914* (Berlin: Metropol, 2002), 217.

[41] Groß, *Ritualmordbeschuldigungen*, 218.

[42] See Schorsch, *Jewish Reactions*; Ragins, *Jewish Responses*; and Marjorie Lamberti, *Jewish Activism in Imperial Germany: The Struggle for Civil Equality* (New Haven: Yale Univ. Press, 1978).

The actions of government officials in anti-Semitic *causes célèbres* such as Neustettin, Skurcz, and Xanten, on the other hand, seem to provide a counter-example. In each of these cases, the same Robert von Puttkamer sent experienced Criminal Commissars from Berlin to take over biased or poorly-run investigations that had singled out local Jews. These criminal investigators then worked vigorously to overcome local prejudice while securing an acquittal of Jewish defendants. This is especially true in the Neustettin case, where Criminal Commissar Höft intervened after an initial conviction to push for a more objective reconsideration of the evidence. Thanks to the involvement of investigators such as Höft and Baumgard, none of these sensational prosecutions resulted in the final conviction of innocent Jewish citizens. At least in these few cases, it appears, the German government finally stepped in to curb the excesses of anti-Semitic agitation and popular prejudice.

Even in these special cases, however, it is clear that there were often ulterior motives that influenced the behavior of government officials and investigators. For example, although Höft and Baumgard frequently mentioned their desire to see justice done, their investigations often proceeded in a way that was not designed to protect the Jewish community or the rights of individual defendants, but instead to safeguard public order. The Pomeranian riots of 1881 had made it clear to government officials that popular anti-Semitic fervor had the potential to turn violent, and scattered rioting surrounding the Neustettin and Xanten trials seemed to reinforce this fear.[43] As Baumgard's anxious letters to Schelling in the Xanten case illustrate, his primary concern was not always the trial of an apparently innocent man, but the threat that dispensing with such a trial might pose to local peace and stability.

In addition to the desire to prevent violent disorder in the countryside, government officials in Berlin were also obsessed with limiting

[43] Helmut Walser Smith has rejected the notion that in these cases the Prussian army prevented what would inevitably have been a large-scale massacre. As Smith puts it: "The riots [in Konitz] were no doubt terrifying, but they did not descend into a tempest of destruction. As enmity deepened and tempers flared, instead of wanton carnage, a familiar routine of ominous threats and symbolic gestures mediated the voices of hatred . . . for the Germans of Konitz it sufficed to ritually enact violence . . ." Smith may be correct; however, there was no way for local Jews or police officials to know that the violence would not continue to escalate. Helmut Walser Smith, *The Butcher's Tale: Murder and Anti-Semitism in a German Town* (New York: Norton, 2002), 166.

the political fallout of these affairs—especially in terms of criticism of the German justice system. According to Johannes Groß, Justice Minister von Schelling arranged for the re-arrest of the Jewish defendant Adolf Buschhoff in the Xanten case primarily in order to deflect public criticism about the influence of Jews on the German government.[44] It is no coincidence, then, that Schelling's announcement of this re-arrest came as part of a parliamentary speech in response to Adolf Stöcker's criticism of the justice system.[45] By insisting that Buschhoff be brought to trial over the objections of many investigators, Schelling not only violated German law, but also failed to demonstrate the very neutrality and impartiality in the German justice system that his actions were designed to publicly vindicate.[46]

Such concerns about politics and public opinion seem to have been fairly typical for justice officials of the time. In his recent book on the criminal justice system in Wilhelmine Berlin, Benjamin Hett notes that "the system was driven from pillar to post by its efforts to harness and contain public opinion, while fighting forlornly to preserve the state's authority."[47] Thus, it is not at all surprising that instead of suspending the prosecutions of Jewish defendants they believed were probably innocent, government officials and investigators sometimes sought to avoid public unrest and deflect claims of pro-Jewish favoritism by allowing trial proceedings to take place. Of course, for Jewish defendants and their families, this kind of demonstration of government "impartiality" was certainly of little comfort. By allowing ritual murder accusations to proceed to trial—even under charges that made no mention of ritual motives—government authorities suggested to the German public at least the possibility that ritual murder accusations might have actual credibility.

In examining the later Konitz ritual murder case (1900), Christoph Nonn suggests another reason why Criminal Commissars may have felt obligated to pursue ritual murder cases to trial despite doubts about the accusations: simple careerism. The lead investigator in

[44] Groß, *Ritualmordbeschuldigungen*, 173.

[45] Report from *Haus der Abgeordneten* February 9, 1892 in GStA PK, I. HA Rep. 84a Nr. 57459, 177 ff.

[46] Groß argues that such an action was a clear violation of German criminal law, which according to §152 of the RStPO forbid prosecutors from filing charges against defendants they believed were innocent. Groß, *Ritualmordbeschuldigungen*, 173, 180.

[47] Benjamin Carter Hett, *Death in the Tiergarten* (Cambridge Mass.: Harvard Press, 2004), 153.

Konitz, Criminal Commissar Wehn, doubted the accusations against the Jewish suspect almost as soon as he set foot in town. Not only did he find the suspect and his friends to be credible, he also expressed his disgust with the ridiculous fantasy stories of local residents that were encouraged by the anti-Semitic press. According to a later statement by Wehn, although he was brought up as an anti-Semite, his experiences in Konitz served to destroy these prejudices.[48] For some reason, however, Wehn still suggested in his final investigative report that ritual murder accusations might have some plausibility. According to Christoph Nonn, Wehn's remarks were not caused by a remaining "latent" anti-Semitism, but by a banal desire to ingratiate his superiors. In an age where many high government officials were known to express a "socially acceptable" anti-Semitism, and at a time where his own job was on the line because of a stalled investigation, acknowledging the plausibility of charges against the Jews may have been a tactic to curry favor with those in Berlin that controlled his professional fate.[49]

Although a fear of public unrest, concerns about political fallout, and simple careerism may all have contributed to the conduct of government officials and investigators in individual cases, we should not underestimate the degree to which an openness to anti-Semitic myths and stereotypes also played an important role.[50] We must remember, for example, that for many contemporary observers, scholarly debates about the nature of Judaism and the contents of the Talmud had not yet yielded any definitive conclusions. As I argued in chapter five, the public refutation and humiliation of individual anti-Semitic pseudo-scholars both in print and in the courtroom never succeeded in destroying myths about the contents of Jewish

---

[48] Christoph Nonn, *Eine Stadt sucht einen Mörder* (Göttingen: Vandenhoeck und Ruprecht, 2002), 172.

[49] Ironically, since social and political elites often condemned popular "Rowdy Anti-Semitism" as socially unacceptable, Nonn argues that this careerism could also pressure local officials to lash out more vigorously at outside anti-Semitic agitators. He describes several cases in Konitz where local officials exaggerated the role of anti-Semitic agitators in inciting violence in order to deflect attention from their own inability to restore order. Nonn, *Eine Stadt,* 172–5.

[50] Unfortunately, other than their published statements in court and a few reports to Berlin, it is difficult to fix the backgrounds or the personal motives of individuals like Höft or Baumgard with much certainty. While they very well may have shared some of the same anti-Jewish stereotypes as men like Kaiser Wilhelm and Puttkamer, these sentiments were not made obvious in their letters or their actions.

teachings. Instead, highly-publicized debates and court confrontations only helped to maintain the illusion that the true nature of Judaism and the Talmud were still a matter open to "scientific dispute". Although individual anti-Semites such as August Rohling might have had their scholarly reputations destroyed in court, the mere weight and constant repetition of their false translations and erroneous conclusions preserved a sense that even the most heinous of anti-Semitic myths might have some kernel of truth. Of course, if some "scholars" still believed in the nefarious character of Talmudic injunctions, could mere government officials or criminal investigators be so sure that ritual murder allegations were pure fantasy or fable?[51]

A few historians have also discerned clear anti-Semitic sentiment at the highest levels of the justice system within the marginalia of reports on ritual murder cases. Bernd Kölling, for example, describes sarcastic notes written by readers in the margins of Baumgard's reports on the Xanten case. For Kölling, these notes, along with the underlining of passages in clippings from anti-Semitic texts, suggest a clear anti-Semitic bias among justice officials.[52] In his analysis of the later Konitz Affair, Bernhard Vogt points to similar handwritten comments by Justice Minister von Schönstedt. While officially denying the possibility of a ritual murder, Schönstedt pushed Criminal Commissars in Konitz to re-examine if the crime could have been perpetrated by Jews out of superstition or other personal motives. Schönstedt also included a copy of a pamphlet by Theodor Fritsch in the official record along with the comment that "I believe, according to the evidence, that an investigation which had kept open the possibility of a ritual murder might have reached an entirely different conclusion!"[53]

---

[51] Bernd Kölling points out that even doctors, judges, and prosecutors who openly mocked popular superstitions still found the need to vigorously investigate and seek expert testimony on the possibility of Jewish blood rituals. This indicates, he claims, that German elites sought to emphasize their superiority to the masses, while they nonetheless played a vital role in the discourse of ritual murder. Bernd Kölling, "Blutige Illusionen. Ritualmorddiskurse und Anti-Semitismus im niederrheinischen Xanten am Ende des 19. Jahrhunderts" in *Agrarische Verfassung und politische Struktur. Studien zur Gesellschaftsgeschichte Preußens 1700–1918*, ed. Wolfgang Neugebauer and Ralf Pröve (Berlin, 1998), 370–371.

[52] Kölling, "Blutige Illusionen," 369.

[53] Bernhard Vogt, "Die 'Atmosphäre eines Narrenhauses'. Eine Ritualmordlegende um die Ermordung des Schülers Ernst Winter in Konitz," in *Zur Geschichte und Kultur der Juden in Ost- und Westpreußen*, ed. Michael Brocke et al. (Hildesheim, 2000), 559–560.

However, if government intervention into anti-Semitic *causes célèbres* was often guided by ulterior or, at best, mixed motives, this did not lessen the anger and frustration of anti-Semitic agitators at government officials. Anti-Semitic leaders such as Adolf Stöcker, Otto Glagau, and Max Liebermann von Sonnenberg repeatedly described the German justice system as thoroughly biased, corrupt, and ineffective. For example, in both the second Neustettin arson trial and the Skurcz ritual murder trial, the intervention of Criminal Commissar Höft not only signaled for anti-Semites an unfair meddling in local affairs by the Berlin government, it also provided "proof" that government officials were operating under Jewish influence. Such complaints about government interference "on behalf of Jewish defendants" continued to occur throughout the *Kaiserreich*, including at the infamous ritual murder accusations in Xanten (1892) and Konitz (1900). Thus, German anti-Semites drew a very different conclusion about the overall response of the German legal system to the "Jewish Question". From their point of view, scattered legal victories were greatly outnumbered by serious political and financial setbacks.

The fact that both Jews and anti-Semites complained about bias within the German legal system should not lead us to agree with the assertion of some government officials that they were objective and neutral in cases dealing with the "Jewish Question". By intervening in a few cases while at the same time failing to forcefully condemn anti-Semitic agitation, government officials undoubtedly helped to provoke and further radicalize anti-Semitic sentiment. On their own, these limited interventions only reinforced the use of anti-Semitic rhetoric by opponents of the regime and encouraged the exaggerated claims of agitators about Jewish control of the government and justice system.

Nevertheless, it is important to draw a clear distinction between the *Judenpolitik* of the Second Reich and the Third. In Neustettin, Skurcz, and Xanten, government intervention in the form of Criminal Commissars helped to assure that Jewish defendants were acquitted, despite the balance of local opinion and the pressure exerted by the anti-Semitic, Conservative, and Catholic press. Although not always sensitive to the complaints of Jews, government officials did realize the dangers that the anti-Semitic movement could pose to public order. Thus, it is clear that the most radical forces of popular anti-Semitism did meet with significant resistance among government officials in Imperial Germany, even if those resisting may have also harbored their own stereotypes and prejudices about the Jews.

* * *

As many historians, including Richard Levy, have previously argued, individual anti-Semitic agitators and their small political organizations had a very difficult time in Imperial Germany. Anti-Semitic politicians failed to build a unified party, failed to establish a profitable anti-Semitic press, failed to maintain substantial electoral support, failed to establish a stable bloc in the Reichstag, and failed to pass any systematic or substantial anti-Jewish legislation. These failures, however, are only half the story. As Massimo Ferrari Zumbini argues in his survey of anti-Semitism in Imperial Germany: "[Anti-Semites achieved] much less than they had hoped for, and yet much more than they could have ever dreamed."[54] While anti-Semitic leaders were never able to form their own stable independent organization, their rhetoric was adopted by many politicians and journalists from more mainstream groups, including the Conservative and Center Parties. The culmination of this, of course, was the Tivoli convention at the end of 1892, where influenced by the furor surrounding Ahlwardt's Judenflinten trial, the Conservative Party officially approved anti-Semitic language in its platform. Although this change was not of lasting significance, it did demonstrate the amount of influence small anti-Semitic parties or individual agitators could often exert. Thus, while individual agitators such as Ahlwardt often faded into obscurity and financial ruin, their impact in making anti-Jewish rhetoric more publicly visible and more palatable as a political weapon should not be underestimated.

Although the courtroom dramas described here are not generally remembered today, it would be a mistake to underestimate their effects on public perceptions of anti-Semitism in Imperial Germany. Certainly, the frequent discussion of these events in the daily press had a significant impact on the German populace—perhaps more than the work of anti-Semitic writers such as Paul de Lagarde and Heinrich von Treitschke. These trials could arouse powerful emotions, could incite anti-Jewish sentiment, and (as in 1892) could even influence election results. Many anti-Semitic agitators, such as Otto Böckel, even reported that watching and reading about such trials

---

[54] Massimo Ferrari Zumbini, *Die Wurzeln des Bösen: Grunderjahre des Anti-Semitismus von der Bismarckzeit zu Hitler* (Frankfurt: Vittorio Klostermann, 2003), 635.

had first motivated them to become anti-Semites.[55] These *causes célèbres* thus played a significant role in the development of anti-Semitism during the early *Kaiserreich*. They added a sense of immediacy and gravity to the Jewish Question and allowed the otherwise small anti-Semitic parties to exert a disproportionate influence on the course of German politics.

Certainly these conclusions suggest a much more nuanced picture of anti-Semitism than allowed by Daniel Goldhagen's polemical account. How axiomatic was anti-Semitism in late nineteenth-century Germany? If anti-Semitism is broadly defined to include the prevalence of social discrimination and anti-Jewish stereotypes, it seems irrefutable that anti-Semitism was common and pervasive in Imperial Germany. However, if the term anti-Semitism refers to an obsessive, paranoid, racial, and "eliminationist" attitude toward Jews that tended toward violent action, it is not at all clear that this kind of judgment is justified.

Political anti-Semitism was indeed a very powerful weapon in Imperial Germany, but it also had many powerful and influential opponents across the political spectrum—including leading liberal politicians, prominent Catholic leaders such as Ludwig Windthorst, and many Protestant clergymen such as Franz Delitzsch and Hermann Strack. Daniel Goldhagen, however, tends to dismiss these "defenders of Judaism," since many of them believed in the existence of a "real" Jewish Question, which they hoped would be resolved peaceably through the conversion or total assimilation of all German Jews. As Goldhagen states:

> The 'solutions' that anti-Semites did propose in the latter part of the nineteenth century ran the gamut from the old liberal hope of causing

[55] David Peal, "Anti-Semitism and Rural Transformation in Kurhessen: The Rise and Fall of the Böckel Movement" (Ph.D. Diss., Columbia University, 1985), 151–152. Böckel refers to the 1884 Marburg trial of Conrad Hedderich for murdering a Jewish couple in their home. After testifying that the couple had foreclosed his farm and ruined him, Hedderich was acquitted of murder. In another speech, Böckel claimed to have been influenced by other courtroom experiences: "If one wants to study the Jewish Question, one must go to the courthouse, like me, to see where the Jew leads his poor farmers. Sometimes I watched at the District Court as the poor victims groveled with lowered heads before the grinning Jews. Yes, gentlemen, it was this sight that made me into an anti-Semite." As quoted in Rüdiger Mack, "Otto Böckel und die antisemitische Bauernbewegung in Hessen 1887–1894," in *900 Jahre Geschichte der Juden in Hessen. Beiträge zum politischen, wirtschaftlichen und kulturellen Leben*, ed. Christiane Heinemann (Wiesbaden: 1983), 386.

> the Jews to disappear through total assimilation . . . to forcible and violent expulsion, and even to total annihilation. All these solutions are but variations, enormously different as they may be, on the eliminationist mind-set. From the anti-Semites' perspective, though not from that of the Jews, these "solutions" were, with their remaining differences, rough functional equivalents.[56]

Again, this definition is problematic. Should men like Delitzsch and Strack, who vigorously attacked anti-Semitism, denounced attempts to take legal measures against Jews, and fostered strong ties to Jewish communities really be categorized as eliminationist anti-Semites alongside those few Germans who called for violence against Jews? Only by adopting an extremely broad definition can Goldhagen obscure the real and important differences between these groups. He "discovers" an eliminationist anti-Semitic German populace by lowering the standards for admission to this category. As Alan Levenson suggests about men like Delitzsch and Strack, "despite a theological starting point inimical to Judaism, their Judaica scholarship, their contacts with Jewish scholars, and their opposition to prevailing trends in German Christianity consistently led them in pro-Jewish directions."[57]

Goldhagen's assertions about the potential lethality of anti-Semitism in Imperial Germany also seem exaggerated. Anti-Semitic rhetoric did tend to be extreme, especially during the 1890s, and some anti-Semitic pamphlets and articles contained veiled references and occasionally even direct mention of violence against Jews. However, instead of analyzing the popular support or resistance to such calls for violence, Goldhagen simply concludes that "*the eliminationist mind-set tended toward an exterminationist one.*"[58] In other words, Goldhagen implies that since eliminationist anti-Semitism was prevalent, and since anti-Semitic literature tended toward extreme racism and violence, the great majority of Germans must have been prepared to accept radical, even genocidal "solutions" to the Jewish Question.

---

[56] Goldhagen, *Hitler's Willing Executioners*, 70.

[57] In discussing Delitzsch and Strack, Levenson uses the concept of "allosemitism" developed by the sociologist Zygmunt Baumann. Allosemitism is "the allocation of a special vocabulary to address the radical otherness of the Jews." This sense of otherness can be accompanied by either negative or positive associations. In the case of these defenders of Judaism, the associations were largely positive. See Alan Levenson, *Between Philosemitism and Antisemitism: Defenses of Jews and Judaism in Germany, 1871–1932* (Lincoln: Univ. of Nebraska Press, 2004), 66–67.

[58] Goldhagen, *Hitler's Willing Executioners*, 71. (Italics in original).

In support of his assertions about the lethality of anti-Semitism in Imperial Germany, Goldhagen cites a 1963 dissertation by Klemens Felden, which includes a content analysis of 51 anti-Semitic publications between 1861 and 1895.[59] Goldhagen concludes from Felden's work that twenty-eight of these works proposed "solutions" to the Jewish Question—nineteen of which called for the physical extermination of the Jews. These statistics are indeed startling and very instructive about the nature of anti-Semitism during the *Kaiserreich.* However, in linking these statistics to his theory of eliminationist anti-Semitism, Goldhagen is guilty of a logical fallacy. In defining eliminationist anti-Semitism, Goldhagen lowered the bar to include even those liberals, Conservatives, and moderate Catholics who explicitly denounced the anti-Semitic movement. The literature surveyed by Felden, however, does not include works from Goldhagen's broad range of eliminationist anti-Semites, but from only a relatively narrow sample of extreme anti-Semites associated with anti-Semitic political parties. Of those books in Felden's survey, many were widely-read and publicly discussed, but most were strongly condemned by liberals and moderate Catholics—groups that Goldhagen included in his broader definition of anti-Semitism. In fact, many of the most vicious anti-Semitic tracts in Felden's survey, including works by Hermann Ahlwardt, Otto Böckel, and Karl Paasch, caused significant shock and consternation not only among Conservatives and Catholics, but also among fellow anti-Semitic agitators. Felden's study thus shows the degree to which violent action against the Jews was conceivable in Imperial Germany, but not the degree of public support attracted by these radical solutions.

Finally, Goldhagen also asserts that anti-Semitism had enormously wide institutional and political support in Germany throughout the nineteenth century. Numerous studies have demonstrated the high degree of anti-Jewish feeling among government officials and the clear discrimination against Jews in the military, the bureaucracy, and the judiciary. But interestingly enough, what Goldhagen does not mention is that the most radical anti-Semitic rhetoric (particularly in the works analyzed by Felden) was often used as part of a campaign

---

[59] See Klemens Felden, "Die Übernahme des antisemitischen Stereotyps als soziale Norm durch die bürgerliche Gesellschaft Deutschlands, 1875–1900" (Dissertation, Ruprecht-Karl-Universität zu Heidelberg, 1963).

of political opposition. The most radical anti-Semites of the 1880s and 1890s were largely hostile to what they saw as a government still under the sway of Jewish-liberalism. While proclaiming their own loyalty and patriotism to the Kaiser, these agitators (sometimes reluctantly and sometimes enthusiastically) pressed their anti-Semitic campaigns in the face of government disapproval and sometimes prosecution. The two major parties that commonly used anti-Semitic rhetoric to attack liberals in the 1870s and 1880s, the Conservative Party and Catholic Center Party, did so primarily as voices of opposition to a continuation of a moderate Bismarckian *Kartell* alliance between National Liberals and moderate Conservatives. Thus, the most vicious anti-Semitic rhetoric in this period was often directed *against* the German government and many of its institutions and policies.

It is clear that historians need to be careful about judging anti-Semitism in early Imperial Germany through the lens of events that occurred half a century later; however, it is also important not to minimize the legacy of anti-Semitism during this period. The fact that men like Glagau, Stöcker, and Ahlwardt did not consciously support a Nazi *Endlösung* does not mean that their contributions to German anti-Semitism were without ultimate effect. And perhaps those in the Conservative and Catholic press who may have used anti-Jewish rhetoric out of sheer political opportunism deserve an even larger share of responsibility for what came after. These men gave focus and direction to existing anti-Jewish sentiment, they lent credibility to the most outrageous of accusations against Jews, they reinforced anti-Jewish stereotypes, and they sought to exploit fear and hatred for political and ideological motives. For all the differences between the Second Reich and the Third, the anti-Semitic demands of a Liebermann von Sonnenberg or Glagau appear moderate only in the shadow of the Nuremberg Laws, as the often vicious rhetoric of a *Germania* or *Kreuzzeitung* appears mild only in comparison to that of Goebbels and Streicher. Anti-Semitism in the *Kaiserreich* did not inevitably lead to Hitler's *Judenpolitik*, but it is difficult to imagine the latter without the powerful influence of the former.

APPENDIX

AN OVERVIEW OF THE GERMAN PRESS IN THE *BISMARCKZEIT*

Because the press was instrumental in publicizing anti-Semitic trials and framing popular debate on the Jewish Question, newspapers form a large proportion of the primary source materials used in this study. In the following pages, I will provide a short description of some of the most important political newspapers in Germany. Although the following discussion will focus primarily on the Berlin press, it will also include newspapers from other German cities that played a prominent role in debates on the Jewish Question and on anti-Semitic trials in particular. This summary is not intended to be a complete list or a comprehensive history of the German press. It is compiled primarily from a variety of secondary sources such as Hans-Dietrich Fischer's *Deutsche Zeitungen des 17. bis 20. Jahrhunderts*, Kurt Koszyk's *Deutsche Presse im 19. Jahrhundert*, and Walther Oschilewski's *Zeitungen in Berlin.*

The Conservative Press

The most prominent German Conservative newspaper of this period was the *Neue Preußische Zeitung*—nicknamed the *Kreuzzeitung* because of the prominent cross on its masthead. The *Kreuzzeitung* was founded in 1848 as an attempt by leading *Junkers* to create a journalistic counterweight to liberal newspapers such as Georg Gervinus's *Deutsche Zeitung*. After several failed attempts, Ludwig von Gerlach created the *Kreuzzeitung* with the support of several wealthy *Junkers*, including Otto von Bismarck.[1] Although the newspaper was first formed to serve as a bulwark against the forces of republicanism, it soon became

[1] Meinolf Rohleder and Burkhard Treude, "Neue Preussische (Kreuz-)Zeitung," In *Deutsche Zeitungen des 17. bis 20. Jahrhunderts*, ed. Hans-Dietrich Fischer (Pullach bei München: Verlag Dokumentation, 1972), 209–210.

a source of reactionary opposition to the "bureaucratic-absolutist Camarilla" centered around Otto von Manteuffel.[2] Once Bismarck assumed power in the early 1860s, however, the *Kreuzzeitung* once again aligned itself more closely with the Prussian government. In fact, by 1870 the *Kreuzzeitung* stood alongside the *Spenerschen Zeitung* as a semi-official Bismarck newspaper.[3]

From unification onward, the political position of the *Kreuzzeitung* was determined primarily by the relations between Bismarck and Conservative Party leaders. Under the stewardship of Philipp von Nathusius-Ludom after 1872, the newspaper rebelled violently against Bismarck, who many Conservatives believed had abandoned their party for the National Liberals. Between 1876 and 1881, however, the newspaper's attacks on Bismarck softened as the Chancellor broke with the liberals and returned to a more conservative course. When Bismarck began to seek a moderate *Kartell* alliance between National Liberals and moderate Conservatives in the mid-1880s, the *Kreuzzeitung* once again began to view Bismarck as a bitter enemy.

Under the editorship of Wilhelm von Hammerstein (after 1881), the *Kreuzzeitung* came to represent the most radical and reactionary wing of the Conservative Party—a faction commonly referred to as the *Kreuzzeitungsgruppe*. The newspaper not only became more strident in its opposition to Bismarck, but also used increasingly vicious anti-Semitic articles in an attempt to drive a wedge between moderate Conservatives and their National Liberal *Kartell* partners. Thus, during the height of Bismarck's *Kartell* between 1887 and 1890, Hammerstein and the *Kreuzzeitungsgruppe* used the newspaper to do battle with Bismarck, with the "Jewish-liberals," and even with the moderate wing of their own party. In a desperate attempt to counter the influence of the ultra-Conservative *Kreuzzeitung* on the Conservative rank-and-file, the leader of the moderate Conservatives, Otto von Helldorf-Bedra, later took control of several other newspapers including the *Conservative Correspondenz*.

Although the *Kreuzzeitung* was by far the most prestigious Conservative newspaper, it reached only a relatively narrow *Junker* readership. The number of subscribers to the newspaper doubled to over 6500 by 1860, but throughout the *Bismarckzeit* the paper never exceeded

[2] Ibid., 214–215.
[3] Ibid., 217.

10,000 subscribers.[4] Thus, the *Kreuzzeitung* could in no way be considered a mass newspaper. In the mid-1870s, the editor of the *Kreuzzeitung*, Nathusius-Ludom, created a new conservative newspaper called the *Reichsbote* that was directed at a broader popular audience. Eventually, the *Reichsbote* surpassed the *Kreuzzeitung* to become the most popular Conservative newspaper of the era. The long-time editor of the *Reichsbote*, Pastor Heinrich Engel, became a close confidant of Adolf Stöcker during the 1880s and 1890s, and his newspaper often gave voice to Stöcker's ideas.

Although Adolf Stöcker made common cause with the *Kreuzzeitungsgruppe*, he also endeavored to create a small independent Christian Social press. In 1882, he founded the *Christlichsoziales Correspondenzblatt*, which functioned as the official party newspaper throughout the 1880s. In 1889, Stöcker supplemented this newspaper by founding *Das Volk*. Like the *Reichsbote*, *Das Volk* was designed as a newspaper for the "*kleinbürgliche Mittelstand*." Although the readership of *Das Volk* remained relatively small, the newspaper became a prominent anti-Semitic voice in the early 1890s through the aggressive editorship of Hans Leuß and Heinrich Oberwinder.

The Catholic Press

For many years, the leading Catholic newspaper in Germany was the *Kölnische Volkszeitung*. Originally founded by Josef Bachem as the *Kölnische Blätter* in 1860, the *Kölnische Volkszeitung* was an independent Catholic newspaper with liberal tendencies. Originally in favor of a *großdeutsch* Germany under Austrian control, the newspaper was one of Bismarck's sharpest critics in the late 1860s.[5] After the founding of the German Reich, the *Kölnische Volkszeitung* continued to speak out against Bismarck's persecution of German Catholics in the *Kulturkampf*. Although the newspaper was often associated with the Center Party leader, Ludwig Windthorst, it remained under Josef Bachem's personal control. The *Kölnische Volkszeitung* was generally known for

---

[4] Ibid., 212.

[5] Rolf Kramer, "Kölnische Volkszeitung," in *Deutsche Zeitungen des 17. bis 20. Jahrhunderts*, ed. Hans-Dietrich Fischer (Pullach bei München: Verlag Dokumentation, 1972), 258.

its relatively moderate tone, but the paper did publish strong anti-Semitic articles in the early 1880s and again in the early 1890s—most directed against the influence of the "Jewish-liberal" press.

While the *Kölnische Volkszeitung* was usually associated with a moderate wing of the Center Party, a group of more conservative Catholics founded their own influential newspaper in Berlin, called the *Germania*. Although formed at the same time as the Catholic Center Party (1871) and commonly referred to as a semi-official organ of this party, the *Germania* often found itself in conflict with more moderate Catholic leaders. Unlike the *Kölnische Volkszeitung*, the *Germania* was not owned by a single family, but by a shifting group of financial backers. Thus, it never officially linked itself to one group of Catholic politicians.[6] Despite this instability, the *Germania* was fairly consistent in its militant anti-Bismarckian, anti-liberal, and anti-Semitic rhetoric. One of its first editors was Christoph Joseph Cremer, who authored vicious anti-Jewish attacks in the mid-1870s and later affiliated himself with Adolf Stöcker and the *Berliner Bewegung*.[7] Cremer's successor, Paul Majunke, was equally dedicated to anti-liberal and anti-Jewish attacks. Although moderate Catholic politicians such as Ludwig Windthorst repeatedly intervened to force out radical journalists like Cremer and Majunke, the *Germania* nevertheless maintained a reputation for being militant in its attacks on the German government and on the Jews. Because of its strong opposition to the *Kulturkampf*, the *Germania* was often considered the leading voice of German Catholics through the 1870s and 1880s. However, as the tensions of the *Kulturkampf* waned, the *Germania* declined in importance compared to the *Kölnische Volkszeitung*.[8]

The "Governmental" Press

The *Norddeutsche Allgemeine Zeitung* was known throughout the 1880s as Otto von Bismarck's semi-official newspaper. Founded in 1861,

---

[6] Margaret Lavinia Anderson, *Windthorst: A Political Biography* (Oxford: Clarendon Press, 1981), 248.

[7] Cremer's association with Stöcker brought a public attack from Windthorst, and eventually caused him to be forced out of the Center Party. Cremer later broke bitterly with Stöcker over Stöcker's suggestion that he had been paid by Gerson von Bleichröder to withdraw as an election candidate. Cremer's bitter counter-accusations launched the Stöcker-Witte Affair.

[8] Anderson, *Windthorst*, 248.

the *NAZ* first became associated with government officials through its chief editor, Dr. August Braß.[9] Bismarck often released statements anonymously through the *NAZ*, which appeared under bylines such as "from Berlin" or "from very high sources"—he occasionally even sent finished manuscripts of articles he wished to have printed. In this way, Bismarck could secretly work to sway public opinion and test out controversial ideas in public that could always be disavowed in official circles.[10] Braß was succeeded as editor of the *NAZ* in the early 1870s by Emil Pindter, who continued the newspaper's close relationship with Bismarck. Although its cooperation with the government made the *NAZ* important for domestic and foreign politicians, the newspaper was never successful in reaching a mass audience. During the 1880s, the total subscriptions of the *NAZ* lagged far behind other prominent political newspapers. After Bismarck's dismissal in 1890, he withdrew his support for the *NAZ* in favor of the *Hamburger Nachrichten*. Pindter responded by quickly forming an alliance with the new Chancellor, Leo von Caprivi—a decision that later brought him into sharp conflict with his former benefactor.[11]

The *Kölnische Zeitung* was one of the oldest liberal newspapers in Germany. Originally founded in 1651 as the *Postzeitung*, it eventually grew to be the largest newspaper in the Rhineland. During the early 1860s, this newspaper fought bitterly with the Conservative *Kreuzzeitung* and Otto von Bismarck. However, as it became clear that Bismarck intended to achieve unification while granting many concessions to the liberals, the *Kölnische Zeitung* soon hailed Bismarck as a hero for Germany. During the early 1870s, the editor of the *Kölnische Zeitung*, Dr. Franz Fischer, developed such close ties to government officials that the newspaper was often reputed to be a semi-official government organ.[12] The newspaper followed Bismarck eagerly

[9] Heinz-Dietrich Fischer, "Deutsche Allgemeine Zeitung," in *Deutsche Zeitungen des 17. bis 20. Jahrhunderts*, ed. Heinz-Dietrich Fischer (Pullach bei München: Verlag Dokumentation, 1972), 269. Ironically, Braß was a former republican from the 1848 revolution and had founded the paper with his friend Wilhelm Liebknecht. As Braß became more friendly toward the German government, Liebknecht quit the newspaper.

[10] Ibid., 271.

[11] Ibid., 271–273.

[12] Georg Potschka, "Kölnische Zeitung," in *Deutsche Zeitungen des 17. bis 20. Jahrhunderts*, ed. Hans-Dietrich Fischer (Pullach bei München: Verlag Dokumentation, 1972), 153.

into the *Kulturkampf*, and thus cultivated a bitter rivalry with its Catholic counterpart in Cologne, the *Kölnische Volkszeitung*. After Bismarck abandoned the liberals in the late 1870s, the *Kölnische Zeitung* shifted toward the political right along with the National Liberal fraction. By the late 1880s, the newspaper was far more sympathetic to moderate Conservatives than to their former allies in the Progressive Party.

Another newspaper that exhibited loyalty to Bismarck during the 1880s was the Free Conservative newspaper *Die Post*. Originally founded by the financier Henry Bethel Strousberg to serve his own political and financial interests, *Die Post* was later purchased by the giant *Disconto-Gesellschaft* and eventually fell into the control of leaders of the Free Conservative Party. Its long-time editor, Leopold Kayßler, turned the paper into a small, but relatively well-respected Berlin newspaper.[13] Although *Die Post* did print several strongly anti-Semitic articles in the early 1880s (when Bismarck gave his tacit support to anti-Semitic candidates), it became more critical of the ultra-Conservatives and anti-Semites throughout the decade.

The *National-Zeitung* was founded in 1848, in the wake of the lifting of press censorship by Friedrich Wilhelm IV. It loosely affiliated itself with liberal politicians and gave strong support to the idea of a unified Germany under Prussian leadership. Ferdinand Salomon inherited the newspaper in 1879 from his uncle Bernhard Wolff, and, along with his chief editor, Friedrich Dernberg, aligned the paper closely to the National Liberal Party. Many prominent industrialists fostered ties to this newspaper; Bismarck, however, tended to favor the *NAZ* and the *Kölnische Zeitung*. After the weakening and splitting of the National Liberal Party in the early 1880s, the newspaper wavered in its political loyalties and its number of public subscriptions dropped. Although it remained an influential newspaper throughout the decade, the *National-Zeitung* continued to decline in importance.[14]

---

[13] Walther Oschilewski, *Zeitungen in Berlin: Im Spiegel der Jahrhunderte* (Berlin: Haude und Spenersche Verlagsbuchhandlung, 1975), 79–80.

[14] Jürgen Kahl, "National Zeitung," in *Deutsche Zeitungen des 17. bis 20. Jahrhunderts*, ed. Hans-Dietrich Fischer (Pullach bei München: Verlag Dokumentation, 1972), 177–190.

The Liberal Press

The *Voßische Zeitung* was one of the oldest newspapers in Berlin. Originally founded in 1617 as the *Frischmann-Zeitung*, it was renamed in 1751 after its new owner Christian Friedrich Voß. Nicknamed "*Tante Voß*" (Aunt Voß) by its Berlin reading public, the newspaper remained relatively apolitical until 1848. After government censorship was relaxed, however, the *Voßische Zeitung* immediately adopted a liberal political identity. Although the newspaper was never explicitly linked to any political party, it usually aligned itself with Progressive liberal politicians. Under the able editorship of Friedrich Stephany, the paper held a respected position in the Berlin press.[15] By the early 1880s, however, the *Voßische Zeitung* had been surpassed in readership by two new liberal newspapers: the *Berliner Tageblatt* and the *Berliner Zeitung*.

The *Berliner Tageblatt* was founded in 1871 by the 27 year-old Rudolf Mosse. Although the newspaper struggled at first, Mosse's previous experience as the business manager for other Berlin newspapers helped him attract a large group of advertisers. By 1880, with the help of the respected editor and journalist Arthur Levysohn, Mosse built the *Berliner Tageblatt* into the most popular newspaper of its kind in Germany.[16] Despite its liberal sympathies in political matters, the *Berliner Tageblatt* was so widely read that many *Junkers* were jokingly accused of secretly slipping the *Tageblatt* inside their copies of the *Kreuzzeitung*. This kind of success made the Jewish Mosse a very unpopular figure for opponents of liberalism—and for proponents of anti-Semitism.

Meanwhile, a rival to Rudolf Mosse, Leopold Ullstein, created his own publishing empire around the liberal *Berliner Zeitung*. The liberal journalist Peter Langmann originally founded this newspaper in the mid-1870s. However, Langmann soon ran into financial difficulties, and Ullstein stepped in to assume control of the newspaper in 1878. The partnership of Ullstein and Langmann quickly turned the small newspaper into one of the most successful institutions in Berlin—with almost 25,000 readers by the end of 1879. Although the *Berliner*

---

[15] Klaus Bender, "Voßische Zeitung," in *Deutsche Zeitungen des 17. bis 20. Jahrhunderts*, ed. Hans-Dietrich Fischer (Pullach bei München: Verlag Dokumentation, 1972), 25–40.

[16] Oschilewski, *Zeitungen in Berlin*, 88.

Zeitung represented a political viewpoint similar to the *Berliner Tageblatt*, it was often more outspoken in its criticism of the government. The newspaper's constant attacks against the Anti-Socialist Laws brought repeated prosecution by government authorities, but also won the loyalty of many Berlin workers.[17]

The *Berliner Börsen-Courier* was founded in 1868 by George Davidsohn. The *Börsen-Courier* was created as a rival to Davidsohn's former employer, the *Berliner Börsen-Zeitung*. Primarily through Davidsohn's connections with prominent bankers and financiers, the *Börsen-Courier* quickly earned a reputation as a respected financial news report. Davidsohn also used his ties to artists, writers, and musicians to make the *Börsen-Courier* an influential force in Berlin culture. Under his control, the newspaper became one of Richard Wagner's earliest and most enthusiastic supporters in the German press.[18] While Davidsohn's previous employer, the *Berliner Börsen-Zeitung*, was considered a "governmental" newspaper and was often affiliated with the National Liberals, his new paper took a much more leftist-liberal or *freisinnig* direction. The *Börsen-Courier* quickly became one of the most outspoken critics of anti-Semitism and perhaps the bitterest enemy of Adolf Stöcker and the *Berliner Bewegung*.

Although published far from Berlin, the *Frankfurter Zeitung* also played a significant role in Berlin politics. Founded in 1856 by a Jewish banker named Leopold Sonnemann, the newspaper was originally conceived as a local report on business and the stock market in Frankfurt am Main. Within a few years, however, it had transformed into a fully developed newspaper. Sonnemann exerted a great amount of influence on the character of the newspaper, which in its early years was *großdeutsch*, liberal, and strongly critical of Bismarck. A convinced democrat, Sonnemann was linked to the *Deutsche Arbeiterverein* and supported the early work of August Bebel.[19] His newspa-

---

[17] Peter De Mendelssohn, *Zeitungsstadt Berlin: Menschen und Mächte in der Geschichte der deutschen Presse* (Berlin: Verlag Ullstein, 1982), 102–111. Mendelssohn's claim that the paper reached 20,000 subscribers by the end of 1878 does not match the government records in the Bundesarchiv Berlin-Lichterfelde, which show a subscription of 2675 in early 1880. However, Mendelssohn's figures match those provided by Kurt Koszyk, *Deutsche Presse im 19. Jahrhundert* (Berlin: Colloquium Verlag, 1966), 284.

[18] Oschilewski, *Zeitungen in Berlin*, 80–81.

[19] Kurt Paupié, "Franfurter Zeitung," in *Deutsche Zeitungen des 17. bis 20. Jahrhunderts*, ed. Hans-Dietrich Fischer (Pullach bei München: Verlag Dokumentation, 1972), 243.

per was also one of the most fervent opponents of the Anti-Socialist Laws and a leading critic of the anti-Semitic movement.

The Jewish Press

In contrast to anti-Semitic stereotypes about Jewish unity, the Jewish community in nineteenth-century Germany was deeply divided along religious and political lines. During this period, many Jews had gradually become more reform-minded, often rejecting old religious traditions in an attempt to adapt their Judaism to the modern world. According to the Prussian Law on the Status of the Jews (1847), individual Jews were required to be affiliated with their local synagogue and Jewish communal organization in order to maintain their legal status as members of the Jewish faith. Because of these legal regulations, Orthodox Jews were not permitted to leave a synagogue that was too modern or too liberal for their tastes and were forced to remain members of Liberal or Reform congregations.[20] Orthodox leaders responded to this predicament with outrage, and demanded that they be given the right to secede from established Jewish organizations and form their own independent religious communities free from the influence of non-Orthodox Jews. Two influential rabbis led this separatist "Neo-Orthodox" movement: Samson Raphael Hirsch in Frankfurt am Main and Ezriel Hildesheimer in Berlin. Partially through the influence of these two men, the liberal politician Eduard Lasker successfully introduced legislation in 1876 that allowed a secession of Orthodox communities.[21]

Samson Hirsch and Ezriel Hildesheimer were not interested in "returning to the Ghetto," nor were they interested in preventing all reforms of Jewish religious practices. In fact, with his slogan "*Torah im derech eretz*" (Torah *and* the ways of the earth), Hirsch insisted that "the Jew does not stand obstinately in his Judaism against all nations and times."[22] Nevertheless, Hirsch and Hildesheimer both hoped to

---

[20] Uriel Tal, *Christians and Jews in Germany* (Ithaca: Cornell Univ. Press, 1969), 113.

[21] Sanford Ragins, *Jewish Responses to Anti-Semitism in Germany 1870–1914* (Cincinnati: Hebrew Union College Press, 1980), 90.

[22] Ragins, *Jewish Responses to Anti-Semitism*, 90; Samson Raphael Hirsch as quoted in Pinchas Rosenblüth, "Die geistigen und religiösen Stromungen in der deutschen

establish the secessionist communities as bulwarks against the complete erosion of Jewish traditions and the growing secularization of the Jewish community. To support this mission, Orthodox leaders were active in creating a specialized Jewish press that would report on Jewish religious and political affairs and encourage solidarity within the Orthodox Jewish community.

Hirsch and Hildesheimer were both vigorous in making their political and religious views known, and they both founded their own newspapers to carry their views to a broad Jewish public. Hirsch founded the monthly *Jeschurun* in Frankfurt as early as 1854, and he later merged this newspaper with the *Israelit* in Mainz. During the 1870s, the *Israelit* appeared in both German and Yiddish and carried the subtitle: "A Central Organ for Orthodox Judaism." As a prominent voice for Orthodox Jews in Central Germany, Hirsch did not hesitate to use his newspaper to attack anti-Semitism as well as to criticize the leaders of Reform Judaism.

Although Ezriel Hildesheimer was also a critic of Reform Judaism, he insisted that it was necessary to maintain strong ties with reform-oriented Jewish communities. Through his contacts with Reform Jews, he hoped to foster inter-confessional solidarity and demonstrate by example that traditional Judaism and modern German culture were compatible. Thus, in addition to founding the Orthodox Rabbinical Seminary in Berlin, Hildesheimer was also an active participant in broader Jewish organizations, including the Berlin *Hochschule für die Wissenschaft des Judenthums*.[23]

Like Samson Hirsch, Ezriel Hildesheimer also used a newspaper to spread his own political and religious point of view. In the early 1880s, Hildesheimer assumed control of the weekly newspaper, the *Jüdische Presse*. Originally founded in 1869 by the Orthodox Rabbi Dr. S. Enoch, this newspaper grew to be the most prominent voice for Orthodox Jews in Berlin. The primary intellectual force behind this newspaper was Ezriel Hildesheimer's son Hirsch, who dedicated his life to Jewish religious teachings, to philanthropic campaigns for Jews in Eastern Europe and Palestine, and to a vigorous battle against the spread of anti-Semitism. Unlike other Orthodox editors, Hirsch

---

Judenheit," in *Juden im Wilhelminischen Deutschland 1890–1914*, ed. Werner Mosse (Tübingen: J.C.B. Mohr, 1976), 586.

[23] Bernhard Poll, *Jüdische Presse im 19. Jahrhundert* (Aachen: Ausstellung zur Eröffnung des Neubaus der Bibliothek; Professor Walther Hirsch in Tel Aviv, 1967), 21.

Hildesheimer generally refrained from using this newspaper to attack or criticize Reform Jews. The pages of the *Jüdische Presse* were, however, commonly filled with polemical attacks and scholarly refutations of various anti-Semitic tracts, and Hildesheimer was also a regular participant in libel trials filed against—and sometimes filed by—anti-Semitic agitators.[24]

The most popular and well-respected Jewish newspaper in Germany was the *Allgemeine Zeitung des Judenthums* in Leipzig. Founded in 1837 by Dr. Ludwig Philippson, the paper was designed to serve as a "central newspaper for all Jewish affairs, a universal and general organ for Jews, their factions, teachings, and opinions . . . offered to both a Jewish and non-Jewish public."[25] Philippson had originally been a Rabbi in Magdeburg before his retirement for health reasons. Afterward, he continued to be a prominent figure in both Jewish scholarship and Jewish political affairs. In fact, Philippson was one of the major opponents of Samson Hirsch and Ezriel Hildesheimer in their efforts to legalize the Orthodox secession of 1876. Philippson worried that abandoning the principle of obligatory religious affiliation would cause Orthodox and Reform Jews to drift further apart and eventually lead to the disintegration of the German-Jewish community.[26] Although he lost this battle, Philippson continued in his attempt to use the *Allgemeine Zeitung des Judenthums* to unite German Jews of all political and religious factions. Under Philippson's direction until his death in 1889, the *AZdJ* maintained a generally liberal outlook, but remained unaffiliated with any particular group of liberal politicians.[27]

Some, but certainly not all, Jewish newspapers followed a generally liberal political outlook. There were strong ties between many liberal and Jewish journalists, but these ties were sometimes strained by significant philosophical differences. Ludwig Philippson of the *AZdJ*, for instance, was fiercely criticized by many liberals for opposing

---

[24] Mordechai Breuer, *Jüdische Orthodoxie im Deutschen Reich* (Frankfurt: Jüdische Verlag bei Athanäum, 1986), 156–157. See Breuer's description of a third important Jewish journal in Regensburg, the *Laubhütte*, that was in many ways modeled as a Jewish version of the popular *Gartenlaube*.

[25] From the prospectus of the *Allgemeine Zeitung des Judenthums* in 1837, quoted in Poll, *Jüdische Presse*, 26–27.

[26] Tal, *Christians and Jews in Germany*, 39–40.

[27] After the death of Philippson, the liberal (and Jewish) publisher Rudolf Mosse assumed control of the *AZdJ*. Mosse published several other newspapers, including the *Berliner Tageblatt*.

an end to compulsory religious affiliation. Liberal intellectuals ridiculed compulsory affiliation because in their opinion it preserved the power of obsolete religious institutions through reactionary legislation and obstructed the freedom of individuals to follow their own religious conscience.[28] Furthermore, the *AZdJ* and other Jewish newspapers were wary of liberals who supported egalitarianism with the eventual goal of wiping out all cultural or religious distinctions in Germany. In fact, during the 1870s, the *AZdJ* urged Jews to separate themselves from liberalism if it prevented the preservation of Jewish uniqueness.[29] This, of course, brought strong criticism from many liberal intellectuals.

Ironically, in Imperial Germany the term "*Judenpresse*" was not specifically an allusion to papers like the *Jüdische Presse*, but a derogatory reference to mainstream liberal newspapers that were supposedly owned or managed by Jews. Use of the epithet "*Judenpresse*" was not restricted to anti-Semitic newspapers. In fact, all political rivals of liberalism, including the Conservative, Catholic, and even the socialist Press commonly used this term. Even Otto von Bismarck repeatedly referred to liberal newspapers that were critical of his policies as "Jew-papers."[30] Most of the time, the label "*Judenpresse*" referred specifically to left-liberal newspapers such as the *Berliner Tageblatt*, *Berliner Börsen-Courier*, *Berliner Zeitung*, and the *Frankfurter Zeitung*. However, many ultra-Conservatives and anti-Semites also used the term for governmental newspapers like the *Norddeutsche Allgemeine Zeitung* and the *National Zeitung*. The anti-Semitic journalist Oswald Zimmerman even taunted rival Conservative editors in Dresden as "Cohnservatives" for being too soft on the Jewish Question.[31]

In reality, a significant proportion of those involved in the liberal press were Jewish, including newspaper owners like George Davidsohn, Rudolf Mosse, Leopold Ullstein, Leopold Sonnemann, and Ferdinand

---

[28] Tal, *Christians and Jews in Germany*, 39–40.

[29] Ibid., 43. Liberal criticism of the Orthodoxy especially emerged during debates on religion—including the debates over the *Volksschulgesetz* of 1892, which provoked the liberal *Berliner Tageblatt* to state "it makes no difference to us if the opponent's name is Stöcker or Hildesheimer!" See Breuer, *Jüdische Orthodoxie im Deutschen Reich*, 308.

[30] Fritz Stern, *Gold and Iron: Bismarck, Bleichröder, and the Building of the German Empire* (New York: Vintage Books, 1979), 276. According to Stern, Bismarck especially used this epithet for the *National Zeitung*.

[31] See, for example, Zimmermann's *Deutsche Wacht* (Dresden) 2 June 1889 #22.

Salomon. There were also a multitude of Jewish journalists, such as Friedrich Dernberg and Arthur Levysohn. Although there were also many non-Jewish editors and journalists in the German liberal press, these men were often accused of hiding their Jewish blood or of being "*Judensprösslinge*" or "*Judenknechte.*" Despite the frequent disagreements and rivalries among liberal editors, their enemies commonly assumed that all members of the "*Judenpresse*" worked closely together in support of Jewish interests.

Unlike their liberal counterparts who employed large staffs and sought a mass audience, most Jewish newspapers were one-man operations that relied on the opinions of their rabbi/scholar/editor and the contributions of occasional correspondents. Although such newspapers would often enter into political debates or exchange barbs with other mainstream papers, they were often occupied with reporting on more narrow Jewish cultural or religious matters.[32]

The Anti-Semitic Press

Most newspapers affiliated with the anti-Semitic movement did not raise enough money to survive more than a few years. One prominent exception was the Berlin *Staatsbürger Zeitung*. Originally founded in 1865 by the *Staatssozialist* Friedrich Wilhelm Held, the newspaper counted Franz Mehring among its early contributors. After Held's death, however, the *Staatsbürger Zeitung* fell into the control of Wilhelm Bruhn, who gradually infused his own anti-Semitic opinions into the paper.[33] Throughout the 1870s and 1880s, the *Staatsbürger Zeitung* remained a constant, but relatively minor voice in Berlin politics. Bruhn never affiliated the newspaper with a particular anti-Semitic faction, although he often included contributions from various anti-Semitic leaders. In the early 1890's, the *Staatsbürger Zeitung* affiliated itself closely with the radical anti-Semitic agitator Hermann Ahlwardt. This association led to increased publicity for the newspaper and briefly made it a more prominent political force. When Ahlwardt faded from the political scene in the mid-1890s, Bruhn began to use the *Staatsbürger Zeitung* to support his own political ambitions.

---

[32] Jacob Borut, "The Jewish Press in Germany in the Late Nineteenth Century as a Source of Historical Information," *Qesher* 11 (May 1992): 23e–24e.

[33] Oschilewski, *Zeitungen in Berlin*, 79.

Other than the *Staatsbürger Zeitung*, most explicitly anti-Semitic newspapers in Berlin were short-lived. In the early 1880s, individual agitators such as Ernst Henrici and Max Lieberman von Sonnenberg founded their own newspapers to help spread their political ideas. Henrici's paper, the *Reichsherold*, lasted only a few months before it collapsed. Liebermann, who like Henrici also suffered from financial difficulties, briefly ran the *Hallesches Thorbote*, which changed into the *Neue Deutsche Volkszeitung* before collapsing in 1885. Several other anti-Semitic newspapers were founded in Berlin during the early 1880s, such as Julius Ruppel's *Berliner Ostend-Zeitung*, Otto de Grahl's *Deutsche Patriot*, and H. de Grousillers' weekly satirical newspaper *Die Wahrheit*. While these newspapers did have a significant effect in arousing public anger against the Jews in the early 1880s, none survived more than a few years.

Largely due to the efforts of one man, Theodor Fritsch, Leipzig replaced Berlin as the primary center for anti-Semitic literature in the late 1880s and 1890s. Fritsch was originally trained as an engineer, but he became active as an anti-Semitic author and publisher after 1881. Although a speech impediment prevented him from becoming a successful politician, Fritsch became the driving force behind a publishing house that distributed several anti-Semitic newspapers and hundreds of pamphlets. Fritsch's publishing house, later known as the Hammer-Verlag, was responsible for the series *Brennende Fragen!* as well as the infamous *Antisemiten-Catechismus*, which was reissued during the Third Reich as the *Handbuch der Judenfrage*. After 1885, Fritsch joined with Max Liebermann von Sonnenberg to form the *Deutsche Antisemitische Vereinigung* and then the *Deutschsoziale Partei*. As their secret party newspaper, Fritsch and Liebermann published the monthly *Antisemitische Korrespondenz*.[34] In late 1888, Fritsch decided to make this newspaper public, and he replaced the subtitle "Forum for Internal Party Matters" with "Central Organ for German Anti-Semites." With this newspaper and the *Deutsch-Soziale Blätter*, Fritsch achieved moderate public success in spreading his racial anti-Semitic message.

The operations of Fritsch and Liebermann were soon joined by anti-Semitic rivals in other German cities. The *Deutsche Reform*, founded

[34] Although the newspaper originally had a very limited and private circulation, copies are still available in several locations. See especially the Sammlung Fechenbach at BAK.

by Alexander Pinkert (Egon Waldegg) in Dresden, was one of the first explicitly anti-Semitic newspapers in Germany. This newspaper had limited success before going bankrupt in 1886, when it was purchased by another anti-Semitic agitator, Oswald Zimmerman. One of the few Catholic leaders in the anti-Semitic movement, Zimmerman used the *Deutsche Reform* to attack his rivals in both the Conservative and Center parties. In 1887, he renamed his newspaper the *Deutsche Wacht* and made it the chief organ of his own political party. Although the *Deutsche Wacht* had only a moderate-sized readership, Zimmerman succeeded in using the newspaper to support his own political ambitions and to amass a personal fortune.[35]

In the late 1880s, both Zimmerman and Fritsch had another serious rival in the small German town of Marburg. By successfully agitating among the rural peasantry of Central Germany, Otto Böckel founded a new political party called the *Antisemitische Volkspartei.* Despite his occasional cooperation with Fritsch and Zimmerman, Böckel was often openly hostile to the Leipzig and Dresden branches of the movement. Although Böckel's newspaper, the *Reichsherold*, never reached a broad audience, it remained an important instrument for spreading anti-Semitic propaganda in Central Germany and for engaging in squabbles with Böckel's anti-Semitic rivals.

The competition between anti-Semitic newspapers was intense in the few instances where more than one anti-Semitic organization existed within a city. In Dresden for instance, one of the editors of the anti-Semitic *Dresdner Nachrichten*, Paul Liman, left for Zimmerman's *Deutsche Wacht.* Liman alleged that his former colleague, Max Lohan, was leading the *Nachrichten* away from racial anti-Semitism. After a long series of polemical exchanges between the two newspapers, Lohan printed the revelation that Liman was descended from Jewish grandparents. Although Liman was dismissed from the *Deutsche Wacht* after these rumors were confirmed, relations between the newspapers remained unfriendly.[36] Local anti-Semitic rivalries were even more intense in the central German town of Kassel, where two similarly

[35] Richard Levy, *The Downfall of the Anti-Semitic Political Parties in Imperial Germany* (New Haven: Yale Univ. Press, 1975), 116. Levy suggests that Zimmerman's wealth came from the over-capitalization of his newspaper (which was a joint-stock company) and other shady financial dealings.

[36] *Volkszeitung* 8 February 1894 #38 in StH Polizeibehörde, Abteilung IV, Politische Polizei: S 576 Teil III a.

named newspapers, the *Geldmonopol* and *Reichsgeldmonopol*, frequently accused each other of accepting Jewish money.[37]

Political Influence on the German Press

It is important to note that the task of evaluating the German press along this kind of political spectrum is dangerous for several reasons. First, as most historians acknowledge, any political spectrum is in itself an artifice and a simplification of political alliances and rivalries. Thus, to designate one politician or newspaper as "to the left of" another is not necessarily to predict how either will react in a given circumstance. Aside from this basic problem, there is also the complication that individual newspapers varied in their degrees of political independence. A newspaper like the *Kreuzzeitung*, for example, was tied to a particular political leader in the 1880s and represented his political opinions. Many other newspapers reflected a fairly consistent political outlook, but remained free of explicit ties to a single political party or clique of public figures. In addition, some newspapers occasionally modified their political loyalties as their editorial staff changed or as political conditions dictated. Thus, any historian who uses newspapers as primary sources must attempt to take into account the complex development of each individual newspaper.

Newspapers in the *Kaiserreich* were often subject to the secret influence of powerful political or financial figures. The most prominent of these secret manipulators of the press was Otto von Bismarck himself. From the beginning of his political career, Bismarck had realized the potential usefulness and potential danger of the political press. He was influential in the creation of the Conservative *Kreuzzeitung* in 1851, and he was an avid reader of newspapers throughout his life. Nevertheless, once he became Prussian Minister-President and later German Chancellor, he vigorously pursued and prosecuted newspapers that criticized his policies. During the 1860s and 1870s, legal prosecution of editors and confiscation of newspapers occurred at an ever-increasing rate. Bismarck realized, however, that repres-

[37] See *Geldmonopol* 25 February 1883 #8 in BAK *ZSg. 113* Sammlung Fechenbach Nr. 22.

sive measures alone would be unsuccessful in shaping public opinion. Thus, in the 1860s the Prussian government founded the *Provinzial-Korrespondenz*, a semi-official newspaper designed as a supplement to larger regional newspapers. Through the *Provinzial-Korrespondenz*, Bismarck hoped to counter what he saw as the dangerous influence of the liberal and democratic press. This government newspaper was only a marginal success, and Bismarck soon turned to other means of influencing the German press.[38]

In the mid-1860s, Bismarck forged a working relationship with the National Liberal *Norddeutsche Allgemeine Zeitung*. He often edited the political articles in the paper and sometimes even contributed anonymous articles of his own. Throughout his career, Bismarck also selected other newspapers to use as personal propaganda vehicles. Although Bismarck never divulged the extent of his ties to the press, several newspapers developed public reputations as semi-official government organs.

In addition to these efforts to establish a government-friendly press, Bismarck embarked on a secret campaign to influence a wide range of political newspapers through bribes to various editors or individual correspondents. Bismarck's source for these bribes was the so-called *Welfenfonds*, the treasuries of the former King of Hanover and the *Kurfürst* of Hessen, which had been confiscated by the Prussian government in the late 1860s. The interest from these funds was first used to fight the influence of radical Hanoverian journalists, but Bismarck soon used the treasury to bribe journalists from across the political and geographical spectrum.[39] Opposition journalists did not know how much money was being dispersed from the *Welfenfonds*, or which newspapers were receiving payments, but they constantly complained about Bismarck's unethical use of these public funds. Public controversy, however, was not enough to stop Bismarck from using these tactics. Until his dismissal in 1890, Bismarck used hundreds of thousands of Marks from the Hanoverian funds to make various newspapers and journalists dependent on his support.[40]

---

[38] The *Provinzial-Korrespondenz* lasted until 1884, but less than 40 newspapers accepted it as a supplement. Koszyk, *Deutsche Presse im 19. Jahrhundert*, 232–234.

[39] Ibid., 238. The funds were sometimes called the *Reptilienfonds* since Bismarck made a public speech in 1869 advocating a use of the money against the "vicious reptiles" in the Hanoverian press.

[40] For more on Bismarck and the press see Irene Fischer-Frauendienst, *Bismarcks Pressepolitik* (Münster: Verlag C.J. Fahle, 1963).

Bismarck was not the only public figure to use his status and financial resources to exert an influence on the German press. His personal banker, Gerson von Bleichröder had exceptionally close ties to National Liberal newspapers like the *Berliner Börsen Zeitung*, the *National Zeitung*, and especially the *Norddeutsche Allgemeine Zeitung*. Bleichröder nurtured longstanding friendships with the editors of these papers, and his enemies assumed he could plant stories anytime he wished. Bleichröder also established contacts with several other influential newspapers such as the *Berliner Börsen-Courier* and the *Allgemeine Zeitung* in Augsburg, and he even thought of acquiring one of these newspapers for himself. In the end, however, Bleichröder remained an influential figure for the liberal press, but one who operated from behind the scenes.[41] Other prominent businessmen also had ties to Berlin newspapers. Adolph von Hansemann and his *Disconto-Gesellschaft*, for example, bought both the *National-Zeitung* and *Die Post* during the 1870s, the latter purchased from the bankrupt railroad magnate Bethel Henry Strousberg. The large Norddeutsche Bank also played an important role in financing the *Norddeutsche Allgemeine Zeitung*.[42]

Lesser-known figures could also have an impact on the press. The wealthy Bavarian aristocrat Friedrich Karl Reichsfreiherr von Fechenbach zu Laudenbach was a prime example. In the early 1880s, Fechenbach was intent on forging an alliance between Catholics and Conservatives. He used his influence to recruit prominent men such as Adolf Stöcker and Wilhelm von Hammerstein to join his so-called Social-Conservative Alliance. But Fechenbach's efforts were largely a failure. The Center Party leader, Ludwig Windthorst, urged other Catholic politicians to keep their distance from Fechenbach, and only 16 of 250 people who attended the first meeting of his Social-Conservative Alliance were Catholic.[43] Moderate Conservatives were also wary of Fechenbach, who they believed wanted to create a new inter-confessional party under his own personal leadership. Once Fechenbach's direct political efforts failed, he resorted to indirect methods of influencing public opinion. Throughout the 1880s, Fechenbach secretly contributed articles to many newspapers, par-

---

[41] Stern, *Gold and Iron*, 276–278.
[42] Ibid., 276–277.
[43] Anderson, *Windthorst*, 254.

ticularly the Catholic *Deutsche Reichszeitung* in Bonn. Fechenbach was also active in financing individual anti-Semitic agitators and their journalistic endeavors. He was one of the major benefactors of the radical anti-Semite, Ernst Henrici, and his *Nachlaß* is full of letters requesting financial support from anti-Semites as far away as Hamburg and Budapest.[44] The full extent of Fechenbach's influence on German anti-Semitism, as well as his ties to leading Conservative and Catholic politicians may never be known, but this influence should not be underestimated.

Although social and political elites often wielded a great influence over the content of German newspapers, it would be a mistake to view the political press simply as a mechanism for the exertion of "top-down forces." That is, newspapers were not mere tools by which elite groups or political organizations could manipulate the broad German masses. While political newspapers usually had goals of political conversion or mobilization in mind, they were also forced to be responsive to public needs and desires. Newspapers were businesses, after all, and individual journalists and editors had to constantly shape the content of their newspapers in a way that would appeal to a general audience. Thus, "bottom-up" forces influenced the content of newspapers as much as "top-down" forces. In other words, public opinion often influenced newspapers as much as it was influenced by them.

[44] Fechenbach's *Nachlaß* is now housed at the Bundesarchiv Koblenz.

BIBLIOGRAPHY

Archival Sources

I.) Landesarchiv Berlin (LAB) A. Pr. Br. Rep. 030, Polizeipräsidium Berlin

No. 8679–8680. Die Deutsche antisemitische Vereinigung, begründet auf dem Antisemiten-Congreß zu Cassel im Juni 1886. (1885–1897)

No. 11453. Überwachung des antisemitischen Redakteurs Liebermann von Sonnenburg und Strafverfahren gegen diesen 1881–1908

No. 11690. Überwachung des antisemitischen Schriftstellers Wilhelm Marr 1853–1889

No. 12322. Überwachung des antisemitischen Schriftstellers Heinrich Rudolf Pleck-Podgorski 1885–1910

No. 14750. Prozeß gegen den Redakteur Heinrich Bäcker in Berlin wegen der Veröffentlichung von Extra-blättern der "Freien Zeitung" in Berlin mit dem Artikel: "Zur Characteristik des Hofpredigers Stöcker" (1884–1886)

No. 14754. Die Verhandlungen gegen Karl Paasch wegen der Herausgabe und Veröffentlichung von antisemitischen Schriften (1892–1901)

No. 14942. Antisemiten-Liga 1879–1883

No. 14961. Deutscher Antisemitenbund 1884–1887

No. 14962. Deutscher Antisemitenbund 1887–1890

No. 14963. Deutscher Antisemitenbund 1890–1893

No. 14964. Deutscher Antisemitenbund 1893–1896

No. 15076–8. Konservative Partei. Enthält u.a.: Druckschrift "Der Juden—Die Könige unserer Zeit"

No. 15219. Die Judenfrage (1880–81) Enthält: u.a.: Antisemitische Druckschriften, Zeitungsauschnitte, Plakate und Karicaturen

No. 15220. Die Judenfrage (1881–1882)

No. 15221. Die Judenfrage (1882–1894)

No. 15222. Die Judenfrage. Darin: Insbesondere Stellung der Studenten zur Judenfrage (1881).

No. 15223. Die Judenfrage. Die Beschlagnahme antisemitischer Karikaturen und Plakate (1881–1883).

No. 15224. Die Judenfrage. Die Henricische Reichshallenversammlung am 17. December 1880 (1880–1882).

No. 15225. Sammlung von Zeitungen mit Artikeln zur Judenfrage 1880–1881.

No. 15226. Internationaler Kongreß zur Wahrung nichtjüdischer Interessen Dresden 10.–12. Sep. 1882 und Chemnitz 27./28. April 1883

II.) Bundesarchiv Koblenz (BAK)

ZSg. 1–Partei- und Verbandrucksachen-Sammlung

Zeitraum 1867–1945

Politische Parteien:

No. E 25: Antisemitische Volkspartei (Böckel)

No. E 73: Christlich Soziale Partei Kl. Erw. 227

No. E 108: Christlich-Soziale Reichspartei

No. 265: Deutsche Reform-Partei

No. 108: Deutsche Zentrumspartei Kl. Erw. 44, 48, 190, 220, 442, 471, 476, 596

No. 170: Deutschkonservative Partei
No. E 75: Deutsch-Nationale Reform-Partei
No. E 2: Deutsch-soziale antisemitische Partei
No. E 24: Deutsch-soziale Reform
Partei Politische Verbände, Vereinigungen und Organisationen:
No. E 101: Deutscher Antisemiten-Bund
No. 244: Verein zur Abwehr des Antisemitismus Mitteilungen
Religionsgesellschaften:
No. 266: Central-Verein deutscher Staatsbürger jüdischen Glaubens

ZSg. 2—Allgemeine Drucksachen-Sammlung
I. 1867–1914
2. Innere Angelegenheiten
Teil 15—Judenfrage und Antisemitismus

ZSg.113—Sammlung Fechenbach
No. 12–23—Antisemitismus
No. 256–299—Deutschkonservatives Partei
No. 740–753—Protestante Angelegenheiten
No. 852–906—Katholische Angelegenheiten

Nachlässe:
NL105—Fechenbach, Freiherr Karl Friedrich von

III.) Bundesarchiv Abteilung Berlin-Lichterfelde (BABL)
R 15.01 Reichsministerium des Innern
Film 14220 No. 19 Band 1—Maßnahmen gegen Ausschreitungen der Presse (Mai 1869–Dez 1910)
Film 14222/1 No. 20 Band 1—Gesuche und Beschwerden in Presseangelegenheiten (Juni 1873–Dez 1886)

R 30.01 Reichsjustizamt/Reichsjustizministerium
No. 3793 Presserecht, Band 1. (1877–1894)
No. 3803 Presseangelegenheiten, Band 1 (1877–1934)
No. 6157 Majestätsbeleidigung, Band 1 (1875–1907)
No. 6251 Äußerungen der Presse zur Wucherfrage, Band 1 (1878–1893)

R 43 Alte Reichskanzlei (Stammakten)
No. 679–681 Angelegenheiten der Juden (1879–1893)
No. 1455 Angriffe des p.v. Diest-Daber auf den Fürsten Bismarck und Rehabilitierungsgesuche
No. 1548–1554 Angelegenheiten der Presse in allgemein (1878–1892)

Nachlässe:
90 Be 5 Bennigsen, Rudolf von
90 Li 1 Liebermann von Sonnenberg, Max

IV.) Geheimes Staatsarchiv Preussischer Kulturbesitz (GStA PK)
I. HA Rep. 76 (III) Kultusministerium—Außen Magazin (Merseburger Teil)
Section I, Abteilung XIIIa
No. 36–Zeitungsartikel und Schriften über das Judenwesen Band I (1890–1902)
No. 49—Die in bezug auf die religiösen und staatsbürgerlichen Verhältnisse der Juden mitgeteilten Aufsätze und Druckschriften

sowie die Herausgeber derselben.
Band I (1821–1884)
No. 56—Die Agitationen gegen die Juden
Band I (1879–1881)
Band II (1881–1883)

I. HA Rep. 77 Preußisches Innenministerium—Außen Magazin
Abteilung II, Sektion 8
Tit. No. 380—Preßsachen general (1848–1923)
No. 1—Die Gesetzgebung und die allgemeinen Anordnungen wegen der Presse
Band 8 (1870–1906)
No. 2—Die Bestrafung der Verfasser und Verbreiter aufrührischer und anstösiger Schriften, Abhandlungen und Artikel
Band 1 (1848–1913)
No. 32—Die Errichtung eines deutschen Reichsgesetzes über die Presse
Band 2 (1871–1873)
Band 3 (1873–1901)
No. 33—Die Beaufsichtigung der Katholischen resp. ultramontanen Presse gegen staatsgefährliche Umtriebe. Haltung der Zentrumspresse gegenüber der Regierungspolitik
Band 1 (1874–1875)
Band 2 (1875)
Band 3 (1875–1877)
Band 4 (1877–1889)

Tit. 54a Zeitungs-Sachen Berlin
No. 10—Die Herausgabe und den Debit der in Berlin erscheinenden "National-Zeitung"
Band 1 (1849–1876)
Band 2 (1876–1891)
No. 13—Die Herausgabe der "Neuen Preußischen Zeitung" auch unter dem Namen "Kreuzzeitung" bebaut
Band 2 (1857–1898)
No. 20—Die Herausgabe der in Berlin erscheinenden sogenannten "Vossischen Zeitung" (1848–1904)
No. 27—Die in Berlin erscheinenden Börsen- und Handels-Zeitungen sowie die Zeitungen in anderen gewerblichen Beziehungen (1855–1890)
No. 45—Die in Berlin unter der Bezeichnung "Germania" erscheinende Zeitschrift (1871–1872)
No. 60—Das von dem Hofprediger Stöcker gegründete Organ "Das Volk" (1889 17.3.–1889 19.3.)

I. HA Rep. 84a—Justizministerium—Innen Magazin (Dahlemer Teil)
No. 4062—Presserecht, Übersichten der beschlagnahmten Erzeugnisse der Tagespresse
Band I (1874–1876)—K29/7993–7996
No. 4063—Presserecht, Übersichten der beschlagnahmten Erzeugnisse der Tagespresse
Band II (1877–1882)—K29/7997–8001
No. 10567—Eidesleistungen der Juden
Bd. 5 (1861–1913)

I. HA Rep. 84a—Justizministerium—Außen Magazin (Merseburger Teil)
No. 47115—Das Judenwesen Bd. 9 (1866–1894)
No. 55739—Strafverfahren gegen das MdR Rektor Hermann Ahlwardt in Berlin wegen der Druckschrift "Der Verzweiflungskampf der arischen Völker mit dem Judentum" (1890–1893)
No. 55740—Strafverfahren gegen Hermann Ahlwardt wegen eines Vortrages in Essen und der Druckschrift "Jüdische Taktik" (1891–1894)
No. 55741—Strafverfahren gegen Hermann Ahlwardt wegen der antisemitischen Druckschrift "Judenflinten" (1892–1894)
No. 55742—Zeitungsausschnitte zum Prozeß gegen Hermann Ahlwardt (1892)
No. 55743—Beschlagnahme der antisemitischen Broschüre "Der Fall Ahlwardt in der öffentlichen Meinung und im Lichte der Wahrheit" von Dr. Paul Förster (1892)
No. 55744—Maßnahmen gegen die Verbreitung der antisemitischen Broschüre "Juden-Bordelle" (1892)
No. 55745—Aufhebung der Beschlagnahme der Broschüre "Juden-Bordelle" (1892)
No. 55746—Strafverfahren auf Anzeige des jüdischen Theologen Prof. Dr. Hermann L. Strack gegen den Redaakteur Dr. Bacher und Drucker Baade wegen Verbreitung eines Flugblattes in der "Staatsbürger-Zeitung" mit Beschimpfungen der jüdischen Religion (1892–1900)
No. 55747—Strafverfahren gegen den Verlagsbuchhändler Paul Glöß in Dresden u.a. wegen Beleidigung Caprivis durch antisemitische Äußerungen im "Politische Bilderbogen" No. 9 "Bismarck in Berlin" (1893–1895)
No. 55748—Ermittlungsverfahren gegen Hermann Ahlwardt wegen Beleidigung des Finanzministers Miquel (1893–1894)
No. 55749—Strafverfahren gegen den Schriftsteller Rudolf von Plack-Podgorski in Berlin u.a. wegen antisemitischer Beleidigung des Finanzministers (1893–1899)
No. 55750—Ermittlungsverfahren gegen das MdR Redakteur Otto Böckel in Berlin, Antisemit, wegen Beleidigung der Offizier der Armee (1895–1897)
No. 56464—Körperverletzung durch den Rabbinatskandidaten Max Bernstein aus Breslau (1889–1890)
No. 57459–57461—Mord durch Adolf Buschoff, Metzger und jüdischer Schlächter aus Xanten
No. 57459 Bd. 1 (1891–1892)
No. 57460 Bd. 2 (1892–1893)
No. 57461 Bd. 3 (1893–1909)
No. 57462—Mord durch Adolf Buschoff, Metzger und jüdischer Schlächter aus Xanten. Zeitungsausschnitte (1892–1893)
No. 57463—Mord durch Adolf Buschoff, Metzger und jüdischer Schlächter aus Xanten. Berichte der "Kölnischen Zeitung" von dem Schwurgericht in Cleve (1892)
No. 57467—Eingabe des Rektors Lang in Chur an den Reichskanzler und Preussischen Ministerpräsidenten zur Justizpraxis und zum Antisemitismus im Hinblick auf den noch immer unaufgeklärten Xantener Knabenmord 1891 (1917 [1918])

I. HA Rep. 89 Zivilkabinett—Außen Magazin (Merseburger Teil)
Band 8—Politische und Sicherheitspolizei (7.3.3)

No. 15091—Unruhen und Ausschreitungen 1863–1879
No. 15092—Unruhen und Ausschreitungen 1880–1889

VI. HA Nachlaß Adolf Stöcker
Abt. I Briefe (an Stöcker)
No. 1c—Kaiser Wilhelm II (1882–1890)
Abt. III Akten
No. 2—Verschiedene Prozesse und Klagssache
No. 4—Prozeß des Redakteurs Bachler (Staatsbürgerzeitung) gegen den sozialdemokratische Abgeordnete Paul Singer (1888)
No. 5—Prozesse gegen Pfarrer Witte, vol 1. (1889–1898)
No. 6—Prozesse gegen Pfarrer Witte, vol. 2. (1889/90)

V.) Staatsarchiv der Freien und Hansestadt Hamburg (StH)
Polizeibehörde, Abteilung IV,
Politische Polizei (Bestandnummer 331–3):
S 576
Teil I—Zeitungsausschnitte über antisemitische Angelegenheiten
Bd. 1. 1890–1892
Bd. 2. 1892–1895
Bd. 3. 1893–1894
Teil II a—Anmeldung öffentlicher Versammlungen durch die Antisemiten (1884–1892)
Teil II b—Überwachung antisemitischer Veranstaltungen (1893–1897)
Teil III a—Gerichtsverhandlungen mit Antisemiten 1893–1895
Teil III b—Versammlungen, Parteitage (außer Hamburg) 1893–1895
Teil III c—Versammlungen, Parteitage (außer Hamburg) 1890–1895

S 3939—Rektor Hermann Ahlwardt.
1. Personalien des Rektors a.D. Hermann Ahlwardt (1893–1896)
2. Berichten über Versammlungen des Rektors Ahlwardt in Hamburg (1891–98)
3. Acten betr. Ahlwardt's Broschüre "Jüdische Taktik" (1892)
4. Zeitungsauschnitte betr. Ahlwardt's Broschüre "Judenflinten" (1892–1899)
5. Akte in Sachen Rector a.d. Hermann Ahlwardt (1890–1914)

Nachlässe:
622–1 Nachlaß Marr, Wilhelm

List of Selected Newspapers

I.) *Anti-Semitic Newspapers*

Antisemitische Correspondenz (Leipzig). ed. Theodor Fritsch.
Berliner Ostend-Zeitung: Organ für die Interessen des deutschen Volkes. ed. Julius Rüppel, 1880–1882. Earlier *Der Ost-District: Organ für kommunale, gewerbliche und Vereins-Interessen des Ost-Districts.*
Deutsch-Soziale Blätter (Leipzig).
Der Deutsche Patriot. ed. O. de Grahl, 1881 only.
Deutsche Reform (Dresden) ed. Alexander Pinkert-Waldegg until 1885, then Oswald Zimmerman, 1879–1887. Later renamed the *Deutsche Wacht.*

Die Deutsche Wacht: Monatsschrift für nationale Entwicklung. ed. Wilhelm Marr, 1879–1881.
Deutsche Wacht: Organ für nationale Politik; Publikations-organ der völkischen Vereine Sachsens (Dresden). ed. Oswald Zimmermann,1887–1933. Continues from *Deutsche Reform.*
Geldmonopol (Cassel).
Hallesches Thorbote. ed. Max Liebermann von Sonnenberg. Later becomes *Neue Deutsche Volkszeitung.*
Der Kulturkämpfer: Zeitschrift für öffentlich Angelegenheiten. ed. Otto Glagau, 1880–1889.
Neue Deutsche Volkszeitung: Organ für Sociale Reform. ed. Max Liebermann von Sonnenberg.
Patriotische Zeitung (Liegnitz).
Das Reichs-Geldmonopol: antisemitisches Volksblatt für wirtschaftlich-sociale Neugestaltung (Cassel). 1882–1889. Later *Antisemitisches Volksblatt.*
Der Reichsherold. ed. Ernst Henrici, 1881 only.
Staatsbürger-Zeitung (Berlin-Fronau). ed. Wilhelm Bruhn, 1865–1914.
Die Wahrheit: humoristish-satirisches Wochenblatt. ed. H. de Grousillers.
Westfälische Reform (Münster).

II.) *Christian Social/Kreuzzeitungsgruppe/Agrarian*

Christlichsoziales Correspondenzblatt: Organ für christliche Socialpolitik; Bekanntmachungs-Organ der Christlich-Socialen Partei. ed. Aschenbrenner.
Deutsches Tageblatt. 1881, ed. J. Cremer, 1880s, M. Giesemann and Dr. O. Hammann, 1881.
Grenzboten: Zeitschrift für Politik und Literatur. 1844–1922.
Die Kreuzzeitung (*Neue Preußische Zeitung*). ed. Dr. Nathusius-Ludom, 1872–1876; Dr. v. Niebelschütz, 1876–1881; Freiherr v. Hammerstein, 1881–1895.
Der Reichsbote: deutsche Wochenzeitung für Christentum und Volkstum. ed. Friedrich Engel, 1873–1936.
Deutsche Reichsglocke. ed. Rudolf Meyer. Formerly *Deutsche Eisenbahn-Zeitung: Organ für Volkswirtschaft, Politik und sociales Leben.*
Das Volk. ed. Hans Leuß and Heinrich Oberwinder.

III.) Kartell/Moderate/Governmental

Conservative Correspondenz. ed. Griesemann,1889–1890.
Kölnische Zeitung. ed. Franz Fischer.
National Zeitung. ed. Friedrich Dernberg.
Norddeutsche Allgemeine Zeitung. ed. Emil Pindter.
Die Post. ed. Leopold Kayssler, 1866–1921.

IV.) Catholic Newspapers

Deutsche Reichszeitung (Bonn).
Germania. ed. Paul Majunke, 1871–1878; Adolf Franz, 1878–1881.
Kölnische Volkszeitung.
Westfälische Merkur (Münster).

V.) Left-Liberal Newspapers

Berliner Börsen-Courier. ed. Robert Davidsohn.
Berliner Tageblatt und Handelszeitung. ed. Arthur Levyson, 1872–1939.
Berliner Zeitung. 1876–1905.
Frankfurter Zeitung.

Freisinnige Zeitung. ed. Eugen Richter.
Die Nation.
Volkszeitung: Organ für Jedermann aus d. Volke. 1853–1904.
Vossische Zeitung. ed. Friedrich Stephany.

VI.) Jewish Newspapers
Allgemeine Zeitung des Judentums: eine unpartheiisches Organ für alles jüdische Interesse in Betreff von Politik, Religion, Literatur, Geschichte, Sprachkunde und Belletristik (Leipzig and Berlin). ed. Dr. Ludwig Philippson, 1837–1922.
Israelit und Jeschurun.
Jüdische Presse. ed. Rabbi Dr. S. Meyer until October 1883; Hirsch Hildesheimer after October 1883. 1870–1923.

Primary Sources

Ahlwardt, Hermann. *Judenflinten.* Dresden: Glöß, 1892.
——. *Die Judenfrage: Ein Vortrag . . . gehalten zu New York, im Januar 1896.* Hoboken, N.J.: American Antisem. Organization, 1896.
——. *Mehr Licht! Die Ermordung Friedrich Schillers, Lessings und Mozarts vor dem Forum moderner Literatur- und Weltgeschichte.* Leipzig-Reudnitz: W. Fischer, 1914.
——. *Meine Verhaftung.* Dresden: Glöß, 1892.
——. *Neue Enthüllungen: Judenflinten.* Dresden: Glöß, 1892.
——. *Die Prozesse Manché und Bleichröder.* Berlin: Dewald, 1891.
——. *Schwerin und Bleichröder: Edelmann und Jude.* Dresden: Glöß, 1893.
——. *Der Verzweiflungskampf der arischen Völker mit dem Judenthum.* Berlin: F. Grobhäuser, 1890.
Ahlwardt und seine Judenflinten: Ansichten eines deutschen Waffenoffiziers. Berlin: Schreiter, 1892.
Akten und Gutachten in dem Prozesse Rohling contra Bloch. Wien: M. Breitenstein, 1890.
Antisemiten-Spiegel. Die Antisemiten im Lichte des Christenthums, des Rechtes und der Moral. Danzig: A.W. Kasemann, 1900.
Der Antisemitismus. Sein Entstehen und Vergehen. Briefe eines Ariers an einen Semiten. Leipzig: E. Thiele, 1886.
Autoemanzipation! Mahnruf an seine Stammesgenossen von einem Russischen Juden. Berlin: Jüdischer Verlag, 1935.
Bauer, Erwin. *Der Fall Bleichröder.* Leipzig: Germanicus Verlag, 1891.
——. *Der Sensationsfall Carl Paasch.* Leipzig: W. Wauer, 1891.
Bey, Osman [Frederick Millingen]. *Die Eroberung der Welt durch die Juden.* Wiesbaden: Rud. Bechtold, 1875.
Bloch, Josef Samuel. *My Reminiscences.* New York: Arno Press, 1973.
——. *Gegen die Antisemiten: Eine Streitschrift.* Wien: D. Löwy, 1882.
——. *Des k. k. Prof. Rohling neueste Fälschungen.* Wien: Separat-Abdruck aus der Wiener Allgemeine Zeitung, 1883.
Der Blutmord in Konitz, mit Streiflichtern auf die staatsrechtliche Stellung der Juden im Deutschen Reiche. Nach Authentischen Quellen von einem besorgten Vaterlandsfreunde. Vorwort von Max Lieberman von Sonnenberg. Berlin: Deutschnationale, 1900.
Buch, Willi [Wilhelm Buchow]. *50 Jahre antisemitische Bewegung.* Munich: Deutscher Volksverlag, 1937.
Conti, Berthold W. *Ahlwardt's Bubenstreiche und die hierfür aplicirten Ohrfeigen ertheilt von dem Race-Juden.* N.p.: April 1893.
——. *Stöcker wider Ahlwardt und Genossen. Offener Brief an dd. Hofprediger a.D. Stöcker.* Berlin: Selbstverlag, n.d.
Cremer, Christoph Josef. *Die angeblichen 10,000 Mark des Herrn von Bleichröder.* Berlin: Luckhardt, 1889.

Delitzsch, Friedrich. *Christentum und Jüdische Presse. Selbsterlebes.* Erlangen: A. Deichert, 1882.

——. *Neueste Traumgeschichte der antisemitischen Propheten. Sendschreiben an Prof. Zöckler in Greifswald.* Erlangen: Deichert, 1883.

——. *Rohlings Talmudjude beleuchtet von Franz Delitzsch.* Leipzig: Dörffling und Franke, 1881.

——. *Schachmatt den Blutlügern Rohling und Justus.* Erlangen: Deichert, 1883.

Deutsche Antisemitenchronik 1888–1894. Zürich: J. Schabelitz, 1894.

Diest-Daber, Otto von. *Actenstücke in Sachen des Herrn von Diest-Daber: Als Manuscript zum discreten Gebrauch gedruckt.* Dresden: Julius Reichel, 1890.

——. *Berichtigung von Unwahrheiten in den Erinnerungen des Fürsten Bismarck und Deutsches Rechtsbewusstsein.* Zurich: C. Schmidt, 1899.

——. *Bismarck und Bleichröder. Deutsches Rechtsbewußtsein und die Gleichheit vor dem Gesetze. Lebenserfahrungen aus Akten, Tagebüchern, Briefen, u.a. Ein ernster Mahnruf an jeden wahrhaften und festen Patrioten.* München: Th. Wenng, 1897.

——. *Geldmacht und Socialismus: einzelne Schlagschatten auf die innere Politik des Fürsten Bismarck mit Original-Correspondenzen desselben.* Berlin: Puttkammer & Muhlbrecht, 1875.

——. *Zur Klarstellung des Anonymen Schriftstückes.* Dresden: Selbstverlag des Verfassers, 1878.

——. *Der sittliche Boden im Staatsleben.* Berlin: Putkammer & Muhlbrecht, 1876.

Draak, F. *Schwarze Banden unter Ärzten und Juristen im neugeeinten deutschen Reiche.* Berlin: Verlag von C. Draak, 1892.

Dühring, Eugen. *Die Judenfrage als Frage der Rassenschändigkeit für Sitte und Kultur der Völker.* Berlin: Reuther, 1892.

——. *Die Judenfrage als Rassen, Sitten, und Culturfrage: Mit einer weltgeschichtliche Antwort.* Leipzig: H. Reuther, 1881.

——. *Die Parteien in der Judenfrage.* Leipzig: Th. Fritsch, 1882.

Engel, Heinrich. *Das Judentum im Staate.* Berlin: Verlag der Redaktion des "Reichsbote," 1884.

Der Fall Buschoff: die Untersuchung über den Xantener Knabenmord von einem Eingeweihten. Berlin: Vaterländische Verlagsanstalt, 1892.

Der Fall Kantorowicz und die Judenfrage vor dem Preußischen Abgeordnetenhause am 20. und 22. November 1880. Berlin: Werkenthin, 1881.

Fechenbach-Laudenbach, Friedrich von. *Fürst Bismarck und die "deutsch"-conservative Partei: oder eine politische Abrechnung.* Frankfurt: Foesser, 1887.

——. *Noch einmal: "Die Partei Bismarck sans Phrase": Beleuchtung und Würdigung meiner gegnerischen Kritiker und ihrer Kritiken nebst Vergleich der Declaranten der 1850er mit diejenigen der 1870er Jahre.* Augsburg: Huttler, 1885.

Förster, Bernhard. *Das Verhältnis des modernen Judenthums zur deutschen Kunst.* Berlin: Schulze, 1881.

Förster, Paul. *Der Fall Ahlwardt in der öffentlichen Meinung und im Lichte der Wahrheit: Eine Streitschrift.* Berlin: Dewald, 1893.

Frank, Friedrich. *Der Ritualmord vor den Gerichtshöfen der Wahrheit und der Gerechtigkeit.* Regensburg: Verlagsanstalt vorm. G.J. Manz, 1901.

Friedländer, Hugo. *Interessante Kriminalprozesse.* Berlin: H. Barsdorf, 1910–.

——. *Der Knabenmord in Xanten vor dem Schwurgericht zu Cleve vom 4. bis 14. Juli 1892.* Cleve: W. Startz, 1892.

Fritsch, Theodor. *Der Streit um Gott und Talmud. Meine Antworten an Strack u.a.* Leipzig: Hammer Verlag, 1922.

——. *Verteidigungsschrift gegen die Anklage wegen groben Unfugs, verübt durch verbreitung antisemitischer Flugblätter.* Leipzig: T. Fritsch, 1891.

Fuchs, Eugen. *Um Deutschtum und Judentum.* Frankfurt a. M.: J. Kauffmann, 1919.

Gehlsen, Joachim. *Aus dem Reiche Bismarck.* Berlin: 1894.

Glagau, Otto. *Der Bankerott des Nationalliberalismus und die "Reaktion"*. Berlin: Verlag von F. Luckhardt, 1878.
——. *Der Börsen und Gründungsschwindel in Berlin.* Leipzig: P. Frohberg, 1876.
——. *Der Börsen und Grundungsschwindel in Deutschland.* Leipzig: P. Frohberg, 1877.
——. *Deutsches Handwerk und historisches Bürgerthum.* Osnabruck: B. Wehberg, 1879.
——. *Des Reiches Noth und der neue Culturkampf.* Osnabruck: B. Wehberg, 1880.
Graf, Armin. *Herrenhaus redivivus. Der Fall Paasch im Preußischen Herrenhause am 1. April 1892. Ein einstimmiges Verdikt dieses Hohen Hauses über die gemeingefährlichen Bestrebungen des internationalen Judentums und über das bisherige Verhalten des Justizministeriums der Judenfrage gegenüber nebst einem Anhang über die Verjudung unserer Aristokratie.* Berlin: Dewald, 1892.
Grumbkow, Richard von. *Die Judenfrage vor Gericht.* Dresden: R. von Grumbkow, 1883.
Henrici, Ernst. *Den Neustettinersynagogenbrand vor Gericht.* Berlin: Schulze, 1883.
——. *Was ist der Kern der Judenfrage? Vortrag gehalten am 13. Januar 1881.* Berlin: Verlag der "Wahrheit," 1881.
Hoffman, David. *Der Schulchan-Aruch und die Rabbinen über das Verhältnis zu Uebergläubigen. Zur Berichtigung des von Prof. Gildemeister in dem "Isaakiade" Prozesse abgegeben gerichtlichen Gutachtens.* Berlin: Verlag d. 'Jüdischen Presse,' 1885.
Der "Judenflinten"-Proceß. Sonderabdr. d. stenogr. Bericht d. "Neuen Deutschen Zeitung..." Leipzig: Verlag d. "Neuen deutschen Zeitung," 1892.
Kleist, L. *Der Apostel Stöcker, seine Jünger und der deutsche Bürgerkrieg: Ein Beitrag zur Entwickelungsgeschichte der antisemitischen Bewegung.* Berlin: Stuhr'sche Buchhandlung, 1881.
König, Adolf. *Ein Bubenstück, ersonnen um eines Mannes Ehre zu vernichten. Aktenmäßige Darstellung s. Prozesses gegen Hirsch Hildesheimer.* Hagen: H. Risel, 1888.
Kopp, Joeseph. *Zur Judenfrage nach den Akten des Prozeßes Rohling-Bloch.* Leipzig: Klinkhardt, 1886.
Leuß, Hans. "Die antisemitische Bewegung." *Die Zukunft*, Bd. 7, No. 33 (Mai 19. 1894): 330.
Liebermann von Sonnenberg, Max. *Beiträge zur Geschichte der antisemitischen Bewegung vom Jahre 1880–1885.* Berlin: M. Liebermann von Sonnenberg, 1885.
Löe, Otto Freiherr von. *Fürst Bismarck.* Basel: Bernheim, 1887.
——. *Fürst Bismarck und die Reichsglocke. Appellations-Rechtfertigungsschrift.* N.p.: Selbstverlag d. Hrsg., 1877.
Löwy, D. *Der Talmudjude von Rohling in der Schwurgerichtsverhandlung vom 28.Oktober 1882: Zur Abwehr und Verständigung.* Wien: Verlag und Buchhandlung D. Löwy, 1882.
Majunke, Paul. *Geschichte des "Culturkampfes" in Preußen-Deutschland.* Paderborn, Münster: Schöningh, 1886.
Marr, Wilhelm. *Der Judenkrieg, seine Fehler und wie er zu organisieren ist.* Chemnitz: E. Schmeitzner, 1880.
——. *Öffnet die Augen, Ihr deutschen Zeitungleser.* Chemnitz: E. Schmeitzner, 1880.
——. *Der Sieg des Judentums über das Germanentum: von nichtconfessionellen Standpunkt aus betrachtet.* Bern: R. Costenoble, 1879.
——. *Vom judischen Kriegsschauplatz: eine Streitschrift.* Bern: R. Costenoble, 1879.
——. *Wählet keinen Jüden! Der Weg zum Siege des Germanenthums über das Judenthum.* Berlin: O. Hentze, 1880.
——. *Wählet keinen Juden! Ein Mahnwort an die deutschen Wähler.* Berlin: O. Hentze, 1881.
Meyer, Rudolph Hermann. *Hundert Jahre conservativ Politik und Literatur.* 2 vols. Wien, Leipzig: Verlag "Austria" Franz Doll, 1895.
——. *Politische Gründer und die Corruption in Deutschland.* Leipzig: E. Bidder, 1877.
Nathan, Paul. *Der Prozess von Tisza-Eszlar.* Berlin: Fontane, 1892.
——. *Xanten-Cleve: Betrachtungen zum Prozess Buschhof.* Separat-Abdruck aus der *Nation.* Berlin: H.S. Hermann, 1892.

Naudh, Heinrich [Heinrich Nordmann]. *Die Juden und der deutschen Staat.* Leipzig: Fritsch, 1861.

Ónody, Géza von. *Tisza Eszlar in der Vergangenheit und Gegenwart.* Budapest: 1883.

Otto von Diest-Daber. Lebensbild eines muthigen Patrioten, zu seinem achtzigsten Geburtstage: dargestellt von einem Deutschen. Berlin: Hermann Walther Verlagsbuchhandlung, 1901.

Paasch, Karl. *Ein deutscher Pentateuch: Rüstzeug zum Kämpfe gegen das Judenthum für Politiker und Abgeordnete aller Parteien.* Leipzig: Verlag von Carl Minde, 1892.

——. *Eine jüdisch-deutsche Gesandtschaft und ihre Helfer. Geheimes Judenthum, Nebenregierungen und jüdische Weltherrschaft.* 2 vols. Leipzig: Selbstverlag, 1891.

——. *Mein gutes Recht.* Zürich: Mayer & Hendeß in Komm., 1906.

——. *Offener Brief an . . . Reichskanzler von Caprivi.* Leipzig: Minde, 1891.

——. *Die Ursache und die Entstehung des Prozesses Leckert-Lützow. Dr. Schumann. Freiherr von Tausch. Liebermann v. Sonnenberg (Ein Spitzel im deutschen Reichtag). Zeitgemäße psychologische Skizzen nebst politischen Dokumenten.* Zurich: Verlags-Magazin [J. Schabelitz], 1897.

Perrot, Franz. "Das Aktienwesen und -unwesen." *Im neuen Reich: Wochenschrift für das Leben des deutschen Volkes im Staat, Wissenschaft und Kultur* 3, Bd. 2 (1873): 488–496.

——. *Bismarck und die Juden: Papierpest und Ära-Artikel von 1=75: Erganzt durch Karl Perrot.* Berlin: M. Galle, 1931.

Plack-Podgorski, Heinrich Rudolf. *Ahlwardt vor Gericht: Eine kritische Beleuchtung des Judenflintenprozesses.* 5th ed. Dresden: Drückerei Glöß, 1893.

——. *Pharisäer und Heuchler, oder die Leuchten des deutschen Parlaments u.d. Stützen d. Staates. Geschildert nach d. Ahlwardtschen Aktenmaterial u. a. Quellen als e. Erg. seiner öffentliche Anklagen im Deutschen Reichstage unter wortgetr. Abdr. von Akten u. Belegen.* Berlin: Dewald, 1893.

——. *Der Prozeß Polke. Ein Rechtsbild aus der Zeit Wilhelm II.* Dresden: Glöß, 1892.

Politischer Bilderbogen. Vols. 1–. Dresden: Glöß Verlag, 1892–1901.

*Der Prozeß Ahlwardt: Ein Zeichen der Zeit und eine lehrreiche Studie. Von *** einem Deutsch-Nationalen.* Berlin: P. Heichen, 1892.

Der Prozeß Ahlwardt; Stenographischer Bericht über die Behandlungen vor der II. Strafkammer . . . am 11. April und 5. Mai 1891. Berlin: G. Höppner, 1891.

Prozeß Buschoff: Der Xantener Knabenmord vor dem Schwurgericht zu Cleve vom 4. bis 14. Juli 1892. Hagen i. W.: Wrietzner, 1892.

Der Prozeß Fenner nach den Akten dargestellt. Marburg: Verlag des "Reichsherold," 1888.

Prozeß Oberwinder: Eine Beleuchtung des Falls Buschoff. Stenographischer Bericht. Berlin: Verlag des Vaterländischen Verlags-Anstalt, 1892.

Schneidt, Karl. *Der Prozeß Ahlwardt und Anderes.* Berlin: Moderner Verlag, 1892.

Stein, Adolf. *Der gefälschte Brief. Stenographischer Bericht über den Witte-Stöcker- Prozeß vom 29. und 30. 1897.* Berlin: Vaterländischen Verlags-Anstalt, 1897.

Strack, Hermann Lebrecht. *Der Blutaberglaube in der Menschheit.* München: C.H. Beck'sche Verlagsbuchhandlung, 1892.

——. *Herr Adolf Stöcker. Christliche Liebe und Wahrhaftigkeit.* Karlsruhe und Leipzig: Verlag von H. Reuther, 1886.

——. *Die Juden, dürfen sie "Verbrecher von religions wegen" genannt werden? Aktenstücke, zugleich als ein Beitrag zur Kennzeichnung der gerechtigkeitspflege in Preussen.* Berlin: H. Walther, 1893.

——. *Jüdische Geheimgesetze? Mit Drei Anhängen: Rohling, Ecker, und kein Ende?* Berlin: C.A. Schwetschkke & Sohn, 1924.

Willmans, C. *Die goldene Internationale und die Nothwendigkeit einer Sozialen Reformpartei.* Berlin: Niendorf, 1876.

Der Xantener Knabenmord. Prozeß Buschoff. Verh. v.d. Schwurgericht zu Cleve vom 4.–14. Juli 1892. S.A. a. d. 'Niederrhein. Volksztg.' Crefeld: 1892.

Der Xantener Knabenmord vor dem Schwurgericht zu Cleve 4.–14. Juli 1892. Berlin: S. Cronbach, 1893.

Zeuge Stöcker: Eine Zeitbild aus dem Jahre 1885. Die Prozeßverhandlungen wegen Beleidigung des Hofpredigers Stöcker vor der II. Strafkammer des Landgerichts Berlin I am 9., 10., 13. Und 16. Juni nebst erläuternden und ergänzenden Anmerkungen. Berlin: Verlag "Fortschritt, Aktiengesellschaft", 1885.

Der zweite Prozeß Ahlwardt wegen Beleidigung des Magistrats und anderer Personen. Nach stenographischen Berichten über die Verhandlungen vor der II. Strafkammer beim kgl. Landgericht I zu Berlin, vom 16. bis 22. Februar 1892. Berlin: Gustav Ad. Dewald, 1892.

Secondary Sources

Ackerman, Nathan W., and Marie Jahoda. *Anti-Semitism and Emotional Disorder: A Psychoanalytic Interpretation.* New York: Harper & Brothers, 1950.

Almog, Schmuel. *Nationalism and Antisemitism in Modern Europe 1815–1945.* New York: Pergamon Press, 1990.

Anderson, Margaret. *Windthorst: A Political Biography.* Oxford: Clarendon Press, 1981.

Arendt, Hannah. *The Origins of Totalitarianism.* Vol. 1, *Anti-Semitism.* New York: Harcourt, Brace & World, 1968

Aschheim, Steven. *Brothers and Strangers: The East European Jew in German and German-Jewish Consciousness, 1800–1923.* Madison: Univ. of Wisconsin Press, 1982.

Bachem, Karl. *Josef Bachem, seine Familie und die Firma J.P. Bachem in Köln, die Rheinische und die Deutsche Volkshalle, die Kölnischen Blätter und die Kölnische Volkszeitung.* 2 Vols. Köln: Verlag und Druck von J.P. Bachem, 1912.

——. *Vorgeschichte, Geschichte und Politik der deutschen Zentrumspartei.* 9 vols. Aalen: Scientia-Verlag, 1967.

Berdahl, Robert M. "Conservative Politics and Aristocratic Landholders in Bismarckian Germany." *Journal of Modern History* XLIV, no. 1 (March 1972): 1–20.

Berding, Helmut. *Moderner Antisemitismus in Deutschland.* Frankfurt a. M.: Suhrkamp, 1988.

Blackbourn, David G. "Catholics, the Center Party and Anti-Semitism." In *Nationalist and Racialist Movements in England and Germany Before 1914,* edited by Paul Kennedy and Anthony Nicholls, 106–129. London: MacMillan Press, 1981.

——. *Populists and Patricians. Essays in Modern German History.* London and Boston: Allen and Unwin, 1987

——. "The Problem of Democratization: German Catholics and the Role of the Centre Party." In *Society and Politics in Wilhelmine Germany,* edited by Richard J. Evans, 160–185. London: Croom Helm; New York: Barnes and Noble, 1978.

Blackbourn, David and Geoff Eley. *The Peculiarities of German History: Bourgeois Society and Politics in Nineteenth-Century Germany.* Oxford: Oxford Univ. Press, 1984.

Boehlich, Walther. *Berliner Antisemitismusstreit.* Frankfurt a. M.: Insel-Verlag, 1965.

Borut, Jacob. "The Rise of Jewish Defence Agitation in Germany, 1890–1895: A Pre-History of the C.V.?" *Leo Baeck Institute Year Book* 36 (1991): 59–96.

——. "The Jewish Press in Germany in the Late Nineteenth Century as a Source of Historical Information." *Qesher* 11 (May 1992): 23e–24e.

Brakelmann, Günter and Martin Rosowski, ed. *Antisemitismus: Von religioser Judenfeindschaft zur Rassenideologie.* Gottingen: Vandenhoeck & Ruprecht, 1989.

Brakelmann, Günter, Martin Greschat, and Werner Jochmann, ed. *Protestantismus und Politik, Werk und Wirkung Adolf Stöckers.* Hamburg: Christians, 1982.

Breuer, Mordechai. *Jüdische Orthodoxie im Deutschen Reich 1871–1918: Sozialgeschichte einer religiösen Minderheit.* Frankfurt a. M.: Athenaum, 1986.

Bronsen, David, ed. *Jews and Germans from 1860 to 1933: The Problematic Symbiosis.* Reihe Siegen 9. Heidelberg: Winter, 1979.

Brown, Malcolm B. "Friedrich Nietzsche und sein Verleger Ernst Schmeitzner: Eine Darstellung ihrer Beziehung." *Archiv für Geschichte des Buchwesens* 28 (1987): 215–291.

Bußmann, Walter. "Bismarck: seine Helfer und seine Gegner." In *Reichsgründung 1870/71. Tatsachen, Kontroversen, Interpretationen*, edited by Theodor Scheider und Ernst Deuerlein, 119–147. Stuttgart: Seewald Verlag, 1970.

Claussen Detlev. *Von Judenhaß zum Antisemitismus: Materialen einer verleugneten Geschichte.* Darmstadt: Luchterhand, 1987.

Cobet, Christoph. *Der Wortschatz des Antisemitismus in der Bismarckzeit.* München: W. Fink, 1973.

Craig, Gordon. *Germany: 1866–1945.* New York: Oxford Univ. Press, 1978.

De Mendelssohn, Peter. *Zeitungsstadt Berlin.* Berlin: Verlag Ullstein, 1982.

Dominick, Raymond. *Wilhelm Liebknecht and the Founding of the German Social Democratic Party.* Chapel Hill: Univ. of North Carolina, 1982.

Doskow, Ambrose and Sidney Jacoby. "Anti-Semitism and the Law in Pre-Nazi Germany." *Contemporary Jewish Record* 3 (1940): 498–509.

Eley, Geoff. *Reshaping the German Right.* New Haven: Yale Univ. Press, 1980.

——. "Anti-Semitism, Agrarian Mobilization, and the Crisis in the Conservative Party: Radicalism and Containment in the Foundation of the Bund der Landwirte, 1892–1893." In *Politics, Parties, and the Authoritarian State: Imperial Germany 1871–1914. Festschrift für Otto Pflanze*, vol. 2, edited by John C. Fout. New York: Holmes and Meier, 1988.

Engelmann, Hans. *Kirche am Abgrund: Adolf Stöcker und seine antijüdische Bewegung.* Studien zu jüdischem Volk und christlicher Gemeinde, Band 5. Berlin: Selbstverlag Institut Kirche und Judentum, 1984.

Erb, Rainer & Werner Bergmann. *Die Nachseite der Judenemanzipation: Der Widerstand gegen die Integration der Juden in Deutschland, 1780–1860.* Berlin: Metropol, 1989.

Evans, Ellen Lovell. *The Center Party 1870–1933: A Study in Political Catholicism.* Carbondale, Illinois: Southern Illinois Univ. Press, 1981.

Farr, Ian. "Populism in the Countryside: The Peasant Leagues in Bavaria in the 1890s." In *Society and Politics in Wilhelmine Germany*, edited by Richard J. Evans, 136–159. London: Croom Helm; New York: Barnes and Noble, 1978.

Felden, Klemens. "Die Übernahme des antisemitischen Stereotyps als soziale Norm durch die bürgerliche Gesellschaft Deutschlands, 1875–1900." Dissertation, Ruprecht-Karl-Universität zu Heidelberg, 1963.

Ferrari Zumbini, Massimo. *Die Wurzeln des Bösen: Gründerjahre des Antisemitismus von der Bismarckzeit zu Hitler.* Frankfurt: Vittorio Klostermann, 2003.

Fischer, Heinz Dietrich, ed. *Deutsche Presseverleger des 18. Bis 20. Jahrhunderts.* Verlag Dokumentation, Pullach bei München, 1975.

——, ed. *Deutsche Zeitungen des 17 bis 20. Jahrhunderts.* Verlag Dokumentation, Pullach bei München, 1972.

——. *Handbuch der politischen Presse in Deutschland 1480–1980.* Düsseldorf: Droste Verlag, 1981.

Fischer-Frauendienst, I. *Bismarcks Pressepolitik.* Münster: Verlag C.J. Fahle, 1963.

Foerder, Ludwig. *Antisemitismus und Justiz.* Berlin: Philo Verlag, 1924.

Frankel, Johnathan. *The Damascus Affair: "Ritual Murder," Politics, and the Jews in 1840.* Cambridge: Cambridge Univ. Press, 1997.

Fricke, Dieter, ed. *Die Bürgerlichen Parteien in Deutschland. Handbuch der Geschichte der bürgerlichen Parteien und anderer bügerlicher Interessenorganizationen vom Vormärz bis zum Jahre 1945*, 2 vols. Berlin: Das Europaische Buch, 1968.

Geschichte der deutschen Presse: Die deutsche Presse in der Periode von 1871 bis zum Ausgang des 19. Jahrhunderts. Lehrbrief 7. Leipzig: Karl-Marx-Universität Sektion Journalistik, 1974.

Gilbert, Felix. *Bismarckian Society's Image of the Jew.* New York: Leo Baeck Institute, 1978.

Gilman, Sander. *Jewish Self-Hatred: Anti-Semitism and the Hidden Language of the Jews.* Baltimore: Johns Hopkins Univ. Press, 1986.

——. *The Jew's Body.* New York: Routledge, 1991.

Grab, Walter, ed. *Jüdische Integration und Indentität in Deutschland und Österreich 1848–1914: Internationales Symposium, April 1983.* Jahrbuch des Instituts für deutsche Geschichte, Beiheft 6. Tel Aviv: Institut für Deutsche Geschichte, 1984.

Grieve, Hermann. *Geschichte des modernen Antisemitismus in Deutschland.* Darmstadt: Wissenschaftliche Buchgesellschaft, 1983.

——. "Zu den Ursachen des Antisemitismus im Deutschen Kaiserreich von 1870–71." *Judaica* 27 (1971): 184–192.

——. "Zur multikausalen Bedingtheit des modernen Antisemitismus." *Judaica* 40 (1984): 133–144.

Groß, Johannes T. *Ritualmordbeschuldigungen gegen Juden im deutschen Kaiserreich, 1871–1913.* Berlin: Metropol, 2002.

Groth, Otto. *Das unerkannte Kulturmacht.* 7 Vols. Berlin: Verlag Walter de Gruyter & Co., 1960–1972.

Gutteridge, Richard. *Open thy Mouth for the Dumb!: The German Evangelical Church and the Jews 1879–1950.* Oxford: Blackwell, 1976.

Haase, Amine. *Katholische Presse und die Judenfrage. Inhaltsanalyse katholischer Periodika am Ende des 19. Jahrhunderts.* Pullach bei München: Verlag Dokumentation, 1975.

Hall, Alex. "The Kaiser, the Wilhelmine State and *Lèse-Majesté.*" *German Life and Letters* (January 1974): 101–115.

——. *Scandal, Sensation, and Social Democracy: The SPD Press and Wilhelmine Germany, 1890–1914.* Cambridge: Cambridge Press, 1977.

Hamburger, Ernest. *Juden im öffentlichen Leben Deutschlands. Regierungmitglieder, Beamte und Palamentarier in der monarchischen Zeit 1848–1918.* Schriftenreihe wissenschaftlicher Abhandlungen des Leo Baeck Instituts 19. Tübingen: Mohr [Siebeck], 1968.

Handler, Andrew. *Blood Libel at Tiszaeszlar.* New York: Columbia Univ. Press, 1980.

Harris, James F. "Franz Perrot: A Study in the Development of German Lower Middle Class Social and Political Thought in the 1870's." In *Studies in Modern European History and Culture* 2 (1976): 73–106.

Hartston, Barnet. "Reluctant Justice: Government Legal Intervention on behalf of Jews in Imperial Germany" *German Studies Review* 27, no. 1 (February 2004): 83–102.

Heffter, Heinrich. "Die Opposition der Kreuzzeitungspartei gegen die Bismarcksche Kartellpolitik in den Jahren 1887 bis 1880." Dissertation, Leipzig: G. Herrmann, 1927.

Heinen, E. "Antisemitische Strömungen im politischen Katholizismus während des Kulturkampfs." In *Geschichte in der Gegenwart. Festschrift für Kurt Kluxen,* edited by E. Heinen and H.-J. Schoeps. Paderborn: Schoningh, 1972.

——. *Beiträge zur Geschichte des politischen Katholizismus: Festgabe zum sechzigsten Geburtstag Ernst Heinen.* Idstein: Schulz-Kirchner, 1993.

Heinrichs, Helmut, ed. *Deutsche Juristen jüdischer Herkunft.* Munich: C.H. Beck'sche Verlagsbuchhandlung, 1993.

Hellwing, I.A. *Der konfessionelle Antisemitismus im 19. Jahrhundert in Österreich.* Vienna: Herder, 1972.

Hett, Benjamin Carter. *Death in the Tiergarten: Murder and Criminal Justice in the Kaiser's Berlin.* Cambridge, Mass.: Harvard Press, 2004.

Hoffmann, Christhard. "Politische Kultur und Gewalt gegen Minderheiten. Die antisemitischen Auschreitungen in Pommern und Westpreußen." *Jahrbuch für Antisemitismusforschung* 3 (1994): 93–120.

——. "Political Culture and Violence against Minorities: The Antisemitic Riots in Pomerania and West Prussia." In *Exclusionary Violence: Antisemitic Riots in Modern German History,* edited by Christhard Hoffmann et al., 67–92. Chicago: University of Michigan Press, 2002.

Hoffmann, Gerd. *Der Prozess um den Brand der Synagoge in Neustettin: Antisemitismus in Deutschland ausgangs des 19. Jahrhunderts.* Schifferstadt: Gerd Hoffman Verlag, 1998.

Horch, Hans Otto and Horst Denkler, ed. *Conditio Judaica. Judentum, antisemitismus, und deutschsprachige Literatur vom 18. Jahrhundert bis zum ersten Weltkrieg: Interdisziplineres Symposion der Werner-Reimers-Stiftung Bad Homber v.d.H.*. 2 vols. Tübingen: Niemeyer, 1988.

Jahr, Christoph. "Ahlwardt on Trial: Reactions to the Antisemitic Agitation of the 1890s in Germany." *Leo Baeck Institute Year Book* 48 (2003): 67–85.

Jahr, Christoph, Uwe Mai and Kathrin Roller, ed. *Feindbilder in der deutschen Geschichte: Studien zur Vorurteilsgeschichte im 19. und 20. Jahrhundert.* Berlin: Metropol, 1994.

Jarausch, Konrad. "Jewish Lawyers in Germany, 1848–1938: The Disintegration of a Profession." *Leo Baeck Institute Year Book* 36 (1991): 173.

——. *The Unfree Professions: German Lawyers, Teachers, and Engineers 1900–1950.* New York: Oxford Univ. Press, 1990. Jochmann, Werner. *Gesellschaftkrise und Judenfeindschaft in Deutschland 1870–1945.* Hamburg: Christians, 1988.

Kampe, Norbert. *Studenten und "Judenfrage" im deutschen Kaiserreich: Die Entstehung einer academischen Tragerschicht des Antisemitismus.* Gottingen: Vandenhoeck & Ruprecht, 1988

Kampmann, Wanda. *Deutsche und Juden: Die Geschichte der Juden in Deutschland vom Mittelalter bis zum Beginn des Ersten Weltkriegs.* Frankfurt a.M.: Fischer Taschenbuch Verlag, 1979.

Kasischke, Daniela. "Moderner Antisemitismus im Spiegel der Hamburger Presse nach dem Gründerkrach, 1873–1882." Magisterarbeit, Hamburg Universität, 1990.

Katz, Jacob. "Die Juden sind unser Unglück." *Tribüne* 92 (1984): 58–66.

——. *Out of the Ghetto. The Social Background of Jewish Emancipation, 1770–1870.* Cambridge: Harvard Univ. Press, 1973.

——. *From Prejudice to Destruction.* Cambridge: Harvard Univ. Press, 1980.

——. *Zur Assimilation und Emanzipation der Juden.* Darmstadt: Wissenschaftliche Buchgesellschaft, 1982.

Kent, George. *Arnim and Bismarck.* Oxford: Oxford Univ. Press, 1968.

Kiefer, Annegret. *Das Problem einer "Jüdischen Rasse": eine Diskussion zwischen Wissenschaft und Ideologie, 1870–1930.* New York: P. Lang, 1991.

Kieval, Hillel J. "The Importance of Place: Comparative Aspects of the Ritual Murder Trial in Modern Central Europe." In *Comparing Jewish Societies,* edited by Todd M. Endelman, 135–165. Ann Arbor: 1997.

Kirchheimer, Otto. *Political Justice.* Westport, CT: Greenwood Press, 1961.

Kolditz, Gerald. "Zur Enwicklung des Antisemitismus in Dresden während des Kaiserreichs." In *Zwischen Integration und Vernichtung: Jüdisches Leben in Dresden im 19. und 20. Jahrhundert.* Dresdner Hefte, vol. 45. Dresden: Dresdner Geschichtsverein, 1996.

Kölling, Bernd. "Blutige Illusionen. Ritualmorddiskurse und Antisemitismus im niederrheinischen Xanten am Ende des 19. Jahrhunderts." In *Agrarische Verfassung und politische Struktur. Studien zur Gesellschaftsgeschichte Preußens, 1700–1918. Hartmut Harnisch zum 65. Geburtstag,* edited by Wolfgang Neugebauer und Ralf Pröve, 249–82. Berlin: 1998.

Koszyk, Kurt. *Deutsche Presse im 19. Jahrhundert.* Berlin: Colloquium Verlag, 1966.

Krach, Tillmann. *Jüdische Rechtsanwälte in Preussen.* Munich: C.H. Beck'sche Verlagsbuchhandlung, 1991.

Krieger, Karsten, ed. *Der "Berliner Antisemitismusstreit," 1879–1881,* 2 vols. München: K.G. Saur, 2004.

Lamberti, Marjorie. *Jewish Activism in Imperial Germany: The Struggle for Civil Equality.* New Haven: Yale Univ. Press, 1978.

Lange, Josef. *Die Stellung der überregionalen katholischen deutschen Tagespresse zum Kulturkampf in Preußen, 1871–78.* Bern: Herbert Lang; Frankfurt a. M.: Peter Lang, 1974.

Ledford, Kenneth. *From General Estate to Special Interest: German Lawyers 1878–1933.* New York: Cambridge Univ. Press, 1996.

Lehr, Stephan. *Antisemitismus—religiöse Motive im sozialen Vorurteil. Aus der Frühgeschichte des Antisemitismus in Deutschland 1870–1914*. München: Chr. Kaiser Verlag, 1974.

Leuschen-Seppel, Rosemarie. *Sozialdemokratie und Antisemitismus im Kaiserreich: die Auseinandersetzungen der Partei mit der Antisemiten*. Bonn: Verlag Neue Gesellschaft, 1978.

Levenson, Alan. *Between Philosemitism ans Antisemitism: Defenses of Jews and Judaism in Germany, 1871–1932*. Lincoln: University of Nebraska Press, 2004.

Levy, Richard, ed. *Antisemitism in the Modern World: An Anthology of Texts*. Toronto: D.C. Heath, 1991.

——. *The Downfall of the Anti-Semitic Political Parties in Imperial Germany*. New Haven: Yale Univ. Press, 1975.

Levy, Richard and Konrad H. Jarausch. "1848 and the Discovery of Political Anti-Semitism in Germany: The Case of Wilhelm Marr." *Consortium on Revolutionary Europe 1750–1850* (1981): 255–264.

Lichtblau, Albert. *Antisemitismus und Soziale Spannung in Berlin und Wien 1867–1914*. Berlin: Metropole Verlag, 1994.

Lindemann, Albert. *Esau's Tears: Modern Anti-Semitism and the Rise of the Jews*. New York: Cambridge University Press, 1997.

——. *The Jew Accused: Three Anti-Semitic Affairs*. New York: Cambridge Univ. Press, 1991.

Losemann, Volker. "Rassenideologien und Antisemitische Publizistik in Deutschland im 19. und 20. Jahrhundert." In *Judentum und Antisemitismus von der Antike bis zur Gegenwart*. Im Auftrag des Fachbereichs Geschichtswissenschaften der Philipps-Universität Marburg, edited by Thomas Klein, Volker Losemann, and Gunther Mai. Düsseldorf: Droste Verlag, 1984.

Low, Alfred David. *Jews in the Eyes of Germans, From the Enlightenment to Imperial Germany*. Philadelphia: Institute for the Study of Human Issues, 1979.

Mack, Rüdiger. "Otto Böckel und die antisemitische Bauernbewegung in Hessen 1887–1894." in *900 Jahre Geschichte der Juden in Hessen. Beiträge zum politischen, wirtschaftlichen und kulturellen Leben*, edited by Christiane Heinemann, 377–410. Wiesbaden: 1983.

Massing, Paul. *Rehearsal for Destruction: A Study of Political Anti-Semitism in Imperial Germany*. New York: Harper & Bros., 1949.

Maier, Hans. *Die Antisemiten*. Deutsches Parteiwesen, Heft 2. München: Buchhandlung Nationalverein, 1910.

Mazura, Uwe. *Zentrumspartei und Judenfrage, 1870/71–1933: Verfassungsstaat und Minderheitenschutz*. Mainz: Mathias Grünewald Verlag, 1994.

McAleer, Kevin. *Dueling: The Cult of Honor in Fin-de-Siècle Germany*. Princeton: Princeton Univ. Press, 1994.

Meyer, Michael. "The Great Debate on Anti-Semitism: Jewish Reaction to new Hostility in Germany, 1879–1881." *Leo Baeck Institute Yearbook* 11 (1966): 167–70

Mosse, George. *Germans and Jews: The Right, the Left, and the Search For a Third Force in Pre-Nazi Germany*. New York: Howard Fertig, 1970.

——. *Toward the Final Solution: A History of European Racism*. New York: Howard Fertig, 1978.

Mosse, Werner, ed. *Juden in Wilhelminischen Deutschland 1890–1914. Ein Sammelband*. Schriftenreihe wissenschaftlicher Abhandlungen des Leo Baeck Instituts, no. 33. Tübingen: J.C.B. Mohr, 1976.

Müller, Klaus. "Zentrumspartei und Agrarische Bewegung im Rheinland 1882–1903." In *Spiegel der Geschichte. Festgabe für Max Braubach zum April 10, 1964*, edited by Konrad Repgen and Stephen Skalweit, 828–857. Münster: Aschendorff, 1964.

Münch, Fritz. *Bismarcks Affäre Arnim*. Berlin: Spitz, 1990.

Naujoks. Eberhard. "Bismarck in der Wahlkampagnen von 1879 und 1881. Der Zusammenhang von innerer und auswärtiger Pressepolitik." In *Historia integra*.

Festschrift f. E. Hassinger, edited by Hans Fenske, Wolfgang Reinhard, and Ernst Schulin, 265–281. Berlin (West): Duncker und Humblot, 1977.

——. "Bismarck und die Organisation der Regierungspresse." *Historische Zeitschrift* 205 (1967): 46–80.

——. *Bismarcks auswärtige Pressepolitik und die Reichsgründung 1865–1871*. Wiesbaden: F. Steiner, 1968.

——. *Die Parlamentarische Entstehung des Reichspressegesetzes in der Bismarckzeit, 1848/74*. Düsseldorf: Droste Verlag, 1975.

Nelson, K.R. "Government and Press in Germany, 1870–1945." *Gazette* 16 (1970): 215–229.

Nicholls, Stephen C.J. *The Burning of the Synagogue in Neustettin: Ideological Arson in the 1880s*. Center for German-Jewish Studies. Research Paper No. 2, Spring 1999.

Nipperdey, Thomas and Reinhard Rürup. "Antisemitismus." in *Geschichtliche Grundbegriffe. Historisches Lexikon zur politisch-sozialen Sprache in Deutschland*, vol. 1, edited by O. Brunner, Werner Conze, and Reinhart Koselleck, 129–153. Stuttgart: E. Klett, 1972.

Nonn, Christoph. *Eine Stadt sucht einen Mörder. Gerücht, Gewalt und Antisemitismus im Kaiserreich*. Göttingen: Vandenhoeck und Ruprecht, 2002.

——. "Zwischenfall in Konitz. Antisemitismus und Nationalismus im preußischen Osten um 1900." *Historische Zeitschrift* 266 (1998): 387–418.

Oberholtzer, Ellis Paxson. *Die Beziehung zwischen dem Staat und der Zeitungspresse im Deutschen Reich*. Berlin: Mayer und Müller, 1895.

Oschilewski, Walther. *Zeitungen in Berlin: Im Spiegel der Jahrhunderte*. Berlin: Haude und Spenersche Verlagsbuchhandlung, 1975.

Overesch, Manfred. *Presse zwischen Lenkung und Freiheit. Preußen und seine offiziöse Zeitung von der Revolution bis zur Reichsgründung, 1848–1871*. München-Pullach: Verlag Dokumentation, 1974.

Parmod, Maximilian. *Antisemitismus und Strafrechtspflege*. 3rd ed. Berlin: S. Chronbach, 1894.

Peal, David. "Jewish Responses to German Antisemitism: The Case of the Böckel Movement, 1887–1894." *Jewish Social Studies* 48, No. 3–4 (Summer-Fall 1986): 269–82.

Pflanze, Otto. *Bismarck and the Development of Germany*. Vol. 2. Princeton: Princeton Univ. Press, 1990.

Pöls, W. "Bleichröder und die Arnim-Affäre." *Historische Zeitschrift* 211 (1970): 65–76.

Pohl, Heinz Alfred. *Bismarcks "Einflußnahme" auf die Staatsform in Frankreich 1871–1877: Zum Problem des Stellenwerts von Pressepolitik im Rahmen der auswärtigen Beziehungen*. Frankfurt: Peter Lang, 1984.

Poll, Bernhard. *Jüdische Presse im 19. Jahrhundert*. Aachen: Ausstellung zur Eröffnung des Neubaus der Bibliothek; Professor Walther Hirsch in Tel Aviv, 1967.

Prutz, Robert Eduard. *Geschichte des deutschen Journalismus*. Gottingen: Vandenhoeck & Ruprecht, 1971.

Puhle, Hans-Jürgen. *Agrarische Interessenpolitik und Preußischer Konservativismus im wilhelminischen Reich, 1893–1914*. Bonn-Bad Godesberg: Verlag Neue Gesellschaft, 1975.

Pulzer, Peter. "Religion and Judicial Appointments in Germany 1869–1918." *Leo Baeck Institute Year Book* 28 (1983): 185–204.

——. *The Rise of Political Anti-Semitism in Germany and Austria*. New York: John Wiley & Sons, 1964.

——. "Why was there a Jewish Question in Imperial Germany?" In *Leo Baeck Institute Yearbook* 25 (1980): 133–146.

Ragins, Sanford. *Jewish Responses to Anti-Semitism in Germany, 1870–1914*. Cincinnati: Hebrew Union College Press, 1980.

Retallack, James. "Anti-Semitism, Conservative Propaganda, and Regional Politics in Late Nineteenth Century Germany." *German Studies Review* (October 1988): 377–403.

——. "Conservatives Contra Chancellor: Official Responses to the Spectre of Conservative Demagoguery From Bismarck to Bülow." *Canadian Journal of History* (August 1985): 203–236.

——. *Notables of the Right. The Conservative Party and Political Mobilization in Germany, 1876–1918.* London and Boston: Allen and Unwin, 1988.

Richarz, Monika, ed. *Jüdisches Leben in Deutschland.* 2 vols. Bloomington: Indiana Univ. Press, 1991.

Rieger, Isolde. *Die wilhelminische Presse im Überblick 1888–1918.* Munich: Pohl, 1957.

Riquarts, Kurt-Gerhard. "Der Antisemitismus als politische Partei in Schleswig-Holstein und Hamburg 1871–1914." Doktorarbeit, Kiel Univ., 1975.

Röhl, J.C.G. "The Disintegration of the Kartell and the Politics of Bismarck's Fall From Power, 1887–1890." *Historical Journal* 9, No. 1 (1966): 60–89.

Rohrbacher, Stefan und Schmidt Michael. *Judenbilder. Kulturgeschichte antijüdischer Mythen und antisemitischer Vorurteile.* Reinbeck bei Hamburg: Rowohlts Taschenbuch Verlag, 1991.

Rose, Paul Lawrence. *Revolutionary Antisemitism in Germany: From Kant to Wagner.* Princeton: Princeton Univ. Press, 1990.

Rosenberg, Hans. *Grosse Depression und Bismarckzeit: Wirtschaftsablauf, Gesellschaft und Politik in Mitteleuropa.* Berlin: W. De Gruyter, 1967.

Rürup, Reinhard. *Emanzipation und Antisemitismus, Studien zur "Judenfrage" der bürgerlichen Gesellschaft.* Kritische Studien zur Geschichtswisenschaft, Bd. 15. Gottingen: Vandenhoeck und Ruprecht, 1975.

Schmolke, Michael. *Die Schlechte Presse. Katholiken und Publizistik zwischen 'Katholik' und 'Publik.'* Münster, Regensburg, 1971.

Schöps, Julius H. and Joachim Schlor, ed. *Antisemitismus: Vorurteile und Mythen.* München: Piper, 1995.

——. "CDU vor 75 Jahren. Die sozialpolitischen Bestrebungen des Reichsfreiherrn Friedrich Carl von Fechenbach, 1836–1907." *Zeitschrift für Religions- und Geistesgeschichte* 9 (1957): 266–277.

Schorsch, Ismar. *Jewish Reactions to German Anti-Semitism, 1870–1914.* New York: Columbia Univ. Press, 1972.

Stern, Fritz. *Gold and Iron: Bismarck, Bleichröder, and the Building of the German Empire.* New York: Knopf, 1977.

——. *The Politics of Cultural Despair: A Study in the Rise of the Germanic Ideology.* Berkeley: Univ. of California Press, 1961

Strenge, Barbara. *Juden im preußischen Justizdienst 1812–1918: Der Zugang zu den juristischen Berufen als Indikator der gesellschaftlichen Emanzipation.* Munich: K.G. Saur, 1996.

Suchy, Barbara. "The Verein zur Abwehr des Antisemitismus (I) From its Beginnings to the First World War." *Leo Baeck Institute Year Book* 28 (1983): 208.

Tal, Uriel. *Christians and Jews in Germany: Religion, Politics and Ideology in the Second Reich, 1870–1914.* Ithaca: Cornell Univ. Press, 1975.

——. *Religious and Anti-Religious Roots of Modern Anti-Semitism.* New York: Leo Baeck Institute, 1971.

Toury, Jacob. *Die politische Orientierungen der Juden in Deutschland.* Tübingen: Mohr [Siebeck], 1966.

——. *Soziale und politische Geschichte der Juden in Deutschland 1847–1871. Zwischen Revolution, Reaktion, und Emanzipation.* Veröffentlichungen des Diaspora Research Institute 20; Schriftenreihe des Instituts für deutsche Geschichte der Universität Tel Aviv 2. Düsseldorf: Droste Verlag, 1977.

Vogt, Bernhard. "Antisemitismus und Justiz in Kaiserreich: Der Synagogenbrand in Neustettin." In *'Halte fern dem ganzen Lande jades Verderben . . .': Geschicht und Kultur der Juden in Pommern*, edited by Margret Heitmann and Julius Schoeps, 379–399. Hildesheim: 1995.

——. "Die 'Atmosphäre eines Narrenhauses': Eine Ritualmordlegende um die Ermordung des Schülers Ernst Winter in Konitz." In *Zur Geschichte und Kultur der Juden in Ost- und Westpreußen*, edited by Michael Brocke et al., 546–77. Hildesheim: 2000.

Volkov, Shulamit. *Jüdisches Leben und Antisemitismus im 19. und 20. Jahrhundert.* München: C.H. Beck, 1990.

——. "Kontinuät und Diskontinuät im deutschen Antisemitismus 1878–1945." *Vierteljahreshefte für Zeitgeschichte* 33, Heft 2 (1985): 221–243.

——. *The Rise of Popular Anti-Modernism in Germany, the Urban Master Artisans 1873–1896.* Princeton: Princeton Univ. Press, 1978.

——. "The Social and Political Function of late 19th Century Anti-Semitism: the Case of the Small Handicraft Masters." In *Sozialgeschichte heute: Festschrift für Hans Rosenberg*, edited by Hans-Ulrich Wehler, 416–431. Gottingen: Vandenhoeck & Ruprecht, 1974.

Wawrzinek, Kurt. *Die Enstehung der deutsche Antisemitenparteien.* Vaduz: Kraus, 1965.

Wetzel, H.W. *Presseinnenpolitik im Bismarckreich, 1874–1900. Das Problem der Repression oppositioneller Zeitungen.* Bern: Herbert Lang; Frankfurt: Peter Lang, 1975.

Zang, Hermann. *Die "Gartenlaube" als politisches Organ: Belletristik, Bilderwerk und literarische Kritik im Dienste der liberalen Politik 1860–1880.* Coburg: A. Rossteuscher, 1935.

Zimmermann, Mosche. "From Radicalism to Anti-Semitism." *Jerusalem Quarterly* 23 (1982): 114–128.

——. "Two Generations in the History of German Anti-Semitism: The Letters of Theodor Fritsch to Wilhelm Marr." *Leo Baeck Institute Yearbook* 23 (1978): 89–99.

——. *Wilhelm Marr: The Patriarch of Anti-Semitism.* New York: Oxford Univ. Press, 1986.

Zmarzlik, Hans-Günther. "Antisemitismus in Deutschen Kaiserreich: 1871–1918." In *Die Juden als Minderheit in der Geschichte*, edited by Bernd Martin and Ernst Schulin. München: Deutscher Taschenbuch, 1981.

INDEX

Studies in Central European Histories

EDITED BY THOMAS A. BRADY AND ROGER CHICKERING

1. BLICKLE, P. *Communal Reformation.* The People's Quest for Salvation in the Sixteenth Century. ISBN 0 391 03730 7
2. ROPER, K. *German Encounters with Modernity.* Novels of Imperial Berlin. ISBN 0 391 03695 5
3. CHICKERING, R. *Karl Lamprecht.* A German Academic Life (1856-1915). ISBN 0 391 03766 8
4. BRADY, Jr., T.A. *Protestant Politics.* Jacob Sturm (1489-1553) and the German Reformation. ISBN 0 391 03823 0
5. Theibault, J.C. *German Villages in Crisis.* Rural Life in Hesse-Kassel and the Thirty Years War, 1580-1720. ISBN 0 391 03839 7
6. WALLACE, P.G. *Communities and Conflict in Early Modern Colmar 1571-1730.* ISBN 0 391 03822 2
7. USHER CHRISMAN, M. *Conflicting Visions of Reform.* German Lay Propaganda Pamphlets, 1519-1530. ISBN 0 391 03944 x
8. SAFLEY, T.M. *Charity and Economy in the Orphanages of Early Modern Augsburg.* ISBN 0 391 03983 0
9. JACKSON, Jr., J.H. *Migration and Urbanization in the Ruhr Valley, 1821-1914.* ISBN 0 391 04033 2
10. LAPP, B. *Revolution from the Right.* Politics, Class and the Rise of Nazism in Saxony, 1919-1933. ISBN 0 391 04027 8
11. SCHECK, R. *Alfred von Tirpitz and German Right-Wing Politics, 1914-1930.* ISBN 0 391 04043 x
12. LOVELL EVANS, E. *Cross and the Ballot.* Catholic Political Parties in Germany, Switzerland, Austria, Belgium and the Netherlands, 1785-1985. ISBN 0 391 04095 2
13. ANDERSON, A.D. *On the Verge of War.* International Relations and the Jülich-Kleve Succession Crises (1609-1614). ISBN 0 391 04092 8
14. BENZ, E. *Fertility, Wealth, and Politics in Three Southwest German Villages, 1650-1900.* ISBN 0 391 04093 6
15. BOWMAN, W.D. *Priest and Parish in Vienna, 1780-1880.* ISBN 0 391 04094 4
16. SUN, R.C. *Before the Enemy is Within Our Walls.* Catholic Workers in Cologne, 1885-1912: A Social, Cultural and Political History. ISBN 0 391 04096 0
17. BÜSCH, O. *Military System and Social Life in Old Regime Prussia, 1713-1807.* The Beginnings of the Social Militarization of Prusso-German Society. Transl. by J.G. Gagliardo. ISBN 0 391 03984 9
18. SONDHAUS, L. *Franz Conrad von Hötzendorf.* Architect of the Apocalypse. ISBN 0 391 04097 9

19. PATROUCH, J.F. *Negotiated Settlement.* The Counter-Reformation in Upper Austria under the Habsburgs. ISBN 0 391 04099 5
20. HAUDE, S. *In the Shadow of "Savage Wolves".* Anabaptist Münster and the German Reformation during the 1530s. ISBN 0 391 04100 2
21. CALDWELL, P.C. & SCHEUERMAN, W.E. *From Liberal Democracy to Fascism.* Legal and Political Thought in the Weimar Republic. ISBN 0 391 04098 7
22. BRENNER, A.D. *Emil J. Gumbel.* Weimar German Pacifist and Professor. ISBN 0 391 04101 0
23. BELL, D.P. *Sacred Communities.* Jewish and Christian Identities in Fifteenth-Century Germany. ISBN 0 391 04102 9
24. MYERS FEINSTEIN, M. *State Symbols.* The Quest for Legitimacy in the Federal Republic of Germany and the German Democratic Republic, 1949-1959. ISBN 0 391 04103 7
25. HOBSON, R. *Imperialism at Sea.* Naval Strategic Thought, the Ideology of Sea Power, and the Tirpitz Plan, 1875-1914. ISBN 0 391 04105 3
26. EDWARDS, K.A. *Families and Frontiers.* Re-creating Communities and Boundaries in the Early Modern Burgundies. ISBN 0 391 04106 1
27. LAVERY, J. *Germany's Northern Challenge.* The Holy Roman Empire and the Scandinavian Struggle for the Baltic 1563-1576. ISBN 0 391 04156 8
28. HEALY, R. *Jesuit Specter in Imperial Germany.* ISBN 0 391 04194 0
29. GEEHR, R.S. *Aesthetics of Horror.* The Life and Thought of Richard von Kralik. ISBN 0 391 04201 7
30. SAFLEY, T.M. (ed.). *Reformation of Charity.* The Secular and the Religious in Early Modern Poor Relief. ISBN 0 391 04211 4
31. LINDEMANN, M. (ed.). *Ways of Knowing.* Ten Interdisciplinary Essays. ISBN 0 391 04184 3
32. ULBRICH, C. *Shulamit and Margarete.* Power, Gender, and Religion in a Rural Society in Eighteenth-Century Europe. Transl. by T. Dunlap. ISBN 0 391 04145 2
33. FUNCK, M. & CHICKERING, R. (eds.). *Endangered Cities.* Military Power and Urban Societies in the Era of the World Wars. ISBN 0 391 04196 7
34. BEACHY, R. *The Soul of Commerce.* Credit, Property, and Politics in Leipzig, 1750-1840. ISBN 0 391 04142 8
35. MAYES, D. *Communal Christianity.* The Life and Loss of a Peasant Vision in Early Modern Germany. ISBN 0 391 04225 4
36. AASLESTAD, K. *Place and Politics.* Local Identity, Civic Culture, and German Nationalism in North Germany during the Revolutionary Era. ISBN 0 391 04228 9
37. BURNETT, S.G. & BELL, D.P. (eds.). *Jews, Judaism, and the Reformation in Sixteenth-Century Germany.* ISBN 0 391 04229 7
38. SAFLEY, T.M. *Children of the Laboring Poor.* Expectation and Experience among the Orphans of Early Modern Augsburg. ISBN 0 391 04224 6
39. HARTSTON, B.P. *Sensationalizing the Jewish Question.* Anti-Semitic Trials and the Press in the Early German Empire. ISBN 90 04 14654 7
40. JANIK, E. *Recomposing German Music.* Politics and Musical Tradition in Cold War Berlin. ISBN 90 04 14661 X

www.ingramcontent.com/pod-product-compliance
Lightning Source LLC
LaVergne TN
LVHW010631300926
849162LV00001B/123
9789004146549